Database Programming with VB.NET

CARSTEN THOMSEN

Apress™

ISBN (pbk): 1-893115-29-1
Printed and bound in the United States of America 12345678910
Trademarked names may appear in this book. Rather than use a trademark symbol with every occurrence of a trademarked name, we use the names only in an
editorial fashion and to the benefit of the trademark owner, with no intention of
infringement of the trademark.

Editorial Directors: Dan Appleman, Gary Cornell, Karen Watterson, Jason Gilmore
Technical Reviewer: Mark Dunn
Managing Editor: Grace Wong
Marketing Manager: Stephanie Rodriguez
Project Manager: Alexa Stuart
Developmental Editor: Valerie Perry
Copy Editor: Ami Knox
Production Editor: Kari Brooks
Page Composition: Impressions Book and Journal Services, Inc.
Artist: Allan Rasmussen
Indexer: Carol Burbo
Cover Design: Tom Debolski

Distributed to the book trade in the United States by Springer-Verlag New York,
Inc., 175 Fifth Avenue, New York, NY, 10010
and outside the United States by Springer-Verlag GmbH & Co. KG, Tiergartenstr.
17, 69112 Heidelberg, Germany
In the United States, phone 1-800-SPRINGER; orders@springer-ny.com;
http://www.springer-ny.com
Outside the United States, contact orders@springer.de;
http://www.springer.de; fax +49 6221 345229

For information on translations, please contact Apress directly at 901 Grayson
Street, Suite 204, Berkeley, CA, 94710
Phone: 510-549-5938; Fax: 510-549-5939; info@apress.com;
http://www.apress.com

The information in this book is distributed on an "as is" basis, without warranty.
Although every precaution has been taken in the preparation of this work, neither the author nor Apress shall have any liability to any person or entity with respect to any loss or damage caused or alleged to be caused directly or indirectly
by the information contained in this work.

The source code for this book is available to readers at http://www.apress.com.
You will need to answer questions pertaining to this book in order to successfully
download the code.

Contents at a Glance

Contents

Foreword

DID YOU HEAR THE LATEST? A paradigm shift has occurred. With the release of Microsoft's Visual Studio.NET and the .NET Framework, Microsoft has forever changed the way we program Web-based and n-tier applications!

The .NET Framework exposes a number of radically new concepts—especially for developers working with database applications. Instead of using the good old COM-based ADO Recordset class, you will now be using ADO.NET's disconnected DataSet and DataTable classes (*disconnected* is the key word here).

When I was asked to write a foreword for Carsten's new book on database access in VB.NET, I was anxious to see how well it measured up to Microsoft's help files. I was not disappointed! This important book zeros in on significant aspects of ADO.NET and how they differ from ADO.

This book will not only serve as a good ADO.NET programmer's guide, but also as a great language reference on VB.NET database access.

Well done, Carsten!

Carl Prothman
Issaquah, Washington
July 30, 2001
http://www.able-consulting.com

Acknowledgments

THIS BOOK IS A DREAM COME true for me; I have finally (okay, maybe I'm being hard on myself since I'm "only" 33) managed to write a complete book all by myself, without coauthors. I'll admit it—I'm really proud of myself, but writing it certainly hasn't been without costs. I have spent many hours researching a technology at beta stage that changed almost as frequently as I changed my underwear. (Don't ask.) When I set out to do this book, I knew that many changes would occur, but I never dreamed that Microsoft would make the number of changes they did from Beta 1 to Beta 2. Anyway, it only "cost" a few extra months writing the book. That said, there were some individuals at Microsoft who leaned over backwards to ease my pain. One guy in particular, Steve Ling, who's handling the .NET documentation, was very good at answering my sometimes odd queries. So, Steve, many thanks to you, for your speedy, accurate, and candid answers.

I also wish to thank the publisher for believing that I (an unpublished author) could actually write this book. This book should have been published a number of months before it actually did, and although I can blame most of this on other parties, it was certainly reassuring for me that Apress stood behind me whenever the schedule was being "extended." Great many thanks to you for this. That's how a book should be made, with the right information, and not necessarily on time. I know one or two other publishers that would consider this a problem, so I guess I'm just so very pleased I picked Apress.

I don't want this to turn into an appraisal of the publisher, but I really do have a lot of good things to say about Apress. Before you ask, I am not looking for a new contract, I already have it, so there!

The publisher and especially the group of people involved in this book need a special thank you, because they let me write the book my way, more or less. I have had a lot of help from the technical reviewer, Mark Dunn, who has proved to be extremely valuable for content of this book. Not only did he find some of the major stinkers that even the best of us sometimes write, but he also came up with a number of good ideas on how to arrange the book and what else to stick in there. When Mark was unavailable for a short period, I had to impose on a former colleague of mine, Michael Thomhav, and he did a great job reviewing one of the chapters. So many thanks to you too, Michael, for jumping in on such short notice. Karen Watterson the editor—hmm, what can I possibly say about her, making sure she doesn't take it the wrong way? Well, it's been fun working with Karen on this book, and we've all exchanged some pretty funny e-mails, so perhaps the best thing to say would be: Thanks for all your input and for making it a little funnier to work with you guys.

When I was writing the book, I published the unedited chapters on my own Web site. I did this not only to get some visitors to my site, but also to get some feedback, which I sure did manage to get. So, thanks to all of you who took the time to read and offer some excellent feedback, especially these guys: Greg Beamer, Per Jørgensen, Jens Allenbæk, John Fasly, Thomas Moore, Peter Wang, and Michael Christensen. Thanks, guys.

Last, but sure not least, there's also "the family thing": I owe a giant special thanks to "the missus" (Mia) and the kids (Caroline and Nicole). You're the ones who've suffered the most when I was writing the book, but hopefully I've learned enough this time around to make sure I'm a better companion and father when I write Book #2. And thanks also for letting me do a "bit" of work on our two-week holiday on the Spanish island of Tenerife. *Tusind tak.*

Carsten, `carstent@vb-joker.com`
Esbjerg, Denmark
July 16, 2001

Introduction

THIS BOOK IS ALL ABOUT accessing databases of various kinds, such as the Active Directory, SQL Server 2000, and Message Queuing. My intention with this book is to give the reader insight into how ADO.NET works, and how you can use the classes from ADO.NET to access a database; use stored procedures, views, and triggers; how to get information from Active Directory; and how to use Message Queuing in your applications. Having said that, my major concern was to make this book as easy to read as possible, and although there are passages in the book that aren't quite as easy to read as I wanted, I think I have managed to do what I set out to do.

This book is targeted at the intermediate user, meaning users who already know a little about Visual Studio.NET and previous versions of Visual Basic. Basic knowledge of Object Oriented Programming (OOP), ADO, and database design is also assumed. Parts of the book are at beginner level and other parts are at a more advanced level. The beginner level stuff is where I feel it is appropriate to make sure you really understand what is being explained.

Since I am using some of the Enterprise functionality of the Visual Studio .NET, you will also need either of the two Enterprise editions to follow all the exercises. However, the Professional edition will do for most of the example code, and it will certainly do if you just want to see how it's all done while learning ADO.NET. This means the only thing extra you get from the Enterprise editions in terms of database access is an additional set of database tools to be used from within the IDE.

Organization

This book is organized into three parts:

- Part One is a general introduction to Visual Studio.NET and the .NET Framework.

- Part Two is the juicy part, the part where you take a look at how to connect to relational and hierarchical databases. You will also learn how to wrap your database access in classes and how to master exception handling. Part Two starts with a look at how to design a relational database.

- Part Three is where you finish the UserMan example application.

Example Code

All the example code for this book can be found on the Apress Web site (http://www.apress.com) in the Downloads section. You will need to answer questions pertaining to this book in order to successfully download the code.

Data Source

The data source for the example code in this book is running on a SQL Server 2000. You get a trial version of SQL Server 2000 when you purchase Visual Studio.NET, so you should be able to run the examples even if you don't currently have SQL Server 2000. Having said that, the example code can easily be modified to work with either MS Access or SQL Server 7.0. The only thing you need to be aware of is that SQL Server 2000 can return a row set as XML, which is not directly possible with MS Access or SQL Server 7.0. SQL Server 7.0 doesn't support referential integrity, which means it must be implemented using triggers.

Feedback

I can be reached at dbpwvbnet@vb-joker.com, and I will gladly answer any e-mail concerning this book. Now, I don't need any unnecessary grief, but I will try and respond to any kind of query you might have regarding this book.

I have set up a Web site for the UserMan example application where you can post and retrieve ideas on how to take it further. The Web site address is http://www.userman.dk. Check it out.

About the Author

**Carsten Thomsen** is a Danish national who currently holds the MCSE and MCSD certifications. He's also a Microsoft MVP in Visual Basic, a recognition he first received in August 1999. Carsten has been programming in VB since the launch of VB 3.0, and, although he has experimented with other programming languages, he pretty much sticks with VB and specializes in accessing various kinds of data stores. Carsten, his girlfriend, Mia, and their two-year old daughter, Caroline, live in the small town of Esbjerg on the west coast of Denmark. Carsten's other daughter, Nicole, lives in Dublin with her mother. Carsten admits to spending too much time with computers, but enjoys spending whatever spare time is left with Mia and his daughters. "We spend a week in Southern Europe or Northern Africa as often as we possibly can."

Carsten can be reached at carstent@vb-joker.com.

About the Technical Reviewer

 Mark Dunn, MCT, MCSD, MCDBA, is a senior consultant/technical instructor with Extreme Logic, Inc. (http://www.extremelogic.com) He has degrees in mathematics and physics and lives in Atlanta, Georgia.

Mark worked many years as a consultant before moving into training, and admits that about 90 percent of his time is currently spent teaching classes—mostly VB and SQL Server. In the past, he's taught Delphi, Java, JavaScript, Oracle, and Power Builder. His experience with VB dates back to VB 1.0, and QBASIC and Microsoft's BASIC PDS before that. He wrote major modules for a program called Tapscan that's still used in the States for ratings analysis by radio stations, and he also wrote the report generation engine and a geographical mapping module for Tapscan. During his consultant years, he did a lot of client/server application consulting, mostly solving problems with VB front ends connecting to Oracle back ends.

Mark, too, admits to being "consumed with computers," and also tries hard to balance his time between work and family. Mark's been married for almost 15 years and has an 8-year-old son (Mark Jr.) and a 6-year-old daughter (Erin). Mark Jr. is very involved with little league baseball as is Erin with gymnastics.

Mark can be contacted at markdunn@mindspring.com.

Part One

Getting Started

CHAPTER 1

A Lightning-Quick
Introduction to VB.NET

THE .NET FRAMEWORK is an environment for building, deploying, and running
services and other applications. This environment is all about code reuse and
specialization, multilanguage development, deployment, administration,
and security. The .NET Framework will lead to a new generation of software that
melds computing and communication in a way that allows the developer to create truly distributed applications that integrate and collaborate with other
complementary services. In other words, you now have the opportunity to create
Web services, such as search engines and mortgage calculators, that will help
transform the Internet as we know it today. No longer will it be about individual
Web sites or connected devices; it is now a question of computers and devices,
such as handheld computers, wristwatches, and mobile phones, collaborating
with each other and thus creating rich services. As an example, imagine calling a
search engine to run a search and then displaying and manipulating the results
of the search in your own application.

There are rumors that the .NET Framework is solely for building Web sites,
but this is not true. You can just as easily create your good old-fashioned Windows applications with the .NET Framework. The .NET Framework is actually
more or less what would have been called COM+ 2.0 if Microsoft had not
changed its naming conventions. Granted, the .NET Framework is now a far cry
from COM+, but initially the development did start from the basis of COM+.
I guess not naming it COM+ 2.0 was the right move after all.

This book is based on the assumption that you already know about the .NET
Framework. However, this chapter does provide a quick run-through of these
concepts and terms. Although the terms are not specific to VB.NET, but indeed to
all .NET programming languages, you will need to know them, if you are serious
about using VB.NET for all your enterprise programming.

Reviewing Programming Concepts

The .NET environment introduces some programming concepts that will be
new even to those who are familiar with a previous version of Visual Basic. In

fact, these concepts will be new to most Windows developers because the .NET programming tools, such as VB.NET, are geared towards enterprise development in the context of Web-centric applications. This does not mean the days of Windows platform–only development are gone, but .NET requires you to change the way you think about Windows programming. The good old Registry is "gone"— that is, it is no longer used for registering your type libraries in the form of ActiveX/COM servers. Components of .NET Framework are self-describing; all information about referenced components, and so on, are part of the component in the form of metadata.

Visual Studio.NET is based on the Microsoft .NET Framework, which obviously means that Visual Basic.NET is as well. VB.NET, which is simply the short form of Visual Basic.NET, is part of the Visual Studio.NET package. Visual Basic is just one of the languages that Microsoft ships for the .NET platform.

At first some of these new terms and concepts seem a bit daunting, but they really aren't that bad. If you need to refresh your memory regarding .NET programming concepts and the .NET Framework, then simply keep reading, because this chapter is indeed a very quick review of these basics.

A Quick Look at Components of the .NET Framework

The .NET Framework adheres to the Common Type System (CTS) for data exchange and the Common Language Specification (CLS) for language interoperability. In short, three main parts make up the .NET Framework:

- Active Server Pages.NET (ASP.NET)

- The Common Language Runtime (CLR)

- .NET Framework Class Library (the base classes)

The .NET Framework consists of these additional components:

- Assemblies

- Namespaces

- Managed components

- Common Type System (CTS)

- MS Intermediate Language

- Just-In-Time (JIT)

All of these components are discussed in the following sections.

Active Server Pages.NET

Active Server Pages.NET is an evolution of Active Server Pages (ASP) into so-called managed space, or rather managed code execution (see "Common Language Runtime" and "Managed Data" later in this chapter). ASP.NET is a framework for building server-based Web applications. ASP.NET pages generally separate the presentation (HTML) from the logic or code. This means that the HTML is placed in a text file with an .aspx extension and the code in a text file with a .vb extension (when you implement your logic/code in VB.NET, that is).

ASP.NET is largely syntax compatible with ASP, which allows you to port most of your existing ASP code to the .NET Framework and then upgrade the ASP files one by one. ASP.NET has different programming models that can be mixed in any way. The programming models are as follows:

- *Web forms* allow you to build Web pages using a forms-based UI. These forms are quite similar to the forms in previous versions of Visual Basic. That means you have proper event and error handling.

- *Web services* are a clever way of accessing functionality on remote servers. Web services are based on the Simple Object Access Protocol (SOAP), which is a firewall-friendly protocol based on XML. SOAP uses the HTTP protocol to work across the Internet.

- *Standard HTML* allows you to create your pages as standard HTML version 3.2 or 4.0.

Common Type System

The .NET environment is based on the Common Type System, which means that all .NET languages share the same data types. This truly makes it easy to exchange data between different programming languages. It does not matter if you exchange data directly in your source code (for example, inheriting classes created in a different programming language) or use Web services or COM+ components. CTS is built into the Common Language Runtime. Have you ever had a problem exchanging dates with other applications? If so, I am sure you know how valuable it is to have the CTS to establish the correct format. You do not have to worry about the format being, say, DD-MM-YYYY; you simply need to pass a **DateTime** data type.

Common Language Specification

The Common Language Specification is a set of conventions that is used for promoting language interoperability. This means that the various programming languages developed for the .NET platform must conform to the CLS in order to make sure that objects, developed in different programming languages, can actually talk to each other. This includes exposing only those features and data types that are CLS compliant. Internally your objects, data types, and features can be different from the ones in the CLS, as long as the exported methods, procedures, and data types are CLS compliant. In other words, the CLS is really nothing more than a standard for language interoperability used in the .NET Framework.

Common Language Runtime

The Common Language Runtime is the runtime environment provided by the .NET Framework. The CLR's job is to manage code execution, hence the term *managed code*. The compilers for Visual Basic.NET, and C# both produce managed code, whereas the Visual C++ compiler by default produces unmanaged code. By unmanaged code, I mean code for the Windows platform like the compilers for the previous versions of Visual C++ produced. You can however use the managed code extensions for Visual C++.

Implications for JScript

Does this mean the end of JScript? Well, not quite. If you are referring to server-side development in the new compiled JScript language, well then I guess it's up to the developer. JScript as it is known today, a.k.a. client-side code execution, will continue to exist, largely because of its all-browser adoption. But if the CLR is ported to enough platforms and supported by enough software vendors, it might well stand a good chance of competing with the Virtual Machine for executing Java applets. Java as a compiled language will be available as a .NET language, or rather come with a .NET compiler from Rational Software.

VBScript, VBA, and VSA

Okay, what about VBScript and Visual Basic for Applications (VBA)? This is obviously another issue that relates to the introduction of VB.NET. A new version of VBA, called Visual Studio for Applications (VSA), will be available for customizing and extending the functionality of your Web-based applications. VSA is based on Visual Basic.NET as much as on VBA, so it is definitely a good and cool thing to do VB.NET programming. Bet on two horses for the price of one. VSA is actually a "merger" of VBScript and VBA, and it uses a script engine runtime for the .NET Framework. Even with backward compatibility between VB.NET and earlier versions of Visual Basic, the language itself has been upgraded significantly, which means that some of your existing VBA/VBScript code will require changes in order to run in the VSA runtime environment.

The CLR also performs the following built-in tasks:

- Managing data

- Performing automatic garbage collection

- Sharing a common base for source code

- Compiling code to the Microsoft Intermediate Language (MSIL)

I discuss these features in the next few sections.

Managed Data

The .NET Framework compilers mainly produce managed code, which is managed by the CLR. Managed code means managed data, which in turn means data with lifetimes managed by the CLR. Managed data will definitely help eliminate memory leaks, but at the same time it means you have less control over your data, because you no longer have deterministic finalization, which is arguably one of the strengths of COM(+).

Automatic Garbage Collection

When objects are managed (allocated and released) by the CLR, you do not have full control over them. The CLR handles the object layout and the references to the objects, disposing of the objects when they are no longer being used, a process called *automatic garbage collection*. This is very different from the process for handling objects in previous versions of Visual Basic, known as *deterministic finalization.* Previous versions of VB are based on COM and as such used the COM model for referencing and counting objects. As a result, whenever your application instantiated an object (Set object = New Class), a counter for this object reference was incremented by one, and when your application destroyed the object reference (Set object = Nothing or when it went out of scope), the counter was decremented. When the counter hit zero, the object would be released automatically from memory. This is something you have to be very aware of now, because you no longer have full control over your object references. If you are a Java programmer, you already know about this.

Source Code Shares Common Base

Because all the CLR-compliant compilers produce managed code, the source code shares the same base, that is, the type system (CTS) and to some extent the language specification (CLS). This means you can inherit classes written in a language other than the one you are using, a concept known as *cross-language inheritance.* This is a great benefit to larger development teams, where the developers' skill sets are likely rather different. Another major benefit is when you need to debug; you can now safely debug within the same environment source code across various programming languages!

Intermediate Language Compilation

When you compile your code, it is compiled to what is called Microsoft Intermediate Language (MSIL) and stored in a Portable Executable (PE) file along with metadata that describes the types (classes, interfaces, and value types) used in the code. Because the compiled code is in an "intermediate state," the code is platform independent. This means the MSIL code can be executed on any platform that has the CLR installed. The metadata that exists in the PE file along with the MSIL enables your code to describe itself, which means there is no need for type libraries or Interface Definition Language (IDL) files. The CLR locates the metadata in the PE file and extracts it from there as necessary when the file is executed.

   At runtime the CLR's JIT compilers then convert the MSIL code to machine code, which is then executed. This machine code is obviously appropriate for the platform on which the CLR is installed. The JIT compilers and the CLR are made by various vendors, and I suppose the most notable one is the Windows CLR made by Microsoft (surprise, eh?).

JIT: Another Word for Virtual Machine?

I believe we have all heard about the virtual machine used by Java applets. In short the CLR's JIT compiler is the same as a virtual machine in the sense that it executes intermediate code and as such is platform independent. However, there is more to the way the CLR's JIT compiler handles the code execution than does the so-called virtual machine. The JIT compiler is dynamic, meaning that although it is made for a specific OS, it will detect and act upon the hardware layer at execution time.

The JIT compiler can optimize the code for the specific processor that is used on the system where the code is being executed. This means once the JIT compiler detects the CPU, it can optimize the code for that particular CPU. Instead of just optimizing code for the Pentium processor, the compiler can also optimize for a particular version of the Pentium processor, such as the Pentium IV. This is good, and although the current execution of managed code is somewhat slower than unmanaged code, we are probably not far from the point in time when managed code will execute faster than unmanaged code.

Another major difference between the Java virtual machine and the CLR is that whereas the former is invoked for every new process/application, this is not true for the latter.

Assemblies and Namespaces

The .NET Framework uses assemblies and namespaces for grouping related functionality, and you have to know what an assembly and a namespace really are. You can develop some very simple .NET applications without really knowing these items, but you will not get very far.

Assembly

An *assembly* is the primary building block for a .NET Framework application, and it is a fundamental part of the runtime. All applications that use the CLR must be made up of more than one or more assemblies. Each assembly provides the CLR with all the necessary information for an application to run. Please note that an application can be and often is made up of more than one assembly, that is, an assembly is not a unit of application deployment. You can think of an assembly in terms of classes in a DLL.

Although I refer to an assembly as a single entity, it might in fact be composed of several files. It is a logical collection of functionality that is deployed as a single unit (even if it is more than one file). This has to do with the way an assembly is put together. Think of an assembly in terms of a type library and the information you find in one. However, an assembly also contains information about everything else that makes up your application, and is therefore said to be self-describing.

Because an assembly is self-describing by means of an assembly manifest, you won't have to deal anymore with shared DLLs in your application and the problems they have created over the years since Windows came of age. However, because you no longer use shared DLLs, your code will take up more memory and disk space, as the same functionality can now be easily duplicated on your hard disk and in memory. It is possible to share assemblies, however, to get around this.

Actually, you can still use COM+ Services (DLLs and EXEs) from within the .NET Framework, and you can even add .NET Framework components to a COM+ application. However, this book will concentrate on using .NET Framework components.

As touched upon a moment before, an assembly contains a *manifest*, which is little more than an index of all the files that make up the assembly. The assembly manifest is also called the assembly's metadata. (As mentioned earlier, metadata is data used to describe the main data.) Within the manifest, you have the components listed in Table 1-1.

Table 1-1. Assembly Manifest Components

ITEM	DESCRIPTION
Identity	Name, version, shared name, and digital signature
Culture, Processor, OS	The various cultures, processors and OSs supported
File Table	Hash and relative path of all other files that are part of the assembly
Referenced Assemblies	A list of all external dependencies, that is, other assemblies statically referenced
Type Reference	Information on how to map a type reference to a file containing the declaration and implementation
Permissions	The permissions your assembly requests from the runtime environment in order to run effectively

Besides the assembly manifest components, a developer can also add custom assembly attributes. These information-only attributes can include title and description of the assembly.

Namespace

A *namespace* is a logical way to group or organize related types (classes, interfaces, or value types). A .NET namespace is a design-time convenience only, which is used for logical naming/grouping. At runtime it is the assembly that establishes the name scope.

The various .NET Framework types are named using a hierarchical naming scheme with a dot syntax. Because the naming scheme is hierarchical, there is also a root namespace. The .NET root namespace is called **System**. For example, for the second-level namespace **IO** in the **System** namespace, the full name is **System.IO**. In code you would include the following to use types within the **System.IO** namespace:

```
Imports System.IO
```

This would give you easy access to the types within the namespace. So to declare an object as an instance of the **File** class in the **System.IO** namespace, you would enter the following:

```
Dim objFile As File
```

When the compiler encounters this declaration statement, it will look for the **File** class within your assembly, but when that fails, it will append **System.IO.** to the **File** class to see if it can find the **File** class in that namespace. However, you can also directly prefix the class with the namespace. So, to declare an object as an instance of the **File** class in the **System.IO** namespace, you would enter the following:

```
Dim objFile As System.IO.File
```

As you can see, using the **Imports** statement could save you a fair bit of typing. I believe it will also make your code easier to read and maintain if you have all your **Imports** statements at the top of your class or module file. One look and you know what namespaces are being used.

A namespace is created using the following syntax:

```
Namespace <NsName>
End Namespace
```

where <*NsName*> is the name you want to give to your namespace. All types that are to be part of the namespace must be placed within the namespace block.

You need namespaces to help prevent ambiguity, which is also known as *namespace pollution*. This happens when two different libraries contain the same names, causing a conflict. Namespaces help you eliminate this problem!

If two namespaces actually do have the same type, and you reference this type, the compiler will find the first one referenced in code and hand it to you. This means that if you have a module or class file, the location of the **Imports** statement will determine which type will be chosen. Say that you have two namespaces, called *Test1* and *Test2*, which both implement the class *Show.* You need to reference the *Show* class of the *Test2* namespace and other classes within both the two namespaces, so you use the **Imports** statement:

```
Imports Test1
Imports Test2
```

Now, what happens when you create an object as an instance of the *Show* class, within the same class or module file as the **Import** statements, like this?

```
Dim objTest As New Show
```

Well, because the *Test1* namespace is referenced first, the compiler will automatically pick the *Show* class from there. So, in this particular case you will need to prefix the class name with the namespace, like this:

```
Dim objTest As New Test1.Show
```

Namespaces can span more than one assembly, making it possible for two or more developers to work on different assemblies, but create classes within the same namespace. Namespaces within the current assembly are accessible at all times, that is, you do not have to import them.

> **NOTE** *Namespaces are explicitly public, and you cannot change that using an access modifier such as **Private**. However, you have full control over the accessibility of the types within the namespace. As stated, the visibility of a namespace is public, but the assembly in which you place it determines the accessibility of a namespace. This means the namespace is publicly available to all projects that reference the assembly into which it is placed.*

The runtime environment does not actually know anything about namespaces, so when you access a type, the CLR needs the full name of the type and the assembly that contains the type definition. With this information the CLR can load the assembly and access the type.

The .NET Framework Class Library

The .NET Framework Class Library includes base classes and classes derived from the base classes. These classes include a lot of functionality, such as server controls, exception handling, and data access of course, which is the subject of this very book. The .NET Framework classes give you a head start when building your applications, because you do not have to design it from the ground up. The class library is actually a hierarchical set of unified, object-oriented, extensible class libraries, also called Application Programming Interfaces (APIs). This differs from previous versions of Visual Basic, in which a lot of system and OS functionality could only be accessed through Windows API calls.

Getting Cozy with the .NET Integrated Development Environment

The Integrated Development Environment (IDE) hosts a slew of new fantastic features, and I will mention the following ones very briefly:

- IDE shared by all languages

- Two interface modes

- Built-in Web browser functionality

- Command window

- Built-in object browser

- Integrated debugger

- Integrated help system

- Macros

- Upgraded deployment tools

- Text editors

- Server Explorer

- Data connections

- Toolbox

- Task list

All Languages Share the IDE

All .NET languages share the same IDE (see Figure 1-1), giving all developers the benefit of the same tools across the various programming languages. This also means that you get the same look and feel, whatever language you are developing in.

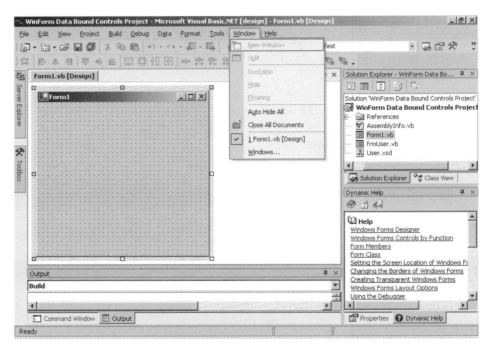

Figure 1-1. One shared IDE

Two Interface Modes

The IDE supports two *interface modes*, which arrange windows and panes:

- *Multiple document interface (MDI) mode*: This is the old mode well known from previous versions of Visual Basic, where you have the MDI parent window hosting a number of MDI children within the MDI parent window context. In Figure 1-2 you can see the two open windows, **Start Page** and **Form1.vb [Design]**, overlap as MDI children windows.

- *Tabs on documents mode*: This is the default mode, and I personally prefer this mode, as it seems easier to arrange all your windows and panes. Either of the two open windows in Figure 1-1 can be displayed by clicking on the appropriate tab, **Start Page** or **Form1.vb [Design]**.

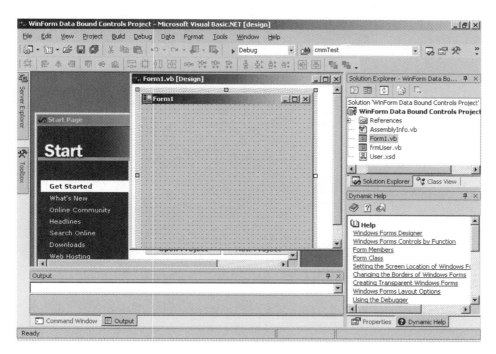

Figure 1-2. MDI mode

Built-in Web Browser Functionality

The IDE has built-in Web browser capabilities so you do not need to have a separate browser installed on your development machine. However, I do recommend installing at least one separate Web browser for testing purposes. The built-in Web browser is great for viewing Web pages without having to compile and run the whole project. See the **Browse – Object Construction Sample** Window in Figure 1-3, which displays an HTML page within the built-in Web browser.

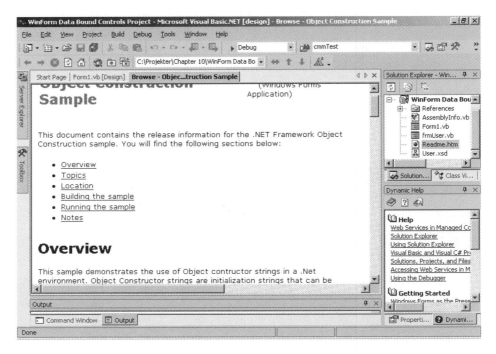

Figure 1-3. Built-in Web browser

Command Window

The Command window has two modes:

- *Command mode* allows you to type your IDE commands and create short name aliases for often-used commands (see Figure 1-4).

- *Immediate mode* lets you evaluate expressions, set or read the value of variables, assign object references, and execute code statements (see Figure 1-5).

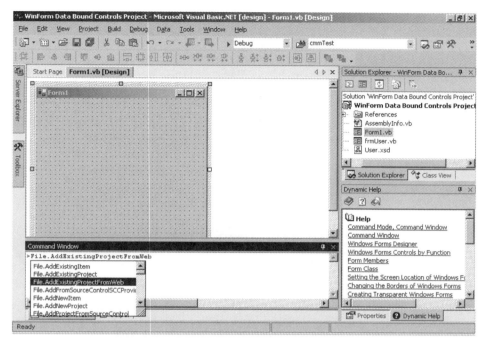

Figure 1-4. Command window in command mode

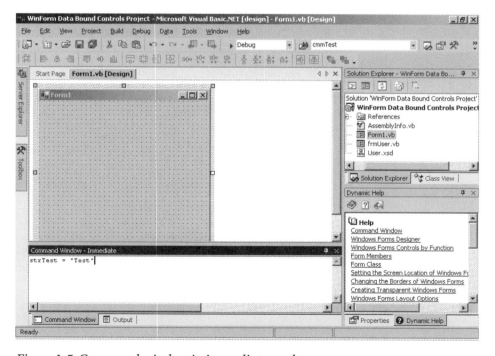

Figure 1-5. Command window in immediate mode

Built-in Object Browser

The built-in Object Browser, which feels and looks like the one in previous versions of Visual Basic, lets you examine objects and their methods and properties. The objects you can examine, also called the Object Browser's browsing scope, can be part of external or referenced components, or components in the form of projects in the current solution. The components in the browsing scope include COM components and .NET Framework components (obviously). Figure 1-6 shows the Object Browser.

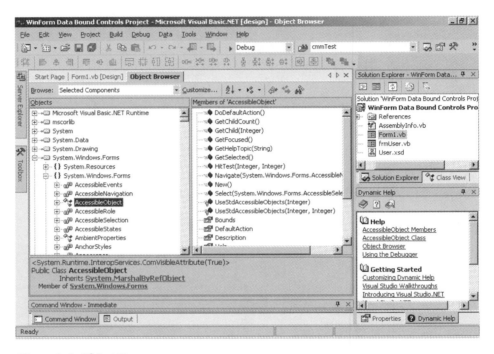

Figure 1-6. Object Browser

Integrated Debugger

The integrated debugger now supports cross-language debugging from within the IDE. You can also debug multiple programs at the same time, either by launching the various programs from within the IDE or by attaching to already running programs or processes (see Figure 1-7).

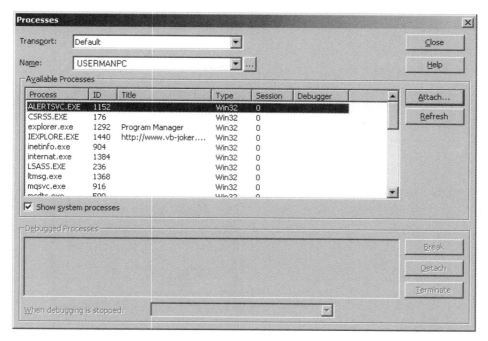

Figure 1-7. Debugger Processes window

Integrated Help System

The Help system in VS.NET is somewhat advanced and consists of the following:

- *Dynamic Help*: The Dynamic Help is great; and I love it, because the content of the Dynamic Help window is based on the current context and selection. This means that the Dynamic Help window, which is located in the lower-right corner of the IDE by default, changes its content when you move around in the code editor to reflect the current selection. This works not only when you are in the Code Editor, but also when you edit HTML code, use the XML Designer, design reports, edit cascading style sheets (CSS) and so on.

   When you want to view one of the topics displayed in the Dynamic Help window, as shown in Figure 1-8, you simply click the topic and the help text pops up, either in the MSDN Library application or within the IDE as a document. This depends or your help settings, external or internal display.

- *MSDN*: The MSDN Library comes as part of Visual Studio.NET as it did with previous versions of Visual Basic. The complete help system for VS.NET is included as is the Platform SDK and the .NET Framework SDK documentation, to mention a few inclusions. The Library browser has been improved, and it is now a browser-style application with links to appropriate information on the various Microsoft Web sites.

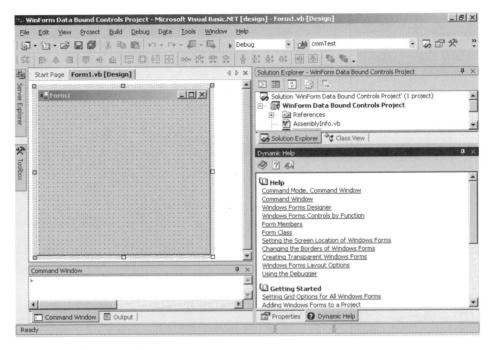

Figure 1-8. Dynamic Help window

Macros

We all know that some tasks or series of tasks are done repeatedly when developing. That is why the VS.NET IDE gives you the opportunity to automate these repetitive tasks with the use of macros. Macros can be created/edited using either the Recorder or the Macros IDE. The Macros IDE is actually a rather familiar friend, if you ever did any VBA programming, as it is quite similar. So too is the language, which looks like VBA. In fact, it is now called Visual Studio for Applications, as discussed earlier, and the macro language is of course based on Visual Basic.NET.

Upgraded Deployment Tools

The Deployment Tools in VS.NET have been heavily upgraded since the previous version of VS. In VS.NET you can perform the following tasks among others:

- Deploy application tiers to different test servers for remote debugging

- Deploy Web applications

- Distribute applications using the Microsoft Windows Installer

Text Editors

The various text editors in the IDE all have the same functionality that you have come to expect from a Windows editor. The shortcuts are the same and most of the accelerator keys are well known.

However, something that may be new to you is the inclusion of line numbers, displayed on the very left of the editor. These optional line numbers are not part of the code or text, but are merely displayed for your convenience (see Figure 1-9).

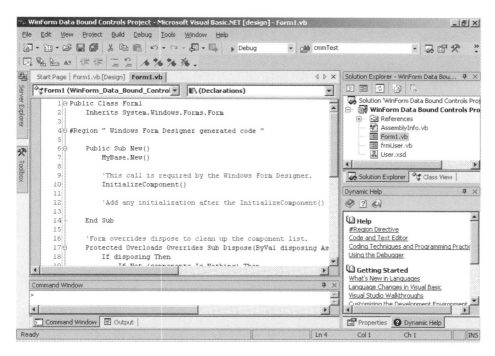

Figure 1-9. The text editor with line numbers

Server Explorer

The Server Explorer window, which is located on the bar on the left side of the IDE by default, can be used for manipulating resources on any server you can access. The resources include the following:

- Database objects

- Performance counters*

- Message queues*

- Services*

- Web services*

- Processes*

- Event logs*

Most of these resources are new (those marked with an *) and can literally be dragged onto a Web form or Windows form and then manipulated from within your code (see Figure 1-10). Please note that it depends on the version of Visual Studio you buy, whether all of these resources can be accessed from the Server Explorer.

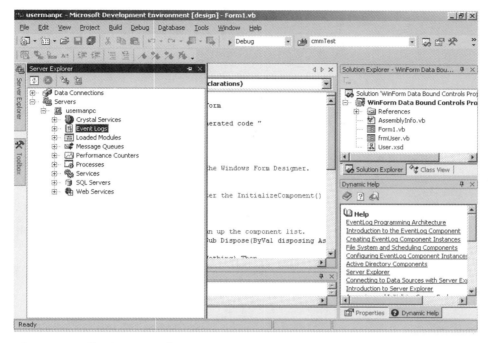

Figure 1-10. The Server Explorer

Data Connections

There are a number of ways you can set up connections to a database and manipulate the database objects. Hey, wait a minute! I will be going into greater detail on this subject from Chapter 3 on, so don't get me started on this subject here!

Toolbox

The Toolbox window, which is located on the bar on the left side of the IDE by default, contains all the intrinsic tools you can use in the various design and editor modes, such as HTML design, Windows Form design, Web Form design, Code Editor, and UML Diagram design. When you have a window open, the content of the Toolbox changes according to what is available to work with in the current window (see Figure 1-11).

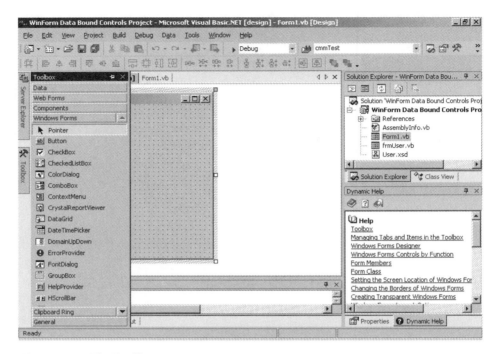

Figure 1-11. The Toolbox

Task List

The Task List window, which is docked at the bottom of the IDE by default, helps you organize and manage the various tasks you need to complete in order to build your solution. The developer and the CLR both use the Task List. This means that the developer can add tasks manually, but the CLR also adds tasks if an error occurs when compiling. When a task is added to the list, it can contain a filename and line number. This way you can double-click the task name and go straight to the problem or unfinished task.

Once you finish a certain task, you can check the appropriate check box to indicate the task has been completed (see Figure 1-12).

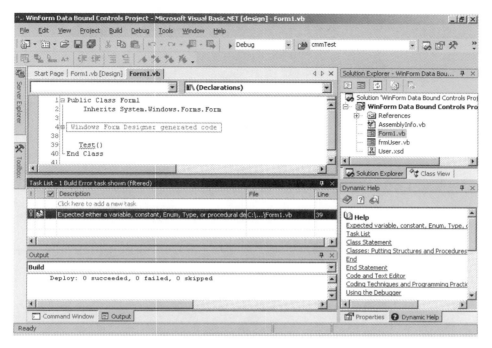

Figure 1-12. The Task List

Summary

This chapter is a quick rundown of the new concepts and terms in Visual Basic.NET. I discussed assemblies and namespaces, and how they fit in the .NET Framework; the Common Language Runtime, which unifies the .NET Programming Languages with a common base; the Common Language Specification, which is the standard all .NET languages must adhere to; the Common Type System, which dictates the base types used for data exchange; server-based Active Server Pages programming; and the Framework Class Library.

Finally, I gave you a quick look at some of the new features of the shared IDE, such as the line numbering in the text editors and the integrated debugger.

The next chapter is a short side trip from Visual Basic.NET. It is a general chapter on how to design and talk to databases. Amongst other concepts you will be looking at how to normalize a database.

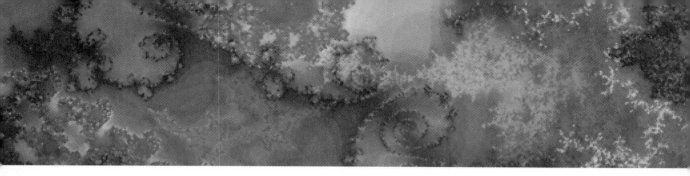

Part Two

Database Programming

CHAPTER 2

Talking to Databases

A short introduction to general database terms and concepts

IN THIS CHAPTER I introduce you to the terms and concepts that I will be using through the rest of the book. Consider this chapter a reference to the following chapters. I will be looking at what a database really is, why you should use a database, and how to design a relational database. Although this chapter is not intended to teach you everything there is to know about designing a relational database, you will get the basics. For additional information, you will find a good article on database design and a link for database normalization at the following address on the Microsoft Product Services site:
`http://support.microsoft.com/support/kb/articles/Q234/2/08.ASP`.

The hands-on exercise at the end of this chapter will reinforce the database concepts I present to you here.

What Exactly Is a Database?

There are probably as many definitions of the term *database* as there are different software implementations of electronic databases. So for that reason, I will try to keep it simple. A database is a collection of data, which can be information about anything really. A phone number is data, a name is data, a book contains data, and so on. What the data is about is not really important in the context of defining data. A database is usually organized in some way.

A phone book is a database usually organized (sorted) alphabetically by surname. The main objective for a phone book is for the reader to be able to locate a phone number. With any given phone number you generally associate a name, consisting of first name and surname, an address, and perhaps the title of the person who "owns" the phone number. Here I am actually in the process of taking the phone book apart, or perhaps I should call it figuring out how the phone book is organized. I will leave this for later paragraphs.

As you can see, a database does not have to be an electronic collection of data, nor does it have to be organized in any particular way. However, this book deals with electronic databases exclusively.

Why Use a Database?

When thinking of reasons for using databases, some keywords spring to mind: storage, accessibility, organization, and manipulation.

- *Storage:* For a database to exist elsewhere other than in your head, you need to store it in some form. You can store it electronically on a disk and bring it with you, if that is what you want to do, or hand it to someone else. Your database could be in the form of a Microsoft Excel spreadsheet or a Microsoft Access database.

- *Accessibility:* Well, if you cannot access your data within the database, the database is of no use to anyone. When using an electronic database, such as one created in Microsoft Access, you generally have a lot of options for accessing it. You can access an MS Access database using the MS Access front-end, or indeed any application capable of communicating with a driver that can talk to the MS Access database. Now obviously accessibility depends on the format the database is saved in, but for argument's sake let us just say that it is standard format known to everyone, such as dBase or MS Access.

- *Organization:* The most logical way to organize a phone book is alphabetically. However, the phone book has a lot of duplicated data, which can take up twice as much space as you would expect nonduplicated data to take. The data is duplicated to allow you to use more than one way to look up data. You can look up a listing under the surname and you can look up a listing using the address, and so on. Duplication is obviously not a problem when speaking of an electronic database, if it has been properly implemented. You can use indexes and keys to give your clients a variety of ways to access the data without duplicating it. Indexes and keys serve as pointers to the data, which means they are valuable tools for avoiding duplicated data.

- *Manipulation:* Editing a phone book is certainly not an easy task. You can strike over the text in case a phone number no longer exists, but what about changing the owner of a phone number or adding a new phone number? In how many places will you have to edit and/or add data? This just will not work, unless you are willing to redo the whole phone book!

When it comes to your electronic database, if it has been properly implemented, it is simply a matter of locating the information you want to edit or delete, enter the data, and off you go. The data is now added and changed in all the right places.

Okay, so to quickly summarize, here are the benefits of using a database:

- Locating and manipulating the data is much easier when your data is in one place.

- Organization of the data is easier when it is in one place and it is stored electronically.

- You can access the data from a variety of applications and locations when all your data is placed in one place, your database.

Database Management System

The term *Database Management System* (DBMS) is used in a variety of contexts, some more correct than others. A complete DBMS consists of hardware, software, data, and users. However, in the context of this book, a DBMS is a software package through which you can administrate one or more databases, manipulate the data within a database, and export/import to and from different data formats. A DBMS is not necessarily a database server system such as MS SQL Server or Oracle; it can also be a so-called desktop database such as Microsoft Access or Lotus Approach. A desktop database does not require a server; it is simply a file (or set of related files) that you can access using the right driver from within your own application or using accompanying front-end software.

Throughout this book, I will be using the terms *database* and *DBMS* interchangeably.

Rows vs. Records

This concept is quite simple, but it used to confuse me when I first started messing about with databases. If you are confused about these terms, then let me help you: *Rows* and *records* are the exact same thing. Remember that when you come across the two terms in the very same context.

Columns vs. Fields

Like rows and records, the terms *column* and *field* are synonymous.

Relational vs. Hierarchical

Today there are two types of databases widely deployed, *relational* and *hierarchical*. The relational database is by far the most popular of these and it is probably the one you already know about. Mind you, you have probably been using a hierarchical database without knowing it! The Windows Registry and the Active Directory in Windows 2000 are both hierarchical databases.

Hierarchical Databases

A *hierarchical database* has an inverted tree-like structure with a root element at the top (see Figure 2-1). The root element has one or more nodes, and the nodes themselves have nodes. It's just like a tree with branches and leaves. You have probably been using the Windows Explorer file manager, which relies on a tree-like structure for representing your disk and files. The Windows Explorer is more like a hierarchical DBMS with multiple databases, that is, My Computer is a database, drive C on your local computer is a node of the root element My Computer, the folders on drive C are nodes of drive C, and so on.

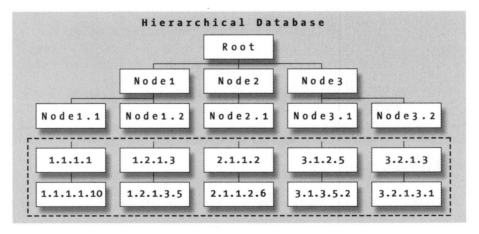

Figure 2-1. Hierarchical database

Hierarchical databases are usually very fast, because the data structures are directly linked, but they are not good for modeling complex relations such as the ones you have in a warehouse system with raw materials, products, boxed products, shelves, rows of shelves, and so on. All these items are somewhat related, and it is difficult to represent these relations in a hierarchical database without duplicating data and loss of performance.

These are some good candidates for hierarchical databases:

- File and directory systems

- Management/organization rankings

I am sure you can think of a few more yourself.

Hierarchical databases are generally hard to implement, set up, and maintain, and they usually require a systems programmer to do so. However, IBM produces a hierarchical database system called the Information Management System (IMS). You can find it at `http://www-4.ibm.com/software/data/ims/`. IMS has tools similar to those in relational databases systems (discussed next) for setting up and implementing your hierarchical database. I will not be implementing a hierarchical database in this book, but I will show you how to access one, the Active Directory. See Chapter 7 for more information on Active Directory and hierarchical databases.

Relational Databases

A *relational database* consists of tables that are related to each other in some way, either directly or indirectly. If you think in terms of objects, tables represent the objects, and these objects/tables are connected using so-called relationships. One example might be an order system, where you have products, customers, orders, and so on. In a rather simple order system you will have separate tables for holding information pertaining to orders, customers, and products. A customer has zero or more orders, and an order consists of one or more products, so you can see how easy it is to create relationships between the tables. Please see "Relational Database Design" a little later in this chapter for more information on how a relational database should be designed.

Relational Database Model

The Relational Database Model, which was "invented" by E. F. Codd, has become the de facto standard for database design today. The idea behind this model is not very complex, although it can be hard to grasp at first.

Relational Database Design

It is very important that you design your database properly the first time around, because it is so much harder to make structural changes after you have deployed it. Other reasons for implementing a good database design are performance and maintainability. Sometimes after you have been working on your database design for a while, you end up redesigning it, simply because you find out that the current design does not facilitate what you are trying to achieve. Design your first database, go over the design, and change it according to your findings. You should keep doing this, until you no longer find any problems with it.

There are many excellent tools for modeling a relational database, but even if these tools are good, you still need to know how to construct a relational database to fully exploit one of these tools. Here is a list of some of the tools available:

- ICT WizERD: `http://www.ict-computing.com/prod01.htm`

- Erwin: `http://www.cai.com/products/alm/erwin.htm`

- Visible Analyst® DB Engineer:
  `http://www.visible.com/dataapp/dappprods/vadbe.htm`

Identifying Objects for Your Database

When you set out to design your relational database, the first thing you need to do is to sit down and find out what objects your database should hold. By *objects,* I mean items representing customers (Customer objects), orders (Order objects), and products (Product objects), which you would find in a typical order system. It can be difficult to identify these objects, especially if you are new to relational database design. If this is so, I am quite sure that the first object you identify, and perhaps the only object you can identify, is the Order object. The important thing to remember here is that while the Order object is a perfectly legitimate object, there is more to it than that. You need to keep breaking the objects apart until you are at the very lowest level. In the example order system, an order is made up of one or more OrderLine objects, a Customer object, and so on. The OrderLine object itself can be broken into more objects. An OrderLine consists of product types and the number of products. The Price object can be derived from the Product object. Here's a list of typical objects for this order system:

- Order

- Customer

- Product

- OrderLine

- Price

Something's wrong with this, however. When you split your objects into smaller ones, the criteria for doing so should be whether the derived object actually has a life of its own. Take a look at the Price object. Should it be an object, or is it simply a property of the Product object? By property I mean something that describes the object. The Price object will probably correspond to more than one Product objects, and as such it will be duplicated. The Price could be a separate object, but it would make more sense to have it be a property of the Product object.

Consider the following questions and answers:

- Does one price correspond to more than one Product, or will the price be duplicated within the Product object?

  The Price probably will correspond to more than one Product, and as such it will be duplicated. You could treat Price as a separate object, but it would make more sense to have it be a property of the Product object. Although the Price will be duplicated, you also have to think about maintainability. If you need to change the price of one Product, what happens when you change the Price object and more than one Product is linked to it? You change the price for all related Products!

- Does a Price describe a Product, or is it generic?

  The Price describes one Product and one Product only.

- Is or will the Price be calculated when invoicing?

  The Price is fixed, so we will have to store it somewhere.

It's necessary to identify these objects so you can start creating tables; the objects I have identified so far are indeed tables. The properties that I have come across, such as the Price, are fields in the table.

Relationships

Now you need to tell the DBMS how the various tables are related by defining *relationships*. There are three kinds of relationships:

- One-to-one

- One-to-many

- Many-to-many

Relationships are established between *parent tables* and *child tables*. The parent table is the primary object in this context and the child tables are the related objects.

One-to-One Relationships

One-to-one relationships are used when you want to create a direct relationship between two objects, a parent table and a child table. Examples of such a relationship can be seen in Table 2-1.

Table 2-1. One-to-One Relationships

PARENT TABLE	CHILD TABLE
OrderLines	Products
Orders	Customers
Customer	Postal Code

One-to-Many Relationships

A *one-to-many relationship* is the most common relationship, and you will implement many of these relationships over the years as a database designer. This type of relationship exists between a parent table and a child table in cases where the parent record can have zero or more child records. Examples of such a relationship can be seen in Table 2-2.

Table 2-2. One-to-Many Relationships

PARENT TABLE	CHILD TABLE
Orders	OrderLines
Customers	Orders
Products	OrderLines

As you can see from the examples of one-to-one relationships in the previous section, the parent and child tables are often reversed. This means that the parent table in a one-to-one relationship can be the child table in a one-to-many relationship.

Many-to-Many Relationships

A *many-to-many relationship* exists in cases where a record in the parent table has many related records in the child table and vice versa. One example of such a relationship can be seen in Table 2-3.

Table 2-3. Many-to-Many Relationships

PARENT TABLE	ASSOCIATED TABLE	CHILD TABLE
Orders	OrderLines	Products

Many-to-many relationships cannot be modeled directly between a parent table and a child table. Instead you define two one-to-many relationships using a third table, called an associated table. This table holds the unique ID of the record in the parent record as well as the unique ID of the record in the child table as one record (see Figure 2-2). So, in order to find a particular record in the associated table, you need the unique IDs of both the parent and child records. The two IDs are very good candidates for a composite primary key.

Figure 2-2 should be read like this:

- One order contains one or more products

- One product belongs to zero or more orders

- An order line belongs to one order only and contains one product only. The OrderLines table is the associated table in this case.

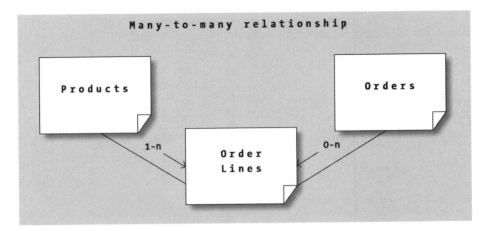

Figure 2-2. Many-to-many relationship

Keys

Keys are important in relational database design, because they are used as record identifiers and for sorting query output. There are two types of keys: primary keys and foreign keys.

Primary Key

The *primary key* of a table is always unique, that is, no two records in the table hold the same value in the field(s) that is designated as the primary key. This means the primary key uniquely identifies each record in the table. This also means that a field that makes up or is part of a primary key, cannot contain Null. A primary key comprising more than one field is called a *composite primary key*. The primary key is often a *lookup key*, which helps you locate a record; you search for a value in the primary key field. In terms of relationships, the primary key is always used in combination with a foreign key (discussed next) in the child table. In Figure 2-3, the primary key in the Orders table is marked PK. There can be only one row in the Orders table that relates to zero or more rows in the Order-Lines table.

Foreign Key

A *foreign key* is used in relationships as the lookup value in the child table. This means it directly corresponds to the value of the primary key in the parent table, so that you can use the value of the primary key to look up a related record in the child table. Note that unlike the primary key, the foreign key can contain a Null value. I don't recommend this, but it's doable. In a one-to-one relationship, the foreign key must be unique. Otherwise it can contain duplicates. In Figure 2-3, the foreign key in the OrderLines table is marked FK. There can be many rows in the OrderLines table that relate to a row in the Orders table. Please note that the Salesman field in the Orders table is a foreign key candidate for looking up Orders belonging to a certain salesman. This obviously requires a separate Salesman table with a unique SalesmanId field as the primary key.

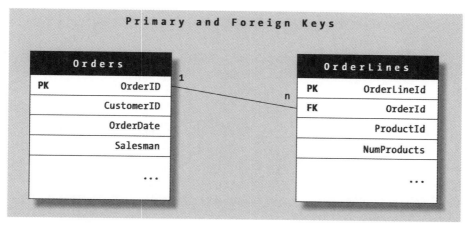

Figure 2-3. Primary and foreign keys

Index

You use indexes to specify lookup fields that are not primary or foreign keys. When you create an index, it is much faster to search for a value in the field(s) that makes up the index. There is some overhead when you create an index, but if you are careful when selecting the fields you want to use in indexes, the advantages outweigh the disadvantages.

The overhead results in extra disk space consumption and a slight performance penalty when adding or editing records. Sometimes you need to try out an index and do some performance testing to see if you will gain or lose performance by implementing it. One candidate for an index is the Name field in a Customer table. You cannot use it as a primary key field as it more than likely will be duplicated, because many people have the same names. However, you will probably need to look up a customer using his or her name, as he or she might not remember his or her customer ID (which could be the primary key) if the customer gives you a call.

Data Integrity

Data integrity indicates if the content of a database can be "trusted," or if it is up-to-date. In other words, data integrity means that no data is outdated or orphaned because of updates to related data. Data integrity can be ensured by checking for one or more of the following:

- Entity integrity

- Referential integrity

- Domain integrity

Entity Integrity

Entity integrity states that no value in a primary key can be NULL. This goes for composite primary keys (primary keys consisting of more than one field) as well as single-field primary keys. The special value NULL refers to an empty or nonassigned value. Since primary keys must be unique, they must not be allowed to contain NULL values, and hence you should apply entity integrity when designing your database.

Referential Integrity

Referential integrity has to do with. . . yes, you guessed it, relationships. Referential integrity ensures that no record in a child table has a foreign key that does not exist as a primary key in the parent table. This means that when you enforce referential integrity, you cannot add a record to the child table with a foreign key that does not match a primary key in the parent table.

Depending on whether you specify restrictions or cascades when you set up referential integrity, the behavior in Table 2-4 is applied. A *cascade* refers to the process whereby related tables are also updated when you update or delete a record in a parent table.

Table 2-4. Referential Integrity Behavior

TASK	CASCADE	RESTRICTION
Delete a record in parent table for which there are related records in a child table.	The related records in the child table are also deleted.	The deletion is disallowed.
Update/change the primary key of a record in parent table for which there is related records in a child table.	The related records in the child table are also updated.	The update/change is disallowed.

Referential integrity ensures that no record in a child table is orphaned, that is, has no related record in the parent table.

Domain Integrity

Domain integrity ensures that values in a particular field conform to the domain description in place. Domain integrity is ensured through physical and logical constraints applied to a specific field. When you try to add an invalid value to a field with domain constraints, the value will be disallowed. Such a domain constraint could be applied to a Phone Number field in the Customers table, like this:

- Physical constraint: data type: string, length: 13

- Logical constraint: input format: (999) 9999999

Normalization

Although normalization is not actually a part of the relational model, it is very much a process that can be applied to relational database design. *Normalization* is a method of data analysis you use when you are designing your database. The normalization process, which is a series of progressive sets of rules, can be referred to as normal forms. The purpose of normalization is to define tables, which you can modify with predictable results, and thus ensure data integrity. A predictable result means that no data inconsistency and/or redundancy occur when you modify the data. The normal forms were defined in the 1970s to overcome problems with table relations. These problems are also called *anomalies*.

Normal Forms

Because the *normal forms* are a progressive set of rules, they should be applied beginning with the First Normal Form, then the Second Normal Form, and so on. (The various levels of forms are discussed later in this section.) Mind you, not all of the normal forms have to be applied to your database design. I would think that a lot of databases out there that have been normalized only adhere to the first three normal forms. I believe it is up to you as a database designer to pull the plug on the process, once you feel you have achieved your goal.

> **NOTE** *I had a hard time understanding the normal forms when I first came across them some years ago. These days I hardly think about them when I design my databases. I just design them and they generally conform to the first three to four normal forms. Actually, if you are going to design a number of databases in your career, I can only suggest you get to know these normal forms by heart. The hard work will pay off, believe me. If you already know about normalization and generally apply it to your database design, then your job for the rest of this book is to catch my mistakes!*

First Normal Form

The *First Normal Form* (1NF) is achieved when all repeating groups of data have been put into separate tables and connected using a one-to-many relationship. One example of this might be if the Orders table had columns for four Order-Lines, as shown in Figure 2-4.

Figure 2-4. 1NF violation

Don't tell me you never made the mistake displayed in Figure 2-4. Think back to when you were first designing databases that were effectively flat file databases, that is, databases where all data is placed in the same table or file. If you want to conform to 1NF, your table design should instead look like Figure 2-5.

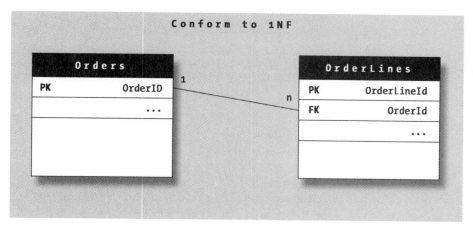

Figure 2-5. 1NF conformance

Second Normal Form

To conform to the *Second Normal Form* (2NF) you must first conform to 1NF. Actually 2NF only applies to tables in 1NF with composite primary keys. So if your database conforms to 1NF and your tables only have primary keys with a single field, then your database automatically conforms to 2NF. However, if your table does have a composite primary key, then you need to eliminate the functional dependencies on a partial key. Putting the violating fields in a separate table does this.

For instance, if you have an OrderLines table and it contains the fields shown in Figure 2-6, then the ProductDescription field violates 2NF. 2NF is violated because the ProductDescription field only relates to the ProductId field and not the OrderId field. This means that to conform to 2NF, you would have to move the ProductDescription field to the Products table. You can use the ProductId as a lookup value to retrieve the product description.

Figure 2-6. 2NF violation

Third Normal Form

Third Normal Form (3NF) conformance can be achieved by conforming to 2NF and by eliminating functional dependencies on non-key fields. As with 2NF, putting the violating fields into a separate table meets this condition. This means all non-key fields will then be dependent on the whole key only.

In Figure 2-7, the Location field is not dependent on the ProductId field, which is the primary key, but instead on the Warehouse field, which is not a key. Therefore the 3NF is violated. You would create a new Warehouse table with the Warehouse and Location fields to conform to the 3NF. You can use the Warehouse field as a lookup value to retrieve the Warehouse location.

```
           3NF  Violation

             Products
      PK           ProductId
                         ...
                   Warehouse
                   Location
```

Figure 2-7. 3NF violation

Fourth Normal Form

To conform to the *Fourth Normal Form* (4NF), the records in your tables must conform to 3NF and they must have no multivalued dependencies. The term *multivalued dependencies* can be explained like this: The record may not contain two or more independent multivalued facts about an entity. Confused, eh? Okay, think about this then:

- A customer can speak one or more languages and one or more customers can speak a language.

- A customer can have one or more payment options and one payment option can apply to zero or more customers.

As you can see, you are dealing with two many-to-many relationships.

In the example shown in Figure 2-8, you have the option of storing a payment option and a language for each customer. The only problem is that the language and the payment option are multivalued, that is, there are more than one language and more than one payment option. This effectively means a single customer who speaks the languages English and Danish and has the payment options Cash On Delivery (COD) and Credit will require more than one customer record. Actually, this customer will require four records if you need to hold all combinations (two languages × two payment options). Can you imagine the nightmare of updating all these records once you change, say, a payment option?

Figure 2-8. 4NF violation

To avoid violating the 4NF, you need to model the two many-to-many relationships using an associated table, as done for the Customers-Payments relationship in Figure 2-9. Please note that the primary key in the

CustomerPayments table is composite, that is, it consists of both fields, whereas there are two single-field foreign keys, one for each relation with the Customers and the Payments tables.

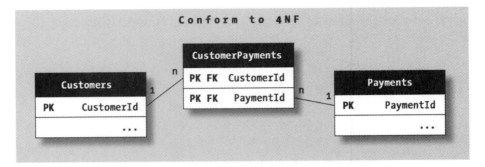

Figure 2-9. 4NF conformance

You need to conform to the 4NF to make sure you do not have data redundancy and to make data updates easy.

Fifth Normal Form

A record conforms to the *Fifth Normal Form* (5NF) when its information cannot be reconstructed from several smaller records. By smaller records I mean records each having fewer fields than the original record. The 5NF is not much different from the 4NF, and I don't think I have ever personally had to apply the 5NF to a database.

Denormalization

Denormalization is the process of reversing the normalization, usually because of a performance loss as a result of the normalization process. However, there are no hard-and-fast rules for when you need to start the denormalization process. Before you start doing any normalization, you can benchmark your current system and establish a baseline. When you are done with the normalization, you can again benchmark your system to see if any performance has been gained or lost. If the performance loss is too great, you start the denormalization process, where you reverse one or more of the changes you made in the normalization process. It is important that you only make one such change at a time in order to test for possible performance gains after every change.

Denormalization is also an important aspect to keep in mind when your database matures, because performance is most often degraded when you start adding data to your database.

UserMan Database Schema

The UserMan sample application that I build on throughout this book will feature a database, of course. The schema for this SQL Server database is shown in Figure 2-10.

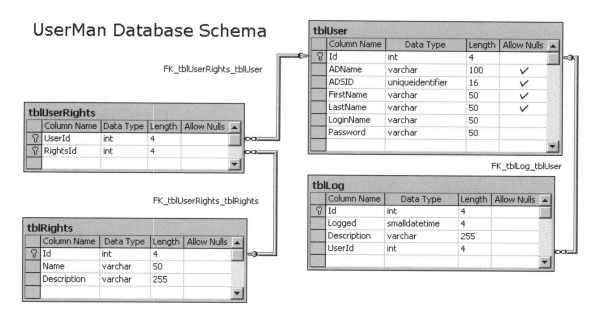

UserMan Database Schema

tblUser

Column Name	Data Type	Length	Allow Nulls
Id	int	4	
ADName	varchar	100	✓
ADSID	uniqueidentifier	16	✓
FirstName	varchar	50	✓
LastName	varchar	50	✓
LoginName	varchar	50	
Password	varchar	50	

FK_tblUserRights_tblUser

tblUserRights

Column Name	Data Type	Length	Allow Nulls
UserId	int	4	
RightsId	int	4	

FK_tblLog_tblUser

tblLog

Column Name	Data Type	Length	Allow Nulls
Id	int	4	
Logged	smalldatetime	4	
Description	varchar	255	
UserId	int	4	

FK_tblUserRights_tblRights

tblRights

Column Name	Data Type	Length	Allow Nulls
Id	int	4	
Name	varchar	50	
Description	varchar	255	

Figure 2-10. UserMan database schema

As you can see in Figure 2-10, the database includes four tables:

- *tblUser:* This is the main table that holds all standard information about a user, such as first name, last name, and so on.

- *tblUserRights:* This is an associated table that holds many-to-many relationships between the tblUser and tblRights tables.

- *tblRights:* This table holds the various rights a user can be assigned in the system, which could allow a user to create a new user, delete an existing user, and so on.

- *tblLog:* The log table holds information on when a user did what. Let's keep those users under tight control!

EXERCISE

Examine the UserMan database schema and see if you can find a way to improve the design according to the various design tools I have covered in this chapter.

As stated before, I will be working on this database throughout this book, and in the final chapter I will give you ideas on how to extend the current schema and the sample application.

Summary

This chapter explained databases and how and when to use them. I briefly outlined the differences between a relational database and a hierarchical database. Then I discussed designing a relational database, and I have shown you most of the concepts involved in building a relational database, such as the normal forms, keys (primary and foreign), the various types of relationships between tables and how to implement them logically, and indexes. I also covered data integrity in the form of entity, referential, and domain integrity.

The last section of this chapter detailed the database schema for the UserMan sample application. I will be working with this database throughout the book.

The following chapter takes you on a journey through most of the classes in ADO.NET and explains how to use them.

CHAPTER 3A

Presenting ADO.NET: The Connected Layer

This chapter and its twin chapter, Chapter 3B, cover ADO.NET. The classes in ADO.NET can be categorized into two groups: the connected layer and the disconnected layer. This chapter covers the connected layer.

Active Data Objects (ADO) has long been the preferred interface for Visual Basic programmers to access various data sources. Think of ADO as the middle layer in your application, the layer between your front-end and the data source. ADO 2.7 is the latest version of this product.

Active Data Objects.NET (ADO.NET) is the all-new singing-and-dancing version of ADO. ADO.NET has been designed to be a disconnected and distributed data access technology based on XML. This fits very well into the new, "hidden" Microsoft strategy of making it run on every platform that supports XML. It also means that you can pass ADO.NET data sets from one location to another over the Internet, because ADO.NET can penetrate firewalls. Actually, it is fair to say that ADO.NET is a revolution and not an evolution.

ADO vs. ADO.NET

This book refers to both of these data access technologies. Here is how you can distinguish one from the other:

- *ADO* will be used to describe the ADO technology that has been with us for some years now. This technology is COM-based and can only be used through COM Interop.

- *ADO.NET* is a new version based entirely on the .NET Framework, and the underlying technology is very different from the COM-based ADO. Although the name ADO is still there, these are different technologies.

However, as you probably know, ADO is still here, although it requires COM Interop (interoperability) if you want to use it from within the .NET Framework. You will get a chance to look at COM Interop in Chapter 3B.

ADO.NET is what you will be using in most of your .NET applications, because of its disconnected architecture. However, you should keep in mind that ADO.NET is firmly targeted at n-tier Web applications, or applications that are distributed over a number of different servers. So if you are building n-tier or client-server solutions for the Windows platform only, you are better off sticking with ADO for the moment, but this will probably change with future versions of ADO.NET.

You will get a look at ADO as well as ADO.NET here, but I will not be covering ADO in the same detail as ADO.NET. If you need more information on ADO, try these books from Apress:

- *Serious ADO: Universal Data Access with Visual Basic*, by Rob Macdonald. ISBN 1-893115-19-4. Published August 2000.

- *ADO Examples and Best Practices*, by William R. Vaughn. ISBN 1-893115-16-X. Published May 2000.

The overall object model looks the same for ADO and ADO.NET. In order to access a data source, you need a provider. A *provider* is really another word for driver, and it is simply a library that can access the data source in binary form. (See "Providers" later in this chapter for details.) Once you have the provider, you need to set up a connection from your application that uses the provider to gain access to the data source. See Figure 3A-1 for a simplified picture. Now that the connection is set up and opened, you can execute queries and retrieve, delete, manipulate, and update data from the data source.

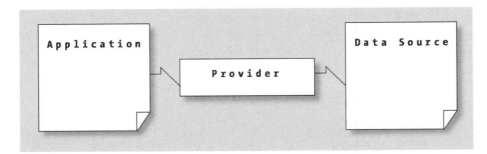

Figure 3A-1. How a provider works

You need data objects in order to manipulate data. I explain these in the following sections.

Data-Related Namespaces

There are a number of namespaces in VB. NET, or rather VS.NET, that are of interest when dealing with data (see Table 3A-1). These namespaces hold the various data classes that you must import into your code in order to use the classes.

Actually, you can prefix these classes with the namespace when you declare and instantiate your objects, but you still need to know where to find the classes in the first place.

> **NOTE** *If you are uncertain about what a namespace really is, see Chapter 1.*

Table 3A-1. Data-Related Namespaces

NAMESPACE	DESCRIPTION
System.Data	Holds the ADO.NET classes and other miscellaneous generic classes or classes that are subclassed in the .NET data providers.
System.Data.SqlClient	Holds the classes specific to MS SQL Server 7.0 or later. This is the MS SQL Server 7.0 or later .NET data provider.
System.Data.OleDb	Describes the collection of classes that are used for accessing an OLE DB data source. This is the OLE DB .NET Data Provider.

You can import namespaces into a class in your code using the **Imports** statement, like this:

```
Imports System.Data
```

Instead of importing the namespaces, you can prefix the classes when declaring and/or instantiating your objects, like this:

```
Dim cnnUserMan As System.Data.SqlClient.SqlConnection ' Declare new connection
cnnUserMan = New System.Data.SqlClient.SqlConnection() ' Instantiate connection
```

Providers

A *provider* is simply just another word for driver, meaning it is a binary library that exposes an API that can be called from within your application. The library is a DLL file, and sometimes this DLL is dependent on other DLLs, so in fact a provider can be made up of several files. The providers discussed here are called OLE DB providers and they can be accessed directly. However, when you use VB.NET, or previous versions of VB, the API exposed by the provider library is actually wrapped in the ADO classes. So, you do not have to worry about this low-level kind of programming. All you need to do is specify the name of the provider when you set up or open a connection.

OLE DB is really a specification that is used by OLE DB providers, and the primary purpose of an OLE DB provider is to translate OLE DB instructions into the language of the target data source and vice versa.

There is one important distinction between ADO and ADO.NET: ADO calls the OLE DB provider through COM Interop whereas ADO.NET uses the **DataAdapter** class, which then calls the OLE DB provider, also through COM Interop (see Figure 3A-2). Actually, this is not quite true; sometimes the **DataAdapter** object directly accesses the API exposed by the DBMS, as can be the case with MS SQL Server 7.0 or later (see Figure 3A-3). The .NET data provider for SQL Server uses a private protocol named tabular data stream (TDS) to talk to SQL Server.

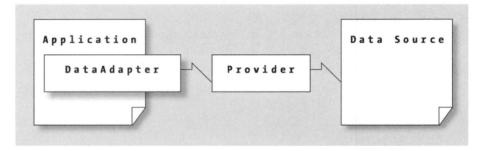

*Figure 3A-2. **DataAdapter** using an OLE DB provider to access the data source*

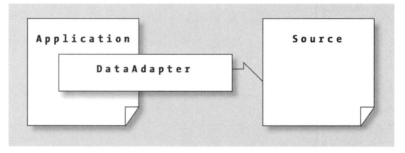

*Figure 3A-3. **DataAdapter** accessing the data source directly*

If you know at compile-time that one of the data sources you need to connect to is a data store for which you have a specific .NET data provider, then use that provider, because it has been optimized for that specific data store. If on the other hand you are creating a generic data wrapper to be used when you do not know the data sources you will be connecting to at runtime, go with the generic OLE DB .NET Data Provider. So, now I have discussed specific .NET data providers, such as the SQL Server .NET Data Provider, and the generic OLE DB .NET Data Provider for use with any OLE DB–compliant provider, but there is also a third and somewhat overlooked .NET data provider that comes with ADO.NET. This is the ODBC .NET Data Provider. This provider is for accessing ODBC data sources exclusively and can only be used in cases where you have the appropriate ODBC driver. ODBC won't be discussed further in this book.

The providers listed in Table 3A-2 work with the OLE DB .NET Data Provider. See ".NET Data Providers" later in this chapter for details.

Table 3A-2. Providers Compatible with the OLE DB .NET Data Provider

PROVIDER NAME	DESCRIPTION
SQLOLEDB	Use with MS SQL Server
MSDAORA	Use with Oracle
Microsoft.Jet.OLEDB.4.0	Use with JET databases (MS Access)

Specifying a Provider When Connecting

There are several ways to open or set up a connection, but here is one way of specifying what provider you want to use:

```
cnnUserMan.ConnectionString = "Provider=Microsoft.Jet.OLEDB.4.0;" & _
  "Data Source=C:\Northwind.mdb"
```

In the **ConnectionString** property of the connection cnnUserMan (declared and instantiated elsewhere, obviously) specify that you want to use the JET provider (Provider= Microsoft.Jet.OLEDB.4.0). See the section "ConnectionString Property" later in this chapter.

.NET Data Providers

.NET data providers are a core part of the new ADO.NET programming model. Although a .NET data provider loosely maps to an OLE DB provider, it is in fact a lot closer to the ADO object model. This is because the OLE DB and ADO layers have been merged in the .NET Framework, giving .NET data providers higher performance. The higher performance results from the fact that when using ADO.NET, you are effectively using only one layer as compared to using ADO and an OLE DB provider, which are two layers.

Another way of looking at this is that previously you would tinker directly with the low-level OLE DB API only if you really knew what you were doing. The reason for doing so was you wanted higher performance. No more, my friend! Now you have ADO.NET with its high-level programming interface, exposed by the ADO.NET object model, and yet you get the same performance as using OLE DB directly. Isn't that great? Okay, before you start celebrating too much, let me make one final point: OLE DB as a specification exposes a data source in a rich way—that is, it exposes all the functionality of all the various types of data sources out there, whereas .NET data providers expose minimal functionality. So OLE DB is not likely to disappear anytime soon, and as such will only be replaced by .NET data providers when in the context of disconnected and distributed data access. For most other instances when you need rich client-side data manipulation, you should probably stick with ADO and OLE DB for now.

A .NET data provider actually consists of the following four data classes:

- **Connection**

- **DataAdapter**

- **Command**

- **DataReader**

These classes are discussed in detail in the following paragraphs. The .NET data provider is the first of two layers that compose the ADO.NET object model. This first layer is also called the *connected layer,* and the other layer is surprisingly called the *disconnected layer.* The disconnected layer is the **DataSet** object. See "Using the DataSet Class" in Chapter 3B for more information.

The Connection Class

The connection class is part of the .NET data provider. You need a connection when you want to access a data source, but if you just want to save some related data in a table, you don't actually need one. I'll cover this topic in the section "Building Your Own DataTable" in Chapter 3B. I will not be discussing the ADO connection in this section, just the ADO.NET connection. From a source code point of view, the ADO connection has the same look and feel as the ADO.NET connection anyway. If you need specific information on the ADO Connection object, you may want to read one of the books mentioned at the beginning of this chapter.

Two of the managed connections that Microsoft provides with the .NET Framework are **OleDbConnection** and **SqlConnection.** *Managed* means executed by and in the context of the Common Language Runtime (CLR).

> **NOTE** *See "Common Language Runtime" in Chapter 1 for details.*

Although the **OleDbConnection** class can be used with SQL Server data sources, you should use the **SqlConnection** for SQL Server 7.0 or later, as it has been optimized for connecting to this specific data source. Use the **OleDbConnection** for all other data sources, unless you can get hold of a third-party .NET data provider (and thus the specific connection class) for your specific data store.

OleDbConnection

Use the managed **OleDbConnection** to connect with all your .NET-enabled applications. The **OleDbConnection** is especially useful for creating a generic data wrapper to use when you need to connect to various data sources. The **OleDbConnection** is for establishing a connection through an OLE DB provider.

SqlConnection

The **SqlConnection** class is only for use with MS SQL Server 7.0 or later. It has been specifically optimized for connecting to this particular data store, and unless you are building a generic data wrapper, I recommend always using this managed connection with your .NET-enabled applications.

ConnectionString Property

The **ConnectionString** property, which is nearly 100 percent similar to an OLE DB connection string in the case of a **SqlConnection** and 100 percent compatible in the case of an **OleDbConnection**, is used for specifying the values for connecting to a data source. You can set and get this property, the default value of which is an empty string, only when the connection is closed. All values may be specified by enclosing them in single quotes or double quotes, but this is optional. All value pairs (*valuename=value*) must be separated with a semicolon (;).

> **NOTE** *The separator used in the **ConnectionString** property is the same at all times. Even if you are an international user with different character sets, separators, and so on, you still need to use the semicolon as the list separator for this property!*

Here is an example of the **ConnectionString** property:

```
"Data Source=USERMANPC;User ID=UserMan;Password=userman;Initial Catalog=UserMan"
```

The value names are case-insensitive whereas some of the values, such as the value for the *Password* value name, are case-sensitive. Table 3A-3 lists the **ConnectionString** property values in alphabetical order.

Table 3A-3. *ConnectionString Property Values*

VALUE NAME	DEFAULT VALUE	REQUIRED	DESCRIPTION	EXAMPLE	PROVIDER SPECIFIC
Addr or *Address*		Yes	The name or network address (e.g., an IP address) of a SQL Server to which you want to connect.	Addr='DBSERVER' or Address='10.0.0.1'	Yes (works with the **SqlConnection** class and the SQLOLEDB provider with the **OleDbConnection** class)
Application Name		No	The name of your application.	Application Name='UserMan'	Yes (works with the **SqlConnection** class and the SQLOLEDB provider with the **OleDbConnection** class)
AttachDBFilename		No	The name of the primary database file to attach. The name of the attachable database includes the full path. This value is typically used with file-based databases such as Microsoft Access.	AttachDBFileName='C:\Program Files\UserMan\Data\UserMan.mdb'	
Database		Yes	The name of your database.	Database='UserMan'	Yes (works with the **SqlConnection** class and the SQLOLEDB provider with the **OleDbConnection** class)
Data Source		Yes	Basically the same as **Addr** or **Address**, but it also works with an MS Access JET database.	Data Source='C:\Program Files\UserMan\Data\UserMan.mdb' or Data Source='USERMANPC'	No
Connect Timeout or *Connection Timeout*	15	No	The number of seconds to wait when connecting to a database before terminating the connection attempt. An exception is thrown if a timeout occurs.	Connection Timeout=15 or Connect Timeout=15	Yes (works with the **SqlConnection** class and the SQLOLEDB provider with the **OleDbConnection** class)

Table 3A-3. **ConnectionString** *Property Values (continued)*

VALUE NAME	DEFAULT VALUE	REQUIRED	DESCRIPTION	EXAMPLE	PROVIDER SPECIFIC
Connection Lifetime	0	No	You can use this value to specify when the connection should be destroyed. This value is only relevant with regards to connection pooling, and as such the value (in seconds) specifies the acceptable time span compared to the time created and the time the connection is returned to the connection pool. In other words, this means the total number of seconds the connection has been alive (time of returning to pool minus time of creation) is compared to this value. If the **Connection Lifetime** value is less than the number of seconds the connection has been alive, then it is destroyed. This value is very useful in load-balancing situations, because if you set the **Connection Lifetime** to a low value, then it is more often than not destroyed upon returning to the connection pool. This means that when the connection is re-created, it might be created on a different server, depending on the load on the servers.	Connection Lifetime=10	Yes (works with the **SqlConnection** class and the SQLOLEDB provider with the **OleDbConnection** class)

Table 3A-3. ConnectionString Property Values (continued)

VALUE NAME	DEFAULT VALUE	REQUIRED	DESCRIPTION	EXAMPLE	PROVIDER SPECIFIC
Connection Reset	'true'	No	This value determines if the connection is reset when it is destroyed or rather removed from the connection pool. If you set this value to 'false' you can avoid an extra round-trip to the server when you require the connection. You should be aware that the connection has not been reset, so the connection will keep whatever values you have set before it was returned to the connection pool.	Connection Reset='false'	Yes (works with the **SqlConnection** class and the SQLOLEDB provider with the **OleDbConnection** class)
Current Language		No	This is the SQL Server Language record name. Check your SQL Server documentation for a list of supported names.	Current Language='English'	Yes (works with the **SqlConnection** class and the SQLOLEDB provider with the **OleDbConnection** class)
Enlist	'true'	No	Enlists the connection in the thread's current transaction, when set to 'true'.	Enlist='false'	Yes (works with the **SqlConnection** class and the SQLOLEDB provider with the **OleDbConnection** class)
File Name		No	For use with a Microsoft Data Link File (UDL).	File Name='Test.udl'	Yes (works with the **OleDbConnection** only)
Initial Catalog (the same as *Database*)					
Initial File Name (the same as *AttachDBFilename*)					

*Table 3A-3. **ConnectionString** Property Values (continued)*

VALUE NAME	DEFAULT VALUE	REQUIRED	DESCRIPTION	EXAMPLE	PROVIDER SPECIFIC
Integrated Security	'false'	No	Specifies if the connection should be secure. The possible values are 'true', 'yes', and 'sspi', which all specify a secure connection, and the default value 'false' and 'no', which obviously specify a nonsecure connection.	Integrated Security='true'	Yes (works with the **SqlConnection** class and the SQLOLEDB provider with the **OleDbConnection** class)
Max Pool Size	100	No	Specifies the maximum number of connections in the connection pool.	Max Pool Size=200	Yes (works with the **SqlConnection** class and the SQLOLEDB provider with the **OleDbConnection** class)
Min Pool Size	0	No	Specifies the minimum number of connections in the connection pool.	Min Pool Size=10	Yes (works with the **SqlConnection** class and the SQLOLEDB provider with the **OleDbConnection** class)
Net or *Network Library*	'dbmssocn'	No	The network library used for connecting to SQL Server. Possible values are 'dbmssocn' (TCP/IP), 'dbnmpntw' (Named Pipes), 'dbmsrpcn' (Multiprotocol), 'dbmsvinn' (Banyan Vines), 'dbmsadsn' (Apple Talk), 'dbmsgnet' (VIA), 'dbmsipcn' (Shared Memory), and 'dbmsspxn' (IPX/SPX). Please note that the corresponding library file (DLL) must be installed on both the system you connect to and the system from which you connect.	Net='dbnmpntw'	Yes (works with the **SqlConnection** class and the SQLOLEDB provider with the **OleDbConnection** class)

Table 3A-3. **ConnectionString** *Property Values (continued)*

VALUE NAME	DEFAULT VALUE	REQUIRED	DESCRIPTION	EXAMPLE	PROVIDER SPECIFIC
Network Address (the same as **Addr** or **Address**)					
Password or *Pwd*		Yes, if your database has been secured	The password that corresponds to the User ID	Password='userman' or Pwd='userman'	No
Persist Security Info	'false'	No	Helps you keep sensitive information like passwords safe. The behavior of this value rather depends on the state of the connection. The possible values are 'true' and 'yes', which don't keep your sensitive information safe, and 'false' and 'no', which obviously do keep it safe.	Persist Security Info='true'	No
Pooling	'true'	No	The connection object is taken from the appropriate pool, if the value is set to 'true'. If there are no available connection objects in the pool, a new one is created and added to the pool.	Pooling='false'	Yes (works with the **SqlConnection** class and the SQLOLEDB provider with the **OleDbConnection** class)
Provider		Yes	Specifies the name of the OLE DB Provider you want to use for accessing your data source.	Provider=SQLOLEDB	Yes (works with the **OleDbConnection** class only)

*Table 3A-3. **ConnectionString** Property Values (continued)*

VALUE NAME	DEFAULT VALUE	REQUIRED	DESCRIPTION	EXAMPLE	PROVIDER SPECIFIC
Server (the same as **Addr** or **Address**)					
Trusted_Connection (the same as **Integrated Security**)					
User ID		Yes, if your database has been secured	The User ID you wish to connect with.	User ID='UserMan'	No
Workstation ID	The name of the client computer or the computer from which you are connecting.	No	The name of the client computer or the computer from which you are connecting.	Workstation ID='USERMANPC'	No

61

Many of these values have corresponding properties, such as the **ConnectionTimeout** property, that can be set separately (see "Connection Class Properties" for more details). Mind you, you can only set these properties when the connection is closed! So if you have an open connection, you need to close it before you try to set any of these properties. The corresponding properties are set when you set the **ConnectionString** property.

When you set the connection string, it will be parsed immediately, which means that any syntax errors will be caught straight away and an exception thrown (a trappable error occurs). Only syntax errors are caught at this time, as other errors are found only when you try to open the connection.

Once you open the connection, the validated connection string is returned as part of the connection object, with properties updated. Mind you, if you don't set the **Persist Security Info** value or if you set it to 'false', then sensitive information will NOT be returned in the **ConnectionString**. The same goes for value names with default values; they are not returned in the connection string. This is important to know, if you want to examine the **ConnectionString** property after it has been set.

If you set a value more than once in the **ConnectionString** property, only the last occurrence of the *valuename=value* pair counts. Also, if you use one of the synonyms, like *Pwd* instead of *Password*, the "official" value name will be returned (*Password* in this case).

Finally, white space is stripped from values and from between value names. Well, this is not quite true, because if you use single quotes or double quotes to delimit the values, then the white space counts!

Connection Class Properties

Instead of using the **ConnectionString** property, you can actually set the various values individually by using their corresponding properties. Tables 3A-4 and 3A-5 list the connection properties in alphabetical order. Please note that the properties with **Protected** accessibility can only be accessed in a class that inherits the connection class. This is very much in line with the new true Object Oriented Programming (OOP) facilities in VB.NET.

Table 3A-4. SqlConnection Class Properties

PROPERTY NAME	ACCESSIBILITY	CONNECTIONSTRING EQUIVALENT	DESCRIPTION	READ	WRITE
ConnectionTimeout	Public	**Connection Timeout**		Yes	No
Container	Public	There is no equivalent **ConnectionString** value.	This property, which is inherited from the **Component** class, gets the **IContainer** interface that contains the component. **Nothing** is returned if the **Component** is NOT encapsulated in an **IContainer**.	Yes	No
Database	Public	**Database** or **Initial Catalog**		Yes	No
DataSource	Public	**Addr** or **Address**		Yes	No
DesignMode (inherited from **Component**)	Protected	There is no equivalent **ConnectionString** value.	This property can be used to check if the component is in design mode. **True** is returned if the component is in design mode and **False** otherwise. Please note that **False** is always returned if the component does not have an associated **ISite**.	Yes	No
Events (inherited from **Component**)	Protected	There is no equivalent **ConnectionString** value.	This property returns an **EventHandlerList** object that holds all the event handlers that have been attached to the component.	Yes	No
PacketSize	Public	There is no equivalent **ConnectionString** value.	This property specifies the packet size for communicating with your data source across the network. The value returned is specified in bytes.	Yes	No

Table 3A-4. SqlConnection Class Properties (continued)

PROPERTY NAME	ACCESSIBILITY	CONNECTIONSTRING EQUIVALENT	DESCRIPTION	READ	WRITE
ServerVersion	Public	There is no equivalent **ConnectionString** value.	This property receives a string from SQL Server containing the version of the current SQL Server. If the **State** property equals **Closed,** when you read this property, the **InvalidOperationException** exception is thrown.	Yes	No
Site (inherited from **Component**)	Public	There is no equivalent **ConnectionString** value.	This property gets or sets the site of the component. An **ISite** object is returned, but the value **Nothing** is returned, if the component does not have an associated **ISite** or if it is not encapsulated in an **IContainer**. **Nothing** is also returned, if the component is being removed from its container (**IContainer**).	Yes	No
State	Public	There is no equivalent **ConnectionString** value.	This property gets the current state of the connection: possible values are **Open** or **Closed**. These values are taken from the **ConnectionState** enum, which is part of the **System.Data** namespace.	Yes	No
WorkstationId	Public	**Workstation ID**	This property returns a string identifying the database client.	Yes	No

Table 3A-5. OleDbConnection Class Properties

PROPERTY NAME	ACCESSIBILITY	CONNECTIONSTRING EQUIVALENT	DESCRIPTION	READ	WRITE
ConnectionTimeout	Public	**Connection Timeout**		Yes	No
Container	Public	There is no equivalent **ConnectionString** value.	This property, which is inherited from the **Component** class, gets the **IContainer** interface that contains the component. **Nothing** is returned if the component is NOT encapsulated in an **IContainer**.	Yes	No
Database	Public	**Database or Initial Catalog**		Yes	No
DataSource	Public	**Addr or Address**		Yes	No
DesignMode (inherited from **Component**)	Protected	There is no equivalent **ConnectionString** value.	This property can be used to check if the component is in design mode. **True** is returned if the component is in design mode, and **False** otherwise. Please note that **False** is always returned if the component does not have an associated **ISite**.	Yes	No
Events (inherited from **Component**)	Protected	There is no equivalent **ConnectionString** value.	This property returns an **EventHandlerList** object that holds all the event handlers that have been attached to the component.	Yes	No
Provider	Public	**Provider**		Yes	No

65

Table 3A-5. **OleDbConnection** *Class Properties (continued)*

PROPERTY NAME	ACCESSIBILITY	CONNECTIONSTRING EQUIVALENT	DESCRIPTION	READ	WRITE
ServerVersion	Public	There is no equivalent **ConnectionString** value.	This property receives a string from the DBMS containing the version number. If the **State** property equals **Closed**, when you read this property, the **InvalidOperationException** exception is thrown. An empty **String** is returned if the OLE DB Provider doesn't support this property.	Yes	No
Site (inherited from **Component**)	Public	There is no equivalent **ConnectionString** value.	This property gets or sets the site of the component. An **ISite** object is returned, but the value **Nothing** is returned if the component does not have an associated **ISite** or if it is not encapsulated in an **IContainer**. **Nothing** is also returned if the component is being removed from its container (**IContainer**).	Yes	No
State	Public	There is no equivalent **ConnectionString** value.	This property gets the current state of the connection: Possible values are **Closed** or **Open**. These values are taken from the **ConnectionState** enum, which is part of the **System.Data** namespace.	Yes	No

Component, Container, IContainer, ISite, and Site Explained

Although detailed discussions of components, containers, IContainer, ISite, and Site are outside the scope of this book, it is important to understand these terms:

- *Component:* Provides object sharing between applications, or a component can manipulate objects supplied by other applications and expose the contained components to other applications. Any given class must implement the **IContainer** interface to be a valid component.

- *Container:* Refers to an object that logically contains zero or more components. A class must implement the **IContainer** interface in order to be a container.

- *IContainer:* Refers to an interface that provides functionality for containers. This functionality includes adding, removing, and retrieving components.

- *ISite:* Refers to an interface that is assigned by the **IContainer** interface, and it provides functionality that is required by sites.

- *Site:* Binds a component to a container, and it provides the container with the functionality needed to manage the components and the communication facilities needed between a container and a site. A class can only be a site if it implements the **ISite** interface.

Connection Class Methods

Tables 3A-6 and 3A-7 list the methods of the **Connection** class. The tables are only reference lists, so if you need information on how to use these methods, such as how to open a connection, then read the explanations following the tables. The same goes if you need to see all the various overloaded functions, which are marked Overloaded. See "Handling Connection Class Exceptions" later in this chapter for details.

Table 3A-6. **SqlConnection** Class Methods

METHOD NAME	ACCESSIBILITY	DESCRIPTION	RETURN VALUE	OVERLOADED
BeginTransaction()	Public	Begins a transaction on the connection object. This method is overloaded, so see "Transactions" later in this chapter for more information.	The instantiated **SqlTransaction** object	Yes
ChangeDatabase(ByVal vstrDatabase As String)	Public	This method, which cannot be overridden, changes the database for the connection to the database passed in the vstrDatabase variable. The connection must be open or else an **InvalidOperationException** exception is thrown.		No
Close()	Public	This method takes no arguments and it simply closes an open connection. Any pending transactions are rolled back when you call this method.		No
CreateCommand()	Public	This method creates an **SqlCommand**. The **SqlCommand** object is associated with the connection object.	The instantiated **SqlCommand** object	No
Dispose() (inherited from **Component**)	Public	This overridden method disposes of the command object and releases any resources used by it.		Yes
Equals()	Public	This method, which is inherited from the **Object** class, can be used to determine if two connections are the same.	Data type **Boolean**	Yes
Finalize()	Protected	This method is inherited from the **Object** class and it is used for attempting to free the resources and perform cleanup operations before the Garbage Collector kills the connection. However, since this method is NOT guaranteed to run, you should look into using the **Dispose** method instead. The method must be overridden in a derived class, if necessary, because it doesn't do anything by default. The reason for this is the Garbage Collector will likely take much longer to run, if it has to deal with running any **Finalize** operations.		No

*Table 3A-6. **SqlConnection** Class Methods (continued)*

METHOD NAME	ACCESSIBILITY	DESCRIPTION	RETURN VALUE	OVERLOADED
GetHashCode()	Public	This method, which is inherited from the **Object** class, returns the hash-code for the connection.	Data type **Integer**	No
GetLifetimeService()	Public	This method, which is inherited from the **MarshalByRefObject** class, returns a lifetime service object. This object controls the lifetime policy for the current instance of the connection class. An object of type **ILease** is returned for the default lifetime service. This method should only be used in conjunction with remotely activated objects. The Leasing Distributed Garbage Collector (LDGC) is in charge of associating a lease (lifetime service) with an object activated remotely. Once the lease expires, the object is removed.	Data type **Object**	No
GetService(ByVal vtypService As Type)	Protected	This method, which is inherited from the **Component** class, returns an object that represents a service (vtypService), which is provided by the component.	Data type **Object**	No
GetType()	Public	This method, which is inherited from the **Object** class, returns the object type or rather the metadata associated with the class from which an object is inherited. If you need the class name, you can get it using cnnUserMan.GetType.ToString.	Data type **Type**	No
InitializeLifetimeService()	Public	This method, which is inherited from the **MarshalByRefObject** class, can be used to provide your own lease to the connection object and thus control its lifetime.	Data type **Object**	No

*Table 3A-6. **SqlConnection** Class Methods (continued)*

METHOD NAME	ACCESSIBILITY	DESCRIPTION	RETURN VALUE	OVERLOADED
MemberwiseClone()	Protected	This method, which is inherited from the **Object** class, creates a copy of the connection. The cloned connection is a shallow copy of the original connection. Shallow in this case means that the original connection is cloned, and so are any references the original connection has to other objects. This means you get a new copy of the original connection with the same object references as the original connection. This is in contrast to what is called a deep copy, where the original connection is copied and so are any objects that are referenced from the original connection.	Data type **Object**	No
Open()	Public	This method, which cannot be overridden, is used for opening the connection to the data source with the current property settings. Different exceptions can be thrown under various circumstances (see "Handling Connection Class Exceptions" later in this chapter.		No
ReferenceEquals(ByVal vobjEqual1 As Object, ByVal vobjEqual2 As Object)	Public	This method is for comparing references, and thus it can be used to check if two connection instances refer to the very same connection.	Data type **Boolean**	No
ToString()	Public	This method, which is inherited from the **Object** class, returns a string representation of the connection. If you call the method using MsgBox(cnnUserMan.ToString()), the message box displayed should contain the text *System.Data.SqlClient.SqlConnection*. This is the name of the object (**SqlConnection**) including the namespace in which it is contained (**System.Data.SqlConnection**).	Data type **String**	No

Table 3A-7. OleDbConnection Class Methods

METHOD NAME	ACCESSIBILITY	DESCRIPTION	RETURN VALUE	OVERLOADED
BeginTransaction()	Public	Begins a transaction on the connection object. This method is overloaded, so see "Transactions" later in this chapter for more information.	The instantiated **OleDbTransaction** object	Yes
ChangeDatabase(ByVal vstrDatabase As String)	Public	This method, which cannot be overridden, changes the database for the connection to the database passed in the vstrDatabase variable. The connection must be open or else an **InvalidOperationException** exception is thrown.		No
Close()	Public	This method takes no arguments, and it simply closes an open connection. Any pending transactions are rolled back when you call this method.	None	No
CreateCommand()	Public	This method creates an **OleDbCommand**. The **OleDbCommand** object is associated with the connection object.	The instantiated **OleDbCommand** object	No
Dispose() (inherited from **Component**)	Public	This overridden method disposes of the command object and releases any resources used by it.		No
Equals()	Public	This method, which is inherited from the **Object** class, can be used to determine if two connections are the same.	Data type **Boolean**	Yes

Table 3A-7. *OleDbConnection Class Methods (continued)*

METHOD NAME	ACCESSIBILITY	DESCRIPTION	RETURN VALUE	OVERLOADED
Finalize()	Protected	This method is inherited from the **Object** class and it is used for attempting to free the resources and perform cleanup operations before the Garbage Collector kills the connection. However, since this method is NOT guaranteed to run, you should look into using the **Dispose** method instead. The method must be overridden in a derived class, if necessary, because it doesn't do anything by default. The reason for this is that the Garbage Collector will likely take much longer to run, if it has to deal with running any **Finalize** operations.	None	No
GetHashCode()	Public	This method, which is inherited from the **Object** class, returns the hash code for the connection.	Data type **Integer**	No
GetLifetimeService()	Public	This method, which is inherited from the **MarshalByRefObject** class, returns a lifetime service object. This object controls the lifetime policy for the current instance of the connection class. An object of type **ILease** is returned for the default lifetime service. This method should only be used in conjunction with remotely activated objects. The Leasing Distributed Garbage Collector (LDGC) is in charge of associating a lease (lifetime service) with an object activated remotely. Once the lease expires, the object is removed.	Data type **Object**	No

*Table 3A-7. **OleDbConnection** Class Methods (continued)*

METHOD NAME	ACCESSIBILITY	DESCRIPTION	RETURN VALUE	OVERLOADED
GetOleDbSchemaTable (ByVal vguiSchema As Guid, ByVal vobjRestrictions As Object)	Public	This method is used for retrieving the schema table and its associated restrictions for the vguiSchema.	Data type **DataTable**	No
GetService(ByVal vtypService As Type)	Protected	This method, which is inherited from the **Component** class, returns an object that represents a service (vtypService), which is provided by the component.	Data type **Object**	No
GetType()	Public	This method, which is inherited from the **Object** class, returns the object type or rather the metadata associated with the class that an object is inherited from. If you need the class name, you can get it using cnnUserMan.GetType.ToString.	Data type **Type**	No
InitializeLifetimeService()	Public	This method, which is inherited from the **MarshalByRefObject** class, can be used to provide your own lease to the connection object and thus control its lifetime.	Data type **Object**	No
MemberwiseClone()	Protected	This method, which is inherited from the **Object** class, creates a copy of the connection. The cloned connection is a shallow copy of the original connection. Shallow in this case means that the original connection is cloned, and so are any references the original connection has to other objects. This means you get a new copy of the original connection with the same object references as the original connection. This is in contrast to what is called a deep copy, where the original connection is copied and so are any objects that are referenced from the original connection.	Data type **Object**	No

*Table 3A-7. **OleDbConnection** Class Methods (continued)*

METHOD NAME	ACCESSIBILITY	DESCRIPTION	RETURN VALUE	OVERLOADED
Open()	Public	This method, which cannot be overridden, is used for opening the connection to the data source with the current property settings. Different exceptions can be thrown under various circumstances (see "Handling Connection Class Exceptions" later in this chapter for details.		No
ReferenceEquals(ByVal vobjEqual1 As Object, ByVal vobjEqual2 As Object)	Public	This method is for comparing references, and thus it can be used to check if two connection instances refer to the very same connection.	Data type **Boolean**	No
ReleaseObjectPool()	Public Shared	This method is used for indicating that the connection pool can be cleared when the last underlying OLE DB provider is released.		No
ToString()	Public	This method, which is inherited from the **Object** class, returns a string representation of the connection. If you call the method using MsgBox(cnnUserMan.ToString()), the MsgBox displayed should contain the text *System.Data.OleDb.OleDbConnection*. This is the name of the object (**OleDbConnection**) including the namespace in which it is contained (**System.Data.OleDb**).	Data type **String**	No

Opening a Connection

Once you have set the properties required to open a connection, it is time to actually open it. This is quite simple if you have set the connection properties correctly. See Listing 3A-1 for an example.

Listing 3A-1. Opening a Connection

```
 1 ' Declare connection object
 2 Dim cnnUserMan As SqlConnection
 3
 4 ' Instantiate the connection object
 5 cnnUserMan = New SqlConnection()
 6 ' Set up connection string
 7 cnnUserMan.ConnectionString = "User ID=UserMan;" & _
 8 "Server=USERMANPC;Password=userman;Initial Catalog=UserMan"
 9 ' Open the connection
10 cnnUserMan.Open()
```

Note that the **Open** method does not take any arguments, so you need to be sure that you have set the properties necessary to connect to your data source. If you haven't set all the required properties or the connection is already open, an exception is thrown. See "ConnectionString Property Exceptions" later in this chapter for details.

Closing a Connection

Close a connection whenever you don't need to use it so it doesn't consume any more memory than needed. Closing a connection also returns it to the connection pool, if it belongs to one. Close a connection like this:

```
cnnUserMan.Close()
```

When you call the **Close** method, it tries to wait for all transactions to finish before closing the connection. If a transaction is not finished up after a period of time, an exception is thrown.

Disposing of a Connection

You can dispose of your connection by calling the **Dispose** method, like this:

```
cnnUserMan.Dispose()
```

The **Dispose** method destroys the reference to the connection and tells the Garbage Collector that it can do its job and destroy the connection itself, assuming of course that this is the only reference to the connection.

Copying Connections

Sometimes you might want or need to copy a connection object. This is fairly easy, but you need to be careful about how you do it. There are two ways to copy a connection object:

- *Shallow copying*: Use this method when you want a clone of the original connection object. This means that any object references that the original connection has at the time of the copying will be copied too. The references are copied, NOT the referenced objects themselves. Shallow copying can be done using the protected **MemberwiseClone** method.

- *Deep copying*: Unlike shallow copying, deep copying is used when you need a copy of all objects referenced from the original connection. This is also called *cloning*, because you get two connections that are exactly the same. If you need this kind of copying, your connection class (inherited from a **SqlConnection** or **OleDbConnection** class) must implement the **ICloneable** interface; you can then use the **Clone** method of this interface to perform the actual cloning.

Comparing Two Connection Objects

If you have been copying a connection object or setting one connection variable equal to another, it can be hard to know if two instances of a connection class in fact are the same connection or if they point to the same location in memory. Mind you, it isn't too difficult to find out programmatically. You can perform a comparison using the following:

- The **Is** operator

- The **Equals** method

- The **ReferenceEquals** method

Comparing Using the Is Operator

Using the **Is** operator is perhaps the easiest way of comparing two connection objects:

```
blnEqual = cnnUserMan1 Is cnnUserMan2
```

The **Boolean** variable blnEqual will be set to **True** if cnnUserMan1 and cnnUserMan2 refer to the same location in memory; otherwise it is set to **False**.

Comparing Using the Equals Method

The **Equals** method, which is inherited from the **Object** class, is actually intended to be used for comparing values and not references. When two connection variables hold a reference to the same location in memory, however, they actually hold the same "value." As such you can use the **Equals** method for connection object comparison. The **Equals** method comes in two flavors. One checks if the passed connection object is equal to the connection object that performs the method:

```
blnEqual = cnnUserMan1.Equals(cnnUserMan2)
```

The **Boolean** variable blnEqual will be set to **True** if cnnUserMan1 and cnnUserMan2 refer to the same connection; otherwise it is set to **False**.

The second, overloaded version of the method takes two connection objects as arguments and checks if these are equal:

```
blnEqual = cnnUserMan1.Equals(cnnUserMan2, cnnUserMan3)
```

The **Boolean** variable blnEqual will be set to **True** if cnnUserMan2 and cnnUserMan3 refer to the same connection; otherwise it is set to **False**. With this overloaded version of the method you can actually compare two connection objects separate from the connection object performing the method.

Comparing Using the ReferenceEquals Method

The **ReferenceEquals** method is for comparing references and as such it should be preferred over the **Equals** method, which is for comparing values. Here is how you use the **ReferenceEquals** method:

```
blnEqual = cnnUserMan1.ReferenceEquals(cnnUserMan2, cnnUserMan3)
```

The **Boolean** variable blnEqual will be set to **True** if cnnUserMan2 and cnnUserMan3 refer to the same connection; otherwise it is set to **False**. **False** is returned if any of the connection arguments contain a Null value.

> **NOTE** *The **Equals** and the **ReferenceEquals** methods are inherited methods, and the arguments are of data type **Object**. This means the comparison can be done using any data type inherited from the base type **Object**.*

Manipulating the Connection State

When dealing with connections, it is often a good idea to check their states before attempting to get or set one of the properties or execute one of the methods. You can use the **Connection** class's **State** property to determine the current state. (See "Connection Class Properties" earlier in this chapter for details.) You check the **State** property against the **ConnectionState** enum. See Table 3A-8 for a list of the members in the **ConnectionState** enum.

*Table 3A-8. Members of the **ConnectionState** Enum*

NAME	VALUE	DESCRIPTION
Closed	0	The connection is closed.
Open	1	The connection is open.
Connecting	2	The connection is currently connecting to the data source.
Executing	4	The connection is executing a command.
Fetching	8	The connection is retrieving data from the data source.
Broken	16	The connection cannot be used as the connection is in error. This usually occurs if the network fails. The only valid method in this state is **Close** and all properties are read-only.

Comparing State to ConnectionState

You can compare the **State** property with the **ConnectionState** enum using the following statement:

```
If CBool(cnnUserMan.State And ConnectionState.Open) Then
```

I use the **And** operator to perform a bitwise comparison between the two enum values. In this case I am checking if the connection is open. If you want to check if the connection is closed, you can do it like this:

```
If CBool(cnnUserMan.State And ConnectionState.Closed) Then
```

Pooling Connections

Connection pooling, or connection sharing and reuse between applications, is automatically applied to the OLE DB .NET Data Provider that comes with ADO.NET. This is important, because connection pooling will reserve resources, as the connections are being reused. However, the SQL Server .NET Data Provider uses an implicit pooling model by default and you can use the **ConnectionString** property to control the implicit pooling behavior of a **SqlConnection** object.

A connection pool is distinct on one count only, the **ConnectionString** property. This means that all connections in any given pool have the exact same connection string. You must know that white space in the connection string will lead to two otherwise identical connections being added to different connection pools. The two instances of **SqlConnection** in Listing 3A-2 will NOT be added to the same pool, because of the white space in the connection string for the cnnUserMan2 connection. There is an extra space character after the separator (semicolon) that separates the **Password** and **Data Source** value names.

Listing 3A-2. White Space in ConnectionString *Property*

```
cnnUserMan1.ConnectionString = "User Id=UserMan;Password=userman;" & _
    "Data Source='USERMANPC';Initial Catalog='UserMan'"
cnnUserMan2.ConnectionString = "User Id=UserMan;Password=userman; " & _
    "Data Source='USERMANPC';Initial Catalog='UserMan'"
```

Testing for the Same Pool

One way to test if your connections go in the same pool or not is to set up two connections with identical connection strings and make sure the **Max Pool Size** value is set to 1. When you open the first connection, a new pool will be created for this specific connection string, and the connection will be added. When you try to open the second connection, the object pooler will try and add it to the existing pool. Because the existing pool doesn't allow any more connections (the maximum pool size has been reached), the request is queued. If the first connection isn't returned to the pool (by closing the connection), a time-out will occur for the second connection, when the **ConnectionTimeout** period elapses. Once you have set up this scenario, you can change the connection strings, and if a time-out occurs at runtime, then your connections do go in the same pool.

Pooling Connections of Data Type SqlConnection

When you set up the **SqlConnection** class's **ConnectionString** property, you must set the **Pooling** value name to the value 'true' or leave out the value pair, as 'true' is the default value for **Pooling**. So by default, a **SqlConnection** object is taken from a connection pool when the connection is opened, and if no pool exists, one is created to hold the connection being opened.

The **Min Pool Size** and **Max Pool Size** value names of the **ConnectionString** property determine how many connections a pool can hold. Connections will be added to a pool until the maximum pool size is reached. Requests will then be queued by the object pooler, and a time-out will occur if no connections are returned to the pool before the time-out period elapses. Connections are only returned to the pool when they are closed using the **Close** method. This is also true even if the connections are broken. Once a broken or invalid connection is returned to the pool, the object pooler removes the connection from the pool. This is done at regular intervals, when the object pooler scans for broken connections.

Another way to remove connections from the pool is to specify a value for the **Connection Lifetime** value name of the **ConnectionString** property. This value is 0 by default, which means that the connection will never automatically be removed from the pool. If you specify a different value (in seconds), this value will be compared to the connection's time of creation and the current time once the connection is returned to the pool. If the lifetime exceeds the value indicated in the **Connection Lifetime** value name, the connection will be removed from the pool.

Resetting Connections in the Connection Pool

The **Connection Reset** value name is used for determining if the connection should be reset when it is returned to the pool. The default value is 'true', indicating the connection is reset upon returning to the pool. This is quite meaningful, if you have tampered with the properties when the connection was open. If you know that your connections stay the same whenever open, you can set the value to 'false' and thus avoid the extra round-trip to the server, sparing network load and saving time.

Pooling Connections of Data Type OleDbConnection

Although the OLE DB .NET Data Provider supplies automatic pooling, you can still manually override or even disable it programmatically.

Disabling OLE DB Pooling

It is possible to disable the automatic connection pooling if you specify the **OLE DB Services** value in your connection string. The following connection will NOT have automatic connection pooling:

```
cnnUserMan.Open("Provider=SQLOLEDB;OLE DB Services=-4;Data Source=USERMANPC" & _
"User ID=UserMan;Password=userman;Initial Catalog=UserMan")
```

You can learn more about the **OLE DB Services** value by reading the document "OLE DB Programmer's Reference" at this address: http://msdn.microsoft.com/library/default.asp?url=/library /en-us/oledb/htm/oledbabout_the_ole_db_documentation.asp.

Clearing Object Pooling

Because the connection pool is being cached when a provider is created, it is important to call the connection's **ReleaseObjectPool** method when you are done using your connection.

Using the ReleaseObjectPool Method

The **ReleaseObjectPool** method tells the connection pooler that the connection pool can be cleared when the last provider is released. You should call this method when you have closed your connection and you know you will not need the connection within the time frame the OLE DB Services normally keeps pooled connections alive (see Listing 3A-3).

Listing 3A-3. Calling the `ReleaseObjectPool` *Method*

```
. . .
' Open the connection
cnnUserMan.Open()
' Do your stuff
. . .
' Close the connection and release pool
cnnUserMan.Close()
cnnUserMan.ReleaseObjectPool()
```

Transactions

Transactions are a way of grouping related database operations so that if one fails, they all fail. Likewise, if they all succeed, the changes will be applied permanently to the data source. So transactions are a safety net, ensuring that your data stays in sync.

One classic example of a transaction is a banking system. Suppose you are moving money from your current account to your savings account. This is an operation that requires two updates: Credit the amount to the current account and debit the amount to the savings account. Let us assume that this operation is under way, and the amount has been credited to the current account. Now, for whatever reason, the system crashes, and the amount is never debited to the savings account. This is no good and will certainly make someone unhappy. If this operation had been performed within a single transaction, the amount credited to the current account would have been rolled back once the system was back up and running. Although I have simplified the whole process, it should be clear why you want to use transactions!

ADO.NET offers you two ways of handling transactions within your application: manual and automatic.

Defining Transaction Boundaries

All transactions have a *boundary*, which is the scope or the "surrounding border" for all the resources within a transaction. Resources within the boundary share the same transaction identifier. This means internally all the resources, such as a database server, are assigned this identifier, which is unique to the transaction boundary. A transaction boundary is abstract, meaning that it's like an invisible frame. The boundary can also be extended and reduced. How this is done all depends on whether you are using automatic (implicit) or manual (explicit) transactions.

Manual Transactions

The .NET data providers that come with ADO.NET support manual transactions through methods of the connection class. When dealing with manual transactions, it is a good idea to check the state of the connection before attempting to perform one of the transaction methods. See "Manipulating the Connection State" earlier in this chapter for details.

Starting a Manual Transaction

To start a transaction, you need to call the **BeginTransaction** method of the connection class. You must call this method before performing any of the database operations that are to take part in the transaction. The call in its simplest form is performed as shown in Listing 3A-4.

Listing 3A-4. Begin Transaction with Default Values
```
traUserMan = cnnUserMan.BeginTransaction()
```

The connection object (cnnUserMan) must be a valid and open connection, or the **InvalidOperationException** is thrown. See "BeginTransaction Method Exceptions" for more details. traUserMan now holds a reference to the transaction object created by the **BeginTransaction** method. The **BeginTransaction** method is overloaded, and Tables 3A-9 and 3A-10 show you the various versions of the method.

*Table 3A-9. The **BeginTransaction** Method of the **SqlConnection** Class*

CALL	DESCRIPTION
BeginTransaction() *As SqlTransaction*	This version takes no arguments, and you should use it when you are not nesting your transactions and you include the default isolation level (see Listing 3A-4).
BeginTransaction(ByVal venuIsolationLevel As IsolationLevel) As SqlTransaction	Takes the transaction's isolation level as the only argument. You should use this version of the method when you want to specify the isolation level (see Listing 3A-5).
BeginTransaction(ByVal vstrName As String) As SqlTransaction	Takes the name of the transaction as the only argument. You should use this version of the method when you want to include the default isolation level and to nest your transactions and thus name them for easier identification (see Listing 3A-6). Please note that `vstrName` cannot contain spaces and has to start with a letter or one of the following characters: # (pound sign) or _ (underscore). Subsequent characters may also be a numeric character (0–9).
BeginTransaction(ByVal venuIsolationLevel As IsolationLevel, ByVal vstrName As String) As SqlTransaction	Takes the transactions isolation level and the name of the transaction as arguments. You should use this version of the method when you want to specify the isolation level and you want to nest your transactions and thus name them for easier identification (see Listing 3A-7). Please note that `vstrName` cannot contain spaces and has to start with a letter or one of the following characters: # (pound sign) or _ (underscore). Subsequent characters may also be a numeric character (0–9).

*Table 3A-10. The **BeginTransaction** Method of the **OleDbConnection** Class*

CALL	DESCRIPTION
BeginTransaction() *As OleDbTransaction*	This version takes no arguments, and you should use it when you are not nesting your transactions and you include the default isolation level (see Listing 3A-4).
BeginTransaction(ByVal venuIsolationLevel As IsolationLevel) As OleDbTransaction	Takes the transactions isolation level as the only argument. You should use this version of the method when you want to specify the isolation level. Refer to Listing 3A-5, but replace **SqlConnection** and **SqlTransaction** in the example with **OleDbConnection** and **OleDbTransaction**.

All the overloaded versions of the **BeginTransaction** method return an instance of transaction class inherited from either the **SqlTransaction** or the **OleDbTransaction** class. The **IsolationLevel** enum, which belongs to the **System.Data** namespace, specifies the local transaction locking behavior for the connection. If the isolation level is changed during a transaction, the server is expected to apply the new locking level to all the remaining statements. See Table 3A-11 for an overview of the **IsolationLevel** enum.

*Table 3A-11. Members of the **IsolationLevel** Enum*

NAME	VALUE	DESCRIPTION
Chaos	16	You cannot overwrite pending changes from more highly isolated transactions.
ReadCommitted	4096	Although the shared locks will be held until the end of the read, thus avoiding dirty reads, the data can be changed before the transaction ends. This can result in phantom data or nonrepeatable reads. This means the data you read is not guaranteed to be the same the next time you perform the same read request.
ReadUncommitted	256	Dirty reads are possible, because no shared locks are in effect and any exclusive locks will not be honored.
RepeatableRead	65536	All data that is part of the query will be locked so that other users cannot update the data. This will prevent nonrepeatable reads, but phantom rows are still possible.
Serializable	1048576	The **DataSet** is locked using a range lock, and this prevents other users from updating or inserting rows in the **DataSet** until the transaction ends (see "Using the DataSet Class" in Chapter 3B).
Unspecified	−1	The isolation level cannot be determined, because a different isolation level than the one specified is being used.

Listing 3A-5. Beginning a Transaction with a Nondefault Isolation Level

```
1 Dim cnnUserMan As SqlConnection
2 Dim traUserMan As SqlTransaction
3
4 ' Open connection etc.
5 ...
6 ' Start transaction with specific isolation level
7 traUserMan = cnnUserMan.BeginTransaction(IsolationLevel.ReadCommitted)
```

Listing 3A-6. Beginning a Named SQL Transaction

```
1 Dim cnnUserMan As SqlConnection
2 Dim traUserMan As SqlTransaction
3 Const STR_MAIN_TRANSACTION_NAME As String = "MainTransaction"
4
5 ' Open connection etc.
6 . . .
7 ' Start named transaction
8 traUserMan = cnnUserMan.BeginTransaction(STR_MAIN_TRANSACTION_NAME)
```

Listing 3A-7. Beginning a Named SQL Transaction with a Nondefault Isolation Level

```
1 Dim cnnUserMan As SqlConnection
2 Dim traUserMan As SqlTransaction
3 Const STR_MAIN_TRANSACTION_NAME As String = "MainTransaction"
4
5 ' Open connection etc.
6 . . .
7 ' Start named transaction with specific isolation level
8 traUserMan = cnnUserMan.BeginTransaction(IsolationLevel.ReadCommitted , _
9   STR_MAIN_TRANSACTION_NAME)
```

In Listings 3A-6 and 3A-7, the transaction is named using a constant, which obviously makes it easier later on to recognize the transaction you want to deal with. See the following section, "Nesting Transactions and Using Transaction Save Points with SqlTransaction," for details.

> **NOTE** *It is actually not necessary to save the returned transaction object, which means that you can leave out the **traUserMan** = bit in Listings 3A-4, 3A-5, 3A-6, and 3A-7. Mind you, there is no point in doing so, since you probably want to commit or roll back the pending changes at a later stage. This is only possible if you save the reference to the transaction object. This differs from ADO, where the rollback and commit functionality were methods of the connection class. In ADO.NET, this functionality is now part of the transaction class.*

Nesting Transactions and Using Transaction Save Points with SqlTransaction

This topic is only valid for the **SqlConnection** and **SqlTransaction** classes. If you are nesting your transactions, it is good idea to give each transaction a name that is readily identifiable, making it easier for yourself later on to tell the transactions apart. Well, I say transactions, but in ADO.NET you cannot have more than one transaction on a single connection. Unlike ADO, where you can start several transactions on a connection by calling the **BeginTransaction** method a number of times and specifying a name for each transaction, you only have the one transaction, also starting with the **BeginTransaction** method. However, the transaction object that is returned from the **BeginTransaction** method has a **Save** method that can be used for the very same purpose. Actually, I think it has become somewhat easier to nest transactions in ADO.NET, but you be the judge of that.

So let's have a look at this new way of nesting transactions. It's actually not nesting as such, but a way of saving specific points in a transaction that you can roll back to. The **SqlTransaction** class's **Save** method is used for saving a reference point in the transaction, as shown in Listing 3A-8.

Listing 3A-8. Saving a Reference Point in a Transaction

```
1 Dim cnnUserMan As SqlConnection
2 Dim traUserMan As SqlTransaction
3 Dim cmmUserMan As SqlCommand
4 Const STR_MAIN_TRANSACTION_NAME As String = "MainTransaction"
5 Const STR_FAMILY_TRANSACTION_NAME As String = "FamilyUpdates"
6 Const STR_ADDRESS_TRANSACTION_NAME As String = "AddressUpdates"
7
8 ' Open connection etc.
9 ...
10 ' Start named transaction
11 traUserMan = cnnUserMan.BeginTransaction(STR_MAIN_TRANSACTION_NAME)
12 ' Update family tables
13 ...
14 ' Save transaction reference point
15 traUserMan.Save(STR_FAMILY_TRANSACTION_NAME)
16 ' Update address tables
17 ...
18 ' Save transaction reference point
19 traUserMan.Save(STR_ADDRESS_TRANSACTION_NAME)
20 ' Roll back address table updates
21 traUserMan.Rollback(STR_FAMILY_TRANSACTION_NAME)
```

In Listing 3A-8 the connection is opened, the transaction started, and the family tables updated. After this a reference point is saved before another update of the database. This time the address table is updated and again a reference point is saved. Finally we come to the real trick: a rollback to a named reference in the transaction occurs, namely the point after the family tables were updated. (For more information on the **Rollback** method of the transaction class, please see "Aborting a Manual Transaction.") When the rollback operation is performed, the updates to the address tables will be undone, whereas the changes to the family tables are still there. When I say still there, I am referring to the fact that the transaction hasn't been committed yet, but if the **Commit** method of the transaction class were executed, using `traUserMan.Commit()`, then the family table updates would be applied permanently.

Nesting Transactions with OleDbTransaction

This topic is only valid for the **OleDbConnection** and **OleDbTransaction** classes. Unlike ADO, where you can start several transactions on a connection by calling the **BeginTransaction** method a number of times, you only have the one transaction, also starting with the **BeginTransaction** method. However, the transaction object that is returned from the **BeginTransaction** method has a **Begin** method that can be used for nesting purposes. An example of using the **OleDbTransaction** class's **Begin** method is shown in Listing 3A-9.

Listing 3A-9. Beginning a Nested OleDb Transaction

```
 1 Dim cnnUserMan As OleDbConnection
 2 Dim traUserManMain As OleDbTransaction
 3 Dim traUserManFamily As OleDbTransaction
 4 Dim traUserManAddress As OleDbTransaction
 5
 6 ' Open connection etc.
 7 . . .
 8 ' Start main transaction
 9 traUserManMain = cnnUserMan.BeginTransaction()
10 ' Update family tables
11 . . .
12 ' Begin nested transaction
13 traUserManFamily = traUserManMain.Begin()
14 ' Update address tables
15 . . .
16 ' Begin nested transaction
17 traUserManAddress = traUserManFamily.Begin()
18 ' Roll back address table updates
19 traUserManAddress.Rollback()
```

Aborting a Manual Transaction

If for some reason you want to abort the transaction—that is, roll back all the changes since you started the transaction—you need to call the transaction class's **Rollback** method. This will ensure that no changes are applied to the data source, or rather the data source is rolled back to its original state. The call is performed like this:

```
traUserMan.Rollback()
```

You can also use the overloaded version of the **Rollback** method with which you specify the name of the transaction, as was done in Listing 3A-8. The **Rollback** method cannot be used before the **BeginTransaction** method of the connection class has been called, and it must be called before the transaction class's **Commit** method is called. An exception is thrown if you don't do as prescribed.

Always Use Named Transactions

Although you can call the **Rollback** method without passing the name of a transaction, it is advisable that you do use a transaction name if you are using the **SqlTransaction** class (the **OleDbTransaction** class doesn't have this feature). When you start the transaction, use one of the overloaded **BeginTransaction** methods that lets you pass the name of an argument as demonstrated in Listings 3A-6, 3A-7, and 3A-8. This way you can always use the overloaded **Rollback** method of the transaction class and pass the name of the transaction. When you use the standard version of the **Rollback** method, all pending changes will be rolled back. Personally I think it makes the code more readable if you always supply the transaction name when you begin the transaction, save a reference point, and roll back a transaction.

Committing a Manual Transaction

When you are done manipulating your data, it's time to commit the changes to the data source. Calling the transaction class's **Commit** method does this. All the changes you have made to the data since you started the transaction with a call to the **BeginTransaction** method will be applied to the data source. Actually, this is only fully true for the **OleDbTransaction** class. If you are using the **SqlTransaction** class, you might save some reference points and use the **Rollback** method to roll back to one or more of these reference points. In such a case the operations that have been rolled back obviously won't be committed.

Determining the Isolation Level of a Running Transaction

If you are uncertain of the isolation level of a running transaction, you can use the **IsolationLevel** property of the transaction class, as shown in Listing 3A-10.

Listing 3A-10. *Determining the Isolation Level of a Running Transaction*

```
' Return the isolation level as text
MsgBox(traUserMan.IsolationLevel.ToString)
' Return the isolation level as an integer value
intIsolationLevel = traUserMan.IsolationLevel
```

Examining the Transaction Class

The transaction class, which can only be instantiated by the connection class's **BeginTransaction** method, cannot be inherited. Once a transaction has been started using **BeginTransaction**, all further transaction operations are performed on the transaction object returned by **BeginTransaction**. In Table 3A-12 you can see the only property of the two transaction classes, **SqlTransaction** and **OleDbTransaction**.

*Table 3A-12. **SqlTransaction** and **OleDbTransaction** Class Property*

PROPERTY NAME	ACCESSIBILITY	DESCRIPTION	READ	WRITE
IsolationLevel	Public	Specifies the level of isolation for the transaction. See "Determining the Isolation Level of a Running Transaction" and "Examining the Isolation Level" earlier in this chapter for more details.	Yes	No

In Table 3A-13 you can see the methods of the two transaction classes, **SqlTransaction** from the **System.Data.SqlClient** namespace and **OleDbTransaction** from the **System.Data.OleDb** namespace. Inherited and overridden methods are not shown.

*Table 3A-13. **SqlTransaction** and **OleDbTransaction** Class Methods*

METHOD NAME	DESCRIPTION	RETURN VALUE	OVERLOADED
Begin() (**OleDbTransaction** only)	Begins a new transaction, nested within the current transaction. See "Nesting Transactions with OleDbTransaction" earlier in this chapter.	**OleDbTransaction** object	Yes
Commit()	Commits the current database transaction. See "Committing a Manual Transaction" earlier in this chapter.		No
Rollback()	Rolls back the pending changes, so they aren't applied to the database. See "Aborting a Manual Transaction" earlier in this chapter.		Yes
Save() (**SqlTransaction** only)	Saves a reference point, which you can roll back to using the **Rollback** method		No

Manual Transaction Summary

Handling transactions manually is not really that big a deal. Here are the few steps you need to remember:

- Start a transaction by using the **BeginTransaction** method of the connection class. You can only execute **BeginTransaction** once per connection, or rather you can't have parallel transactions. You need to commit a running transaction before you can use the **BeginTransaction** method again on the same connection. The **BeginTransaction** returns the transaction object needed for rolling back or committing the changes to the data source.

- Roll back a transaction by using the **Rollback** method of the transaction class.

- Commit a transaction by using the **Commit** method of the transaction class.

Automatic Transactions

Automatic transactions are a little different from manual transactions in the sense that they are not necessarily applied. When I say not necessarily, I mean the following: If the object in which you are using the .NET data provider data classes is not enlisted in a transaction, your data source won't be either. So to cut it short, if you're using transactions for your application, then the data source will be enlisted automatically.

The two .NET data providers OLE DB .NET Data Provider and SQL Server .NET Data Provider automatically enlist in a transaction and obtain the details of the transaction from the Windows 2000 Component Services context.

Handling Connection Class Exceptions

This section describes how you deal with exceptions when you work with connections. An exception, which is more or less the same as what used to be called a trappable error, can be caught using the Try. . .Catch. . .End Try statement construct. If you are using the **SqlConnection** class, please look up the property or method in the section that follows, "SqlConnection Exceptions," for the correct exception. Please note that only exceptions to noninherited properties and methods are mentioned. So exceptions caused by the **Equals** method, which is inherited from the **Object** class, are not shown. The list is also not exhaustive, but merely shows the more common exceptions you will encounter. **OleDbConnection** exceptions are discussed under "OleDbConnection Exceptions" later in this chapter.

SqlConnection Exceptions

Below I will show you how to deal with exceptions thrown when working with the **SqlConnection** class.

Why Did You Get an Exception?

For each exception, I show you a piece of code that can help you determine why an exception occurred. This is useful when the code in the Try section of a Try...Catch...End Try construct contains multiple procedure calls that can throw an exception. Be aware that this is simple code, and it is only there to help you get an idea of how to proceed with your exception handling. In the examples provided I show you how to find out what method, property, and so on threw the exception. However, some methods and properties can throw more than one type of exception, and this is when you need set up multiple catch blocks, like this:

```
Try
. . .
Catch objInvalid As InvalidOperationException
. . .
Catch objArgument As ArgumentException
. . .
End Try
```

For more information on exception handling, please refer to Chapter 5.

BeginTransaction Method Exceptions

The **InvalidOperationException** exception is thrown when you call the **Begin-Transaction** method on an invalid or closed connection. You can check if the connection is closed, like this:

```
' Check if the connection is open
If CBool(cnnUserMan.State And ConnectionState.Open) Then
```

The **InvalidOperationException** exception is also thrown if you try to start parallel transactions by calling the **BeginTransaction** method twice, before committing or rolling back the first transaction.

Listing 3A-11 shows you how you can check if the exception was thrown because of the **BeginTransaction** method.

Listing 3A-11. Checking if BeginTransaction *Caused the Exception*

```
1 . . .
2 Try
3 . . .' Begin transaction
4 Catch objException As Exception
5    ' Check if a BeginTransaction method threw the exception
6    If objException.TargetSite.Name = "BeginTransaction" Then
```

ConnectionString Property Exceptions

The **InvalidOperationException** exception is thrown when the connection is open or broken and you try to set the property. Listing 3A-12 shows you how you can check if the **InvalidOperationException** exception was thrown because of the **ConnectionString** property.

Listing 3A-12. Checking if ConnectionString *Caused the Exception*

```
1 . . .
2 Try
3 . . .' Set connection string
4 Catch objException As Exception
5    ' Check if setting the ConnectionString threw the exception
6    If objException.TargetSite.Name = "set_ConnectionString" Then
```

ConnectionTimeout Property Exceptions

The **ArgumentException** exception is thrown when you try to set the property to a value less than 0. Actually, the **ConnectionTimeout** property is read-only, so you cannot set it directly. However, you can set this property through the **Connection Timeout** value name in the **ConnectionString** property. The **ConnectionString** property will let you set the value name to a value less than 0, but the validation will not take place until you open the connection. This is when the **ArgumentException** exception is thrown. Listing 3A-13 shows you how you can check if the **Argument Exception** exception was thrown because of the **ConnectionTimeout** property.

Listing 3A-13. Checking if ConnectionTimeout *Caused the Exception*

```
1 . . .
2 Try
3 . . .' Set connection timeout
4 Catch objException As Exception
5    ' Check if we tried to set the connectiontimeout to an invalid value
6    If objException.TargetSite.Name = "SetConnectTimeout" Then
```

Database Property and ChangeDatabase Method Exceptions

The **InvalidOperationException** exception is thrown if the connection is not open. Actually, the **Database** property is read-only, so you cannot set it directly. However, you can set this property through the **ChangeDatabase** method or using a Transact-SQL statement. So in fact you can change from the current database to the master database by executing the simple SQL statement USE master using the **ExecuteNonQuery** method of the **SqlCommand** class. The **Database** property is then dynamically updated, and it is after this that an exception can be thrown.

> **NOTE** *Transact-SQL, which is used in SQL Server, is Microsoft's dialect of the ANSI SQL standard. Transact-SQL is fully ANSI compliant, but it also features many enhancements.*

Listing 3A-14 shows you how you can check if the **InvalidOperationException** exception was thrown because of the **Database** property.

Listing 3A-14. Checking if Database *Caused the Exception*

```
1 . . .
2 Try
3 . . .' Set database
4 Catch objException As Exception
5    ' Check if we tried to change database on an invalid connection
6    If objException.TargetSite.Name = "ChangeDatabase" Then
```

Open Method Exceptions

The **InvalidOperationException** exception is thrown when you try to open an already open or broken connection. When this exception is thrown, simply close the connection and open it again. Listing 3A-15 shows you how you can check if the **InvalidOperationException** exception was thrown because of the **Open** method.

Listing 3A-15. Checking if Open *Caused the Exception*

```
1 . . .
2 Try
3 . . .' Open database
4 Catch objException As Exception
5    ' Check if Open caused the exception
6    If objException.TargetSite.Name = "Open" Then
```

OleDbConnection Exceptions

Whenever an error occurs when you are working with the OLE DB .NET Data Provider, an **OleDbException** is thrown. This exception class, which cannot be inherited, is derived from the **ExternalException** class. The **OleDbException** class holds at least one instance of the **OleDbError** class. It is up to you to traverse through all the instances of **OleDbError** classes contained in the **OleDbException** class, in order to check what errors occurred. Listing 3A-16 shows how you can do it. The example catches exceptions that occur when you try to open a connection, but the code in the **Catch** section can be used for any OLE DB exceptions encountered.

Listing 3A-16 Traversing through an `OleDbException` *Class*

```
 1 ...
 2 Try
 3     ' Open the connection
 4     cnnUserMan.Open()
 5 Catch objException As OleDbException
 6     Dim objError As OleDbError
 7
 8     For Each objError In objException.Errors
 9         MsgBox(objException.Message)
10     Next
11 End Try
```

Listing 3A-16 shows you how to extract all instances of the **OleDbError** class in the **Errors** collection of the **OleDbException** class.

Examining the OleDbError Class

In Listing 3A-16, all I've specified is to display the error message, but there are actually a few more properties in the **OleDbError** class that are of interest. See Table 3A-14 for a list of all these properties. Incidentally, the **OleDbError** class, which is noninheritable, is inherited directly from the **Object** class.

Table 3A-14. **OleDbError** *Class Properties*

PROPERTY NAME	ACCESSIBILITY	DESCRIPTION
Message	Public	Returns a description of the error as a variable of data type **String.**
NativeError	Public	Returns the database-specific error information as a variable of data type **Integer.**
Source	Public	Returns the name of the provider in which the exception occurred or was generated from as a variable of data type **String.**
SQLState	Public	Returns the ANSI SQL standard error code as a variable of data type **String.** This error code is always five characters long.

All the properties in Table 3A-14 are read-only. They don't look all that different from the ones in the ADO errors collection, do they?

Examining the OleDbException Class

Besides the **Errors** collection, the **OleDbException** class has a few other properties and methods as you can see in Tables 3A-15 and 3A-16. Both tables are in alphabetical order.

Table 3A-15. OleDbException Class Properties

PROPERTY NAME	ACCESSIBILITY	DESCRIPTION	RETURN VALUE	READ	WRITE
ErrorCode	Public	This property, which is inherited from the **ExternalException** class, returns the error identification number for the error. The identification number is either an HRESULT or a Win32 error code.	Data type **Integer**	Yes	No
Errors	Public	This is actually a collection of the **OleDbError** class. See the preceding section, "Examining the OleDbError Class."	Data type **OleDbErrorCollection**	Yes	No
HelpLink	Public	This property, which is inherited from the **Exception** class, returns or sets the URN or URL that points to a HTML help file.	Data type **String**	Yes	Yes
HResult	Protected	This property, which is inherited from the **Exception** class, returns or sets the HRESULT for an exception. Check out general error handling in Chapter 5.		Yes	Yes
InnerException	Public	This property, which is inherited from the **Exception** class, returns a reference to the inner exception. This property generally holds the previously occurring exception or the exception that caused the current exception.	Data type **Exception**	Yes	No
Message	Public	This property is overridden, so check out the **Message** property of the **OleDbError** class.		Yes	No
Source	Public	This property is overridden, so check out the **Source** property of the **OleDbError** class.		Yes	No
StackTrace	Public	This property, which is inherited from the **Exception** class, returns the stack trace. You can use the stack trace to identify the location in your code where the error occurred.	Data type **String**	Yes	No
TargetSite	Public	This property, which is inherited from the **Exception** class, returns the method that threw the exception. Check out general error handling in Chapter 5, for more information the **MethodBase** object.	Data type **MethodBase**	Yes	No

*Table 3A-16. **OleDbException** Class Methods*

METHOD NAME	ACCESSIBILITY	DESCRIPTION	RETURN VALUE
Equals()	Public	This method, which is inherited from the **Object** class, has already been described in Table 3A-6. Please also see "Comparing Using the Equals Method" earlier in this chapter.	Data type **Boolean**
Finalize()	Protected	This method, which is inherited from the **Object** class, has already been described in Table 3A-6.	None
GetBaseException()	Public	This method, which is inherited from the **Exception** class, returns the original exception thrown. It is useful in cases where one exception has triggered another and so forth. The reference returned will point to the current exception, if this is the only exception thrown.	Data type **Exception**
GetHashCode()	Public	This method, which is inherited from the **Object** class, has already been described in Table 3A-6.	Data type **Integer**
GetObjectData(ByVal vobjInfo As SerializationInfo, ByVal vobjContext As StreamingContext)	Public	This method, which is inherited from the **Exception** class, sets the **SerializationInfo** object with information related to the exception. Check out general error handling in Chapter 5 for more information on the **SerializationInfo** object.	None
GetType()	Public	This method, which is inherited from the **Object** class, has already been described in Table 3A-6.	Data type **Type**
MemberwiseClone()	Protected	This method, which is inherited from the **Object** class, has already been described in Table 3A-6. Please also see "Copying Connections" earlier in this chapter.	Data type **Object**
ToString()	Public	This method, which is inherited from the **Object** class, has already been described in Table 3A-6. When used on the **OleDbException** class, it returns the fully qualified exception name. The error message (**Message** property), the inner exception name (**InnerException** property), and the stack trace (**StackTrace** property) might also be returned.	Data type **String**

Using Command Objects

A *command object* is used when you need to execute a query against your database. The command object is the simplest and easiest way of doing this. The two command classes within ADO.NET that are of interest are **OleDbCommand** and **SqlCommand**. The **OleDbCommand** class is part of the **System.Data.OleDb** namespace, and the **SqlCommand** class is part of the **System.Data.SqlClient** namespace.

> **TIP** *If you are uncertain about which namespace a certain class in your code belongs to, then simply move the cursor over this class and the namespace will be displayed in the little tool tip that pops up.*

OleDbCommand and SqlCommand

As with the provider and connection classes, you should make up your mind if you are going to connect to a MS SQL Server 7.0 or later data source or a different data source. The **SqlCommand** should be used with SQL Server and the **OleDbCommand** with any other OLE DB data source. Because the **SqlCommand** class has been optimized for use with SQL Server, it outperforms the **OleDbCommand** class. However, if you want you can use the **OleDbCommand** instead of the **Sql-Command** in much the same way. In Listing 3A-17 you can see how to declare and instantiate a **SqlCommand**.

Listing 3A-17. Instantiating a SqlCommand

```
 1 Dim cnnUserMan As SqlConnection
 2 Dim cmmUserMan As SqlCommand
 3 Dim strSQL As String
 4
 5 ' Instantiate the connection
 6 cnnUserMan = New SqlConnection()
 7 cnnUserMan.ConnectionString = "User ID=UserMan;" & _
 8   "Server=USERMANPC;Password=userman;Initial Catalog=UserMan"
 9 ' Open the connection
10 cnnUserMan.Open()
11 ' Build query string
12 strSQL = "SELECT * FROM tblUser"
13 ' Instantiate the command
14 cmmUserMan = New SqlCommand(strSQL, cnnUserMan)
```

In Listing 3A-17 I reuse the same connection code shown previously, so no need to explain that. In addition, I declare the command object cmmUserMan and the query string strSQL. Once the connection has been opened, the query string is built and the command instantiated using the query string and the open connection. The way the command object is instantiated here is one of four different instantiation procedures available, because the method is overloaded.

Instantiating the SqlCommand Object

There are the four different ways you can instantiate a **SqlCommand** object (the command object, the query string, and the connection string have all been declared elsewhere):

- cmmUserMan = New SqlCommand() instantiates cmmUserMan with no arguments. If you use this way to instantiate your command, you need to set some of the properties, such as **Connection**, before you execute or otherwise use the command. The following properties are set to initial values when you instantiate:

  ```
  CommandText = ""
  CommandTimeout = 30
  CommandType = CommandType.Text
  Connection = Nothing
  ```

- cmmUserMan = New SqlCommand(ByVal vstrSQL As String) instantiates cmmUserMan with the query command text (vstrSQL). You also need to supply a valid and open connection by setting the **Connection** property. The following properties are set to initial values when you instantiate:

  ```
  CommandText = vstrSQL
  CommandTimeout = 30
  CommandType = CommandType.Text
  Connection = Nothing
  ```

- cmmUserMan = New SqlCommand(ByVal vstrSQL As String, ByRef rcnnUserMan As SqlConnection) instantiates cmmUserMan with the query command text (vstrSQL) and a valid and open connection, rcnnUserMan. The following properties are set to initial values when you instantiate:

  ```
  CommandText = vstrSQL
  CommandTimeout = 30
  CommandType = CommandType.Text
  Connection = rcnnUserMan
  ```

- cmmUserMan = New SqlCommand(ByVal vstrSQL As String, _ByRef rcnnUserMan As SqlConnection, ByRef rtraUserMan As SqlTransaction) instantiates cmmUserMan with the query command text and a connection object. The rcnnUserMan must be a valid and open connection and rtraUserMan must a valid and open transaction that has been opened on rcnnUserMan. This version should be used when you have started a transaction using the **BeginTransaction** method of the connection class. The following properties are set to initial values when you instantiate:

```
CommandText = vstrSQL
CommandTimeout = 30
CommandType = CommandType.Text
Connection = rcnnUserMan
```

Instantiating the OleDbCommand Object

Here are the four different ways you can instantiate an **OleDbCommand** object (the command object, the query string, and the connection string have all been declared elsewhere):

- cmmUserMan = New OleDbCommand() instantiates cmmUserMan with no arguments. If you use this way to instantiate your command, you need to set some of the properties, such as **Connection**, before you execute or otherwise use the command. The following properties are set to initial values when you instantiate:

```
CommandText = ""
CommandTimeout = 30
CommandType = CommandType.Text
Connection = Nothing
```

- cmmUserMan = New OleDbCommand(ByVal vstrSQL As String) instantiates cmmUserMan with the query command text (vstrSQL). You also need to supply a valid and open connection by setting the **Connection** property. The following properties are set to initial values when you instantiate:

```
CommandText = vstrSQL
CommandTimeout = 30
CommandType = CommandType.Text
Connection = Nothing
```

- cmmUserMan = New OleDbCommand(ByVal vstrSQL As String, ByRef rcnnUserMan As SqlConnection) instantiates cmmUserMan with the query command text (vstrSQL) and a valid and open connection rcnnUserMan. The following properties are set to initial values when you instantiate:

```
CommandText = vstrSQL
CommandTimeout = 30
CommandType = CommandType.Text
Connection = rcnnUserMan
```

- cmmUserMan = New OleDbCommand(ByVal vstrSQL As String, _ByRef rcnnUserMan As SqlConnection, ByRef rtraUserMan As SqlTransaction) instantiates cmmUserMan with the query command text and a connection object. rcnnUserMan must be a valid and open connection and rtraUserMan must be a valid and open transaction that has been opened on rcnnUser-Man. This version should be used when you have started a transaction with the **BeginTransaction** method of the connection class. The following properties are set to initial values when you instantiate:

```
CommandText = vstrSQL
CommandTimeout = 30
CommandType = CommandType.Text
Connection = rcnnUserMan
```

Which of the ways to instantiate your command object (**SqlCommand** or **OleDbCommand**) you should choose really depends on the context and what you are trying to achieve. In most cases I guess you would pick cmmUserMan = New OleDbCommand() or cmmUserMan = New OleDbCommand(ByVal vstrSQL As String), which are really the same except for the connection argument in option cmmUserMan = New OleDbCommand(ByVal vstrSQL As String, ByRef rcnnUserMan As SqlConnection). Always use cmmUserMan = New OleDbCommand(ByVal vstrSQL As String, ByRef rcnnUserMan As SqlConnection, ByRef rtraUserMan As SqlTransaction) when a transaction has been started on the connection object.

Command Class Properties

Tables 3A-17 and 3A-18 list all the public command class properties in alphabetical order and shows the equivalent Command class constructor argument (see the preceding sections "Instantiating the SqlCommand Object" and "Instantiating the OleDbCommand Object"). Please note that in most cases the properties are only checked for syntax when you set them. The real validation takes place when you perform one of the **Execute**. . . methods.

Table 3A-17. **SqlCommand** Class Properties

PROPERTY NAME	DESCRIPTION	COMMAND CONSTRUCTOR EQUIVALENT	DEFAULT VALUE	READ	WRITE
CommandText	The query text or the name of a stored procedure to execute. When you set this property to the same value as the current one, the assignment is left out. You need to set this property to the name of a stored procedure, when the **CommandType** property is set to **CommandType.StoredProcedure.**	vstrSQL	"" (empty string)	Yes	Yes
CommandTimeout	This is the number of seconds to wait for the command to execute. If the command has not been executed within this period, an error is generated.		30	Yes	Yes
CommandType	This property determines how the **CommandText** property is interpreted. The following **CommandType** enum values are valid: **StoredProcedure**: The **CommandText** property must hold name of a stored procedure. **Text**: The **CommandText** property is interpreted as a query like a SELECT statement, and so on.		Text	Yes	Yes
Connection	This is the connection to the data source.	rcnnUserMan	**Nothing**	Yes	Yes

*Table 3A-17. **SqlCommand** Class Properties (continued)*

PROPERTY NAME	DESCRIPTION	COMMAND CONSTRUCTOR EQUIVALENT	DEFAULT VALUE	READ	WRITE
DesignTimeVisible	Used to indicate if the command object should be visible in a Windows Forms Designer control		**False**	Yes	Yes
Parameters	Retrieves the **SqlParameterCollection**, which holds the parameters of the Transact-SQL statement		Empty collection	Yes	No
Transaction	If a transaction has been started on the connection this command is attached to, then this property holds the transaction object	rtraUserMan	**Nothing**	Yes	Yes
UpdatedRowSource	Gets or sets how and if the command results are applied to the row source after the command has been executed. This property needs to be set to one the following **UpdateRowSource** enum values: **Both:** The sum of the **FirstReturnedRecord** and **OutputParameters** values **FirstReturnedRecord:** Only data in the first returned record is mapped to the changed row in the data set. **None:** Returned parameters and/or rows will be ignored. **OutputParameters:** Only the output parameters are mapped to the changed row in the Dataset.		Both (None, if the command is automatically generated)	Yes	Yes

Table 3A-18. *OleDbCommand Class Properties*

PROPERTY NAME	DESCRIPTION	COMMAND CONSTRUCTOR EQUIVALENT	DEFAULT VALUE	READ	WRITE
CommandText	The query text or the name of a stored procedure to execute. When you set this property to the same value as the current value, the assignment is left out. You need to set this property to the name of a stored procedure when the **CommandType** property is set to **CommandType.StoredProcedure**. You can only set this property when the connection is open and available, which means that the connection cannot be fetching rows when you set this property.	vstrSQL	"" (empty string)	Yes	Yes
CommandTimeout	This is the number of seconds to wait for the command to execute. If the command has not been executed within this period, an error is generated.		30	Yes	Yes
CommandType	This property determines how the **CommandText** property is interpreted. The following values are valid: **StoredProcedure**: The **CommandText** property must hold the name of a stored procedure **TableDirect**: The **CommandText** property must hold name the of a table. All columns for this table will be returned. This is instead of using a query such as "SELECT * FROM TableName" **Text**: The **CommandText** property is interpreted as a query like a SELECT statement, and so on.		Text	Yes	Yes

Table 3A-18. OleDbCommand Class Properties (continued)

PROPERTY NAME	DESCRIPTION	COMMAND CONSTRUCTOR EQUIVALENT	DEFAULT VALUE	READ	WRITE
Connection	This is the connection to the data source.	rcnnUserMan	**Nothing**	Yes	Yes
DesignTimeVisible	Used to indicate if the command object should be visible in a Windows Forms Designer control.		**False**	Yes	Yes
Parameters	Retrieves the **OleDbParameterCollection**, which holds the parameters of the **CommandText** property.		Empty collection	Yes	No
Transaction	If a transaction has been started on the connection this command is attached to, then this property holds the transaction object.	rtraUserMan	**Nothing**	Yes	Yes
UpdatedRowSource	Gets or sets how and if the command results are applied to the row source after the command has been executed. This property needs to be set to one the following **UpdateRowSource** enum values: **Both:** The sum of the **FirstReturnedRecord** and **OutputParameters** values. **FirstReturnedRecord**: Only data in the first returned record is mapped to the changed row in the data set. **None:** Returned parameters and/ rows will be ignored. **OutputParameters:** Only the output parameters are mapped to the changed row in the Dataset.		Both (None, if the command is automatically generated)	Yes	Yes

Command Class Methods

Table 3A-19 lists all the command class (**SqlCommand** and **OleDbCommand**) methods in alphabetical order.

Table 3A-19. Command Class Methods

METHOD NAME	DESCRIPTION
Cancel()	Cancels the executing command, if there is one. Otherwise nothing happens.
CreateParameter()	This method can be used to create and instantiate an **SqlParameter** or **OleDbParameter** object. This is the equivalent of instantiating a **SqlParameter** object using `prmTest = New SqlParamater()` or **OleDbParameter** using `prmTest = New OleDbParameter()`. Mind you, there is actually one not-so-small difference between these two ways of instantiating the parameter object: The **CreateParameter** method adds the instantiated parameter object to the parameters collection and thus saves you the extra line of code. The parameters collection can be retrieved using the **Parameters** property.
ExecuteNonQuery	Executes the query specified in the **CommandText** property. The number of rows affected is returned. Even if the **CommandText** property contains a row-returning statement, no rows will be returned. The value -1 is returned if you specify a row-returning statement as command text. This is also true if you specify any other statement that doesn't affect the rows in the data source.
ExecuteReader()	Executes the query specified in the **CommandText** property. The returned object is a forward-only data object of type **SqlDataReader** or **OleDbDataReader**. This method is used when you execute a row-returning command, such as a SQL SELECT statement. Although it is possible to execute a non–row-returning command using this method, it is recommended that you use the **ExecuteNonQuery** method for that purpose. The reason for this is that even though the query doesn't return rows, the method still tries to build and return a forward-only data object. This method is overloaded (see "Executing a Command").

Table 3A-19. Command Class Methods (continued)

METHOD NAME	DESCRIPTION
ExecuteScalar()	This method is for retrieving a single value, such as an aggregate value like COUNT(*). There is less overhead and coding involved in using this method than in using the **ExecuteReader** method (see "Executing a Command").
ExecuteXmlReader()	This method is for retrieving a result set as XML (see "Executing a Command").
Prepare()	This method is used for compiling (preparing) the command. You can use this method when the **CommandType** property is set to **Text** or **StoredProcedure**. If, however, the **CommandType** property is set to **TableDirect**, nothing happens. The method takes no arguments, and it is simply called like this: `cmmUserMan.Prepare()`
ResetCommandTimeout()	Resets the **CommandTimeout** property to the default value. The method takes no arguments, and it is called like this: `cmmUserMan.ResetCommandTimeout()`

Executing a Command

Now you know how to set up and instantiate a command object, but you really need to execute it as well in order to fully exploit a command object's potential. As you can see from the various methods of the command class, the **ExecuteNonQuery**, **ExecuteReader**, **ExecuteScalar,** and **ExecuteXmlReader** methods are the ones you need for this purpose. Actually, this is fairly simple, and if you carefully read the names of the methods, you should have no doubt about which one to use (see Table 3A-20).

Table 3A-20. Executing a Command

METHOD NAME	WHEN TO USE	EXAMPLE
ExecuteNonQuery	Use this method when you want to execute a non–row-returning command, such as a DELETE statement. Although you use this method with row-returning statements, it doesn't make much sense, as the result set is discarded.	See Listing 3A-18, which shows how to insert a new user (*User99*) into the tblUser table.
ExecuteReader	This method should be used when you want to execute a row-returning command, such as a SELECT statement. The rows are returned in a **SqlDataReader** or an **OleDbDataReader** depending on which .NET data provider you are using. Please note that the **DataReader** class is a read-only, forward-only data class, which means that it should only be used for retrieving data to display or similar purposes. You cannot update data in a **DataReader**!	See Listing 3A-19, which shows how to retrieve all users from the tblUser table.
ExecuteScalar	You should use this method when you only want the first column of the first row of the result set returned. If there is more than one row in the result set, they are ignored by this method. This method is faster and has substantially less overhead than the **ExecuteReader** method. So use it when you know you will only have one row returned, or when you are using an aggregate function such as COUNT.	See Listing 3A-20, which shows how the number of rows in the tblUser table is returned.
ExecuteXmlReader (**SqlCommand** only)	This method is similar to the **ExecuteReader** method, but the returned rows must be expressed using XML.	See Listing 3A-21, which shows how all the rows in the tblUser table are returned as XML.

Listings 3A-18 to 3A-21 all use the SQL Server .NET Data Provider, but you can simply replace it with the OLE DB .NET Data Provider, if you want to use a different data source. Don't forget to change the **ConnectionString** property according to the data source you want to use.

Listing 3A-18. *Using the* ExecuteNonQuery *Method*

```
1 Dim cnnUserMan As SqlConnection
2 Dim cmmUserMan As SqlCommand
3 Dim strSQL As String
4
5 ' Instantiate the connection
6 cnnUserMan = New SqlConnection()
7 cnnUserMan.ConnectionString = "User ID=UserMan;" & _
8   "Server=USERMANPC;Password=userman;Initial Catalog=UserMan"
9 ' Open the connection
10 cnnUserMan.Open()
11 ' Build query string
12 strSQL = "INSERT INTO tblUser (LoginName) VALUES('User99')"
13 ' Instantiate and execute the command
14 cmmUserMan = New SqlCommand(strSQL, cnnUserMan)
15 cmmUserMan.ExecuteNonQuery()
```

Listing 3A-19. *Using the* ExecuteReader *Method*

```
1 Dim cnnUserMan As SqlConnection
2 Dim cmmUserMan As SqlCommand
3 Dim drdTest As SqlDataReader
4 Dim strSQL As String
5
6 ' Instantiate the connection
7 cnnUserMan = New SqlConnection()
8 cnnUserMan.ConnectionString = "User ID=UserMan;" & _
9   "Server=USERMANPC;Password=userman;Initial Catalog=UserMan"
10 ' Open the connection
11 cnnUserMan.Open()
12 ' Build query string
13 strSQL = "SELECT * FROM tblUser"
14 ' Instantiate and execute the command
15 cmmUserMan = New SqlCommand(strSQL, cnnUserMan)
16 drdTest = cmmUserMan.ExecuteReader()
```

Listing 3A-20. *Using the* ExecuteScalar *Method*

```
1 Dim cnnUserMan As SqlConnection
2 Dim cmmUserMan As SqlCommand
3 Dim intNumRows As Integer
4 Dim strSQL As String
5
6 ' Instantiate the connection
7 cnnUserMan = New SqlConnection()
8 cnnUserMan.ConnectionString = "User ID=UserMan;" & _
```

```
 9  "Server=USERMANPC;Password=userman;Initial Catalog=UserMan"
10  ' Open the connection
11  cnnUserMan.Open()
12  ' Build query string
13  strSQL = "SELECT COUNT(*) FROM tblUser"
14  ' Instantiate the command
15  cmmUserMan = New SqlCommand(strSQL, cnnUserMan)
16  ' Save the number of rows in the table
17  intNumRows = CInt(cmmUserMan.ExecuteScalar().ToString)
```

Listing 3A-21. Using the ExecuteXmlReader ***Method***

```
 1 Dim cnnUserMan As SqlConnection
 2 Dim cmmUserMan As SqlCommand
 3 Dim drdTest As XmlReader
 4 Dim strSQL As String
 5
 6 ' Instantiate the connection
 7 cnnUserMan = New SqlConnection()
 8 cnnUserMan.ConnectionString = "User ID=UserMan;" & _
 9  "Server=USERMANPC;Password=userman;Initial Catalog=UserMan"
10 ' Open the connection
11 cnnUserMan.Open()
12 ' Build query string to return result set as XML
13 strSQL = "SELECT * FROM tblUser FOR XML AUTO"
14 ' Instantiate the command
15 cmmUserMan = New SqlCommand(strSQL, cnnUserMan)
16 ' Retrieve the rows as XML
17 drdTest = cmmUserMan.ExecuteXmlReader()
```

In Listing 3A-21, the result set is retrieved as XML, because the FOR XML AUTO clause appears at the end of the query. This instructs SQL Server 2000 to return the result set as XML.

Handling Command Class Exceptions

There are a number of exceptions that can be thrown when you work with the properties and exceptions of the command class. The following sections discuss the most common ones and how to deal with them.

CommandTimeout Property

The **ArgumentException** exception is thrown when you try to set the **Command-Timeout** property to a negative value. Listing 3A-22 shows you how you can check if the **ArgumentException** exception was thrown when the command time-out was changed.

Listing 3A-22. Checking if the Exception Was Caused When Setting Command Time-Out

```
1 . . .
2 Try
3 . . .' Change command timeout
4 Catch objException As ArgumentException
5    ' Check if we tried to set command timeout to an invalid value
6    If objException.TargetSite.Name = "set_CommandTimeout" Then
```

CommandType Property

The **ArgumentException** exception is thrown if you try to set the property to an invalid command type. Listing 3A-23 shows you how you can check if the **ArgumentException** exception was thrown when the command type was changed.

Listing 3A-23. Checking if the Exception Was Caused When Setting Command Type

```
1 . . .
2 Try
3 . . .' Change command type
4 Catch objException As ArgumentException
5    ' Check if we tried to set command type to an invalid value
6    If objException.TargetSite.Name = "set_CommandType" Then
```

Prepare Method

The **InvalidOperationException** exception is thrown if the connection variable is set to **Nothing** or not open. Listing 3A-24 shows you how you can check if the **InvalidOperationException** exception was thrown when preparing the command.

Listing 3A-24. Checking if the Exception Was Caused When Trying to Prepare the Command

```
1 . . .
2 Try
3 . . .' Prepare command
4 Catch objException As InvalidOperationException
5    ' Check if we tried to prepare the command on an invalid connection
6    If objException.TargetSite.Name = "ValidateCommand" Then
```

UpdatedRowSource Property

The **ArgumentException** exception is thrown if the row source update property was set to a value other than an **UpdateRowSource** enum value. Listing 3A-25 shows you how to check if the **ArgumentException** exception was thrown.

Listing 3A-25. Checking if the Exception Was Thrown When Trying to Change Row Source Update

```
1 ...
2 Try
3 ...' Change Row source Update
4 Catch objException As ArgumentException
5    ' Check if we tried to set the row source update to an invalid value
6    If objException.TargetSite.Name = "set_UpdatedRowSource" Then
```

Using the DataReader Class

The **DataReader** class is a read-only, forward-only data class, and it is very efficient when it comes to memory usage, because only one row is ever in memory at a time. This is in contrast to the **DataTable** class (discussed in Chapter 3B), which allocates memory for all rows retrieved.

You can only instantiate an object of type **DataReader** by using the **ExecuteReader** method of the **Command** class (see "Executing a Command" earlier in this chapter for details). When you use the **DataReader**, the associated connection cannot perform any other operations. This is because the connection as such is serving the **DataReader**, and you need to close the **DataReader** before the connection is ready for other operations. The **DataReader** class is one of the ADO.NET classes that resemble the ADO **Recordset** class the most. Well, it is, if you think **Recordset** with a read-only, forward-only cursor. One of the differences is how you get the next row (see "Reading Rows in a DataReader" later in this chapter).

SqlDataReader and OleDbDataReader

As with the **Connection** and **Command** classes, there are also two general **DataReader** classes of interest: **SqlDataReader** is for use with MS SQL Server 7 or later and **OleDbDataReader** is for use with any other data source. Please note that if you are using an **SqlConnection** object, then you cannot use **OleDbCommand** and/or an **OleDbDataReader** class with the connection. The same goes the other way around. In other words, you cannot mix OleDb and SQL data classes; they cannot work together!

Declaring and Instantiating a DataReader Object

The **DataReader** class cannot be inherited, which effectively means that you cannot create your own data class based on the **DataReader** class.

The following sample code is wrong:

```
Dim drdTest As New SqlDataReader()
```

It is wrong because it tries to instantiate drdTest using the **New** keyword. Listing 3A-26 shows you what you need to do to instantiate a **SqlDataReader** object.

Listing 3A-26. Instantiating a SqlDataReader Object
```
' Declare data reader
Dim drdTest As SqlDataReader
' Excute command and return rows in data reader
drdTest = cmmUserMan.ExecuteReader()
```

In Listing 3A-26 there is no code for declaring, instantiating, and opening the command object, but if you reuse the code from any of the previous listings, you should have fully functioning code. Now, just to underline the way a **DataReader** object is instantiated, here is another example that seems logical, but just will not work:

```
drdTest = New SqlDataReader ()
```

This code will not work because the **DataReader** class doesn't have a constructor.

Reading Rows in a DataReader

Since the **DataReader** class is a forward-only data class, you need to read the rows sequentially from start to finish if you need to read all the returned rows. In Listing 3A-27 you can see how to loop through a populated data reader.

Listing 3A-27. Looping through All Rows in a DataReader
```
1 Dim cnnUserMan As SqlConnection
2 Dim cmmUserMan As SqlCommand
3 Dim strSQL As String
4 Dim drdTest As SqlDataReader
5 Dim lngCounter As Long = 0
6
7 ' Instantiate the connection
8 cnnUserMan = New SqlConnection()
9 cnnUserMan.ConnectionString = "User ID=UserMan;" & _
```

```
10  "Server=USERMANPC;Password=userman;Initial Catalog=UserMan"
11  ' Open the connection
12  cnnUserMan.Open()
13  ' Build query string
14  strSQL = "SELECT * FROM tblUser"
15  ' Instantiate the command
16  cmmUserMan = New SqlCommand(strSQL, cnnUserMan)
17  ' Excute command and return rows in data reader
18  drdTest = cmmUserMan.ExecuteReader()
19  ' Loop through all the returned rows
20  Do While drdTest.Read
21      lngCounter = lngCounter + 1
22  Loop
23
24  ' Display the number of rows returned
25  MsgBox(CStr(lngCounter))
```

Listing 3A-27 loops through the rows in the data reader and counts the number of rows. This is obviously just an example of how to sequentially go through all the rows returned by the **ExecuteReader** method of the **Command** class.

Closing a DataReader

Because the **DataReader** object keeps the connection busy while it is open, it is good practice to close the **DataReader** once you are done with it. The **DataReader** is closed using the **Close** method, like this:

```
drdTest.Close()
```

You can use the **IsClosed** property to check if the data reader is closed, as follows:

If Not drdTest.IsClosed Then

Checking for Null Values in Columns

When you have instantiated your data reader and positioned it in a valid row using the **Read** method, you can check if a particular column contains a Null value. This is done by using the **IsDBNull** method, which compares the content of a specific column in the current row with the **DBNull** class. If the column doesn't contain a known value, also named a Null value, the **IsDBNull** method returns **True**. Otherwise **False** is returned. This is how you can perform the check:

```
' Check if column 3 (zero based array) contains a Null value
If drdTest.IsDBNull(2) Then
```

Handling Multiple Results

The **DataReader** class can handle multiple results returned by the command class. If the command class returned multiple results by specifying a batch of SQL statements separated by a semicolon, you can use the **NextResult** method to advance to the next result. Please note that you can only move forward, so as much as it would be nice to have a **PreviousResult** method, it just isn't possible.

DataReader Properties

The **DataReader** class has the properties shown in ascending order in Table 3A-21.

*Table 3A-21. **DataReader** Class Properties*

NAME	DESCRIPTION
Depth	This read-only property is used with hierarchical result sets, such as XML data. The return value indicates how far down a node you currently are or the depth of the current element in the stack of XML elements. This is not supported by the SQL Server .NET Data Provider.
FieldCount	This read-only property returns the number of columns in the current row. The **NotSupportedException** is thrown, if the **DataReader** is not connected to a data source.
IsClosed	This property, which is read-only, indicates if the data reader is closed. **True** is returned if the data reader is closed and **False** if not.
Item	This read-only property is used to indicate what column or field you want to return the value from. The property, which cannot be overridden, can be specified using a string, indicating the name of the column, or a number, indicating the column ordinal. As with all arrays, the columns are numbered ascending starting with zero, so the first column is retrieved using drdTest.Item(0). Actually, you can leave out the **Item** property and specify the property like this: drdTest(0). Oops, I nearly forgot: You can use the name of the column as well, so if the first column is called Id, then this is how you might set the property: drdTest.Item("Id"). Please note that no formatting is applied to the returned value, meaning that whatever the column contains, it will be returned in its native format!
RecordsAffected	This read-only property retrieves the number of records that was affected (inserted, updated, or deleted) by the command. This property will not be set until you have read all the rows and closed the data reader.

DataReader Methods

Table 3A-22 lists the noninherited and public methods of the **DataReader** class in alphabetical order. Please note that all the methods marked with an asterisk (*) require that the data contained in the specified column to be of the same type as the method indicates. This is because no conversion is performed on the content of the specified column. If you try to use any of the methods on a column containing content of a different data type, the **InvalidCastException** is thrown. Also, these methods cannot be overridden in an inherited class.

*Table 3A-22. **DataReader** Class Methods*

NAME	DESCRIPTION	EXAMPLE
Close()	Closes the data reader. You must call this method before you can use the connection for any other purpose. This is because the data reader keeps the connection busy as long as it is open.	`drdTest.Close()`
*GetBoolean(ByVal vintOrdinal As Integer)	Returns the **Boolean** value of the specified column vintOrdinal. The corresponding SQL Server data type is **bit**.	`blnTest = drdTest.GetBoolean(0)`
*GetByte(ByVal vintOrdinal As Integer)	Returns the value of the specified column vintOrdinal as a **Byte**. The corresponding SQL Server data type is **tinyint**.	`bytTest = drdTest.GetByte(0)`
*GetBytes(ByVal vintOrdinal As Integer, ByVal vintDataIndex As Integer, ByVal varrbytBuffer() As Byte, ByVal vintBufferIndex As Integer, ByVal vintLength As Integer)	Returns the value of the specified column vintOrdinal as an array of **Byte**s in the varrbytBuffer argument. The length of the specified column is returned as the result of the method call. vintLength specifies the maximum number of bytes to copy into the byte array. vintBufferIndex is the starting point in the buffer. When the bytes are copied into the buffer, they are placed starting from the vintBufferIndex point. The bytes are copied from the data source starting from the vintDataIndex point. You can use this method when you need to read large images from the database and the method largely corresponds to the **GetChunk** method in ADO. The corresponding SQL Server data types are **binary**, **image**, and **varbinary**.	`intNumBytes = drdSql.GetBytes(1, 0, Nothing, 0, Integer.MaxValue ReDim arrbytTest(intNumBytes) drdSql.GetBytes(1, 0, arrbytTest, 0, intNumBytes)`

*Table 3A-22. **DataReader** Class Methods (continued)*

NAME	DESCRIPTION	EXAMPLE
*GetChar(ByVal vintOrdinal As Integer)	Returns the value of the specified column (vintOrdinal) as a **Char**. The corresponding SQL Server data type is **char**.	`chrTest = drdTest.GetChar(0)`
*GetChars(ByVal vintOrdinal As Integer, ByVal vintDataIndex As Integer, ByVal varrchrBuffer() As Char, ByVal vintBufferIndex As Integer, ByVal vintLength As Integer)	Returns the value of the specified column (vintOrdinal) as an array of **Char**s in the varrchrBuffer argument. The length of the specified column is returned as the result of the method call. vintLength specifies the maximum number of characters to copy into the character array. vintBufferIndex is the starting point in the buffer. When the characters are copied into the buffer, they are placed starting from the vintBufferIndex point. The characters are copied from the data source starting from the vintDataIndex point. The corresponding SQL Server data types are **char**, **nchar**, **ntext**, **nvarchar**, **text**, and **varchar**.	`intNumChars = drdSql.GetChars(1, 0, Nothing, 0, Integer.MaxValue)` `ReDim arrchrTest(intNumChars)` `drdSql.GetChars(1, 0, arrchrTest, 0, intNumChars)`
GetData(ByVal vintOrdinal As Integer)	Not currently supported.	
GetDataTypeName(ByVal vintOrdinal As Integer)	Returns the name of the data type used by the data source for the specified column	`strDataType = drdTest.GetDataTypeName(0)`
*GetDateTime(ByVal vintOrdinal As Integer)	Returns the **DateTime** value stored in the column specified by vintOrdinal. The corresponding SQL Server data types are **datetime** and **smalldatetime**.	`dtmTest = drdTest.GetDateTime(0)`
*GetDecimal(ByVal vintOrdinal As Integer)	Returns the **Decimal** value stored in the column specified by vintOrdinal. The corresponding SQL Server data types are **decimal**, **money**, **numeric,** and **smallmoney**.	`decTest = drdTest.GetDecimal(0)`
*GetDouble(ByVal vintOrdinal As Integer)	Returns the **Double** value stored in the column specified by vintOrdinal. The corresponding SQL Server data type is **float**.	`dblTest = drdTest.GetDouble(0)`
GetFieldType(ByVal vintOrdinal As Integer)	Returns the data type of the column specified by vintOrdinal. The returned object is of type **Type**.	`typTest = drdTest.GetFieldType(0)`

Table 3A-22. **DataReader** *Class Methods (continued)*

NAME	DESCRIPTION	EXAMPLE
GetFloat(ByVal vintOrdinal As Integer)	Returns the floating-point number stored in the column specified by vintOrdinal. The returned object is of data type **Single**. The corresponding SQL Server data type is **real**.	sglTest = drdTest.GetFloat(0)
GetGuid(ByVal vintOrdinal As Integer)	Returns the globally unique identifier stored in the column specified by vintOrdinal. The returned object is of data type **Guid**. The corresponding SQL Server data type is **uniqueidentifier**.	guiTest = drdTest.GetGuid(0)
GetInt16(ByVal vintOrdinal As Integer)	Returns the 16-bit signed integer stored in the column specified by vintOrdinal. The returned object is of data type **Short**. The corresponding SQL Server data type is **smallint**.	shrTest = drdTest.GetInt16(0)
GetInt32(ByVal vintOrdinal As Integer)	Returns the 32-bit signed integer stored in the column specified by vintOrdinal. The returned object is of data type **Integer**. The corresponding SQL Server data type is **int**.	intTest = drdTest.GetInt32(0)
GetInt64(ByVal vintOrdinal As Integer)	Returns the 64-bit signed integer stored in the column specified by vintOrdinal. The returned object is of data type **Long**. The corresponding SQL Server data type is **bigint**.	lngTest = drdTest.GetInt64(0)
GetName(ByVal vintOrdinal As Integer)	Returns the name of the column specified by vintOrdinal. The returned object is of data type **String**. This method is the reverse of **GetOrdinal**.	strTest = drdTest.GetName(0)
GetOrdinal(ByVal vstrName As String)	Returns the ordinal for the column specified by vstrName. The returned object is of data type **Integer**. This method is the reverse of **GetName**.	intTest = drdTest.GetOrdinal(0)
*GetSqlBinary(ByVal vintOrdinal As Integer) (**SqlDataReader** only)	Returns the variable-length binary data stream stored in the column specified by vintOrdinal. The returned object is of data type **SqlBinary**. The corresponding SQL Server data types are **binary** and **image**.	sbnTest = drdTest.GetSqlBinary(0)

Table 3A-22. **DataReader** *Class Methods (continued)*

NAME	DESCRIPTION	EXAMPLE
*GetSqlBoolean(ByVal vintOrdinal As Integer) (**SqlDataReader** only)	Returns the value stored in the column specified by vintOrdinal. The returned object is of data type **SqlBoolean** and can only be one of the values **True, False,** or **Nothing.** The corresponding SQL Server data type is **bit**. Although this method works with the same SQL Server data type as the **GetBoolean** method, the return value is different.	sbtTest = drdTest.GetSqlBit(0)
*GetSqlByte(ByVal vintOrdinal As Integer) (**SqlDataReader** only)	Returns the 8-bit unsigned integer stored in the column specified by vintOrdinal. The returned object is of data type **SqlByte**. The corresponding SQL Server data type is **tinyint**.	sbyTest = drdTest.GetSqlByte(0)
*GetSqlDateTime(ByVal vintOrdinal As Integer) (**SqlDataReader** only)	Returns the date and time value stored in the column specified by vintOrdinal. The returned object is of data type **SqlDateTime**. The corresponding SQL Server data types are **datetime** and **smalldatetime**.	sdtTest = drdTest.GetSqlDateTime(0)
*GetSqlDecimal(ByVal vintOrdinal As Integer) (**SqlDataReader** only)	Returns the **SqlDecimal** value stored in the column specified by vintOrdinal.	sdbTest = drdTest.GetSqlDouble(0)
*GetSqlDouble(ByVal vintOrdinal As Integer) (**SqlDataReader** only)	Returns the **SqlDouble** value stored in the column specified by vintOrdinal. The corresponding SQL Server data type is **float**.	sdbTest = drdTest.GetSqlDouble(0)
*GetSqlGuid(ByVal vintOrdinal As Integer) (**SqlDataReader** only)	Returns the globally unique identifier stored in the column specified by vintOrdinal. The returned object is of data type **SqlGuid**. The corresponding SQL Server data type is **uniqueidentifier**.	sguTest = drdTest.GetSqlGuid(0)
*GetSqlInt16(ByVal vintOrdinal As Integer) (**SqlDataReader** only)	Returns the 16-bit signed integer stored in the column specified by vintOrdinal. The returned object is of data type **SqlInt16**. The corresponding SQL Server data type is **smallint**.	s16Test = drdTest.GetSqlInt16(0)
*GetSqlInt32(ByVal vintOrdinal As Integer) (**SqlDataReader** only)	Returns the 32-bit signed integer stored in the column specified by vintOrdinal. The returned object is of data type **SqlInt32**. The corresponding SQL Server data type is **int**.	s32Test = drdTest.GetSqlInt32(0)

Table 3A-22. **DataReader** *Class Methods (continued)*

NAME	DESCRIPTION	EXAMPLE
*GetSqlInt64(ByVal vintOrdinal As Integer) (**SqlDataReader** only)	Returns the 64-bit signed integer stored in the column specified by vintOrdinal. The returned object is of data type **SqlInt64**. The corresponding SQL Server data type is **bigint**.	`s64Test = drdTest.GetSqlInt64(0)`
*GetSqlMoney(ByVal vintOrdinal As Integer) (**SqlDataReader** only)	Returns the **SqlMoney** value stored in the column specified by vintOrdinal. The corresponding SQL Server data types are **money** and **smallmoney**.	`smoTest = drdTest.GetSqlMoney(0)`
*GetSqlSingle(ByVal vintOrdinal As Integer) (**SqlDataReader** only)	Returns the **SqlSingle** value stored in the column specified by vintOrdinal. The corresponding SQL Server data type is **real**.	`ssgTest = drdTest.GetSqlSingle(0)`
*GetSqlString(ByVal vintOrdinal As Integer) (**SqlDataReader** only)	Returns the **SqlString** value stored in the column specified by vintOrdinal. The corresponding SQL Server data types are **char**, **nchar**, **ntext**, **nvarchar**, **text**, and **varchar**.	`sstTest = drdTest.GetSqlString(0)`
GetSqlValue(ByVal vintOrdinal As Integer) (**SqlDataReader** only)	Returns an object that represents the underlying data type and value stored in the column specified by vintOrdinal. The returned object is of data type **Object**. You can use **GetType**, **ToString**, and other methods on the returned object to get the information wanted.	`objTest = drdTest.GetSqlValue(0)`
GetSqlValues(ByVal varrobjValues() As Object) (**SqlDataReader** only)	Returns all the attribute fields for the current column in the varrobjValues array. The array must be initialized before you execute this method. The returned **Integer** is the number of objects in the array.	`Dim arrobjValues() As Object` `ReDim arrobjValues (Integer.MaxValue)` `intNumFields = drdTest.GetSqlValues (arrobjValues)` `ReDim Preserve arrobjValues(intNumFields)`
*GetString(ByVal vintOrdinal As Integer)	Returns the **String** value stored in the column specified by vintOrdinal. The corresponding SQL Server data types are **char**, **nchar**, **ntext**, **nvarchar**, **text**, and **varchar**.	`strTest = drdTest.GetString(0)`

Table 3A-22. **DataReader** Class Methods (continued)

NAME	DESCRIPTION	EXAMPLE
GetTimeSpan(ByVal vintOrdinal As Integer) (OleDbDataReader only)	Returns the **TimeSpan** value stored in the column specified by vintOrdinal	`tmsTest = drdTest.GetTimeSpan(0)`
GetValue(ByVal vintOrdinal As Integer)	Returns the value stored in the column specified by vintOrdinal as a variable of data type **Object**. The value returned is in native .NET format.	`objTest = drdTest.GetValue(0)`

GetValues(ByVal varrobjValues () As Object)	Returns all the attribute column values for the current row in the varrobjValues array. The returned **Integer** is the number of objects in the array. You can use the **FieldCount** property to size the array like this:
	
	`Dim arrobjValues() As Object`
	`ReDim arrobjValues(drdTest.FieldCount)`
	`drdTest.GetValues(arrobjValues)`	

IsDBNull(ByVal vintOrdinal As Integer)	This method returns **True** if the column specified by vintOrdinal is equal to **DBNull**; otherwise it returns **False**. **DBNull** means that the column does not hold a known value or a Null value.	`If drdTest.IsDBNull(0) Then`
NextResult()	This method positions the data reader at the next result in the result set returned by the command. This method has no effect if the command query does not contain a batch of row-returning SQL statements or if the current result is the last in the result set. **True** is returned if there are more results and **False** otherwise. The data reader is positioned at the first result by default when instantiated.	`If drdTest.NextResult() Then`
Read()	This method positions the data reader at the next row. Please note that you must call this method after the data reader has been instantiated before you can access any of the data in the data reader. This is because the data reader, unlike the **Recordset** object in ADO, is not positioned at the first row by default. **True** is returned if the data reader is positioned at the next row and **False** if not.	`If drdTest.Read() Then`

All the **GetSql. . .** methods such as **GetSqlBinary**, which are relevant to the **SqlDataReader** class only, belong to the **System.Data.SqlTypes** namespace. Most of these methods have corresponding methods that work with all the data reader classes. They work with the same data types in the data source (SQL Server), but the data type returned is different. So which method you should pick really depends on the data types you want to work with in your application: Do you want native SQL Server data types or do you want .NET Framework data types?

Handling DataReader Exceptions

The properties and methods of the **DataReader** class can throw the exceptions shown in Table 3A-23.

*Table 3A-23. **DataReader** Exceptions in Alphabetical Order*

NAME	DESCRIPTION	THROWN BY PROPERTY/METHOD
ArgumentException	This exception is thrown when an argument is out of range.	
InvalidCastException	If you try to implicitly cast or convert a database value using one the **Get*** methods, then this exception is thrown.	All the methods marked by an asterisk (*)
InvalidOperationException	When you try to perform an operation (property or method) that is not valid in the objects current state, this exception is thrown.	
NotSupportedException	This exception is thrown when you try to use an I/O property or method on a **DataReader** object that is closed or otherwise not connected.	

When to Use the DataReader Class

The **DataReader** class should be used in cases where you want a minimal overhead in terms of memory usage. Now obviously you do not want to use a **DataReader** object if you are expecting hundreds of thousands of rows returned, because it could take forever to sequentially loop through all these rows.

If you are looking at only one or even a few rows returned, in which you just need to read one or two fields or columns, then the **DataReader** is definitely a good choice. The **DataReader** class is read-only, so if you need to update your data, then the **DataReader** class is obviously NOT a good choice!

XmlReader

Okay, so I lied when I said there are only two **DataReader** classes, because there is also the **XmlReader** class. It should be obvious that this class is for handling data formatted as XML. Actually, the **XmlReader** class, which is part of the System.Xml namespace, must be overridden, and this has already been done in the .NET Framework. You can still choose to override the **XmlReader** class yourself, but there are already three classes that all implement the **XmlReader** class and they are **XmlTextReader**, **XmlValidatingReader,** and **XmlNodeReader**.

- *XmlTextReader:* This class is for fast, noncached, forward-only stream access. The class checks for well-formed XML, but if you need data validation, you must use the **XmlValidatingReader** class.

- *XmlValidatingReader:* This class provides XDR, XSD, and DTD schema validation of the XML data.

- *XmlNodeReader:* The **XmlNodeReader** class reads XML data from an **XmlNavigator** class, which means it can read data stored in an **XmlDocument** or **XmlDataDocument**.

I won't go into more detail on these three derived XML readers, but I will take a closer look at the parent class **XmlReader**.

XmlReader Properties

The **XmlReader** class has the properties, shown in alphabetical order, in Table 3A-24.

*Table 3A-24. **XmlReader** Class Properties*

NAME	DESCRIPTION
AttributeCount	Returns the number of attributes, including default attributes, on the current node. Only the **Element, DocumentType,** and **XmlDeclaration** type nodes have attributes, which means that this property is only relevant to these types of nodes. If you have used the **ExecuteXmlReader** method of a command class, then the **AttributeCount** property will return the number of non-Null values in the current row. This property is read-only.
BaseURI	Returns the base URI of the current node. An empty string is returned if there is no base URI. This property is read-only, and it has no real meaning if your **XmlReader** has been returned by the **ExecuteXmlReader** method of a command class.
CanResolveEntity	This property is read-only, and it returns a value that indicates if the reader can parse and resolve entities.
Depth	The return value indicates how far down a node you currently are or the depth of the current in the stack of XML elements. This property is read-only and it must be overridden.
EOF	This property, which is read-only, returns a **Boolean** value that indicates if the XmlReader is positioned at the end of the stream.
HasAttributes	This property, which is read-only, returns a **Boolean** value that indicates if the current node has any attributes.
HasValue	This read-only property returns a **Boolean** value that indicates if the current node can hold a value. The value is of property type **Value**.
IsDefault	This property, which is read-only, returns a **Boolean** value that indicates if the current node is an attribute generated from a default value, which is defined in a schema or DTD.
IsEmptyElement	This property, which is read-only, returns a **Boolean** value that indicates if the current node is an empty element. An empty element can be defined like this: <DataElement/>.
Item()	This property, which is read-only, returns the value of the attribute that is specified with either an index, as in Item(Index As Integer); a name, as in Item(Name As String); or the **LocalName** and **NameSpaceURI** properties, as in Item(LocalName As String, NameSpaceURI As String). See the entries for **LocalName** and **NameSpaceURI** properties for more information. You can leave out the **Item()** property in most cases and simply use the parentheses instead.
LocalName	This property, which is read-only, returns the name of the current node without the namespace prefix. An empty string is returned for node types that do not have a name. If you have used the **ExecuteXmlReader** method of a command class, then the **LocalName** property will return the name of the table.

*Table 3A-24. **XmlReader** Class Properties (continued)*

NAME	DESCRIPTION
Name	This property, which is read-only, returns the qualified name of the current node or the name with the namespace prefix.
NameSpaceURI	This property, which is read-only, returns the namespace URI for the current node.
NameTable	This property, which is read-only, returns the **XmlNameTable** that is associated with the implementation.
NodeType	This read-only property returns the type for the current node. The data type returned is **XmlNodeType**.
Prefix	This property returns the namespace prefix for the current node. This property is read-only.
QuoteChar	This property returns the quotation mark used for enclosing values of attribute nodes. This property is read-only and it returns either a single quotation mark (') or a double quotation mark ("). The property only applies to attribute nodes.
ReadState	This property returns the read state of the stream. This property is read-only and it returns a member of the **ReadState** enum. The following members can be returned:
	Closed: The Close method has been executed on the **XmlReader**.
	EndOfFile: End of stream has been reached (successfully).
	Error: An error has occurred. This means that **XmlReader** cannot continue reading the stream.
	Initial: You have not called the **Read** method yet, so the reader is at its initial position.
	Interactive: A read operation is currently in progress.
Value	This read-only property returns the text value of the current node. If the current node does not have a value to return, an empty string is returned.
XmlLang	This read-only property returns the xml:lang scope currently being used. Please note that this property value is also part of the **XmlNameTable** returned from the **NameTable** property.
XmlSpace	This read-only property returns the xml:space scope currently being used as a member of the **XmlSpace** enum. The **XmlSpace** enum has the following members:
	Default: The xml:space scope is "default".
	None: There is no xml:space scope.
	Preserve: The xml:space scope is "preserve".

XmlReader Methods

Table 3A-25 lists the noninherited and public methods of the **XmlReader** class in alphabetical order. Please note that all the methods marked with an asterisk (*) require the data contained in the specified column to be of the same type as the method indicates. This is because no conversion is performed on the content of the specified column. If you try to use any of the methods on a column containing content of a different data type, the **InvalidCastException** is thrown. Also, these methods cannot be overridden in an inherited class.

*Table 3A-25. **XmlReader** Class Methods*

NAME	DESCRIPTION	EXAMPLE
Close()	Resets all properties and changes the **ReadState** property to **Closed**	`xrdTest.Close()`
GetAttribute()	This overloaded method returns the value of an attribute. See the example code, which returns the LoginName for the current node or row in the tblUser table. The reader has been instantiated elsewhere with the **ExecuteXmlReader** method of the command class.	`xrdTest.GetAttribute(3)`, `xrdTest.GetAttribute ("LoginName")`
IsStartElement()	This overloaded method returns a **Boolean** value indicating if the current content node is a start tag or an empty element tag.	`If xrdTest.IsStartElement() Then`
LookupNamespace (ByVal vstrPrefix As String)	This method must be overridden in derived implementations of the **XmlReader** class. It resolves vstrPrefix in the current elements scope.	`xrdTest.LookupNamespace ("MyNameSpace")`
MoveToAttribute()	This overloaded method moves to the attribute matching the passed argument. If your **XmlReader** has been returned by the **ExecuteXmlReader** method of a command class, this method can be used to move between the columns in the current row.	`xrdTest.MoveToAttribute(0)`, `xrdTest.MoveToAttribute ("LoginName")`

*Table 3A-25. **XmlReader** Class Methods (continued)*

NAME	DESCRIPTION	EXAMPLE
MoveToContent()	This method checks if the current node is a content node, and skips to the next content node, or EOF, if no content node is found. If the current node is an attribute node, then the reader's position is moved back to the element that owns the attribute node.	xrdTest.MoveToContent()
MoveToElement()	This method that must be overridden moves to the element in which the current attribute node exists. A **Boolean** value is returned based on whether the current attribute is owned by an element. If your **XmlReader** has been returned by the **ExecuteXmlReader** method of a command class, this method can be used in conjunction with the **MoveToAttribute** method to move to a specific attribute/column and then back to the element or row that owns the attribute or column. A **Boolean** value is returned indicating if the move was successful.	xrdTest.MoveToElement()
MoveToFirstAttribute()	This method moves to the first attribute in an element. If your **XmlReader** has been returned by the **ExecuteXmlReader** method of a command class, this method can be used to move to the first column in the current row. A **Boolean** value is returned indicating if the move was successful.	xrdTest.MoveToFirstAttribute()
MoveToNextAttribute()	This method moves to the next attribute in an element. If your **XmlReader** has been returned by the **ExecuteXmlReader** method of a command class, this method can be used to move to the next column in the current row.	xrdTest.MoveToNextAttribute()

*Table 3A-25. **XmlReader** Class Methods (continued)*

NAME	DESCRIPTION	EXAMPLE
Read()	Reads the next node in the stream. This method must be called before any other properties or methods can be called. Actually this is not quite true, as the initial value can be returned from some properties if the reader has not yet been positioned at the first row or element.	xrdTest.Read()
ReadAttributeValue()	This method parses the attribute value into **Text** and **EntityReference** node types. A **Boolean** value is returned indicating if there are any nodes to return. This method has no real meaning if your **XmlReader** has been returned by the **ExecuteXmlReader** method of a command class.	xrdTest.ReadAttributeValue()
ReadElementString()	This overloaded method is used for reading simple text elements.	xrdTest.ReadElementString() or xrdTest.ReadElementString ("ElementName")
ReadEndElement()	This method is for checking if the current node is an end tag. If the current node is an end tag, the reader position is advanced to the next node. This method has no real meaning if your **XmlReader** has been returned by the **ExecuteXmlReader** method of a command class.	xrdTest.ReadEndElement()
ReadInnerXml()	The **ReadInnerXml** method returns all the content of the current node as a string. The returned string includes markup text. This method has no real meaning if your **XmlReader** has been returned by the **ExecuteXmlReader** method of a command class.	xrdTest.ReadInnerXml()

*Table 3A-25. **XmlReader** Class Methods (continued)*

NAME	DESCRIPTION	EXAMPLE
ReadOuterXml()	The **ReadOuterXml** method returns all the content of the current node and all the children nodes as a string. The returned string includes markup text. If your **XmlReader** has been returned by the **ExecuteXmlReader** method of a command class, this method will return the current row as an XML node. Please note that only non-Null columns will be returned as attributes.	`xrdTest.ReadOuterXml()`
ReadStartElement()	This method is for checking if the current node is an element. If the current node is an element, the reader position is advanced to the next node. This method has no real meaning if your **XmlReader** has been returned by the **ExecuteXmlReader** method of a command class.	`xrdTest.ReadStartElement()`
ReadString()	This method, which must be overridden, is for reading the contents of an element and returning it as a string.	`xrdTest.ReadString()`
ResolveEntity()	This method is for use with EntityReferences nodes. It resolves the entity reference for this type of node.	`xrdTest.ResolveEntity()`
Skip()	Skips the current element or moves to the next element. Depending on where the reader is positioned, the **Skip** method can perform the same function as the **Read** method. This happens when the reader is positioned on a leaf node. Please note that this method checks for well-formed XML.	`xrdTest.Skip()`

Declaring and Instantiating an XmlReader Object

The **XmlReader** class must be overridden, which means that you cannot create an instance of the **XmlReader** class.

The following sample code is wrong:

```
Dim xrdTest As New XmlReader()
```

It is wrong because it tries to instantiate xrdTest using the **New** keyword. Listing 3A-28 shows you how to perform the instantiation correctly.

Listing 3A-28. Instantiating an XmlReader *Object*

```
' Declare xml reader
Dim xrdTest As XmlReader
' Excute command and return rows in xml reader
xrdTest = cmmUserMan.ExecuteXmlReader()
```

In Listing 3A-28 there is no code for declaring, instantiating, and opening the command object, but if you reuse the code from the any of the previous listings, you should have fully functioning code.

Reading Rows in an XmlReader

Since the **XmlReader** is a forward-only data class, you need to read the rows sequentially from start to finish if you need to read all the returned rows. In Listing 3A-29 you can see how we loop through a populated XML reader.

Listing 3A-29. Looping through All Rows in an XmlReader

```
1 Dim cnnUserMan As SqlConnection
2 Dim cmmUserMan As SqlCommand
3 Dim strSQL As String
4 Dim xrdTest As XmlReader
5 Dim lngCounter As Long = 0
6
7 ' Instantiate the connection
8 cnnUserMan = New SqlConnection()
9 cnnUserMan.ConnectionString = "User ID=UserMan;" & _
10   "Server=USERMANPC;Password=userman;Initial Catalog=UserMan"
```

```
11 ' Open the connection
12 cnnUserMan.Open()
13 ' Build query string
14 strSQL = "SELECT * FROM tblUser"
15 ' Instantiate the command
16 cmmUserMan = New SqlCommand(strSQL, cnnUserMan)
17 ' Excute command and return rows in data reader
18 xrdTest = cmmUserMan.ExecuteXmlReader()
19 ' Loop through all the returned rows
20 Do While xrdTest.Read
21    lngCounter = lngCounter + 1
22 Loop
23
24 ' Display the number of rows returned
25 MsgBox(CStr(lngCounter))
```

The code in Listing 3A-29 loops through the rows in the data reader and counts the number of rows. This is obviously just an example on how to sequentially go through all the rows returned by the **ExecuteXmlReader** method of the **Command** class.

Closing an XmlReader

Because the **XmlReader** object keeps the connection busy while it is open, it is good practice to close the XML reader once you are done with it. The XML reader is closed using the **Close** method, as follows:

```
xrdTest.Close()
```

The DataAdapter Explained

The **DataAdapter** class is used for retrieving data from your data source and populating your **DataSet** and related classes such as the **DataTable**; see Chapter 3B for more information on these disconnected data classes. The **DataAdapter** class is also responsible for propagating your changes back to the data source. In other words, the data adapter is the "connector" class that sits between the disconnected and the connected parts of ADO.NET. It would indeed be very appropriate to say that the **DataAdapter** class is your toolbox when you want to manipulate data in your data source!

The data adapter connects to a data source using a **Connection** object and then it uses **Command** objects to retrieve data from the data source and to send data back to the data source. With the exception of the **DataReader** class, all data access in ADO.NET goes through the data adapter. Actually, this can be put differently: All disconnected data access works through the data adapter. The data adapter is the bridge between the data source and the data set!

When the data adapter needs to retrieve or send data to and from the data source, it uses **Command** objects. You must specify these command objects. Now, this is very different from what happens in ADO, where you have little control over the way queries are executed. You specify the command objects for selecting, updating, and deleting rows in the data source. This is done by creating your command objects, and then assigning them to the appropriate data adapter property: **SelectCommand**, **InsertCommand**, **UpdateCommand,** or **DeleteCommand**.

The **DataAdapter** class comes in two flavors, the **OleDbDataAdapter** class and the **SqlDataAdapter** class.

DataAdapter Properties

The **DataAdapter** class has the properties shown in Table 3A-26 in alphabetical order. Please note that only the public, noninherited properties are shown. Actually, this is not entirely true, because only properties that are inherited from base classes like **Object** are left out. This means that properties inherited from the **DataAdapter** class are shown. The properties listed are the same for both the **SqlDataAdapter** and the **OleDbDataAdapter** classes.

Table 3A-26. **DataAdapter** *Class Properties*

NAME	DESCRIPTION
AcceptChangesDuringFill	This read-write property returns or sets a **Boolean** value indicating if the **AcceptChanges** method is called on the **DataRow** class after it has been added to a **DataTable**. The default value is **True**.
DeleteCommand	This read-write property returns or sets the SQL statement that will be used when rows are deleted from the data source.
InsertCommand	This read-write property returns or sets the SQL statement that will be used when rows are inserted into the data source.
MissingMappingAction	This read-write property returns or sets a value that indicates if unmapped source tables or source columns should be parsed with their source names, or if an exception should be thrown. This means that this property decides which action to take when there is no mapping for a source table or source column. The valid values are all the members of the **MissingMappingAction** enum and the default value is **Passthrough**.
MissingSchemaAction	This read-write property returns or sets a value that indicates if missing source tables, source columns, and relationships should be added to the schema in the data set, if they should be ignored, or if an exception should be thrown. This means that this property decides which action to take when a table, column, and/or relationship in the data source is missing from the data set. The valid values are all the members of the **MissingSchemaAction** enum and the default value is **Add**.
SelectCommand	This read-write property returns or sets the SQL statement that will be used when rows are selected/retrieved from the data source.
TableMappings	This read-only property returns a value that indicates how a table in the data source should be mapped to a table in the data set. The returned value is a collection of **DataTableMapping** objects. The default value is an empty collection.
UpdateCommand	This read-write property returns or sets the SQL statement that will be used when rows are updated in the data source.

DataAdapter Methods

Table 3A-27 lists the noninherited and public methods of the **DataAdapter** class in ascending order. The methods listed are the same for both the **SqlDataAdapter** and the **OleDbDataAdapter** class, unless otherwise stated.

*Table 3A-27. **DataAdapter** Class Methods*

NAME	DESCRIPTION	EXAMPLE
Fill() (**SqlDataAdapter** only)	The **Fill** method is overloaded and inherited from the **DbDataAdapter** class. The method is used for adding and/or updating rows in the data set. This means you will have a copy of the requested data in the data source in your data set.	See "Populating Your Data Set Using the DataAdapter" in Chapter 3B for examples.
Fill() (**OleDbDataAdapter** only)	The **Fill** method is overloaded and some of the overloaded versions of the method are inherited from the **DbDataAdapter** class. The method is used for adding and/or updating rows in the data set based on the rows in an ADO **Recordset** or ADO **Record** object, or from your data source.	See "Populating Your Data Set Using the DataAdapter" in chapter 3B for examples.
FillSchema()	The **FillSchema** method is overloaded and inherited from the **DbDataAdapter** class. The method is used for adding a **DataTable** object to the data set. This **DataTable** object is configured according to the arguments passed.	See "Using the DataTable Class" in Chapter 3B for some examples.
GetFillParameters()	The **GetFillParameters** method is inherited from the **DbDataAdapter** class. The method retrieves all the parameters that are used when the SELECT statement is executed. The returned value should be stored in an array of data type **IDataParameter**.	`arrprmSelect = dadUser.GetFillParameters()`

Table 3A-27. **DataAdapter** *Class Methods (continued)*

NAME	DESCRIPTION	EXAMPLE
Update()	The **Update** method is overloaded and inherited from the **DbDataAdapter** class. The method is used for updating the data source with the changes from the data set. This means the command object associated with the **InsertCommand**, **UpdateCommand**, and **DeleteCommand** properties will be executed for each inserted, modified, and deleted row respectively.	See "Updating Your Data Source Using the DataAdapter" in Chapter 3B for some examples.

Instantiating a DataAdapter

As with all other objects, the **DataAdapter** must be instantiated before you can use it. The **DataAdapter** class is instantiated using the **New** constructor, which is overloaded. Listings 3A-30 and 3A-31 show you some examples.

Listing 3A-30. Instantiating a SqlDataAdapter

```
1 Const STR_SQL_USER As String = "SELECT * FROM tblUser"
2 Const STR_CONNECTION As String = "Data Source=USERMANPC;" & _
3   "User ID=UserMan;Password=userman;Initial Catalog=UserMan"
4
5 Dim cnnUserMan As SqlConnection
6 Dim cmmUser As SqlCommand
7 Dim dadDefaultConstructor As SqlDataAdapter
8 Dim dadSqlCommandArgument As SqlDataAdapter
9 Dim dadSqlConnectionArgument As SqlDataAdapter
10 Dim dadStringArguments As SqlDataAdapter
11
12 ' Instantiate and open the connection
13 cnnUserMan = New SqlConnection(STR_CONNECTION)
14 cnnUserMan.Open()
15 ' Instantiate the command
16 cmmUser = New SqlCommand(STR_SQL_USER)
17
18 ' Instantiate data adapters
19 dadDefaultConstructor = New SqlDataAdapter()
20 dadSqlCommandArgument = New SqlDataAdapter(cmmUser)
```

```
21 dadSqlConnectionArgument = New SqlDataAdapter(STR_SQL_USER, cnnUserMan)
22 dadStringArguments = New SqlDataAdapter(STR_SQL_USER, STR_CONNECTION)
23 ' Initialize data adapters
24 dadDefaultConstructor.SelectCommand = cmmUser
25 dadDefaultConstructor.SelectCommand.Connection = cnnUserMan
```

Listing 3A-31. Instantiating an `OleDbDataAdapter`

```
 1 Const STR_SQL_USER As String = "SELECT * FROM tblUser"
 2 Const STR_CONNECTION As String = "Provider=SQLOLEDB;Data Source=USERMANPC" & _
 3   ";User ID=UserMan;Password=userman;Initial Catalog=UserMan"
 4
 5 Dim cnnUserMan As OleDbConnection
 6 Dim cmmUser As OleDbCommand
 7 Dim dadDefaultConstructor As OleDbDataAdapter
 8 Dim dadOleDbCommandArgument As OleDbDataAdapter
 9 Dim dadOleDbConnectionArgument As OleDbDataAdapter
10 Dim dadStringArguments As OleDbDataAdapter
11
12 ' Instantiate and open the connection
13 cnnUserMan = New OleDbConnection(STR_CONNECTION)
14 cnnUserMan.Open()
15 ' Instantiate the command
16 cmmUser = New OleDbCommand(STR_SQL_USER)
17
18 ' Instantiate data adapters
19 dadDefaultConstructor = New OleDbDataAdapter()
20 dadOleDbCommandArgument = New OleDbDataAdapter(cmmUser)
21 dadOleDbConnectionArgument = New OleDbDataAdapter(STR_SQL_USER, cnnUserMan)
22 dadStringArguments = New OleDbDataAdapter(STR_SQL_USER, STR_CONNECTION)
23 ' Initialize data adapters
24 dadDefaultConstructor.SelectCommand = cmmUser
25 dadDefaultConstructor.SelectCommand.Connection = cnnUserMan
```

If you use the default constructor for the data adapter (Lines 7, 19, 24, and 25), you have to specify the command object for the actions you will perform. This means that if you want to retrieve rows from the data source, you will at least have to set the **SelectCommand** property. (See the next section, "Setting the Command Properties," for more information on how to set command properties.) On Line 24 I have set the command property to a valid command object. However, this is not necessary, as I could have specified a string be selected (`STR_SQL_USER`) instead.

The other three constructors do not need any further initialization for retrieving rows from your data source. However, if you want to insert, delete, and

update your data source, you must specify the corresponding command properties. (See the next section, "Setting the Command Properties," for more
information on how to do this.)

Which method you want to use is really up to you, but if you are using the
same connection with all your command objects, why not specify it when you
instantiate the data adapter?

As you can see from Listings 3A-30 and 3A-31, there is no real difference
between instantiating an **OleDbDataAdapter** and an **SqlDataAdapter** object. The
real difference between these two classes appears when you want to populate
your data set. See "Populating Your Data Set Using the DataAdapter" in Chapter
3B for more information on how to do this.

Setting the Command Properties

If you only use the data adapter to retrieve data from your data source, you don't
have to set the command properties of your data adapter, if you have already
specified the **SelectCommand** property using the data adapter constructor (see
"Instantiating a DataAdapter" earlier). However, if you need to insert, update,
and/or delete rows from your data source and/or if you haven't set the **Select-
Command** property when instantiating the data adapter, you will have to set
these properties before you start using the data adapter. The **SelectCommand** is
for retrieving rows from the data source, whereas the other three command properties are for updating the data source when the **Update** method is called.

The four command properties are

- **SelectCommand**

- **InsertCommand**

- **DeleteCommand**

- **UpdateCommand**

ADO doesn't give you these choices, which provide you full control over how
data is passed to and from the data source. If you assign command objects to
these properties, you will also be able to control what these objects do through
events like errors. Yes, there is a little more coding involved, but you definitely get
to be in the driver's seat when it comes to data source flow control.

With regards to setting the properties, it is actually quite simple. If you have
created command objects, you only have to assign them to the corresponding
property, as shown in Listings 3A-32 and 3A-33.

Listing 3A-32. Setting the Command Properties of an SqlDataAdapter

```
1 Const STR_SQL_USER_SELECT As String = "SELECT * FROM tblUser"
2 Const STR_SQL_USER_SELECT As String = "DELETE FROM tblUser WHERE Id=@Id"
3 Const STR_SQL_USER_SELECT As String = "INSERT INTO tblUser(FirstName, " & _
4  "LastName, LoginName) VALUES(@FirstName, @LastName, @LoginName)"
5 Const STR_SQL_USER_UPDATE As String = "UPDATE tblUser SET FirstName=" & _
6  "@FirstName, LastName=@LastName, LoginName=@LoginName WHERE Id=@Id"
7 Const STR_CONNECTION As String = "Data Source=USERMANPC;" & _
8  "User ID=UserMan;Password=userman;Initial Catalog=UserMan"
9
10 Dim cnnUserMan As SqlConnection
11 Dim cmmUserSelect As SqlCommand
12 Dim cmmUserDelete As SqlCommand
13 Dim cmmUserInsert As SqlCommand
14 Dim cmmUserUpdate As SqlCommand
15 Dim dadUserMan As SqlDataAdapter
16 Dim prmSQLDelete, prmSQLUpdate, prmSQLInsert As SqlParameter
17 ' Instantiate and open the connection
18 cnnUserMan = New SqlConnection(STR_CONNECTION)
19 cnnUserMan.Open()
20 ' Instantiate the commands
21 cmmUserSelect = New SqlCommand(STR_SQL_USER_SELECT, cnnUserMan)
22 cmmUserDelete = New SqlCommand(STR_SQL_USER_DELETE, cnnUserMan)
23 cmmUserInsert = New SqlCommand(STR_SQL_USER_INSERT, cnnUserMan)
24 cmmUserUpdate = New SqlCommand(STR_SQL_USER_UPDATE, cnnUserMan)
25
26 ' Instantiate data adapter
27 dadUserMan = New SqlDataAdapter(STR_SQL_USER_SELECT, cnnUserMan)
28 ' Set data adapter command properties
29 dadUserMan.SelectCommand = cmmUserSelect
30 dadUserMan.InsertCommand = cmmUserInsert
31 dadUserMan.DeleteCommand = cmmUserDelete
32 dadUserMan.UpdateCommand = cmmUserUpdate
33
34 ' Add Delete command parameters
35 cmmUserDelete.Parameters.Add("@FirstName", SqlDbType.VarChar, 50, _
36  "FirstName")
37 cmmUserDelete.Parameters.Add("@LastName", SqlDbType.VarChar, 50, "LastName")
38 cmmUserDelete.Parameters.Add("@LoginName", SqlDbType.VarChar, 50, _
39  "LoginName")
40 prmSQLDelete = dadUserMan.DeleteCommand.Parameters.Add("@Id", _
41  SqlDbType.Int, Nothing, "Id")
42 prmSQLDelete.Direction = ParameterDirection.Input
```

```
43 prmSQLDelete.SourceVersion = DataRowVersion.Original
44 ' Add Update command parameters
45 cmmUserUpdate.Parameters.Add("@FirstName", SqlDbType.VarChar, 50, _
46  "FirstName")
47 cmmUserUpdate.Parameters.Add("@LastName", SqlDbType.VarChar, 50, "LastName")
48 cmmUserUpdate.Parameters.Add("@LoginName", SqlDbType.VarChar, 50, _
49  "LoginName")
50 prmSQLUpdate = dadUserMan.UpdateCommand.Parameters.Add("@Id", _
51  SqlDbType.Int, Nothing, "Id")
52 prmSQLUpdate.Direction = ParameterDirection.Input
53 prmSQLUpdate.SourceVersion = DataRowVersion.Original
54 ' Add insert command parameters
55 cmmUserInsert.Parameters.Add("@FirstName", SqlDbType.VarChar, 50, _
56  "FirstName")
57 cmmUserInsert.Parameters.Add("@LastName", SqlDbType.VarChar, 50, "LastName")
58 cmmUserInsert.Parameters.Add("@LoginName", SqlDbType.VarChar, 50, _
59  "LoginName")
```

Listing 3A-33. Setting the Command Properties of an OleDbDataAdapter

```
 1 Const STR_SQL_USER_SELECT As String = "SELECT * FROM tblUser"
 2 Const STR_SQL_USER_DELETE As String = "DELETE FROM tblUser WHERE Id=@Id"
 3 Const STR_SQL_USER_INSERT As String = "INSERT INTO tblUser(FirstName, " & _
 4  "LastName, LoginName) VALUES(@FirstName, @LastName, @LoginName)"
 5 Const STR_SQL_USER_UPDATE As String = "UPDATE tblUser SET FirstName=" & _
 6  "@FirstName, LastName=@LastName, LoginName=@LoginName WHERE Id=@Id"
 7 Const STR_CONNECTION As String = "Provider=SqlOleDb;Data Source=USERMANPC" & _
 8  ";User ID=UserMan;Password=userman;Initial Catalog=UserMan"
 9
10 Dim cnnUserMan As OleDbConnection
11 Dim cmmUserSelect As OleDbCommand
12 Dim cmmUserDelete As OleDbCommand
13 Dim cmmUserInsert As OleDbCommand
14 Dim cmmUserUpdate As OleDbCommand
15 Dim dadUserMan As OleDbDataAdapter
16 Dim prmSQLDelete, prmSQLUpdate, prmSQLInsert As OleDbParameter
17 ' Instantiate and open the connection
18 cnnUserMan = New OleDbConnection(STR_CONNECTION)
19 cnnUserMan.Open()
20 ' Instantiate the commands
21 cmmUserSelect = New OleDbCommand(STR_SQL_USER_SELECT, cnnUserMan)
22 cmmUserDelete = New OleDbCommand(STR_SQL_USER_DELETE, cnnUserMan)
23 cmmUserInsert = New OleDbCommand(STR_SQL_USER_INSERT, cnnUserMan)
24 cmmUserUpdate = New OleDbCommand(STR_SQL_USER_UPDATE, cnnUserMan)
```

```
25
26 ' Instantiate data adapter
27 dadUserMan = New OleDbDataAdapter(STR_SQL_USER_SELECT, cnnUserMan)
28 ' Set data adapter command properties
29 dadUserMan.SelectCommand = cmmUserSelect
30 dadUserMan.InsertCommand = cmmUserInsert
31 dadUserMan.DeleteCommand = cmmUserDelete
32 dadUserMan.UpdateCommand = cmmUserUpdate
33
34 ' Add Delete command parameters
35 cmmUserDelete.Parameters.Add("@FirstName", OleDbType.VarChar, 50, _
36  "FirstName")
37 cmmUserDelete.Parameters.Add("@LastName", OleDbType.VarChar, 50, "LastName")
38 cmmUserDelete.Parameters.Add("@LoginName", OleDbType.VarChar, 50, _
39  "LoginName")
40 prmSQLDelete = dadUserMan.DeleteCommand.Parameters.Add("@Id", _
41  OleDbType.Integer, Nothing, "Id")
42 prmSQLDelete.Direction = ParameterDirection.Input
43 prmSQLDelete.SourceVersion = DataRowVersion.Original
44 ' Add Update command parameters
45 cmmUserUpdate.Parameters.Add("@FirstName", OleDbType.VarChar, 50, _
46  "FirstName")
47 cmmUserUpdate.Parameters.Add("@LastName", OleDbType.VarChar, 50, "LastName")
48 cmmUserUpdate.Parameters.Add("@LoginName", OleDbType.VarChar, 50, _
49  "LoginName")
50 prmSQLUpdate = dadUserMan.UpdateCommand.Parameters.Add("@Id", _
51  OleDbType.Integer, Nothing, "Id")
52 prmSQLUpdate.Direction = ParameterDirection.Input
53 prmSQLUpdate.SourceVersion = DataRowVersion.Original
54 ' Add insert command parameters
55 cmmUserInsert.Parameters.Add("@FirstName", OleDbType.VarChar, 50, _
56  "FirstName")
57 cmmUserInsert.Parameters.Add("@LastName", OleDbType.VarChar, 50, "LastName")
58 cmmUserInsert.Parameters.Add("@LoginName", OleDbType.VarChar, 50, _
59  "LoginName")
```

There are only minor differences between Listings 3A-32 and 3A-33, and they are all due to what .NET data provider you are using, the SQL Server .NET Data Provider or the OLE DB .NET Data Provider. Besides setting the command properties of the data adapter, the parameters of the command objects are also configured to work with the tblUser table in the UserMan database. I have used named parameters exclusively, because I do believe it makes code easier to read.

Summary

This chapter introduced you to the two different data access technologies, ADO and ADO.NET. ADO.NET is for building distributed n-tier Web applications, whereas ADO is your best bet for traditional Windows client-server/n-tier applications programming in a heterogeneous networking environment, where you are connected at all times on a LAN link. The object model for the connected layer of ADO.NET was introduced and comparisons were made to the ADO object model wherever needed. As well as being an introduction to the connected layer of ADO.NET and to some extent ADO, this chapter serves as a reference to the various connected classes, methods, and properties of this data access technology.

This chapter covered the following ground:

- *Connection, Command, DataReader and DataAdapter data classes:* The ADO.NET classes were compared to their equivalents in ADO and suggestions were offered about when to use which data class.

- *Transactions, automatic and manual:* I showed you transaction boundaries and how to use them with the **Connection** and **Transaction** classes.

- *Two .NET data providers that come with the .NET Framework, the OLE DB.NET provider and The SQL Client.NET provider:* They both have their own set of related, but not interchangeable, data classes. In other words you cannot mix connections from the OLE DB .NET Data Provider with command classes from the SQL Server .NET Data Provider or vice versa.

- *The SQL Server .NET Data Provider versus the OLE DB .NET Data Provider:* I discussed the use the SQL Server .NET Data Provider whenever you access a SQL Server 7.0 or later and the OLE DB .NET Data Provider for all other data sources for which you have an OLE DB Provider.

The following chapter covers the classes in the disconnected layer of ADO.NET.

CHAPTER 3B

Presenting ADO.NET: The Disconnected Layer

THIS CHAPTER AND ITS TWIN chapter, Chapter 3A, cover ADO.NET. The classes in ADO.NET can be categorized into two groups: the connected layer and the disconnected layer. This chapter exclusively covers the disconnected layer.

I suggest you read Chapter 3A first, if you're new to ADO.NET, before continuing with this chapter. However, this chapter will serve you very well as a reference on its own.

Using the DataSet Class

The **DataSet** class is a fairly complex one to deal with and understand. Well, at least until you have had a closer look at it and realize that you don't really need to know everything there is to know about it. I will go through all aspects of the **DataSet** class and then you can pick for yourself what information you need. The **DataSet** class is part of the **System.Data** namespace.

First things first: A data set is rather closely related to a relational database in structure. When I say that it resembles a relational database, I mean that the **DataSet** class actually exposes a hierarchical object model (which has nothing to do with hierarchical databases). This object model consists of tables, rows, and columns and it also contains relations and constraints. In fact the **DataSet** and **DataTable** classes hold collections containing the following objects:

- **DataSet** class holds the **Tables** collection, which contains objects of data type **DataTable**, and the **Relations** collection, which contains objects of data type **DataRelation**.

- **DataTable** class holds the **Rows** collection, which contains objects of data type **DataRow,** and the **Columns** collection, which contains objects of data type **DataColumn**. The **Rows** collection holds all the rows in the table and the **Columns** collection is the actual schema for the table.

In order to exploit the full potential of the **DataSet** class, you need to use it in conjunction with at least the **DataTable** class.

If nothing else, the **DataSet** class is a local container or in-memory cache for the data you retrieve from the database. You can call it a virtual data store, because all the data retrieved from the database, including the schema for the data, is stored in the disconnected cache, known as the data set. The real trick of the **DataSet** is that although you are disconnected from the data source, you can work with the data in it in much the same way you would with the data in the database. If you are thinking, "Ah, so the data in the **DataSet** is really a copy of the real data," you would be correct, my friend! Now you may be wondering if updating the real data is difficult. Well, yes and no. Yes, because it requires more than just using the good old ADO **Recordset** class, but no, because you have several options available for this purpose. I will get to this in a moment.

So how do you get the data from the database and into the **DataSet**? This is a job for the **DataAdapter** class, the connected part of ADO.NET. The **DataAdapter** is the class that either works directly with the data source, as is the case with SQL Server 7.0 or later, or uses the underlying OLE DB provider to talk to the database. The **DataAdapter** class is explained in Chapter 3A.

One more thing to notice about the **DataSet** class is that it is NOT subclassed, or rather this is the class you will work with no matter what provider you are dealing with. There is no **SqlDataSet** or **OleDbDataSet** class!

Recordset vs. DataSet

If you are familiar with ADO, then you probably know the **Recordset** object and how it can be used with various cursors and so on. Although the **Recordset** class doesn't have a direct equivalent in ADO.NET, I will show you some of the things that make the **DataSet** class and its associated data class, **DataTable**, behave in similar ways to the **Recordset** object. When ADO.NET was on the drawing board, one of the major obstacles was to find a way of making the connected ADO **Recordset** class a disconnected class. The ADO **Recordset** class has been mapped to a few different classes in ADO.NET. This includes the disconnected **DataSet** class, which uses the connected **DataAdapter** class for retrieving data. Even though ADO has introduced the concept of a disconnected recordset through Remote Data Services (RDS), the connected part of the setup is still evident behind the scenes.

Simply put, the **DataSet** class is really a collection of disconnected **Recordset** objects, which are exposed using the **DataTable** class. So if you like using the ADO **Recordset** object, but want to use ADO.NET at the same time, you do have the option, and this option is called the **DataTable** class. The **DataTable** class works much the same way as an ADO recordset. See "Using the DataTable Class" later in this chapter for details.

Data Source Independence

One of the strengths of a **DataSet** is the fact that is completely independent of the data source. It is in other words a container, or cache, of data that is copied from the data source. The fact that a **DataSet** is disconnected and thereby independent of the data source makes it ideal for containing data from multiple data sources, such as tables from various databases.

XML Is the Format

When data is moved from a data source, such as a database, to the data set (or the other way around), the format used to facilitate this is XML. This is one of key concepts of ADO.NET; everything is XML-based! Because the format is XML, not only can you transfer data sets across process and machine boundaries, but you can also transfer data sets across networks that use a firewall! That's right, XML makes this possible! Now you truly have a way of manipulating data coming across the Internet from any data source that understands XML.

Okay, so the format used for transferring the data is XML, but this is not the only place ADO.NET uses XML. XML is the underlying format for all data in ADO.NET, and if you need to persist or serialize your data to a file, the format used is again XML. This means that you can read the persisted file using any XML-capable reader.

One point should be made very clear before you continue: Although the underlying or fundamental data format in ADO.NET is XML, the data in a data set is NOT expressed using XML. The ADO.NET data APIs automatically handle the creation of XML data when you exchange data between data sets and data sources, but the data inside the data set is in a format that is much more efficient to work with. So you don't actually have to know anything about XML in order to use ADO.NET. However, I would recommend that you do learn at least the basics of XML, because it is such an integral part of Visual Studio.NET.

Typed vs. Untyped Data Sets

A data set can be *typed* or *untyped*. The difference is that the typed data set has a schema and the untyped data set doesn't. You can choose to use either type of data set in your application, but you need to know that there is more support for the typed data sets in Visual Studio, and as such there are more tools for your convenience.

A typed data set gives you easier access to the content of table fields through strongly typed programming. Strongly typed programming uses information from the underlying data scheme. This means you're programming directly against your declared objects and not the tables you're really trying to manipulate. A typed data set has a reference to an XML schema file. This schema file (*.xsd) describes the structure of all the tables contained within the data set.

> **NOTE** *See Chapter 4 for more information on how to create a typed* **DataSet***.*

In Listing 3B-1 you can see how strong typing changes the way you would normally access the content of a column in a table.

Listing 3B-1. Strong Typing vs. Weak Typing

```
1 ' Display value from ADO Recordset
2 MsgBox(rstUser.Fields("FirstName").Value)
3 ' Display value from ADO.NET DataSet using strong typing
4 MsgBox(dstUser.tblUser(0).FirstName)
5 Display value from ADO.NET DataSet using weak typing
6 MsgBox(dstUser.Tables("tblUser").Columns(3).ToString)
```

As you can see from Listing 3B-1, the syntax is much simpler when you use strong typing. Simply reference the table and field by using the table name and field name directly (see Line 4). The rstUser recordset and the dstUser data set have been declared, instantiated, and opened or populated elsewhere.

DataSet Properties

The **DataSet** class has the properties shown in Table 3B-1 in alphabetical order. Please note that only the public, noninherited properties are shown.

Table 3B-1. **DataSet** *Class Properties*

NAME	DESCRIPTION
CaseSensitive	This read-write property determines if string comparisons in the **DataTable** objects, contained in the **Tables** collection, are case-sensitive. The default value is **False**. This property also affects how filter, sort, and search operations are performed. When you set this property you also by default set the same property of the **DataTable** objects in the **Tables** collection.
DataSetName	Returns or sets the name of the **DataSet**
DefaultViewManager	Returns a view of the data in the data set. This view can be filtered or sorted, and you can search and navigate through it. The returned value is of data type **DataViewManager**.
EnforceConstraints	This property value determines if the constraint rules are enforced when an update operation is executed. The default value is **True**. The **ConstraintException** exception is thrown if one or more constraints cannot be enforced.
ExtendedProperties	Returns the collection of custom properties or custom user information. The returned data type is a **PropertyCollection** class. You can add information to the property collection by using the **Add** method of the collection as follows: `dstUserMan.ExtendProperties.Add("New Property", "New Property Value")`
HasErrors	Returns a **Boolean** value indicating if there are any errors in the rows in the data set tables. You can use this property before checking any of the individual tables that also have a **HasErrors** property.
Locale	This read-write property holds the locale information that is used for comparing strings in a table. The value is of data type **CultureInfo**. The default is **Nothing**.
Namespace	This read-write property holds the namespace for the data set. It is used when you read an XML document into the data set or when you write an XML document from the data set.
Prefix	This read-write property holds the namespace prefix for the data set. The prefix is used in an XML document for identifying which elements belong to the namespace of the data set object. The namespace is set with the **NameSpace** property.
Relations	Returns the collection of relations from the **DataSet**. The returned value is of data type **DataRelationCollection**, and it holds objects of data type **DataRelation**. **Nothing** is returned if no data relations exist.
Tables	Returns the collection of tables from the data set. The returned value is of data type **DataTableCollection**, and it holds objects of data type **DataTable**. **Nothing** is returned if no data tables exist.

DataSet Methods

Table 3B-2 lists the noninherited and public methods of the **DataSet** class in alphabetical order.

*Table 3B-2. **DataSet** Class Methods*

NAME	DESCRIPTION	EXAMPLE
AcceptChanges()	This method accepts or commits all the changes that have been made to the data set since the last time the method was called or since the data set was loaded. Be aware that this method will call the **AcceptChanges** method on ALL tables in the **Tables** collection, which in turn calls the **AcceptChanges** method on all **DataRow** objects in the **Rows** collection of each **DataTable**. So if you need to only accept changes to a specific table, then call the **AcceptChanges** method in this table.	dstUser.AcceptChanges()
BeginInit()	The **BeginInit** method, which cannot be overridden, is used to indicate that the data set has not yet been initialized. The method begins the initialization of a data set used on a form. Actually, it could also be used by another component. This initialization occurs at runtime, and together with the **EndInit** method it ensures that the data set is not used before it is completely initialized.	dstUser.BeginInit()
Clear()	This method clears the data set for data, which means that all rows are being removed from all tables. This method does NOT clear the data structure, only the data itself.	dstUser.Clear()
Clone()	The **Clone** method is for cloning or copying the data structure of the data set. This does NOT include the data itself, but only the tables, schemas, relations, and constraints. If you need to copy the data as well, you need to use the **Copy** method.	dstClone = dstUser.Clone()

Table 3B-2. **DataSet** *Class Methods (continued)*

NAME	DESCRIPTION	EXAMPLE
Copy()	The **Copy** method is for cloning the data structure of the data set and copying the data from the data set into the new data structure. If you only need to clone the data structure, you need to use the **Clone** method.	`dstCopy = dstUser.Copy()`
EndInit()	The **EndInit** method is for use in conjunction with the **BeginInit** method. When you call it, you indicate that data set has fully initialized.	`dstUser.EndInit()`
GetChanges()	This overloaded method is used for retrieving a copy of the data set that contains all the changes that have been made since the last time the **AcceptChanges** method was called or since the data set was loaded. You can use the method without an argument, or you can indicate what kind of changes you want returned in the data set by specifying a member of the **DataRowState** enum.	`dstChanges = dstUser.GetChanges()` or `dstAdded = dstUser.GetChanges (DataRowState.Added)`
GetXml()	The **GetXml** method returns the data in the data set as XML data in a **String** variable.	`strXMLData = dstUser.GetXml()`
GetXmlSchema()	The **GetXmlSchema** method returns the XSD schema for data in the data set in a **String** variable.	`strXMLSchema = dstUser.GetXmlSchema()`
HasChanges()	This method can be used to detect if there are any changes to the data in the data set. The method is overloaded, and one version takes a member of the **DataRowState** enum as an argument. This way you can specify whether you only want to detect a specific change, such as added rows. A **Boolean** value indicating if there are any changes is returned.	`blnChanges = dstUser.HasChanges()` or `blnChanges = dstUser.HasChanges (DataRowState.Added)`

Table 3B-2. **DataSet** *Class Methods (continued)*

NAME	DESCRIPTION	EXAMPLE
InferXmlSchema(ByVal Schema, ByVal varrstrURI() As String)	This overloaded method infers or copies the XML schema from an **XmlReader**, a **Stream**, a **TextReader**, or a file into the data set. The varrstrURI argument is an array of namespace URIs to exclude from the inference/copy.	`dstUser.InferXmlSchema(xrdUser, arrstrURIExclude)`
Merge()	The **Merge** method is overloaded and is used for merging the data set with other data, in the form of an array of **DataRow** objects, into another **DataSet** or with a **DataTable**.	`dstUser.Merge(arrdrwMerge)` or `dstUser.Merge(dtbMerge)` or `dstUser.Merge(dstMerge)`
ReadXml()	This overloaded method is for reading XML schema and data into the data set. The XML schema and data is read from a **Stream,** a file, a **TextReader**, or an **XmlReader**. If you only want to read the XML schema, you can use the **ReadXmlSchema** method.	`dstUser.ReadXml(stmUser)` or `dstUser.ReadXml(strXMLFile)` or `dstUser.ReadXml(trdUser)` or `dstUser.ReadXml(xrdUser)`
ReadXmlSchema()	This overloaded method is for reading XML schema into the data set. The XML schema is read from an **XmlReader**, a **Stream**, a file, or a **TextReader**. If you want to read the XML schema and the data, you can use the **ReadXml** method.	`dstUser.ReadXmlSchema(xrdUser)` or `dstUser.ReadXmlSchema(stmUser)` or `dstUser.ReadXmlSchema (strXMLFile)` or `dstUser.ReadXmlSchema(trdUser)`
RejectChanges()	This method rejects or rolls back the changes made to the data set since the last time the **AcceptChanges** method was called or since the **DataSet** was loaded. Be aware that this method will call the **RejectChanges** method on ALL tables in the **Tables** collection, which in turn calls the **RejectChanges** method on all **DataRow** objects in the **Rows** collection of each **DataTable**. So if you need to reject changes only to a specific table, then call the **RejectChanges** method on this table.	`dstUser.RejectChanges()`
Reset()	This method, which can be overriden, resets the data set to its original state.	`dstUser.Reset()`

Table 3B-2. **DataSet** *Class Methods (continued)*

NAME	DESCRIPTION	EXAMPLE
WriteXml()	This overloaded method is for writing XML schema and data from the data set. The XML schema and data is written to an **XmlWriter**, a **Stream**, a file, or a **TextWriter**. If you want to write only the XML schema, you can use the **WriteXmlSchema** method.	`dstUser.WriteXml(xwrUser)` or `dstUser.WriteXml(stmUser)` or `dstUser.WriteXml(strXMLFile)` or `dstUser.WriteXml(twrUser)`
WriteXmlSchema()	This overloaded method is for writing the XML schema from the data set. The XML schema is written to an **XmlWriter**, a **Stream**, a file, or a **TextWriter**. If you want to write the XML schema and the data, you can use the **WriteXml** method.	`dstUser.WriteXmlSchema(xrdUser)` or `dstUser.WriteXmlSchema(stmUser)` or `dstUser.WriteXmlSchema(strXMLFile)` or `dstUser.WriteXmlSchema(trdUser)`

Instantiating a DataSet

There is not much fuzz to instantiating a **DataSet** object. It can be done when declaring it, as demonstrated here:

```
Dim dstUnnamed As New DataSet()
Dim dstNamed As New DataSet("UserManDataSet")
```

As you can see from the two lines of code, the only difference is the name I have given to the dstNamed data set. Giving a data set a name like this is especially useful when it is persisted as XML, because the XML document element is then given a name you can recognize.

You can also declare the variable first and then instantiate like this:

```
Dim dstUnnamed As DataSet
Dim dstNamed As DataSet

dstUnnamed = New DataSet()
dstNamed = New DataSet("UserManDataSet")
```

Populating Your DataSet Using the DataAdapter

Once you have set up the data adapter and the data set, you need to populate the data set. The **Fill** method of the **DataAdapter** class is used for populating and refreshing the **DataSet** object. The **Fill** method is overloaded, and there are more method versions for the **OleDbDataAdapter** class than the **SqlDataAdapter** class. This is because the **OleDbDataAdapter** class supports populating a data set from an ADO **Recordset** object or an ADO **Record** object. Yes, that's right—you can mess about with the good old ADO **Recordset** object and the somewhat newer ADO **Record** object. In Table 3B-3 I show you the various versions of the **Fill** method. The sample code here assumes that you have instantiated and initialized the various objects. You can see in the previous listings how it is done, because I am essentially building on the same code.

Table 3B-3. The Various Versions of the Overloaded Fill Method (DataAdapter)

EXAMPLE CODE	DESCRIPTION
intNumRows = dadUserMan.Fill(dstUser)	This version of the method populates the dstUser data set and saves the number of rows returned in intNumRows. Because you haven't specified the table name anywhere, the new data table in the **Tables** collection is called "Table". You can check the table name using a statement similar to the following: MsgBox(dstUserMan.Tables(0).TableName).
intNumRows = dadUserMan.Fill(dstUser, "tblUser")	This version of the method populates the dstUser data set and returns the number of rows returned in intNumRows. Because you have specified the source table name, the new data table in the **Tables** collection in the data set is called "tblUser", like in the data source. You can check the table name using a statement similar to the following: MsgBox(dstUserMan.Tables(0).TableName).
intNumRows = dadUserMan.Fill(dstUser, 0, 2, "tblUser")	This version of the method populates the dstUser data set and returns the number of rows returned in intNumRows. Because you have specified the source table name, the new data table in the **Tables** collection in the data set is called "tblUser", like in the data source. The two arguments in the middle (0 and 2) indicate that only rows starting with index 0 (the first row) and then 2 in total are returned. This method should be used if you don't want all rows returned. You can check the number of rows returned in the intNumRows variable.
intNumRows = dadUserMan.Fill(dtbUser)	This version of the method doesn't actually populate a data set, but a **DataTable** object instead. The number of rows returned is saved in intNumRows. Because you haven't specified the source table name, the data table doesn't have a name. You can prevent this by giving the **DataTable** a name when you instantiate it, using a statement like dtbUser = New DataTable("tblUser"), or you can do it after you instantiate the data table. This is done by setting the **TableName** property.

*Table 3B-3. The Various Versions of the Overloaded **Fill** Method (**DataAdapter**) (continued)*

EXAMPLE CODE	DESCRIPTION
intNumRows = dadUserMan.Fill(dtbUser, rstADO) (**OleDbDataAdapter** only)	This version of the method doesn't actually populate a data set, but a **DataTable** object instead. The number of rows returned is saved in intNumRows. The rows from the ADO **Recordset** object are copied to the data table. You can also specify an ADO **Record** object instead of the rstADO **Recordset** object.
intNumRows = dadUserMan.Fill(dstUser, rstADO, "tblUser") (**OleDbDataAdapter** only)	This version of the method populates the dstUser data set and returns the number of rows returned in intNumRows. The number of rows returned is saved in intNumRows. Because you have specified the source table name, the new data table in the **Tables** collection in the data set is called "tblUser". The rows from the ADO **Recordset** object are copied to the data table. You can also specify an ADO **Record** object in case of the rstADO **Recordset** object.

Since I won't be going over how to use ADO **Recordset** and ADO classes in general, perhaps this is a good time to show you a complete code example that opens an ADO **Recordset** and uses this **Recordset** to fill a **DataSet**. Listing 3B-2 shows you how to do this.

Listing 3B-2. Populating a DataSet *from an ADO Recordset*

```
1  Public Sub FillDataSetFromRecordset()
2    Const STR_SQL_USER_SELECT As String = "SELECT * FROM tblUser"
3    Const STR_CONNECTION As String = "Provider=SQLOLEDB;" & _
4      "Data Source=USERMANPC;User ID=UserMan;Password=userman;" & _
5      "Initial Catalog=UserMan"
6
7    Dim cnnUserMan As OleDbConnection
8    Dim dadUserMan As OleDbDataAdapter
9    Dim dstUserMan As DataSet
10
11   Dim rstUser As ADODB.Recordset
12   Dim cnnADOUserMan As ADODB.Connection
13
14   Dim intNumRows As Integer
15
16   ' Instantiate and open the connections
17   cnnUserMan = New OleDbConnection(STR_CONNECTION)
18   cnnUserMan.Open()
19   cnnADOUserMan = New ADODB.Connection()
```

```
20   cnnADOUserMan.Open(STR_CONNECTION)
21
22   ' Instantiate data adapter
23   dadUserMan = New OleDbDataAdapter(STR_SQL_USER_SELECT, cnnUserMan)
24
25   ' Instantiate dataset
26   dstUserMan = New DataSet()
27   ' Instantiate recordset
28   rstUser = New ADODB.Recordset()
29
30   ' Populate recordset
31   rstUser.Open(STR_SQL_USER_SELECT, cnnADOUserMan)
32   ' Fill dataset
33   intNumRows = dadUserMan.Fill(dstUserMan, rstUser, "tblUser")
34 End Sub
```

In Listing 3B-2 I make use of some ADO classes, and in order to do this, you must add a reference to the ADO COM libraries from your project. See "COM Interop" later in this chapter for information on how to this. There isn't much wizardry to the code in Listing 3B-2; I open two connections, one ADO.NET connection and one ADO connection. I then instantiate the data adapter and the record set, populate the record set, and then use the record set to populate the data set. You can use an ADO **Record** object instead of the **Recordset** object and/or you can populate a **DataTable** instead of a **DataSet**. See Table 3B-3 for more information on how you can do this using the **Fill** method of the **DataAdapter**.

Updating Your Data Source Using the DataAdapter

When you are finished manipulating the data in your data set, it is time to update the data source. This is done using the **Update** method of the **DataAdapter** class. This method is responsible for examining the **RowState** property of each of the **DataRow** objects in the **Rows** collection. The **Rows** collection is a member of each of the **DataTable** objects contained in the **Tables** collection of the data set. So the data adapter starts by looping through all the tables in the **Tables** collection in the data set, and for each table it loops through the **Rows** collection to examine the **RowState** property. If a row has been inserted, updated, or deleted, the **DataAdapter** uses one of the command properties to handle the update. This means that the **InsertCommand** property is used if you are inserting a new row, the **UpdateCommand** property is used if you are updating an existing row, and the **DeleteCommand** is used if you are deleting an existing row.

In Listing 3B-3 I set up a data adapter, a data set, and some command objects to manipulate the tblUser table in the UserMan database. Then I add, modify, and delete a row from the table. I then use the **HasChanges** method to check if there are any changes to the data in the data set. If so, I specify that all the changed rows be loaded into the dstChanges data set using the **GetChanges** method. The changes are rejected if there are any errors; otherwise the data source is updated using the **Update** method. The code in Listing 3B-3 doesn't handle exceptions when I try to update the data source, but check out Chapter 5 for example code and recommendations on how to handle exceptions.

Listing 3B-3. Propagating Changes Back to the Data Source

```
1  Public Sub UpdateSqlDataSet()
2    Const STR_SQL_USER_SELECT As String = "SELECT * FROM tblUser"
3    Const STR_SQL_USER_DELETE As String = "DELETE FROM tblUser WHERE Id=@Id"
4    Const STR_SQL_USER_INSERT As String = "INSERT INTO tblUser(FirstName" & _
5      ", LastName, LoginName) VALUES(@FirstName, @LastName, @LoginName)"
6    Const STR_SQL_USER_UPDATE As String = "UPDATE tblUser SET FirstName=" & _
7      "@FirstName, LastName=@LastName, LoginName=@LoginName WHERE Id=@Id"
8    Const STR_CONNECTION As String = "Data Source=USERMANPC" & _
9      ";User ID=UserMan;Password=userman;Initial Catalog=UserMan"
10
11   Dim cnnUserMan As SqlConnection
12   Dim cmmUserSelect As SqlCommand
13   Dim cmmUserDelete As SqlCommand
14   Dim cmmUserInsert As SqlCommand
15   Dim cmmUserUpdate As SqlCommand
16   Dim dadUserMan As SqlDataAdapter
17   Dim dstUserMan, dstChanges As DataSet
18   Dim drwUser As DataRow
19   Dim prmSQLDelete, prmSQLUpdate, prmSQLInsert As SqlParameter
20
21   ' Instantiate and open the connection
22   cnnUserMan = New SqlConnection(STR_CONNECTION)
23   cnnUserMan.Open()
24
25   ' Instantiate the commands
26   cmmUserSelect = New SqlCommand(STR_SQL_USER_SELECT, cnnUserMan)
27   cmmUserDelete = New SqlCommand(STR_SQL_USER_DELETE, cnnUserMan)
28   cmmUserInsert = New SqlCommand(STR_SQL_USER_INSERT, cnnUserMan)
29   cmmUserUpdate = New SqlCommand(STR_SQL_USER_UPDATE, cnnUserMan)
30
31   ' Instantiate data adapter
32   dadUserMan = New SqlDataAdapter(STR_SQL_USER_SELECT, cnnUserMan)
33   ' Set data adapter command properties
34   dadUserMan.SelectCommand = cmmUserSelect
35   dadUserMan.InsertCommand = cmmUserInsert
```

```
36    dadUserMan.DeleteCommand = cmmUserDelete
37    dadUserMan.UpdateCommand = cmmUserUpdate
38
39    ' Add Delete command parameters
40    cmmUserDelete.Parameters.Add("@FirstName", SqlDbType.VarChar, 50, _
41      "FirstName")
42    cmmUserDelete.Parameters.Add("@LastName", SqlDbType.VarChar, 50, _
43      "LastName")
44    cmmUserDelete.Parameters.Add("@LoginName", SqlDbType.VarChar, 50, _
45      "LoginName")
46    prmSQLDelete = dadUserMan.DeleteCommand.Parameters.Add("@Id", _
47      SqlDbType.Int, Nothing, "Id")
48    prmSQLDelete.Direction = ParameterDirection.Input
49    prmSQLDelete.SourceVersion = DataRowVersion.Original
50    ' Add Update command parameters
51    cmmUserUpdate.Parameters.Add("@FirstName", SqlDbType.VarChar, 50, _
52      "FirstName")
53    cmmUserUpdate.Parameters.Add("@LastName", SqlDbType.VarChar, 50, _
54      "LastName")
55    cmmUserUpdate.Parameters.Add("@LoginName", SqlDbType.VarChar, 50, _
56      "LoginName")
57    prmSQLUpdate = dadUserMan.UpdateCommand.Parameters.Add("@Id", _
58      SqlDbType.Int, Nothing, "Id")
59    prmSQLUpdate.Direction = ParameterDirection.Input
60    prmSQLUpdate.SourceVersion = DataRowVersion.Original
61    ' Add insert command parameters
62    cmmUserInsert.Parameters.Add("@FirstName", SqlDbType.VarChar, 50, _
63      "FirstName")
64    cmmUserInsert.Parameters.Add("@LastName", SqlDbType.VarChar, 50, _
65      "LastName")
66    cmmUserInsert.Parameters.Add("@LoginName", SqlDbType.VarChar, 50, _
67      "LoginName")
68
69    ' Instantiate dataset
70    dstUserMan = New DataSet()
71    ' Populate the data set
72    dadUserMan.Fill(dstUserMan, "tblUser")
73
74    ' Add new row
75    drwUser = dstUserMan.Tables("tblUser").NewRow()
76    drwUser("FirstName") = "New User"
77    drwUser("LastName") = "New User LastName"
78    drwUser("LoginName") = "NewUser"
79    dstUserMan.Tables("tblUser").Rows.Add(drwUser)
```

```
 80
 81    ' Update an existing row (with index 5)
 82    dstUserMan.Tables("tblUser").Rows(5)(5) = "OldUser"
 83
 84    ' Delete row with index 6
 85    dstUserMan.Tables("tblUser").Rows(6).Delete()
 86
 87    ' Check if any data has changed in the data set
 88    If dstUserMan.HasChanges() Then
 89       ' Save all changed rows in a new data set
 90       dstChanges = dstUserMan.GetChanges()
 91       ' Check if the changed rows contains any errors
 92       If dstChanges.HasErrors() Then
 93          ' Reject the changes
 94          dstUserMan.RejectChanges()
 95       Else
 96          ' Update the data source
 97          dadUserMan.Update(dstChanges, "tblUser")
 98       End If
 99    End If
100 End Sub
```

Clearing Data from a DataSet

When you have added tables, relations, constraints, and so on to a data set, or
what makes up the structure in your data set, you frequently need a way of clearing all the data from the data set. This can easily be accomplished using the **Clear**
method, as shown in Listing 3B-4.

Listing 3B-4. Clearing the Data from a DataSet

```
 1 Dim cnnUserMan As SqlConnection
 2 Dim cmmUser As SqlCommand
 3 Dim dadUser As SqlDataAdapter
 4 Dim dstUser As DataSet
 5
 6 ' Instantiate and open the connection
 7 cnnUserMan = New SqlConnection("Data Source=USERMANPC;" & _
 8   "User ID=UserMan;Password=userman;Initial Catalog=UserMan")
 9 cnnUserMan.Open()
10 ' Instantiate the command
11 cmmUser = New SqlCommand("SELECT * FROM tblUser", cnnUserMan)
12 ' Instantiate and initialize the data adapter
13 dadUser = New SqlDataAdapter()
```

```
14 dadUser.SelectCommand = cmmUser
15 ' Instantiate data set
16 dstUser = New DataSet()
17 ' Fill the data set
18 dadUser.Fill(dstUser, "tblUser")
19 ' Do your stuff
20 ...
21 ' Clear the data from the data set
22 dstUser.Clear()
```

Copying a DataSet

Sometimes it is necessary to copy a data set for various reasons. If you need to manipulate some data for testing purposes, copying a data set is a good way of leaving the original data intact. Depending on what you actually need to do, there are two ways you can approach this: copy just the data structure, or copy the data structure and the data within it. The next sections describe each of these methods.

Copying the Data Structure of a DataSet

Do you need to copy, or rather clone, the structure of a data set? There is a method of the data set called **Clone** that does exactly this. See Listing 3B-5 for an example.

Listing 3B-5. Cloning the Data Structure from a DataSet

```
 1 Dim cnnUserMan As SqlConnection
 2 Dim cmmUser As SqlCommand
 3 Dim dadUser As SqlDataAdapter
 4 Dim dstUser As DataSet
 5 Dim dstClone As DataSet
 6
 7 ' Instantiate and open the connection
 8 cnnUserMan = New SqlConnection("Data Source=USERMANPC;" & _
 9   "User ID=UserMan;Password=userman;Initial Catalog=UserMan")
10 cnnUserMan.Open()
11 ' Instantiate the command and data set
12 cmmUser = New SqlCommand("SELECT * FROM tblUser", cnnUserMan)
13 dstUser = New DataSet()
14 ' Instantiate and initialize the data adapter
15 dadUser = New SqlDataAdapter("SELECT * FROM tblUser", cnnUserMan)
16 dadUser.SelectCommand = cmmUser
```

```
17 ' Fill the data set
18 dadUser.Fill(dstUser, "tblUser")
19 ' Clone the data set
20 dstClone = dstUser.Clone()
```

Copying the Data and Structure of a DataSet

When you need a complete copy of the data structure and data contained therein from a data set, you can use the **Copy** method for this purpose. See Listing 3B-6 for an example.

Listing 3B-6. Copying the Data Structure and Data from a DataSet

```
 1 Dim cnnUserMan As SqlConnection
 2 Dim cmmUser As SqlCommand
 3 Dim dadUser As SqlDataAdapter
 4 Dim dstUser As DataSet
 5 Dim dstCopy As DataSet
 6
 7 ' Instantiate and open the connection
 8 cnnUserMan = New SqlConnection("Data Source=USERMANPC;" & _
 9   "User ID=UserMan;Password=userman;Initial Catalog=UserMan")
10 cnnUserMan.Open()
11 ' Instantiate the command and data set
12 cmmUser = New SqlCommand("SELECT * FROM tblUser", cnnUserMan)
13 dstUser = New DataSet()
14 ' Instantiate and initialize the data adapter
15 dadUser = New SqlDataAdapter("SELECT * FROM tblUser", cnnUserMan)
16 dadUser.SelectCommand = cmmUser
17 ' Fill the data set
18 dadUser.Fill(dstUser, "tblUser")
19 ' Copy the data set
20 dstCopy = dstUser.Copy()
```

Merging Data in a DataSet with Other Data

From time to time you'll probably want to combine data from a data set and data that exists in another form. For example, say you have a **DataSet** that you filled with data structure and data using the **Fill** method of the **DataAdapter**, and you want to combine this with a **DataSet** or **DataTable** that you have created programmatically. Once you are done manipulating the data, you want to merge the data in the two objects. You can achieve this by merging the data into the data set. Data in the form of an array of **DataRow** objects, a **DataTable** object, or a **DataSet** object can be merged using the **Merge** method of the **DataSet**. The resulting merged data set replaces the data in the data set, which executes the **Merge** method. See Listings 3B-7, 3B-8, and 3B-9 for some examples of the using the Merge method.

Listing 3B-7. Merging a DataSet *object with an array of* DataRow *objects*

```
1 Dim cnnUserMan As SqlConnection
2 Dim cmmUser As SqlCommand
3 Dim dadUser As SqlDataAdapter
4 Dim dstUser As DataSet
5 Dim dtbUser As DataTable
6 Dim arrdrwUser(0) As DataRow
7 Dim drwUser As DataRow
8
9 ' Instantiate and open the connection
10 cnnUserMan = New SqlConnection("Data Source=USERMANPC;" & _
11   "User ID=UserMan;Password=userman;Initial Catalog=UserMan")
12 cnnUserMan.Open()
13 ' Instantiate the command, data set and data table
14 cmmUser = New SqlCommand("SELECT * FROM tblUser", cnnUserMan)
15 dstUser = New DataSet()
16 dtbUser = New DataTable()
17 ' Instantiate and initialize the data adapter
18 dadUser = New SqlDataAdapter("SELECT * FROM tblUser", cnnUserMan)
19 dadUser.SelectCommand = cmmUser
20 ' Fill the data set
21 dadUser.Fill(dstUser, "tblUser")
22 ' Create new row and fill with data
23 drwUser = dstUser.Tables("tblUser").NewRow()
24 drwUser("LoginName") = "NewUser1"
25 drwUser("FirstName") = "New"
26 drwUser("LastName") = "User"
27 arrdrwUser.SetValue(drwUser, 0)
28 ' Merge the data set with the data row array
29 dstUser.Merge(arrdrwUser)
```

Listing 3B-8. Merging Two DataSet *Objects*

```
1 Dim cnnUserMan As SqlConnection
2 Dim cmmUser As SqlCommand
3 Dim dadUser As SqlDataAdapter
4 Dim dstUser As DataSet
5 Dim dstCopy As DataSet
6
7 ' Instantiate and open the connection
```

```
 8 cnnUserMan = New SqlConnection("Data Source=USERMANPC;" & _
 9   "User ID=UserMan;Password=userman;Initial Catalog=UserMan")
10 cnnUserMan.Open()
11 ' Instantiate the command and data set
12 cmmUser = New SqlCommand("SELECT * FROM tblUser", cnnUserMan)
13 dstUser = New DataSet()
14 ' Instantiate and initialize the data adapter
15 dadUser = New SqlDataAdapter("SELECT * FROM tblUser", cnnUserMan)
16 dadUser.SelectCommand = cmmUser
17 ' Fill the data set
18 dadUser.Fill(dstUser, "tblUser")
19 ' Copy the data set
20 dstCopy = dstUser.Copy()
21 ' Do your stuff with the data sets
22 ...
23 ' Merge the two data sets
24 dstUser.Merge(dstCopy)
```

Listing 3B-9. Merging a DataSet Object with a DataTable Object

```
 1 Dim cnnUserMan As SqlConnection
 2 Dim cmmUser As SqlCommand
 3 Dim dadUser As SqlDataAdapter
 4 Dim dstUser As DataSet
 5 Dim dtbUser As DataTable
 6
 7 ' Instantiate and open the connection
 8 cnnUserMan = New SqlConnection("Data Source=USERMANPC;" & _
 9   "User ID=UserMan;Password=userman;Initial Catalog=UserMan")
10 cnnUserMan.Open()
11 ' Instantiate the command, data set and data table
12 cmmUser = New SqlCommand("SELECT * FROM tblUser", cnnUserMan)
13 dstUser = New DataSet()
14 dtbUser = New DataTable()
15 ' Instantiate and initialize the data adapter
16 dadUser = New SqlDataAdapter("SELECT * FROM tblUser", cnnUserMan)
17 dadUser.SelectCommand = cmmUser
18 ' Fill the data set and data table
19 dadUser.Fill(dstUser, "tblUser")
20 dadUser.Fill(dtbUser)
21 ' Do your stuff with the data set and the data table
22 ...
23 ' Merge the data set with the data table
24 dstUser.Merge(dtbUser)
```

Please note that in Listings 3B-7 through 3B-9 I have chosen to create the data structure and fill the data table using the data adapter's **Fill** method. You can obviously create the data structure yourself and fill it with data from a variety of sources before you merge it with the data set. See "Using the DataTable Class" later in this chapter for more information on how to do this.

Detecting and Handling Changes to Data in a DataSet

Sometimes it is necessary to know if the data in your data set has been changed. Changes in this context include new rows and deleted rows as well as modified rows. The **DataSet** class has the **HasChanges** method that can be used for this purpose. This method actually exists for the individual **DataTable** objects in the **Tables** collection, but if you just want to know if any of the data in the data set has changed, you need to use the data set's method.

The **HasChanges** method is overloaded and you can see how to use the various versions in Listings 3B-10 and 3B-11.

Listing 3B-10. Detecting All Data Changes in a DataSet Object

```
 1 Dim cnnUserMan As SqlConnection
 2 Dim cmmUser As SqlCommand
 3 Dim dadUser As SqlDataAdapter
 4 Dim dstUser As DataSet
 5 Dim dstChanges As DataSet
 6
 7 ' Instantiate and open the connection
 8 cnnUserMan = New SqlConnection("Data Source=USERMANPC;" & _
 9   "User ID=UserMan;Password=userman;Initial Catalog=UserMan")
10 cnnUserMan.Open()
11 ' Instantiate the command and data set
12 cmmUser = New SqlCommand("SELECT * FROM tblUser", cnnUserMan)
13 dstUser = New DataSet()
14 ' Instantiate and initialize the data adapter
15 dadUser = New SqlDataAdapter("SELECT * FROM tblUser", cnnUserMan)
16 dadUser.SelectCommand = cmmUser
17 ' Fill the data set
18 dadUser.Fill(dstUser, "tblUser")
19 ' Do your stuff with the data set
20 . . .
21 ' Check if any data has changed in the data set
22 If dstUser.HasChanges() Then
23   ' Save all changes in a new data set
24   dstChanges = dstUser.GetChanges()
25 End If
```

In Listing 3B-10 all the data changes are simply saved to a new data set. Obviously this doesn't do anything to do the data, but once you have changes isolated you can manipulate the data and check for errors. This is particularly useful when you want to update the data source. Don't forget that the **DataSet** is disconnected from the data source and any changes will not be propagated back to the data source until you explicitly update the data source!

Listing 3B-11 has been cut a little short because it is basically the same code as in Listing 3B-10, but it shows how to filter the different changes into different data sets.

Listing 3B-11. Detecting the Different Data Changes in a DataSet *Object*

```
1 Dim cnnUserMan As SqlConnection
2 Dim cmmUser As SqlCommand
3 Dim dadUser As SqlDataAdapter
4 Dim dstUser As DataSet
5 Dim dstChanges As DataSet
6 Dim dstAdditions As DataSet
7 Dim dstDeletions As DataSet
8
9 ' Instantiate and open the connection
. . .
21 ' Check if any data has changed in the data set
22 If dstUser.HasChanges() Then
23    ' Save all modified rows in a new data set
24    dstChanges = dstUser.GetChanges(DataRowState.Modified)
25    ' Save all added rows in a new data set
26    dstAdditions = dstUser.GetChanges(DataRowState.Added)
27    ' Save all deleted rows in a new data set
28    dstDeletions = dstUser.GetChanges(DataRowState.Deleted)
29 End If
```

Accepting or Rejecting Changes to Data in a DataSet

When changes have been made to data in the data set, you can choose to reject or accept them. The **DataSet** class has two methods for doing this: the **AcceptChanges** and **RejectChanges** methods. One thing you have to note about these methods is that they work on the data in the data set and NOT in the data source itself. This goes back to the fact that the data set is disconnected and as such doesn't interact with the data source.

The AcceptChanges Method

When using this method, any changes to a row in a data table in the **Tables** collection will be accepted. This is done by calling the **AcceptChanges** method on each of the **DataTable** objects in the table collection. When the **AcceptChanges** method is called on a data table, the data table invokes the **AcceptChanges** method on each **DataRow** object in the **Rows** collection. What happens then is the **RowState** property of each data row is examined. If the row state is **Added** or **Modified**, then the **RowState** property is changed to **Unchanged**. Rows with **Deleted** row state are removed from the respective data table. If a **DataRow** is being edited when the **AcceptChanges** method is called, the row in question will successfully end edit mode. See Listing 3B-12 in the next section for an example of how **AcceptChanges** can be used and how it affects a **DataSet**. If you call **AcceptChanges** just before calling the **Update** method of the data adapter, no changes will be written back to the data source because you have just accepted the changes and they are now marked **Unchanged**!

> **NOTE** *If a data set contains any **ForeignKeyConstraint** objects, the **AcceptRejectRule** property is enforced once the **AcceptChanges** method is called. The **AcceptRejectRule** property is used to determine if the changes or deletions should be cascaded across a relationship.*

The RejectChanges Method

When using the **RejectChanges** method, any changes to a row in a data table in the **Tables** collection will be rejected. This is done by calling **RejectChanges** on each of the **DataTable** objects in the table collection. When the **RejectChanges** method is called on a data table, the data table invokes the **AcceptChanges** method on each **DataRow** object in the **Rows** collection. What happens then is the **RowState** property of each data row is examined. If the row state is **Added**, then the row is removed from the respective data table. The **RowState** property for rows with **Modified** and **Deleted** row states is changed to **Unchanged** and the original content of the rows restored. If a **DataRow** is being edited when the **RejectChanges** method is called, the row in question will cancel edit mode. See Listing 3B-12 for an example of how **RejectChanges** can be used and how it affects a **DataSet** object.

Listing 3B-12. Accepting or Rejecting Changes to the Data in a DataSet *Object*

```
1 Dim cnnUserMan As SqlConnection
2 Dim cmmUser As SqlCommand
3 Dim dadUser As SqlDataAdapter
```

```
 4 Dim dstUser, dstChanges As DataSet
 5 Dim drwUser As DataRow
 6 Dim intCounter As Integer
 7
 8 ' Instantiate and open the connection
 9 cnnUserMan = New SqlConnection("Data Source=USERMANPC;" & _
10    "User ID=UserMan;Password=userman;Initial Catalog=UserMan")
11 cnnUserMan.Open()
12 ' Instantiate the command and the data set
13 cmmUser = New SqlCommand("SELECT * FROM tblUser"cnnUserMan)
14 dstUser = New DataSet()
15 ' Instantiate and initialize the data adapter
16 dadUser = New SqlDataAdapter("SELECT * FROM tblUser", cnnUserMan)
17 dadUser.SelectCommand = cmmUser
18 ' Fill the data set
19 dadUser.Fill(dstUser, "tblUser")
20 ' Create a new data row with the schema from the user table
21 drwUser = dstUser.Tables("tblUser").NewRow()
22 ' Enter values in the data row columns
23 drwUser("LoginName") = "NewUser1"
24 drwUser("FirstName") = "New"
25 drwUser("LastName") = "User"
26 ' Add the data row to the user table
27 dstUser.Tables("tblUser").Rows.Add(drwUser)
28 ' Check if any data has changed in the data set
29 If dstUser.HasChanges() Then
30    ' Save all changed rows in a new data set
31    dstChanges = dstUser.GetChanges()
32    ' Check if the changed rows contains any errors
32    If dstChanges.HasErrors() Then
33       ' Display the row state of all rows before rejecting changes
34       For intCounter = 0 To dstUser.Tables(0).Rows.Count - 1
35          MsgBox("HasErrors=True, Before RejectChanges, RowState=" & _
36             dstUser.Tables(0).Rows(intCounter).RowState.ToString & _
37             ", LoginName=" & _
38             dstUser.Tables(0).Rows(intCounter)("LoginName").ToString)
39       Next
40       ' Reject the changes to the data set
41       dstUser.RejectChanges()
42       ' Display the row state of all rows after rejecting changes
43       For intCounter = 0 To dstUser.Tables(0).Rows.Count - 1
44          MsgBox("HasErrors=True, After RejectChanges, RowState=" & _
45             dstUser.Tables(0).Rows(intCounter).RowState.ToString & _
46             ", LoginName=" & _
```

```
47              dstUser.Tables(0).Rows(intCounter)("LoginName").ToString)
48       Next
49    Else
50      ' Display the row state of all rows before accepting changes
51      For intCounter = 0 To dstUser.Tables(0).Rows.Count - 1
52        MsgBox("HasErrors=False, Before AcceptChanges, RowState=" & _
53          dstUser.Tables(0).Rows(intCounter).RowState.ToString & _
54          ", LoginName=" & _
55          dstUser.Tables(0).Rows(intCounter)("LoginName").ToString)
56      Next
57      ' Accept the changes to the data set
58      dstUser.AcceptChanges()
59      ' Display the row state of all rows after accepting changes
60      For intCounter = 0 To dstUser.Tables(0).Rows.Count - 1
61        MsgBox("HasErrors=False, After AcceptChanges, RowState=" & _
62          dstUser.Tables(0).Rows(intCounter).RowState.ToString & _
63          ", LoginName=" & _
64          dstUser.Tables(0).Rows(intCounter)("LoginName").ToString)
65      Next
66    End If
67 End If
```

Listing 3B-12 shows how to use the **AcceptChanges** and **RejectChanges** methods of the **DataSet** class. It also shows you how to check for changes and errors in the changed rows. As the example stands, the **HasErrors** method returns **False**, which means that the changes are accepted. You can manipulate the example code so that the changes are rejected and the **RejectChanges** method will be used instead.

Using the DataTable Class

The **DataTable** class is used for manipulating the content of a table contained in the **Tables** collection of the **DataSet** class. The **DataTable** class is part of the **System.Data** namespace. The **DataTable** is an in-memory cache of the data from exactly one table. One last thing to notice about the **DataTable** class is that, like the **DataSet** class, it is NOT subclassed—in other words, this is the class you will work with no matter what provider you are dealing with.

> **NOTE**   *There is no SqlDataTable or OleDbDataTable class.*

DataTable Properties

The **DataTable** class has the properties shown in alphabetical order in Table 3B-4. Please note that only the public, noninherited properties are shown.

Table 3B-4. ***DataTable*** *Class Properties*

NAME	DESCRIPTION
CaseSensitive	This property indicates if a string comparison in the table is case sensitive. A **Boolean** value is set or returned. If the **DataTable** is part of a data set, this property is set to the value of the data set's **CaseSensitive** property. However, if the **DataTable** has been created programmatically, this property is set to **False** by default.
ChildRelations	The **ChildRelations** property returns a collection of child relations for the data table. This property is read-only and the data type returned is **DataRelationCollection**. If no relations exist, **Nothing** is returned.
Columns	This property returns the **DataColumnCollection** collection of columns/fields that makes up the data table. This property is read-only. **Nothing** is returned if no columns exist.
Constraints	The **Constraints** property returns the collection of constraints belonging to the data table. This property is read-only and the data type returned is **ConstraintCollection**. If no constraints exist, **Nothing** is returned.
DataSet	This read-only property returns the data set the table belongs to. This means the returned object is of data type **DataSet**.
DefaultView	This read-only property returns a **DataView** object that is a customized view of the table. The returned data view can be used for filtering, sorting, and searching a data table. See "Using the DataView Class" later in this chapter for more information on the DataView class.
DisplayExpression	The **DisplayExpression** property returns or sets an expression, which returns a value that is used to represent the table in the UI. This property can be used to dynamically create text based on the current data.
ExtendedProperties	This read-only property returns a **PropertyCollection** collection of customized user information. You can use the **Add** method of this property to add custom information to a data table.
HasErrors	This read-only property returns a **Boolean** value indicating if any errors occurred in any of the rows in the data table.

Table 3B-4. **DataTable** *Class Properties (continued)*

NAME	DESCRIPTION
Locale	The **Locale** property returns or sets the **CultureInfo** object. This object provides the locale information that is used for comparing strings in the data table. This means you can specify the locale that matches the data contained in the data table and thus make sure specific characters are sorted correctly and string comparisons are performed according to the rules of the locale. By default this property is set to the value of the data set's **Locale** property. However, if the data table doesn't belong to a data set, this property is set to the culture of the current system.
MinimumCapacity	This property returns or sets the initial starting size for the data table. The property is of data type **Integer** and the default value is 25. The value specifies the number of rows that the data table will be able to hold initially before creating extra resources to accommodate more rows. You should set this property when performance is critical, because it is faster to allocate the resources before you start populating the data table. So set the property to the smallest value appropriate for the number of rows returned when performance is critical.
Namespace	The **Namespace** property returns or sets the namespace used for XML representation of the data in the data table.
ParentRelations	The **ParentRelations** property returns a collection of parent relations for the data table as a **DataRelationCollection** object. This property is read-only. **Nothing** is returned if no parent relations exist.
Prefix	This read-write property holds the namespace prefix for the data table. The namespace prefix is used when the data table is represented as XML. The data type for this property is **String**.
PrimaryKey	The **PrimaryKey** property is read-write enabled, and it returns or sets an array of **DataColumn** objects that are the primary keys for the data table. A **DataException** exception is thrown if you try to set a column that is already a foreign key.
Rows	This read-only property returns the **DataRowCollection** object that holds all the **DataRow** objects that make up the data in this data table. **Nothing** is returned if there are no rows in the table.
TableName	This read-write property holds the name for the data table. The name property is used when the table is looked up in the **Tables** collection of the data set. The data type for this property is **String**.

DataTable Methods

Table 3B-5 lists the noninherited and public methods of the **DataTable** class in alphabetical order.

*Table 3B-5. **DataTable** Class Methods*

NAME	DESCRIPTION	EXAMPLE
AcceptChanges()	This method accepts or commits all the changes that have been made to the data table since the last time the method was called or since the data table was loaded. Because this method changes the row state of all changed rows in the data table, you should not call this method until after you attempt to call the **Update** method on the data adapter. If **AcceptChanges** is called before you update the data set, no changes will be propagated back to the data set because the **RowState** property of the changed rows will be changed back to **Unchanged**, meaning they won't appear to have been changed.	`dtbUser.AcceptChanges()`
BeginInit()	The **BeginInit** method is used to indicate that the data table has not yet been initialized. The method begins the initialization of a data table used on a form or by another component. This initialization occurs at runtime and together with the **EndInit** method it ensures that the data table is not used before it is completely initialized.	`dtbUser.BeginInit()`
BeginLoadData()	The **BeginLoadData** method is used in conjunction with the **EndLoadData** method. This method turns off index maintenance, constraints, and notifications while loading the data with the **LoadDataRow** method.	`dtbUser.BeginLoadData()`
Clear()	This method clears all rows from the data table. If any of the rows has child rows in other tables with which the current data table has an enforced relationship, an exception is thrown.	`dtbUser.Clear()`

*Table 3B-5. **DataTable** Class Methods (continued)*

NAME	DESCRIPTION	EXAMPLE
Clone()	The **Clone** method is for cloning or copying the data structure of the data table. This does NOT include the data itself, but only the schemas, relations, and constraints. If you need to copy the data as well, you have to use the **Copy** method.	`dtbClone = dtbUser.Clone()`
Compute(ByVal vstrExpression As String, ByVal vstrFilter As String)	The **Compute** method computes vstrExpression on the current rows that pass the vstrFilter criteria. Please note that the vstrExpression expression must contain an aggregate function, such as SUM or COUNT.	`objCompute = dtbUser.Compute ("COUNT(FirstName)", "LastName IS NOT NULL")`
Copy()	The **Copy** method is for cloning the data structure of the data table and copying the data from the data table into the new data table. If you only need to clone the data structure, you should use the **Clone** method.	`dtbCopy = dtbUser.Copy()`
EndInit()	The **EndInit** method is for use in conjunction with the **BeginInit** method. When you call it, you indicate that data set has fully initialized.	`dtbUser.EndInit()`
EndLoadData()	The **EndLoadData** method turns back on index maintenance, constraints, and notifications after it has been turned off with the **BeginLoadData** method. Use the **EndLoadData** and **BeginLoadData** methods when loading the data with the **LoadDataRow** method.	`dtbUser.EndLoadData()`
GetChanges()	This overloaded method is used for retrieving a copy of the data table that contains all the changes that have been made since the last time the **AcceptChanges** method was called or since the data table was loaded. You can use the method without arguments or you can indicate what kind of changes you want returned in the data table by specifying a member of the **DataRowState** enum.	`dtbChanges = dtbUser.GetChanges() or dtbAdded = dtbUser.GetChanges (DataRowState.Added)`

*Table 3B-5. **DataTable** Class Methods (continued)*

NAME	DESCRIPTION	EXAMPLE
GetErrors()	The **GetErrors** method returns an array of **DataRow** objects. The array includes all rows in the **DataTable** that contain errors.	`arrdrwErrors =` `dtbUser.GetErrors()`
ImportRow(ByVal vdrwImport As DataRow)	The **ImportRow** method copies a **DataRow** object into a **DataTable**. The copy includes original and current values, errors, and **DataRowState** values. In short, everything from the **DataRow** object is copied across.	`dtbUser.ImportRow(drwImport)`

LoadDataRow(ByVal varrobjValues() As Object, ByVal vblnAcceptChanges As Boolean)	The **LoadDataRow** method finds a specific row using the values in the varrobjValues array. The values in the array are used to match with primary key column(s). If a matching row is found, it is updated. Otherwise a new row is created using the varrobjValues values.	`drwLoad =`
		`dtbUser.LoadDataRow`
		`(arrobjValues, False)`

NewRow()	The **NewRow** method creates a new **DataRow** object with the same schema as the data table.	`drwNew = dtbUser.NewRow()`
RejectChanges()	This method rejects or rolls back the changes made to the data table since the last time the **AcceptChanges** method was called or since the **DataTable** was loaded.	`dtbUser.RejectChanges()`

Select()	The **Select** method is overloaded and is used for retrieving an array of **DataRow** objects. The returned data rows are ordered after the primary key. If no primary key exists, the rows are returned ordered the way they were added to the data table. Actually, this is only true if you use one of the overloaded versions that doesn't take the sort order as an argument.	`arrdrwAllDataRows =`
		`dtbUser.Select() or`
		`arrdrwFirstNameUnsortedDataRows`
		`= dtbUser.Select("FirstName =`
		`'John'") or`
		`arrdrwFirstNameSortedDataRows =`
		`dtbUser.Select("FirstName =`
		`'John'", "LastName ASC") or`
		
		`arrdrwFirstNameSortedOriginal`
		`DataRows =`
		`dtbUser.Select("FirstName =`
		`'John'", "LastName ASC",`
		`DataViewRowState.OriginalRows)`

Declaring and Instantiating a DataTable

There are various ways to instantiate a **DataTable** object. You can use the over-loaded class constructors or you can reference a specific table in the **Tables** collection of a data set. Here is how you instantiate a data table when you declare it:

```
Dim dtbNoArguments As New DataTable()
Dim dtbTableNameArgument As New DataTable("TableName")
```

You can also declare it and then instantiate it when you need to, as follows:

```
Dim dtbNoArguments As DataTable
Dim dtbTableNameArgument As DataTable

dtbNoArguments = New DataTable()
dtbTableNameArgument = New DataTable("TableName")
```

I have used two different constructors, one with no arguments and one that takes the table name as the only argument. Your other option is to first declare the **DataTable** object, and then have it reference a table in the **Tables** collection of a populated data set, like this:

```
Dim dtbUser As DataTable

dtbUser = dstUser.Tables("tblUser")
```

Building Your Own DataTable

Sometimes you need storage for temporary data that has a table-like structure, meaning several groups of data sequences with the same structure. Because of the table-like structure, a **DataTable** is an obvious choice for storage, although not your only one. Listing 3B-13 demonstrates how to create a data structure from scratch like the one in the tblUser table in the UserMan database.

Listing 3B-13. Building Your Own DataTable

```
1 Dim dtbUser As DataTable
2 Dim drwUser As DataRow
3 Dim dclUser As DataColumn
4 Dim arrdclPrimaryKey(0) As DataColumn
5
6 dtbUser = New DataTable("tblUser")
7
```

```
 8 ' Create table structure
 9 dclUser = New DataColumn()
10 dclUser.ColumnName = "Id"
11 dclUser.DataType = Type.GetType("System.Int32")
12 dclUser.AutoIncrement = True
13 dclUser.AutoIncrementSeed = 1
14 dclUser.AutoIncrementStep = 1
15 dclUser.AllowDBNull = False
16 ' Add column to data table structure
17 dtbUser.Columns.Add(dclUser)
18 ' Add column to PK array
19 arrdclPrimaryKey(0) = dclUser
20 ' Set primary key
21 dtbUser.PrimaryKey = arrdclPrimaryKey
22
23 dclUser = New DataColumn()
24 dclUser.ColumnName = "ADName"
25 dclUser.DataType = Type.GetType("System.String")
26 ' Add column to data table structure
27 dtbUser.Columns.Add(dclUser)
28
29 dclUser = New DataColumn()
30 dclUser.ColumnName = "ADSID"
31 dclUser.DataType = Type.GetType("System.Guid")
32 ' Add column to data table structure
33 dtbUser.Columns.Add(dclUser)
34
35 dclUser = New DataColumn()
36 dclUser.ColumnName = "FirstName"
37 dclUser.DataType = Type.GetType("System.String")
38 ' Add column to data table structure
39 dtbUser.Columns.Add(dclUser)
40
41 dclUser = New DataColumn()
42 dclUser.ColumnName = "LastName"
43 dclUser.DataType = Type.GetType("System.String")
44 ' Add column to data table structure
45 dtbUser.Columns.Add(dclUser)
46
47 dclUser = New DataColumn()
48 dclUser.ColumnName = "LoginName"
49 dclUser.DataType = Type.GetType("System.String")
50 dclUser.AllowDBNull = False
51 dclUser.Unique = True
```

```
52 ' Add column to data table structure
53 dtbUser.Columns.Add(dclUser)
54 dclUser = New DataColumn()
55 dclUser.ColumnName = "Password"
56 dclUser.DataType = Type.GetType("System.String")
57 dclUser.AllowDBNull = False
58 ' Add column to data table structure
59 dtbUser.Columns.Add(dclUser)
```

The example code in Listing 3B-13 uses the **DataColumn** and **DataRow** classes as well as the **DataTable** class. The **DataRow** class is covered later in this chapter. The data table created in the listing can now be used for storage by using the **Add** method of the **Rows** collection of the **DataTable** and/or you can add the data table to a **DataSet**.

Populating a DataTable

Populating a **DataTable** can be done in various ways. You can manually add rows to the data table by creating a **DataRow** object, set the column values, and then add it to the data table using the **Add** method of the **Rows** property. There is an example of how to create your own **DataTable** in Listing 3B-13.

Otherwise you can use the **Fill** method of the **DataAdapter** class for this purpose, as demonstrated in the next section in Listing 3B-14.

Clearing Data from a DataTable

When you have added relations, constraints, and so on to a data table, or what makes up the structure in your data table, you frequently need a way of clearing all the data from the data table. This is quite easy and it can be accomplished using the **Clear** method, as shown in Listing 3B-14.

Listing 3B-14. Clearing the Data from a DataTable
```
 1 Dim cnnUserMan As SqlConnection
 2 Dim cmmUser As SqlCommand
 3 Dim dadUser As SqlDataAdapter
 4 Dim dtbUser As DataTable
 5
 6 ' Instantiate and open the connection
 7 cnnUserMan = New SqlConnection("Data Source=USERMANPC;" & _
 8   "User ID=UserMan;Password=userman;Initial Catalog=UserMan")
 9 cnnUserMan.Open()
10 ' Instantiate the command
11 cmmUser = New SqlCommand("SELECT * FROM tblUser", cnnUserMan)
```

```
12 ' Instantiate and initialize the data adapter
13 dadUser = New SqlDataAdapter()
14 dadUser.SelectCommand = cmmUser
15 ' Instantiate data table
16 dtbUser = New DataTable("tblUser")
17 ' Fill the data table
18 dadUser.Fill(dtbUser)
19 ' Do your stuff
20 . . .
21 ' Clear the data from the data table
22 dtbUser.Clear()
```

Copying a DataTable

It is sometimes necessary to copy a data table. If you need to manipulate some data for testing purposes, work on a copy of a data table in order to leave the original data intact. Depending on what you actually need to do, there are two ways you can approach this: You can copy just the data structure (similar to working with a data set), or you can copy the data structure and the data within it. See the example code for both techniques in the next two sections.

Copying the Data Structure of a DataTable

If you need to clone the data structure, the **Clone** method does exactly this. See Listing 3B-15 for an example of cloning data structure.

Listing 3B-15. Cloning the Data Structure from a DataTable

```
 1 Dim cnnUserMan As SqlConnection
 2 Dim cmmUser As SqlCommand
 3 Dim dadUser As SqlDataAdapter
 4 Dim dtbUser As DataTable
 5 Dim dtbClone As DataTable
 6
 7 ' Instantiate and open the connection
 8 cnnUserMan = New SqlConnection("Data Source=USERMANPC;" & _
 9    "User ID=UserMan;Password=userman;Initial Catalog=UserMan")
10 cnnUserMan.Open()
11 ' Instantiate the command and data table
12 cmmUser = New SqlCommand("SELECT * FROM tblUser", cnnUserMan)
13 dtbUser = New DataTable()
14 ' Instantiate and initialize the data adapter
15 dadUser = New SqlDataAdapter("SELECT * FROM tblUser", cnnUserMan)
```

```
16 dadUser.SelectCommand = cmmUser
17 ' Fill the data table
18 dadUser.Fill(dtbUser)
19 ' Clone the data table
20 dtbClone = dtbUser.Clone()
```

Copying the Data and Structure of a DataTable

When you need a complete copy of the data structure and data contained therein from a data table, you can use the **Copy** method for this purpose, as shown in Listing 3B-16.

Listing 3B-16. Copying the Data Structure and Data from a DataTable

```
1 Dim cnnUserMan As SqlConnection
2 Dim cmmUser As SqlCommand
3 Dim dadUser As SqlDataAdapter
4 Dim dtbUser As DataTable
5 Dim dtbCopy As DataTable
6
7 ' Instantiate and open the connection
8 cnnUserMan = New SqlConnection("Data Source=USERMANPC;" & _
9   "User ID=UserMan;Password=userman;Initial Catalog=UserMan")
10 cnnUserMan.Open()
11 ' Instantiate the command and data table
12 cmmUser = New SqlCommand("SELECT * FROM tblUser", cnnUserMan)
13 dtbUser = New DataTable()
14 ' Instantiate and initialize the data adapter
15 dadUser = New SqlDataAdapter("SELECT * FROM tblUser", cnnUserMan)
16 dadUser.SelectCommand = cmmUser
17 ' Fill the data table
18 dadUser.Fill(dtbUser)
19 ' Copy the data table
20 dtbCopy = dtbUser.Copy()
```

Searching a DataTable and Retrieving a Filtered Data View

The **DataTable** class doesn't have any direct methods for finding a specific row as such. However, with the help of the **DefaultView** property you can actually accomplish this. This property—or should I say class, as the property returns or sets a **DataView** object—has a **RowFilter** property that works pretty much the same as the **Filter** property of an ADO **Recordset** object. See Listing 3B-17 for some example code that filters all the users in the tblUser table with the last name of Doe.

Listing 3B-17. Searching in a DataTable *Class*

```
1 Dim cnnUserMan As SqlConnection
2 Dim cmmUser As SqlCommand
3 Dim dadUser As SqlDataAdapter
4 Dim dtbUser As DataTable
5 Dim intCounter As Integer
6 ' Instantiate and open the connection
7 cnnUserMan = New SqlConnection("Data Source=USERMANPC;" & _
8   "User ID=UserMan;Password=userman;Initial Catalog=UserMan")
9 cnnUserMan.Open()
10 ' Instantiate the command and data table
11 cmmUser = New SqlCommand("SELECT * FROM tblUser", cnnUserMan)
12 dtbUser = New DataTable()
13 ' Instantiate and initialize the data adapter
14 dadUser = New SqlDataAdapter("SELECT * FROM tblUser", cnnUserMan)
15 dadUser.SelectCommand = cmmUser
16 ' Fill the data table
17 dadUser.Fill(dtbUser)
18 ' Filter the data table view
19 dtbUser.DefaultView.RowFilter = "LastName = 'Doe'"
20
21 ' Loop through all the rows in the data table view
22 For intCounter = 0 To dtbUser.DefaultView.Count - 1
23    MsgBox(dtbUser.DefaultView(0).Row("LastName").ToString())
24 Next
```

Please note that the number of visible rows in the data table itself does NOT change when you filter the data table view as in the preceding listing. If you were to check the number of rows in the data table (using `dtbUser.Rows.Count`) before and after the filtering, the number would be the same.

Earlier, I stated that you cannot search using any methods or properties of the **DataTable** class itself, but this is not quite true. You can actually use the **Select** method of the **DataTable** class, although this is only useful when you want to retrieve specific rows and manipulate them in a separate array of **DataRow** objects. So if you were to retrieve all users with the last name Doe, as in Listing 3B-17, but you wanted these rows in an array of **DataRow** objects, you would do it this way:

```
Dim arrdrwFilter() As DataRow

arrdrwFilter = dtbUser.Select("LastName = 'Doe'")
```

Please note that the **Select** method can also be used for other purposes, such as retrieving all rows that have not been changed. You can specify the **RowState** of the rows you want to return. Check out the **Select** method in Table 3B-5 earlier.

Using the DataView Class

The **DataView** class is used for having more than just one view of a database. The **DataView** class is part of the **System.Data** namespace. As stated, this class is for creating a different view of your data table than your default view. You can use this class for filtering, sorting, searching and navigating, and even editing the rows in your data table.

Like the **DataSet** and the **DataTable** class, the **DataView** it is NOT subclassed, or rather this class you will work with no matter what provider you are dealing with.

> **NOTE** *There is no SqlDataView or OleDbDataView class!*

DataView Properties

The **DataView** class has the properties shown in Table 3B-6 in alphabetical order. Please note that only the public, noninherited properties are shown.

*Table 3B-6. **DataView** Class Properties*

NAME	DESCRIPTION
AllowDelete	The **AllowDelete** property returns or sets a **Boolean** value that indicates if deletions in the data view are allowed.
AllowEdit	The **AllowEdit** property returns or sets a **Boolean** value that indicates if editing of the rows in the data view is allowed.
AllowNew	The **AllowNew** property returns or sets a **Boolean** value that indicates if you can add new rows to the data view with the **AddNew** method.
ApplyDefaultSort	This property returns or sets a **Boolean** value that indicates if the default sort should be used.
Count	This read-only property returns the number of visible rows in the view. By visible I mean rows that are not affected by the settings of the **RowFilter** and **RowStateFilter** properties.
DataViewManager	The **DataViewManager** property is read-only and it returns the **DataViewManager** that is associated with this data view or rather the data view manager that owns the data set and hence created this data view. **Nothing** is returned if no **DataViewManager** exists.
Item	This property is read-only, and it is used to specify the index of the row you want returned from the data table. Actually, you don't have to specify the **Item** property; you can just use the parentheses on their own. For instance, dvwUser(0) and dvwUser.Item(0) will both retrieve the row with index 0.
RowFilter	The **RowFilter** property is a **String** property that retrieves or sets the expression that is used to filter which rows are visible in the **DataView**. See Listing 3B-17 for an example of how to use this property.
RowStateFilter	This property retrieves or sets the row state filter that is used in the **DataView**. This means that you can filter the rows based on their row state, such as **Unchanged**, **Added**, or **Deleted**. The value must be a member of the **DataViewRowState** enum.
Sort	The **Sort** property retrieves or sets the sort column(s) and the sort order for the table. The data type for the **Sort** property is **String**. You specify the columns separated by a comma and then followed by the sort order, **ASC** or **DESC** for ascending or descending, like this: dvwUser.Sort = "LastName, FirstName ASC"
Table	This property returns or sets the source **DataTable**, meaning the data table that supplies the data view with data. This property can be set only if the current value is **Nothing**.

DataView Methods

Table 3B-7 lists the noninherited and public methods of the **DataView** class in ascending order.

*Table 3B-7. **DataView** Class Methods*

NAME	DESCRIPTION	EXAMPLE
AddNew()	The **AddNew** method adds a new row to the **DataView**. The return value is of data type **DataRowView**.	`drvNew = dvwUser.AddNew()`
BeginInit()	The **BeginInit** method, which cannot be overridden, is used to indicate that the data view has not yet been initialized. The method begins the initialization of a data view used on a form or by another component. This initialization occurs at runtime, and together with the **EndInit** method it ensures that the data view is not used before it is completely initialized.	`dvwUser.BeginInit()`
Delete(ByVal vintIndex As Integer)	This method deletes a row at the specified index, vintIndex. If you regret deleting a row, you can undo it by calling the **RejectChanges** method on the **DataTable**. You can use the **Find** method to locate the index for a specific row.	`dvwUser.Delete(5)`
EndInit()	The **EndInit** method is for use in conjunction with the **BeginInit** method. When you call it, you indicate that data view has fully initialized.	`dvwUser.EndInit()`
Find()	This overloaded method is used for locating a row in the **DataView** by looking up one or more primary key values.	`intIndex = dvwUser.Find(objValue) or intIndex = dvwUser.Find(arrobjValues)`
GetEnumerator()	This method, which cannot be overridden, returns an enumerator for navigating through the list.	`enmDataView = dvwUser.GetEnumerator()`

Declaring and Instantiating a DataView

There are various ways to instantiate a **DataView** object. You can use the over-loaded class constructors, or you can reference the **DefaultView** property of the **DataTable** object. Here is how you instantiate a data view when you declare it:

```
Dim dvwNoArguments As New DataView()
Dim dvwTableArgument As New DataView(dstUser.Tables("tblUser"))
```

You can also declare it and then instantiate it when you need to, like this:

```
Dim dvwNoArguments As DataView
Dim dvwTableArgument As DataView

dvwNoArguments = New DataView()
dvwTableArgument = New DataView(dstUser.Tables("tblUser"))
```

I have used two different constructors, one with no arguments and one that takes the data table as the only argument. The other option is to first declare the **DataView** object and then have it reference the **DefaultView** property of the **DataTable** object, as shown here:

```
Dim dvwUser As DataView

dvwUser = dstUser.DefaultView()
```

Searching a DataView

You can use the **Find** method for finding a specific row. This method, which is overloaded, takes an object or an array of objects as the only argument. See Listing 3B-18 for some sample code that finds the user with an ID of 1 in the tblUser table in the UserMan database.

Listing 3B-18. Searching in a DataView **Class**
```
1 Dim cnnUserMan As SqlConnection
2 Dim cmmUser As SqlCommand
3 Dim dadUser As SqlDataAdapter
4 Dim dtbUser As DataTable
5 Dim dvwUser As DataView
6 Dim objPKValue As Object
7 Dim intIndex As Integer
8
9 ' Instantiate and open the connection
```

```
10 cnnUserMan = New SqlConnection("Data Source=USERMANPC;" & _
11   "User ID=UserMan;Password=userman;Initial Catalog=UserMan")
12 cnnUserMan.Open()
13 ' Instantiate the command and data table
14 cmmUser = New SqlCommand("SELECT * FROM tblUser", cnnUserMan)
15 dtbUser = New DataTable()
16 ' Instantiate and initialize the data adapter
17 dadUser = New SqlDataAdapter("SELECT * FROM tblUser", cnnUserMan)
18 dadUser.SelectCommand = cmmUser
19 ' Fill the data table
20 dadUser.Fill(dtbUser)
21 ' Filter the data table view
22 dtbUser.DefaultView.RowFilter = "LastName = 'Doe'"
23 ' Create the new data view
24 dvwUser = dtbUser.DefaultView
25 ' Specify a sort order
26 dvwUser.Sort = "Id ASC"
27 ' Find the user with an id of 1
28 objPKValue = 1
29 intIndex = dvwUser.Find(objPKValue)
```

Even if you can specify as many values as you like in the form of objects in the object array, the values in the array are only intended to be matched with the primary key columns in the **DataView**. It is no good specifying more than one value if your data view only has one primary key column.

Using the DataRow Class

The **DataRow** class is used for representing a single row in the **DataTable** class. You can use a **DataRow** object on its own, but its only real purpose is to be used in conjunction with the **DataTable** class. The **DataRow** together with the **Data-Column** class are in fact the primary building blocks of the **DataTable** class.

This makes sense really, because when you have a table in a database it also consists of rows and columns. So why make this object model any different?

Okay, let's take a look at the properties and methods of this class. Table 3B-8 shows you all the noninherited, public properties of the **DataRow** class.

*Table 3B-8. **DataRow** Class Properties.*

PROPERTY NAME	DESCRIPTION
HasErrors	The **HasErrors** property returns a **Boolean** value that indicates if there are any errors in the columns collection. This property is read-only.
Item	This overloaded property returns or sets the data stored in the specified column. This property is the default property for the **DataRow** class, which is why you don't have to use this property when you want to access a specific column. Using the parentheses is enough. This means that drwUser.Item(2) and drwUser(2) do exactly the same thing.
ItemArray	The **ItemArray** property returns or sets the values for all the columns in this **DataRow** object. This is done through an array of **Object**s.
RowError	This property returns or sets a custom error description for a **DataRow**. You can use this property to indicate that a particular row is in error.
RowState	The **RowState** property, which is read-only, returns the current state of the **DataRow**. The returned value is one of the **DataRowState** enum values. The state of a row is used by the **GetChanges** and **HasChanges** methods.
Table	This read-only property returns the **DataTable** to which the row belongs.

Table 3B-9 shows you all the noninherited, public methods of the **DataRow** class.

*Table 3B-9. **DataRow** Class Methods*

METHOD NAME	DESCRIPTION	EXAMPLE
AcceptChanges()	This method commits all changes made to the DataRow since the last time **AcceptChanges** was called or since the row was loaded.	drwUser.AcceptChanges()
BeginEdit()	The **BeginEdit** method starts an edit operation on the **DataRow**. When the row is in edit mode, all events are disabled. This means that you can make changes to the contents of the row, without any events firing or validation rules triggering. Use this method in conjunction with the **EndEdit** method and/or the **CancelEdit** method.	drwUser.BeginEdit()
CancelEdit()	This method cancels the current row editing. Use this method in conjunction with the **BeginEdit** method.	drwUser.CancelEdit()
ClearErrors()	Use this method to clear all errors for the **DataRow**. This includes the **RowError** property and also errors that has been set with the **SetColumnError** method.	drwUser.ClearErrors()
Delete()	This method deletes the **DataRow**. Actually, this isn't entirely true. If the **RowState** of the row is **Added**, the row is deleted, but if not, the **RowState** is changed to **Deleted**. This means the row will not actually be deleted until you call the **AcceptChanges** method or the **Update** method on the data set. This also means that you can undo the deletion of the row by calling the **RejectChanges** method. If you try to delete a row that has already been marked **Deleted**, a **DeletedRowInaccessibleException** exception is thrown.	drwUser.Delete()
EndEdit()	This method ends the current editing of the row. Use this method in conjunction with the **BeginEdit** method.	drwUser.EndEdit()

*Table 3B-9. **DataRow** Class Methods (continued)*

METHOD NAME	DESCRIPTION	EXAMPLE
GetChildRows()	This overloaded method is used for retrieving the child rows of the **DataRow**. This is done using a **DataRelation** object; the name of a **DataRelation** object; a **DataRelation** object and a **DataRowVersion** object; or the name of a **DataRelation** object and a **DataRowVersion** object.	`arrdrwChildRows = drwUser.GetChildRows(drlUser) or arrdrwChildRows = drwUser.GetChildRows (strRelationName) or arrdrwChildRows = drwUser.GetChildRows(drlUser, drvUser) or arrdrwChildRows = drwUser.GetChildRows(strRelation Name, drvUser)`
GetColumnError()	This overloaded method returns the error description for the specified column using either a **DataColumn** object, an **Integer**, or a **String**.	`strError = drwUser.GetColumnError(dtcName) or strError = drwUser.GetColumnError (intColumn) or strError = drwUser.GetColumnError(strColumn)`
GetColumnsInError()	The **GetColumnsInError** method returns an array of **DataColumn** objects that all have errors. You should use the **HasErrors** method of the **DataRow** object to determine if any errors exist in the row before calling this method.	`arrdtcError = drwUser.GetColumnsInError()`
GetParentRow()	This overloaded method is used for retrieving the parent row of the **DataRow**. This is done using a **DataRelation** object; the name of a **DataRelation** object; a **DataRelation** object and a **DataRowVersion** object; or the name of a **DataRelation** object and a **DataRowVersion** object.	`drwParent = drwUser.GetParentRow(drlUser) or drwParent = drwUser.GetParentRow (strRelationName) or drwParent = drwUser.GetParentRow(drlUser, drvUser) or drwParent = drwUser.GetParentRow (strRelationName, drvUser)`
GetParentRows()	This overloaded method is used for retrieving the parent rows of the **DataRow**. This is done using a **DataRelation** object; the name of a **DataRelation** object; a **DataRelation** object and a **DataRowVersion** object; or the name of a **DataRelation** object and a **DataRowVersion** object.	`arrdrwParent = drwUser.GetParentRows(drlUser) or arrdrwParent = drwUser.GetParentRows (strRelationName) or arrdrwParent = drwUser.GetParentRows(drlUser, drvUser) or arrdrwParent = drwUser.GetParentRows (strRelationName, drvUser)`

*Table 3B-9. **DataRow** Class Methods (continued)*

METHOD NAME	DESCRIPTION	EXAMPLE

HasVersion(ByVal vdrvVersion As DataRowVersion)	This method returns a **Boolean** value that indicates if the specified version (vdrvVersion) exists. The argument (vdrvVersion) must be one of the members of the **DataRowVersion** enum.	`blnExist =`
		`drwUser.HasVersion`
		`(DataRowVersion.Default)`

IsNull()	This overloaded method returns a **Boolean** value that indicates if the specified column contains a null value (**Nothing**).	`blnNull =`
		`drwUser.IsNull(dtcNull) or`
		`blnNull =`
		`drwUser.IsNull(intColumn) or`
		`blnNull =`
		`drwUser.IsNull(strColumn) or`
		`blnNull =`
		`drwUser.IsNull(dtcNull,`
		`drwVersion)`

RejectChanges()	Rejects all changes made to the row since **AcceptChanges** was last called or since the **DataRow** was loaded.	`drwUser.RejectChanges()`

SetColumnError()	The **SetColumnError** method, which is overloaded, sets the error description or the specified column.	`drwUser.SetColumnError(dtcError,`
		`strError) or`
		`drwUser.SetColumnError`
		`(intColumn, strError) or`
		`drwUser.SetColumnError(strColumn,`
		`strError)`

SetParentRow()	This overloaded method is used for setting the parent row of the **DataRow**. This is done using a **DataRow** object or using a **DataRow** object and a **DataRelation** object.	`drwUser.SetParentRow(drwParent)`
		`or drwUser.GetParentRow`
		`(drwParent, drlParent)`

SetUnspecified (dtcUnspecified)	This method sets the value of the dtcUnspecified **DataColumn** to unspecified.	`drwUser.SetUnspecified` `(dtcUnspecified)`

Declaring and Instantiating a DataRow

There is only one way to instantiate a **DataRow** object. The **DataRow** object doesn't have a constructor, which means you rely on the **DataTable** to help you out. The **NewRow** method of the **DataTable** is what you need:

```
Dim drwUser As DataRow

drwUser = dtbUser.NewRow()
```

Building Your Own DataRow

In Listing 3B-13 you can see how to create your own **DataRow**. This listing also shows you how to create a **DataTable** that looks like the tblUser table in the User-Man database.

Cursors

Cursors are for use with relational databases, and they are merely pointers to a specific row in a result set. In ADO and ADO.NET this result set is usually represented as a data class such as the ADO **Recordset** object or the ADO.NET **DataReader** or **DataTable** classes. In ADO you have a lot of choices for how to deal and work with cursors, whereas your options in ADO.NET are quite limited. This is because of the disconnected architecture of ADO.NET and its data source independence, but I suspect you will see some improvement in later versions.

Cursor Types

There are numerous cursor types. The following sections briefly describe the ones you can use in ADO and ADO.NET, which are listed here:

- Forward-only cursors

- Static cursors

- Dynamic cursors

- Keyset cursors

Forward-Only Cursor

This cursor type requires the least amount of overhead. As the name suggests, you can only move forward one-row at a time in a result set with this kind of cursor. Well, this is not entirely true—you can close the data class holding the result set and then reopen it to move the cursor to the first row or BOF (Beginning-Of-File), which is just before the first row (see Figure 3B-1).

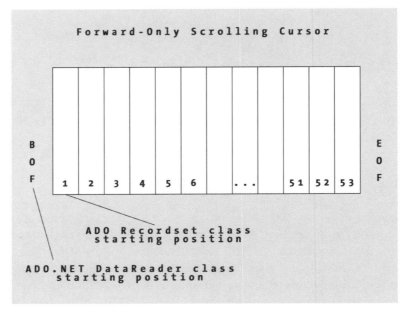

Figure 3B-1. BOF (Beginning-Of-File)

A forward-only cursor is dynamic by default, meaning that when a row is accessed it is read from the data source, so that changes that have been committed to the row after the result set was generated will be seen. This, however, is NOT the case with the ADO.NET **DataReader** class. Changes to the underlying rows in an open **DataReader** object cannot be seen!

This cursor type is the only one used by the ADO.NET **DataReader** class, and it is one of four cursor types used by the ADO **Recordset** class.

Static Cursor

A static cursor is exactly what the name says, static! This means the content of a result set is static, or that the content of the result set will not change after you have opened it. Changes made to the result set after it is opened will not be detected, although changes made by the static cursor itself generally are detected and reflected in the result set, depending on the implementation.

Unlike a forward-only cursor, the static cursor has the ability to scroll both forward and backwards. This cursor is one of four cursor types used by the ADO **Recordset** class.

Dynamic Cursor

The dynamic cursor is very good for dealing with concurrency issues, because it detects all changes made to the result set after the cursor is open. The dynamic cursor can of course scroll both forward and backward. The dynamic cursor has the most overhead of the four cursor types described and as such it can prove costly to use, especially in situations where one of the other cursor types can be used instead.

This cursor is one of four cursor types used by the ADO **Recordset** class.

Keyset Cursor

The keyset cursor can be thought of as a cross between a static cursor and a dynamic cursor, because it has functionality that is unique to one or the other. Changes to values in data columns are detected. Insertions made by the cursor will be appended to the result set, whereas insertions made by others will only be visible if the cursor is closed and opened again. Deletions are a completely different ball game when you have a keyset cursor. Deletions made by other cursors can be detected, but deletions made by the keyset cursor itself cannot be detected.

This cursor is one of four cursor types used by the ADO **Recordset** class.

Cursor Location

In regard to location, cursors come in two different flavors: client-side cursors and server-side cursors. As the names imply, they refer to pointers to data on either the client-side or server-side. There are advantages and disadvantages to both types, as discussed in the following sections.

Client-Side Cursors

Client-side cursors, or local cursors, are used for navigating in a result set located locally, or on the client. This means that all the rows you select in your query and so forth will have to be transferred to the client in one form or another.

Depending on the number of rows, this can be costly in terms of network traffic and storage space on the client. Storage space can be memory as well as disk space, depending on the cursor type and/or available memory on the client.

Server-Side Cursors

Server-side cursors, or remote cursors, are used for navigating in a result set located remotely, or on the server. ADO.NET doesn't currently have intrinsic support for the use of server-side cursors, so your only choice here is ADO. The reason may be that the various data sources differ a lot in the way they are implemented. This means it is extremely difficult to expose server-side cursors (and other server-side functionality) in a way that hides the complexity that goes into dealing with many different data sources. What you want is for the server-side cursor to behave and operate the same way, whatever data source you are accessing!

I am sure there will be some server-side functionality in later versions, however. Having said that, note that the **DataReader** class uses a server-side cursor. Mind you, you can't really control the **DataReader** class—you can only move forward one row at a time—so what you would normally expect from server-side cursor functionality is not exactly what you get from the **DataReader** class.

ADO.NET only uses client-side cursors (except for the **DataReader** class), whereas you can specify your cursor location preference with ADO. So to cut a long story short, if you need the functionality of server-side cursors, ADO is currently your only choice! Actually, if you are after server-side processing, then look into using stored procedures and triggers, as discussed in Chapter 6.

COM Interop

Because previous versions of ADO are built as COM components, you also need to use COM Interop for this purpose. COM Interop provides a way of interfacing with COM components in order to use them and vice versa for that matter. I will only be discussing the COM-to-.NET usage in this section.

You need to use COM Interop whenever you want to access a COM component. There is much more to COM Interop than I am going to cover in this section, so if you need some more information I suggest you check out *Moving to Visual Basic.NET: Strategies, Concepts and Code* by Dan Appleman, ISBN 1893115976, published in 2001 by Apress.

There are several ways of using COM components from within the .NET Framework. They all involve exposing a COM component to the world of managed code. The CLR expects all types to be defined as metadata in an assembly. This goes for COM types as well. So the job at hand is to convert your COM types to metadata, or rather generate metadata for your COM types.

I will show you the two easy ways of generating the metadata, and I suggest that you pick either method for use with previous versions of ADO. The first involves running the command-line Type Library Importer, **TlbImp.exe**, on the COM component to generate metadata in an assembly. Please note that the component must contain a type library. If it doesn't, then there is probably a separate type library file for importing (*.tlb). Any client that writes managed code can use the resulting assembly. Say you want to import the ADO 2.7 library, which is usually located in the Program Files\Common Files\System\Ado folder. To do so, you would open a command prompt, go to the Ado folder, and then execute the following command: TlbImp msado27.tlb. The output is the ADODB.DLL assembly, which holds the ADODB namespace. Surely this must look familiar to you. . . Adding a reference to your project can reference this assembly. See the next option for generating metadata. If you need to see all the command options available to you, just run **TlbImp** with no arguments from the command line. The options will then be displayed.

The second way to generate the metadata involves adding a reference to the COM components in your project, as shown in Figure 3B-2. This way the IDE generates the metadata for you. You can access the **Add Reference** dialog box by clicking on the **Add Reference** command in the **Project** menu.

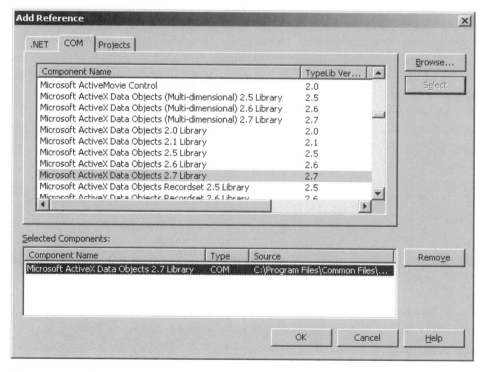

*Figure 3B-2. The **Add Reference** dialog box*

You can use either of these two methods to access any COM types, and as such all of your COM components can still be part of your applications. Mind you, it is advisable to port all of these components to .NET classes, because there is overhead when using COM Interop. Once you have added a reference to a COM component in your project, you can use the Object Browser to see all the types.

Okay, now that I have suggested you do all this, I might as well reveal that it isn't really necessary. It's not necessary because Microsoft has decided to include some Primary Interop Assemblies with VS.NET. Guess what, ADO is one of them. This means a .NET Framework wrapper already exists for the ADO COM libraries. So all you really have to do is add a reference to this wrapper. You can access the **Add Reference** dialog box by clicking on the **Add Reference** command in the **Project** menu. In the **Add Reference** dialog box the wrapper assembly can be found on the .NET tab with the component name adodb. Select it from the list, click on **Select**, and then click on **OK**.

Summary

This chapter, together with the proceeding chapter, introduced you to the two different data access technologies ADO and ADO.NET. ADO.NET is for building distributed n-tier Web applications, whereas ADO is your best bet for traditional Windows client-server/n-tier applications programming in a heterogeneous networking environment, in which you are connected at all times on a LAN link. The object model for the disconnected layer of ADO.NET was introduced and a comparison was made with the ADO object model wherever needed. As well as being an introduction to the disconnected layer of ADO.NET and to some extent ADO, this chapter is a reference to the various classes, methods, and properties of this data access technology.

This chapter also covered the following:

- **DataSet**, **DataTable**, **DataView**, and **DataRow** data classes were discussed. The ADO.NET classes were compared to their equivalents in ADO and suggestions were offered about when to use which data class.

- I also talked about cursors and COM Interop, the latter of which is required in order to use ADO 2.7 or earlier.

The following chapter takes you through the various data-related features of the IDE, such as how to create database projects.

CHAPTER 4

Presenting the IDE from a Database Viewpoint

A presentation of the various designers and projects that are related to databases

THIS CHAPTER INTRODUCES you to the Integrated Development Environment (IDE) and more specifically how it relates to databases. I will be discussing how you create database projects and how you let the various designers do the hard work for you—in other words, how you perform tasks from the IDE that you would otherwise do through code or using other external tools.

In this chapter, I have included several hands-on exercises that will take you through creating a database project and adding scripts, queries, and command files. Just look for the Exercise items that appear throughout this text.

Using the Server Explorer

The Server Explorer is located on the left-hand side of the IDE, and it is displayed if you move the mouse cursor over the Server Explorer tab or if you press Ctrl+Alt+S. The Server Explorer is hidden again if you click on any other part of the IDE, such as the Code Editor. The Server Explorer window contains a tree view of the data connections that have been created and the servers to which you have connected.

> **NOTE** *The resources shown in the Server Explorer window are NOT specific to the project that is currently open.*

When you open up the Visual Studio.NET IDE for the first time, the Server Explorer does not display any data connections or servers, and it looks like the example shown in Figure 4-1.

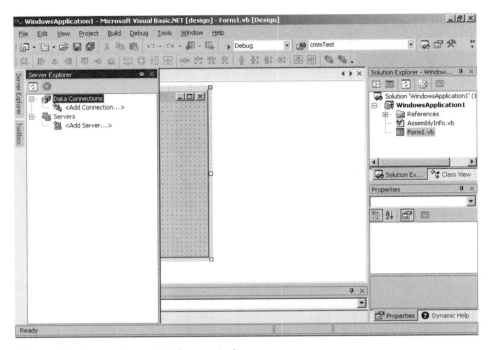

Figure 4-1. Empty Server Explorer window

Handling Data Connections

If you need to manipulate a database or create a strongly typed data set, you have to create a data connection first. Depending on your access privileges, you can perform most database tasks from the Server Explorer.

Adding a Data Connection

You can add a data connection by right-clicking the Data Connections node and selecting Add Connection from the pop-up menu. This brings up the Data Link Properties dialog box. You might need to click the Provider tab to see the dialog box shown in Figure 4-2. If you have ever created data connections from the VB6 Data View, then this dialog box should be very familiar to you.

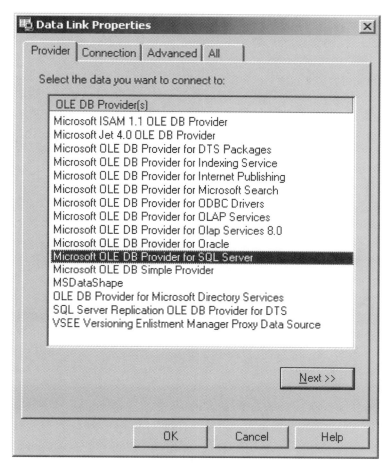

Figure 4-2. Provider tab in Data Link Properties dialog box

On the Provider tab of the Data Link Properties dialog box, you must select the appropriate provider for the data source you are going to connect to, and click Next. This brings the Connection tab, shown in Figure 4-3, to the front.

EXERCISE

On the Provider tab of the Data Link Properties dialog box, select Microsoft OLE DB Provider for SQL Server.

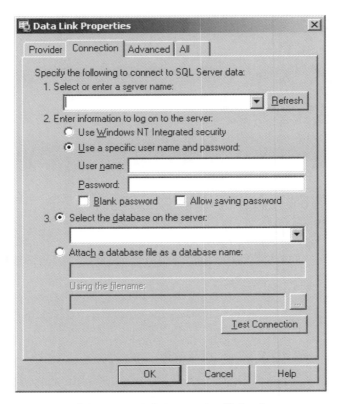

Figure 4-3. Connection tab in Data Link Properties dialog box

On the Connection tab you must enter the appropriate details concerning the database to which you are connecting.

1) On the Connection tab of the Data Link Properties dialog box, you must enter the following text:

    USERMANPC (or the name of your SQL Server)

    See Figure 4-4. The password is *userman* and you must replace *USER-MANPC* with the name of your SQL Server.

2) Click OK.

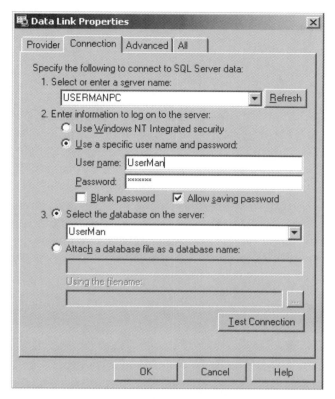

Figure 4-4. SQL Server setup on the Connection tab in Data Link Properties

Deleting a Data Connection

When a data connection is no longer relevant to you, you should delete it from the Server Explorer. There are three ways in which you can delete a data connection from the Server Explorer. First you must select the appropriate node in the tree view and then do one of the following:

- Press the Delete key.

- Right-click on the tree-view node and select the Delete command from the pop-up menu.

- Select the Delete command from the Edit menu.

Please note that this procedure only deletes the connection, and not the database to which you are connecting! If you need to delete a SQL Server database, please see "Deleting/Dropping a SQL Server Database" later in this chapter.

Creating Database Objects

If you want to create database objects such as tables, diagrams, views, stored procedures, or functions, you can do this by first selecting the corresponding tree-view node. Next, right-click on the node, and select the New. . . command from the pop-up menu. Check out Chapter 6 for more information on how to create database objects. Chapter 2 holds information on how to build a relational database the "right" way.

Handling Servers

Under the Servers node in the Server Explorer you can add any server to which you have access. You should add at least all the servers that the current project will be accessing, because it is easier to control and manipulate the servers once they are shown, with their resources, in the Server Explorer window.

Adding a Server

You can add a server by right-clicking the Servers node and selecting Add Server from the pop-up menu. The Add Server dialog box, shown in Figure 4-5, appears.

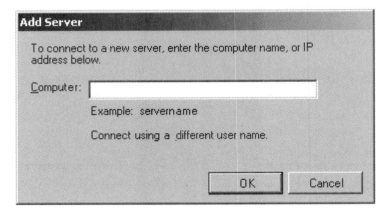

Figure 4-5. Add Server dialog box

In the Add Server dialog box you can add a server by typing the name of the server in the Computer text box. The name can be specified in one of two ways:

- Using the NETBIOS name if the server is on a local network—for example, *USERMANPC*.

- Using the IP-address of the server—for example, *192.129.192.15*.

Type the name of your server in the Name text box of the Add Server dialog box and click OK.

If you want to connect to the server as a different user, you must click on Connect using a different user name. This brings up the Connect As dialog box as shown in Figure 4-6.

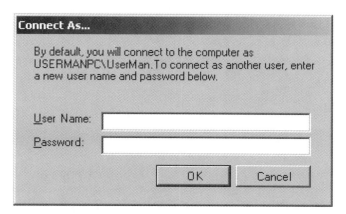

Figure 4-6. Connect As dialog box

The Connect As dialog box has two text boxes you must fill in:

- *User Name:* Type the name of the user you want to connect as. If this user is in a different domain, you must also specify the domain name; use the format *DomainName\UserName*.

- *Password:* Type the password that corresponds to the user name entered. Leave this text box empty if the user doesn't have a password.

Once you have added a server to the Server Explorer, you can view all the resources this server has to offer by expanding the tree node (click on the + icon next to the node if it isn't already expanded).

There are a number of different resources on a server, and I will only cover the ones that are database related, including message queues and SQL Server databases.

Using Server Resources

The following sections describe how to use the database-related resources on the server of your choice.

Using Message Queues

Chapter 8 covers message queues extensively, so I won't go into too many details here. Having said this, I will show you how to create, manipulate, and delete a message queue from the Server Explorer. Another thing you need to be aware of is that you can only access message queues on a server with a dependent message queue. This means workgroup message queue setup is not supported. A workgroup setup is an independent message queue, which means that it is not dependent on a server for storage of messages.

There are three types of message queues that can be seen in the Server Explorer although which message you can actually see depends on your permissions:

- *Private queue:* This is a queue registered on the local computer and is not part of a directory service. Generally this kind of queue cannot be located by other applications. See Chapter 8 for more information.

- *Public queue:* This is a queue registered in the directory service. This queue can be located by any other message queuing application. See Chapter 8 for more information.

- *System queue:* This kind of queue is generally used by the OS for internal messaging. See Chapter 8 for more information.

Figure 4-7 shows you the expanded Message Queue node in the Server Explorer.

Figure 4-7. Expanded Message Queue node in the Server Explorer

Creating a Message Queue

Right-click on the queue node where you want to create the new queue, and select Create Queue from the pop-up menu. This brings up the Create Message Queue dialog box as shown in Figure 4-8.

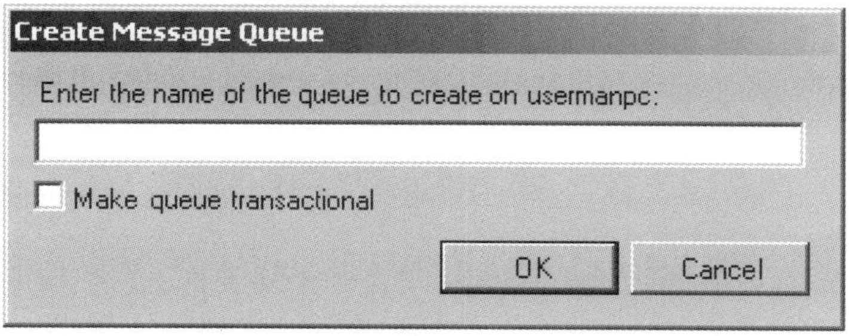

```
┌─────────────────────────────────────────────────────┐
│ Create Message Queue                                 │
├─────────────────────────────────────────────────────┤
│                                                      │
│  Enter the name of the queue to create on usermanpc: │
│                                                      │
│  ┌─────────────────────────────────────────────┐    │
│  │                                             │    │
│  └─────────────────────────────────────────────┘    │
│                                                      │
│  ☐ Make queue transactional                          │
│                                                      │
│            ┌──────────┐     ┌──────────┐             │
│            │   OK     │     │  Cancel  │             │
│            └──────────┘     └──────────┘             │
└─────────────────────────────────────────────────────┘
```

Figure 4-8. Create Message Queue dialog box

You give the message queue a name by typing it in the text box. Select the Make queue transactional check box to accept only those messages that are part of a transaction. Note that you need permissions to create a message queue on the server to which you are connected. Click OK to create the queue.

Deleting a Message Queue

If a message queue is no longer of use to you, you can delete it. This is done by right-clicking on the message queue and selecting Delete from the pop-up menu. A confirmation of the deletion is required. All messages in the queue will be deleted permanently.

Deleting Messages from a Message Queue

If you need to clear one or more messages from a queue, there are two ways of doing so from the Server Explorer. You can delete one at a time, or you can delete all messages from a queue. Clearing all messages from a queue is done by expanding the queue node and right-clicking on the Queue Messages node. Select Clear Messages from the pop-up menu and then confirm the deletion. A single message is cleared from the queue by selecting it, right-clicking on it, and selecting Delete from the pop-up menu.

Using SQL Server Databases

You can use the SQL Server resources to see if a specific server actually hosts a SQL Server. Click on the + icon to expand the SQL Server Databases node. If you click on a SQL Server, the SQL Server service will automatically be started if it isn't already running. This is in contrast to using Data Connections, where the service must be started for you to add a connection!

Creating a SQL Server Database

If you haven't created the database you want to connect to yet, this is how it is done. In the Server Explorer window, expand the server on which the SQL Server is running, expand SQL Server Databases, and right-click on the SQL Server where you want to create a database. This brings up a pop-up menu from which you select the New Database command. The Create Database dialog box appears, as shown in Figure 4-9, and this is where you specify the properties for the database.

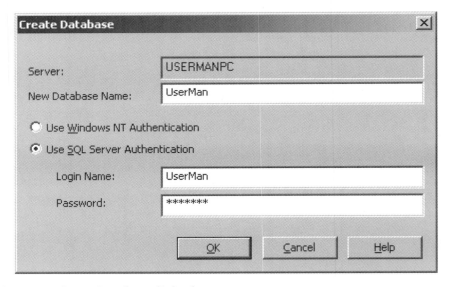

Figure 4-9. Create Database dialog box

If you have ever used the Server Explorer in SQL Server 7.0 or later, you'll probably recognize the content of this dialog box.

- *Server:* This is the name of the server that hosts the SQL Server. If you need to change this, you have to cancel this dialog box and bring up the same dialog box on the required server.

- *New Database Name:* This is the name you want to give your new database.

- *Use Windows NT Authentication:* Select this option if you want to use Windows NT authentication for connecting to the SQL Server. Whatever user name you used to connect will be serve as the basis for authentication on the server that hosts the SQL Server. (I will not be demonstrating the use of this option in this book.)

- *Use SQL Server Authentication:* Select this option if you want to use SQL Server's own authentication. With this option, you have to create a login to use if you are not going to use the system administrator account, **sa**.

- *Login Name:* This is where you must indicate the name of the login you want to use. This text box is not enabled if you use Windows NT authentication.

- *Password:* Type the password that corresponds to the login name. This text box is not enabled if you use Windows NT authentication.

EXERCISE

You might already have created a UserMan database on your SQL Server. However, if you'd like to create a new database, simply follow these instructions on how to fill in the Create Database dialog box:

1) Type or select the name of your server in the Server combo box.

2) Type **Test** in the New Database Name text box.

3) Select the Use SQL Server Authentication option.

4) Type a login name that has create database privileges in the Login Name text box.

5) Type the corresponding password for the login account used in Step 4.

Click on OK to create the new database and have the display refreshed so that it includes the new database. I cover connecting to SQL Server databases earlier in this chapter in the section "Handling Data Connections."

> **NOTE** *When you create a SQL Server database this way, all the default values for a new database will be used. These values are set on the server. If you want to create a database with nondefault values or properties, you must either do so in code using a **CREATE DATABASE** SQL statement or from the SQL Server Enterprise Manager Microsoft Management Console (MMC) snap-in. Alternatively you can create your database as shown and then change some of the default values, like where the database and/or log files are located, through code using an **ALTER DATABASE** SQL statement.*

You cannot create a file-based database, like an MS Access JET database, using the Server Explorer. For this purpose you need to use the corresponding front-end tool (MS Access in this case). You can also execute a **CREATE DATABASE** SQL statement from code using the appropriate provider.

Deleting/Dropping a SQL Server Database

You cannot delete or drop a SQL Server database automatically from the Server Explorer window. You need to do this from the SQL Server Enterprise Manager or through code using a **DROP DATABASE** SQL statement.

EXERCISE

If you created the Test database in the previous exercise, and you want to delete or drop it again, work through the instructions in the following tip.

TIP   *Actually, it is possible to delete or drop a SQL Server database from the Server Explorer window, if you have the rights to access the master database and the permissions to drop a database. If you do, you can do the following:*

1) *Open a database other than the master database on the server in question. This has to be a database in which you have a login name that has the right permissions, as just described.*

2) *Expand the Tables node and right-click on a table.*

3) *Select the Retrieve Data from Table command from the pop-up menu.*

4) *Click on the Show SQL Pane button on the Query Toolbar (check the Tool Tip).*

5) *Delete the SELECT *. . . SQL statement from the SQL Pane.*

6) *Type **USE master** and click on the Run Query button on the Query toolbar.*

7) *Click OK in the resulting dialog box.*

8) *Delete the content of the SQL Pane and type **DROP DATABASE** databasename (where databasename is the actual name of the database you want to delete or drop) and click on Run Query.*

9) *Click OK.*

Deleting a Server

If a server becomes obsolete to you, you should delete it from the Server Explorer. There are three ways in which you can delete a server from the current project. First you must select the appropriate node in the tree view, and then do one of the following:

- Press the Delete key.

- Right-click on the tree-view node and select the Delete command from the pop-up menu.

- Select the Delete command from the Edit menu.

Looking at Database Projects

A database project is used for storing connections, SQL scripts, and command files (such as those for batching scripts and/or scheduled script execution). Besides this, through a database project you can also use Visual SourceSafe for handling the various versions of your database objects. In other words, a database project is for manipulating your database objects directly!

You can create a database project by following these steps:

1. Select the File/New/Project menu command or press Ctrl+Shift+N. This brings up the New Project dialog box, as shown in Figure 4-10.

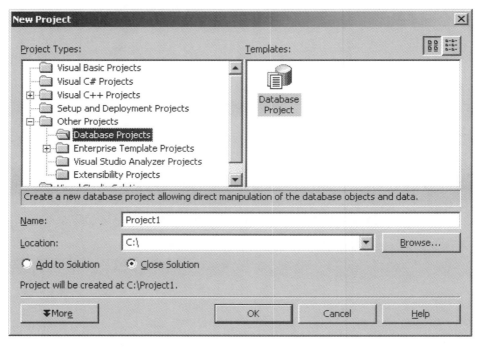

Figure 4-10. The New Project dialog box

2. In the New Project dialog box, expand the Other Projects node and select Database Projects.

3. Give the project a name by typing the name in the Name text box, and specify the location in the Location text box.

4. Finally you need to specify if the new project should be added to the current solution or if the current solution should be closed and a new one

created. Select the Add to Solution option or the Close Solution option to specify which you want. Please note that the Add to Solution option and the Close Solution option are only available if you currently have a project open.

In the New Project dialog box type **UserMan DB Project** in the Name text box. Save the project to your hard disk.

5. Click on OK. Now the Add Database Reference dialog box appears. This dialog box is shown in Figure 4-11.

   The Add Database Reference dialog box has a list of all the data connections from the Server Explorer; see "Handling Data Connections" earlier in this chapter for details. Select the desired data connection. If the database you want to reference is not shown on the list, you can add it by clicking on Add New Reference. This will bring up the Data Link Properties dialog box, which is described under "Adding a Data Connection" earlier in this chapter. Click on OK and the new project will now appear in the Solution Explorer.

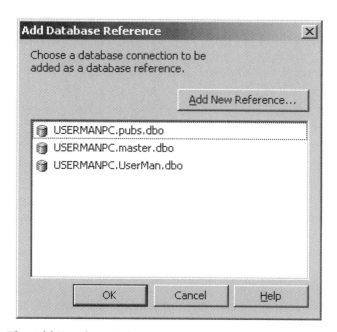

Figure 4-11. The Add Database Reference dialog box

Type **UserMan DB Project** in the Name text box.

6. If you need to add more database references to your project, right-click on the Database References node in the Solution Explorer and select Add Reference from the pop-up menu.

> **NOTE** *When you add a database reference to a database project that doesn't exist under Data Connections in the Server Explorer, it is automatically added to the Data Connections node.*

If you have more than one database reference in your project, you can set one of them to be the default reference. As a result of specifying a default reference, when you create, for example, a script, the list of tables to add to the script will consist of tables from the default database. In addition, the default database reference is the one used when you run scripts and queries within your project. You can set the default database reference by right-clicking on the root project folder and selecting Set Default Reference from the pop-up menu. This brings up the Set Default Reference dialog box, which looks very similar to the Add Database Reference dialog box in Figure 4-11. Select the database you want as your default, and click OK. After you do so, you will notice the Database References node in the Solution Explorer has changed. The default database reference has a new icon, indicating that it is the default reference.

Creating a Database Project Folder

If you look in the Solution Explorer for a database project (make sure the database project is expanded), you can see that three subfolders have already been created. These folders are used for grouping your database objects as described here:

*   The Change Scripts folder is for holding delete and update scripts, and so on.

*   The Create Scripts folder is for creation scripts (tough one to guess, eh?), such as those for creating a database or a table.

*   The Queries folder is for scripts that return rows or single/scalar values and the like.

If you need more folders or just want to create your own set of folders for grouping your database objects, then feel free to do so. All you need to do is right-click on a database project node in the Solution Explorer and select New Folder from the pop-up menu. The new folder is automatically added to the Solution Explorer. You can give the new folder a meaningful name and create subfolders as you would in any normal file system.

> **TIP** *Although you can group your database objects any way you want, following a commonsense folder-naming scheme, like the one used for the default folders, and making sure that the database objects are placed in the appropriate folders is the best approach. This will make it a lot easier to find a specific database object, and obviously it will also make it easier to create command files that only contain scripts from one folder.*

Deleting a Database Project Folder

You can delete folders as well as you can create them for your database objects. You do this by right-clicking on the folder you want to delete, selecting Remove from the pop-up menu, and confirming the deletion of the folder. Actually, you can choose to just remove the folder from the project or to delete the folder from your hard disk as well as remove it from the project.

> **WARNING** *You have to be careful when you delete a folder, because all database objects in the folder will be deleted as well.*

Adding Database Objects to a Database Project

You can add both new and existing database objects to your database project. See the following sections for information on how to do both tasks.

Adding New Database Objects

If you want to add a new database object to any of the folders in a project, including the project root folder, right-click on the desired folder and select Add New Item from the pop-up menu. Actually, there are other options for this purpose on the pop-up menu, but the Add New Item command covers both the Add SQL

Script and Add Query commands. After you make the selection, the Add New Item dialog box pops up (see Figure 4-12).

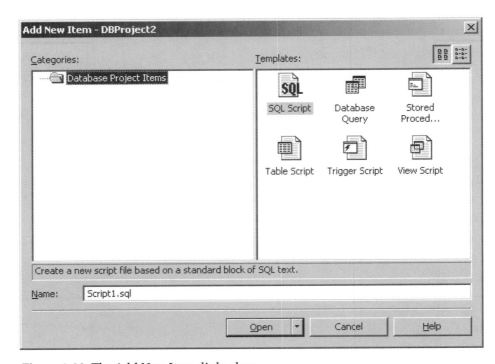

Figure 4-12. The Add New Item dialog box

As you can see from Figure 4-12, there are a few different database objects that can be added to your database project. When you add a new database object to your project, it must be based on a template. Available templates are shown in the right-hand pane of the Add New Item dialog box. Except for the Database Query template, they all open up the SQL Editor for editing once you click Open. (See "Script Editing Using the SQL Editor" later in this chapter for more information on how to use this feature.) If you create a new database object based on the Database Query template, the Query Designer is opened once you click Open. (See "Designing Queries with the Query Designer" later in this chapter for more information on how to use the Query Designer.)

The Query Designer and the SQL Editor overlap in a few areas when it comes to creating scripts or queries. What I mean is that some things can be achieved by using either of the two, and which one you choose is simply a matter of preference. The Query Designer, with its drag-and-drop features, is easier to use, whereas you can perform more complex tasks using the SQL Editor. Table 4-1 lists the templates available and describes which template is best for creating certain database objects as well as which tool to use.

Table 4-1. Database Object Templates

TEMPLATE NAME	DEFAULT TOOL	DESCRIPTION
Database Query	Query Designer	Use a database query for creating row-returning queries, delete and update queries, make/create table queries, and insert queries. You can use the SQL Editor for this purpose as well, but the Query Designer is perfectly designed for this task. It is much simpler because of its query grid and the drag-and-drop features.
SQL Script	SQL Editor	You should use the SQL Script template when you want to create a script that isn't covered by any of the other templates.
Stored Procedure Script	SQL Editor	Use the Stored Procedure template to create stored procedures for fast server-side processing of repeating queries or functions. See Chapter 6 for more information on stored procedures.
Table Script	SQL Editor	Use the Table Script template to make **CREATE TABLE SQL** scripts. Personally I think it's easier to use the Query Designer for this purpose, but sometimes you might add an existing create table script and then you can use the SQL Editor to edit it. It's your call.
Trigger Script	SQL Editor	The Trigger Script template should be used to create triggers for server-side processing or validation of data manipulation. See Chapter 6 for more information on triggers.
View Script	SQL Editor	The View Script template should be used for creating views that make row-returning queries faster. See Chapter 6 for more information on views.

Running Scripts in the IDE

Once you have a created a script, you can actually test it in the IDE. Right-click on the script in the Solution Explorer and select Run from the pop-up menu. This will execute the script on the default database. If you want to execute the script on a different database, select Run On from the aforementioned pop-up menu. This brings up the Run On dialog box, as shown in Figure 4-13.

Figure 4-13. The Run On dialog box

The Run On dialog box is quite similar to the Add Database Reference dialog box in Figure 4-11, but with one exception, the temporary reference (represented by <temporary reference>). You can use this temporary reference to create a temporary database connection, which runs the script and is destroyed as soon as the script ends.

Once you have selected the reference you require, click on OK to run the script on the selected reference.

Adding a Command File

If you want to execute several scripts at a time, it is a good idea to put them all in a single command file. This way you can execute a batch of scripts at any time by executing the command file. Actually, since a command file can be executed at the command line, it is also a good candidate for scheduled execution. This means that it even makes sense to put one script in a command file. The command file is a Windows command file with the *.cmd extension.

You create a command file by right-clicking on the folder in the Solution Explorer in which you want the command file to be placed. The Create Command File dialog box appears after you select Create Command File from the pop-up menu (see Figure 4-14).

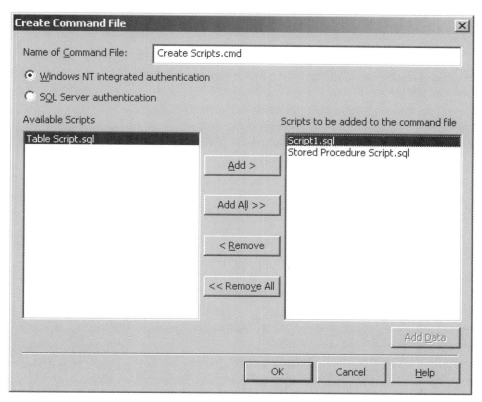

Figure 4-14. The Create Command File dialog box

In the Create Command File dialog box you can give the command file a name and choose which scripts should be part of the command file. The scripts listed under Available Scripts are taken from the folder in which you are creating the command file. You cannot select scripts from other folders. This is why it is so important to organize your scripts in the correct folders. (This goes for queries as well!)

Use the Add or Add All buttons to add the scripts to the command file. Once you have added one or more scripts, you can remove any you've decided not to include by selecting them and clicking on either Remove or Remove All. Please note that the Remove and Remove All buttons are only visible when you have added scripts to the command file.

The last thing you need to do is to choose if you want to use Windows NT authentication or SQL Server authentication. If you choose Windows NT authentication, the scripts will be executed with the permissions of the logged-in user or the user account assigned to the scheduler service. However, if you choose SQL Server authentication, you must provide the login name and password at the command prompt when you execute the script. Click OK when done, and the command file is placed in the folder you right-clicked on when you first began creating the file.

When you execute the command file, you need to supply the name of the server and the name of the database, like this:

```
CommandFileName.cmd ServerName DatabaseName
```

Adding Existing Database Objects

If you have already created one or more of the database objects that you want to add to your project, all you have to do is add them using the pop-up menu. Right-click on the folder that you want to add the object to, and select Add Existing Item from the pop-up menu. This brings up the Add Existing Item dialog box, in which you can browse and select the database objects. You can select more than one database object from the same folder at one time by holding down the Ctrl key when clicking on the objects you want. Click Open once you have selected the desired object(s). The selected objects are added to your project immediately and shown in the updated Solution Explorer window.

> **NOTE** *There is no validation of the existing items you add to your project, so it is up to you to add the correct types of database objects.*

Designing Databases with the Database Designer

The Database Designer is a visual tool for designing your databases. You can use it for creating tables, including keys, indexes, and constraints, and relationships between tables. The Database Designer creates a diagram through which you can visualize your database objects as you add and manipulate them. The database diagram depicts the database graphically, showing the database structure. This means that a database diagram can only hold database objects from one database. In other words, you can have several diagrams in one database, but only one database in any diagram.

Creating a Database Diagram

The *database diagram* is a visual tool for creating your database. You can add or create tables, add relationships between tables, and perform just about all the tasks you would normally when you design your database. You can create a database diagram from the Server Explorer. Expand the Data Connections node and the database for which you want to create the diagram. Right-click the Database Diagrams node and select New Diagram from the pop-up menu. This brings up the Add Table dialog box, as shown in Figure 4-15. In this dialog box you can select the tables from the database that you want on the diagram. Select the desired table(s) and click Add. Click Close to close the dialog box and continue with the diagram.

> **NOTE** *Database diagrams are NOT available for Microsoft Access (JET Engine) databases, only SQL Server and Oracle databases!*

EXERCISE

Create a new database diagram and add all the tables in the UserMan database that start with *tbl*.

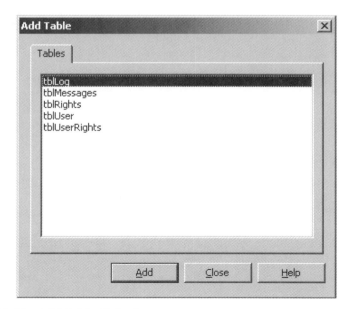

Figure 4-15. The Add Table dialog box

When the diagram opens, the tables you selected are automatically added to the diagram, and if you have set up relations between any of the tables, they are automatically shown as well (see Figure 4-16).

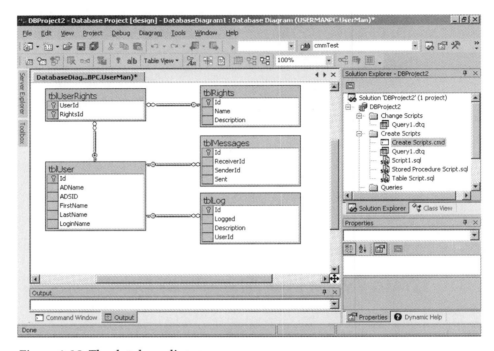

Figure 4-16. The database diagram

Adding Tables

If you need to add more tables to the diagram, you can right-click on any blank space in the diagram and select Add Table from the pop-up menu. This brings up the Add Table dialog box shown in Figure 4-15. Select the tables you want on the diagram and click Add. Click Close to close the dialog box and continue with the database diagram.

Deleting and Removing Tables

If you have added a table to the diagram that you don't really need, all you have to do is remove it. Well, there's more to it than that, because removing a table from the diagram is one thing, deleting a table from the database is a completely different story. Here is what you do to remove a table from a diagram:

1. Right-click on the table in question.

2. Select Remove Table from Diagram from the pop-up menu.

Please note that no confirmation is required for this task! If on the other hand you actually want to delete the table from the database, then this is how you do it:

1. Right-click on the table in question.

2. Select Delete Table from Database from the pop-up menu.

3. Click Yes in the confirmation dialog box.

Creating a New Table

If you haven't already created the table you want to add to the database diagram, you can create it from within the diagram. Right-click on any blank space on the diagram and select New Table from the pop-up menu. This brings up the Choose Name dialog box (see Figure 4-17) in which you enter the name of the new table. Click OK when done entering the name.

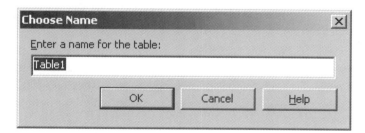

Figure 4-17. The Choose Name dialog box

EXERCISE

Type **tblTest** in the text box of the Choose Name dialog box and click OK.

When you have entered the name and clicked OK, the new table is displayed on the database diagram (see Figure 4-18).

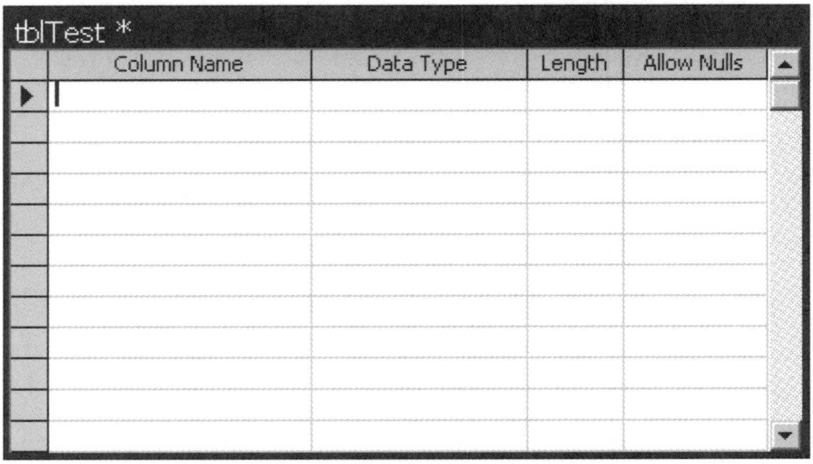

Figure 4-18. The new table on the database diagram

For each field, or column, in the new table, you can specify a column name, data type, and length, and indicate whether the column allows Null values. So to add a new column, simply fill in these attributes as appropriate under Column Name, Data Type, Length, and Allows Nulls, and move to the next row. I know this may seem a little weird and confusing, what with the columns that make up a table being represented as rows in this table design view, but just hang in there, and you'll get it eventually.

EXERCISE

Fill in the column attributes as shown in Figure 4-19 and press Ctrl+S.

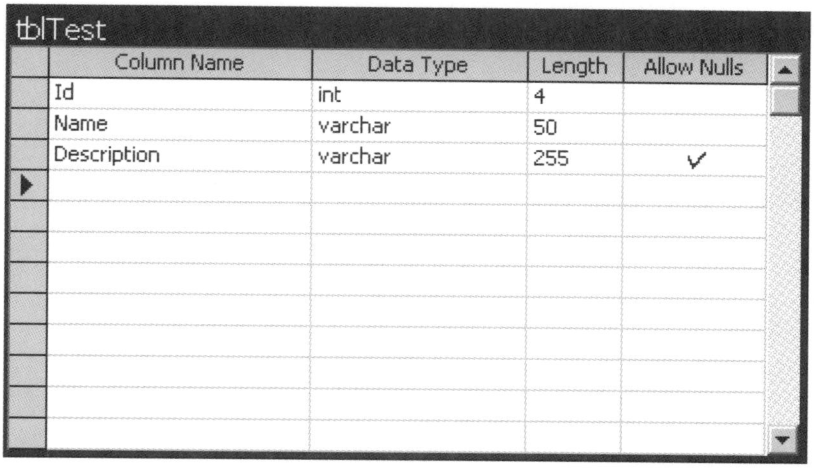

tblTest

Column Name	Data Type	Length	Allow Nulls
Id	int	4	
Name	varchar	50	
Description	varchar	255	✓

Figure 4-19. Column attributes

One of the first things you may notice is that the Data Type Column attribute is DBMS specific. This means the drop-down list of data types is filled with valid data types for the database the diagram is created in.

Once you are done entering the columns and the column attributes, press Ctrl+S to save the diagram and to create the new table. Although it is convenient to create and edit tables with the Database Designer (database diagram), it can be of greater help to use the Table Designer. See "Using the Table Designer" later in this chapter for more information.

Adding Relationships

Relationships are used for indicating relations between data in different tables. Once you have created your tables, all you need to do is create relationships by dragging a field from a table to the related field in another table. This brings up the Create Relationship dialog box, where you can define your relationship.

> **NOTE** *See Chapter 2 for a more detailed description of relationships.*

Deleting Relationships

If a relationship has become obsolete for some reason, you can delete it by right-clicking on the relationship and selecting Delete Relationship from Database from the resulting pop-up menu. You are required to confirm this deletion. As with all other changes you make to the database diagram, the deletion isn't saved to the database until you save the diagram.

Editing Database Properties

If you need to change the properties of the database, such as the keys of a table or the relationship between two tables, you simply right-click on any table or relationship and select Property Pages from the pop-up menu. This brings up the Property Pages dialog box, where you can edit the keys, indexes, and constraints of a table and the relationships between tables.

Database Diagram Overview

I am sure you have had the same problems as me in previous versions of MS database tools: Once you have added many tables to a diagram, it is nearly impossible to get the full overview of the diagram. Well, there are actually a few features available to help you:

- *Zoom in to view just one table or so, or zoom out to view the entire diagram*: You can zoom using the shortcut menu; right-click on any blank space on the diagram, select Zoom from the pop-up menu, and specify the percentage you want to zoom to. The current zoom percentage is checked on the menu if you have previously changed the zoom percentage. There is one command on the Zoom submenu that is of special interest: the To Fit command. This command will automatically choose the zoom percentage that will let you view the entire database diagram in the current view.

- *Move the view port, or rather change the viewable area of the diagram:* Locate the view port icon in the lower-right corner of the diagram (see Figure 4-20). If you click on the view port icon, you can see the entire diagram in the overview window, as shown in Figure 4-21. If you hold down the left mouse button, you can move the view port around the diagram. The view port is the dotted rectangle you can see in the middle of the overview window when you first click on the view port icon.

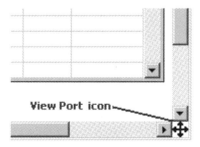

Figure 4-20. The database diagram view port icon

EXERCISE

Zoom the database diagram to 200% and click on the view port icon. Hold down the left mouse button and move the view port around the database diagram. Once you have selected the right area of the diagram, let go of the mouse button. Now the area you can see of the database diagram should be the same as the one you just selected using the overview window.

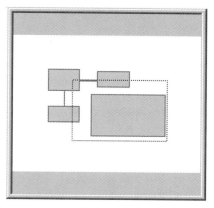

Figure 4-21. The database diagram overview window

- *Arrange all tables so that related tables sit together nice and orderly:* Right-click on any blank space on the diagram, and select Arrange Tables.

- *Show relationship names:* Right-click on any blank space on the diagram, and select Show Relationship Labels. This will display a name label next to the relationship.

- *Add descriptive free text labels to the diagram:* Right-click on any blank space on the diagram, and then select New Text Annotation. This will open a text field where you right-clicked on the diagram. When you have finished typing your text, you simply click on any other part of the diagram to finish editing the text annotation. Use these text annotations to add descriptive text that makes your diagram easier to read. These text annotations are NOT part of the database in any way. If you need to edit an existing text annotation, just click on the text on the diagram and the text field opens up for editing.

- *Change the table view:* If you want to see more or fewer table attributes than what is displayed, you can select the table(s) in question and right-click on one of the selected tables. Next, select Table View from the pop-up menu and click on the desired view. Standard View is very useful when designing a database, whereas the Column Names view is good as an outline.

- *Automatically size the tables:* If the size of one or more tables doesn't fit the number of rows and/or columns, you can select the table(s) in question, right-click on one of the selected tables, and then click on Autosize Selected Tables.

Saving the Database Diagram

When you have the database diagram open, you can press Ctrl+S any time to save the diagram. The diagram is validated before it is saved to the database. If any existing data violates any new relationships and/or constraints, the diagram cannot be saved. A dialog box detailing the error will appear. You will have to correct the error before you can save the diagram and thus save the changes to the database.

Using the Table Designer

The Table Designer is by far the most comprehensive tool for creating a new table in a database. Although you can use the Database Designer to add a new table to a diagram and thus the database, you have a much better overview of a table when you use the Table Designer.

To create a new table using the Table Designer, you must open up Server Explorer, expand the desired database, and right-click on the Tables node in this database. Selecting New Table from the pop-up menu brings up the Table Designer, as shown in Figure 4-22.

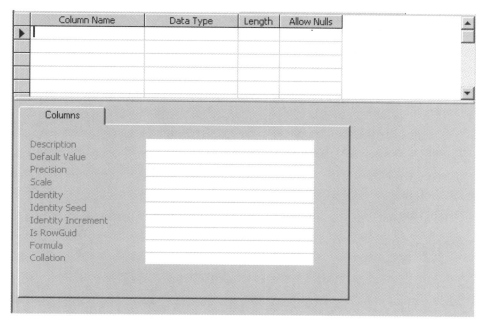

Figure 4-22. The Table Designer

At first the Table Designer looks similar to the table view you see when you use the New Table feature of the Database Designer (see "Adding Tables" earlier in this chapter), but it's a little more sophisticated.

Adding Columns

To add a new column to your table, you simply type the name of the column in the Column Name column. The Data Type attribute must also be filled in with the desired data type for the column. Please note that the data types in the drop-down list box are DBMS specific, which means that the list only contains data types that are valid for the database you are connected to. The Length attribute is also required when you specify a data type that can have varying lengths such as the varchar data type of SQL Server. The Allow Nulls attribute is always checked by default when you create a new column (by typing in the name of the column). If a column allows Null values, it cannot be a key field, so be sure you clear this attribute for your key field before you start adding data to a table, as it can be quite hard to change this attribute afterwards.

What I have described so far is pretty much the same as using the Database Designer to add a new table. Here is the big difference: the Columns attributes pane at the bottom of the Table Designer (see Figure 4-22). The Columns attributes pane varies depending on the database to which you are connected. In the case of Figure 4-22, I am using SQL Server. Some attributes are the same, however, as is the case with the following:

- *Description:* Use this attribute to add a description of the column, such as what kind of values it holds. This can be very valuable to someone taking over your database at a later stage in the life of the database.

- *Default Value:* The Default value is used for specifying a value that will be saved with rows that don't contain a value for this particular column. This can be used in place of allowing Null values, which can be hard to handle from code.

Setting the Primary Key

You can set the primary key by right-clicking on the grid next to Column Name for the column you want to have as the primary key. Next, click on Set Primary Key to set the column as the primary key (see Figure 4-23). If you need to have a composite primary key, then you have to select all the columns that make up the primary key before you right-click on the grid next to the Column Name column. You can select several columns the same way you would select multiple items on a list, that is, by holding down Ctrl when selecting the columns one by one. If the columns are contiguous, you can select the first column and then hold the Shift key and select the last column before you right-click on the grid next to the Column Name column.

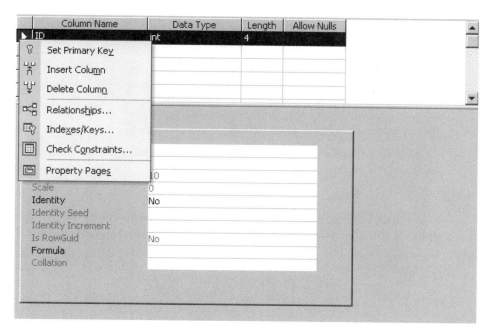

Figure 4-23. Setting the primary key

Adding Indexes and Keys

It is often a good idea to create an index on a column that is used for searching a table. You can create an index by right-clicking anywhere on the table grid in the Table Designer and selecting Indexes/Keys from the pop-up menu. This brings up the Property Pages dialog box with the Indexes/Keys tab shown (see Figure 4-24). Please note that the tab looks different if you have already created an index and/or primary key. The Selected Index list box in this case is populated and one of the existing indexes is selected. Another thing to observe is that the content of this tab is also DBMS specific so it changes depending on the database you are connected to. The Indexes/Keys tab in Figure 4-24 shows a connection to a SQL Server database.

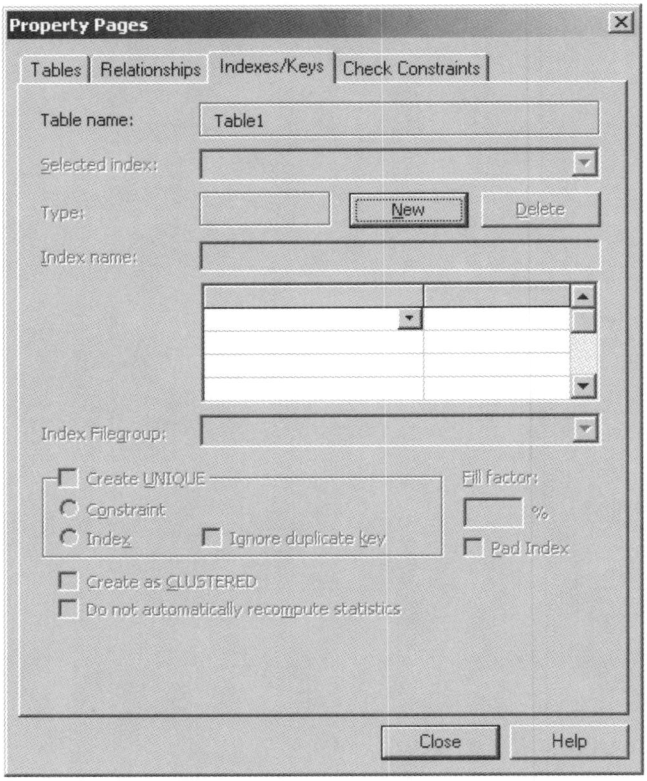

Figure 4-24. The Indexes/Keys tab of the Property Pages dialog box

To create a new index, you click on the New button. This enables some of the text boxes and check boxes on the tab. Start out by giving your index a name in the Index name text box, and then add the columns that make up the index in the grid below the Index name text box. For each column you add to the grid, you must specify if the sorting order is ascending or descending. This obviously depends on the data in the index and how it will be searched. The other options shown in Figure 4-24 are SQL Server specific, and I recommend you read the help files for SQL Server, if you are in doubt about these options. Once you click Close the index is saved. Well, this is not quite true, as it is only saved to memory. This means the index will not be saved to the database until you save the diagram. Just to avoid confusion any more than necessary, only the primary key is designated as a key. So if you want to add a foreign key to use in a relationship, you just add an index to the column(s) in question.

Adding Constraints

Sometimes the values in a particular column in your table must be in a particular range. If so, it is a good idea to create a constraint that will enforce your rules, or ensure that the values are indeed within the required range. You can create a constraint by right-clicking anywhere on the table grid in the Table Designer and selecting Check Constraints from the pop-up menu. This brings up the Property Pages dialog box with the Check Constraints tab shown (see Figure 4-25).

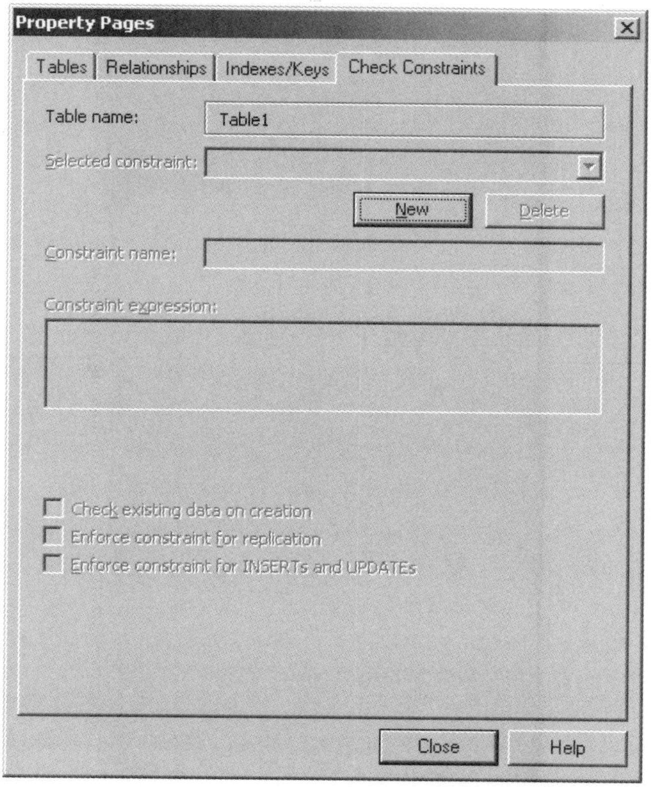

Figure 4-25. The Check Constraints tab of the Property Pages dialog box

To create a new constraint, click on the New button. This enables some of the text boxes and check boxes on the tab. Start out by giving your constraint a name in the Constraint name text box, and then type the constraint expression in the Constraint expression text box. Here's an example of a constraint:

```
Test <> ''
```

This means the field Test cannot hold an empty string. Following is a description of the check box options on the tab:

- *Check existing data on creation:* When the table is saved, any existing data is validated to see if it conflicts with the constraint. Unlike an index, it is possible to have values in a table that do not conform to a column constraint.

- *Enforce constraint for replication:* This option enforces the constraint when the table is replicated to another database.

- *Enforce constraint for INSERTs and UPDATEs:* This option enforces the constraint when data is inserted or updated. This means that an insert or update will fail if it does not conform to the constraint.

The constraint is saved to memory when you click Close.

Creating a Relationship

Although the Table Designer should be the preferred tool for creating a table, it is not the easiest way to create a relationship. Once you have created your tables using the Table Designer, you should open up a database diagram and use the Database Designer to create your relationships. For information on how to do this, see "Adding Relationships" earlier in this chapter.

Designing Queries with the Query Designer

The Query Designer is to queries what the Table Designer is to tables, a visual tool that makes it easy to create your queries. This should be your preferred tool for creating even the simplest of queries, because it has drag-and-drop features as well as a text pane in which you can type in your query manually. Here is how you create a simple select query (if you are uncertain on how to perform the following tasks, please see "Adding New Database Objects" earlier in this chapter):

1. Open up the UserMan DB Project if it isn't already open in the IDE.

2. Add a new query named Select Users.

3. Add the tblUser table to the query.

The Query Designer should now look like Figure 4-26. The top part where the table is placed is called the Diagram pane. The part beneath this is called the Grid pane, followed by a pane displaying free text, which is called the SQL pane. The Results pane resides in the bottom part of the designer.

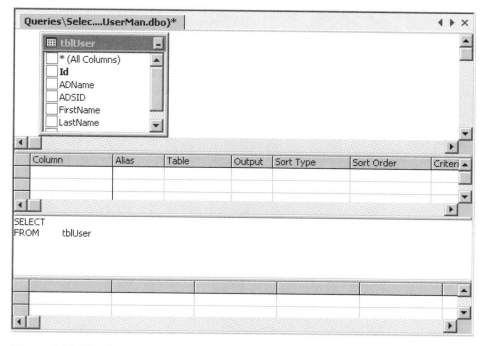

Figure 4-26. The Query Designer

Taking a Closer Look at the Query Designer Panes

As mentioned in the preceding section, there are four panes in the Query Designer:

- Diagram pane

- Grid pane

- SQL pane

- Results pane

These panes all have a function to perform, but with the exception of the Results pane, they overlap in functionality. Actually, the Diagram, Grid, and SQL panes do more than just overlap in functionality; they perform the very same function, and if you look at the other two panes when you edit one pane, you will find that these three panes stay synchronized. I guess it is really a matter of preference which pane you use. See the following sections on what each of the panes can do for you.

The Diagram Pane

The Diagram pane, which is the top part of the Query Designer, is where you add and show the tables used in the query. You can add tables by dragging them from the Server Explorer, or by right-clicking anywhere in the Diagram pane and selecting Add Table from the pop-up menu. For each table in the Diagram pane, you can select which columns are part of the query. This is done by checking the check box next to the column name. If you want all rows output, simply check the option * (All Columns). You can also right-click on the table, click on Select All Columns, and toggle the check marks by pressing the Space key.

> **NOTE** *If you check all the columns in a table as well as the option * (All Columns), you will get all the rows as output of your query twice.*

Removing Tables

Right-click on a table and select Remove from the pop-up menu to remove the table from the Diagram pane. The number of tables allowed in the Diagram pane depends on the query type. SELECT, Make Table and INSERT Results queries can hold any number of tables, whereas the UPDATE, DELETE and INSERT VALUES queries can only hold one table. If the tables in the Diagram pane are related or if there are relationships between any two of the tables, they are shown on the Diagram. However, you cannot change or delete the relationships in the Query Designer. Actually this is not quite true. If any two tables have an inner or outer join, and you remove this join from the Diagram pane, the join is changed to a cross join. A cross join outputs all selected columns from the tables in question in all possible combinations. In other words, you cannot delete a join between two tables using the Diagram pane. You only change the join in the Diagram pane and not the database itself. You need to use the Table Designer or the Database Designer if you want to change a relationship between two tables.

Changing the Join Type

You can also change the join type by right-clicking on the join and selecting Property Pages from the pop-up menu. In the Property Pages dialog box you can change the join to include all rows from one or both of the joined tables or simply just the selected columns in the tables. The types of joins available are LEFT OUTER JOIN, RIGHT OUTER JOIN, FULL OUTER JOIN, and INNER JOIN. In addition, you can change the way the tables are joined by changing the column comparison symbol to one of the following: = (equal to), <> (not equal to), < (less than), <= (less than or equal to), > (greater than), or >= (greater than or equal to). I am of course talking about the column in each table that is used for joining the tables. When the Property Pages dialog box is not shown, you can see from the join itself how the tables are joined. In the middle you can see the comparison sign, and if the join is an OUTER JOIN, a box is added to the diamond shape. See Figure 4-27 for examples of the various combinations of diamond and rectangle shapes that represent joins.

Figure 4-27. Various joins depicted in the Diagram pane

The four join shapes in Figure 4-27 depict the following, from left to right:

- FULL OUTER JOIN, joining columns not equal

- FULL OUTER JOIN, joining columns equal

- LEFT OUTER JOIN, joining columns equal

- INNER JOIN, joining columns equal

If you have many tables in the Diagram pane, then you can choose to show only the name of a table and thus save some real estate onscreen for more tables. This is done by right-clicking the table and selecting Name Only from the pop-up menu. Right-click on the table and click Column Names to show the full table again.

Grouping and Sorting the Output

The output can be sorted (ordered) and grouped as in any normal SQL statement using the Diagram pane. Sorting the columns is done by right-clicking the column in a table and selecting Sort Ascending or Sort Descending. A sort symbol is placed next to the column name when you want output sorted by a specific column. You can cancel the sorting by right-clicking on the column in the table and clicking the checked sort order.

Grouping is done nearly the same way as sorting, except you need to click on the Group By button on the Query toolbar first. In Figure 4-28 the Group By button is the second from the right. Once the Group By button is pressed, you can select the columns you want to group by. When a column is part of the output grouping, a grouping symbol like the one the Group By button displays is placed to the far right of the column name. You can remove grouping by pressing the Group By button again. Please note that the grouping is done in the order you select the columns. As in any SQL query, at least all output columns must be part of the grouping.

Figure 4-28. The Query toolbar

If you are in doubt about how to create a SQL statement in the SQL pane, then using the Diagram pane is a good way to learn, because you can see what effect a change in the Diagram pane has on the corresponding SQL statement in the SQL pane.

The Grid Pane

Recall that the Grid pane allows you to make the same changes as the Diagram pane and the SQL pane. However, there is one difference to the Grid pane: You cannot add tables to it. So in order to add tables to the query, you must use the functionality of the Diagram pane or the SQL pane. Okay, when I say the functionality isn't there, I mean there is no pop-up menu with an Add Table command for the Grid pane, but you can actually use the Add Table command on the Query menu to add a table.

> **NOTE** *When you enter data in the various columns, the data is validated, or verified, as soon as you move to another row or column.*

The Grid pane holds a number of named columns (what a surprise, eh?), and in Table 4-2 you can see a description of each these named columns. Please note that not all columns are visible for all the different query types. Check the Valid Query Types column to see if the column is valid for a particular query.

Table 4-2. Grid Pane Columns Explained

COLUMN NAME	VALID QUERY TYPES	DESCRIPTION
Column	All query types	This is the name of the column in the table referenced in the Table column.
Alias	SELECT, INSERT Results, and Make Table	If you give a column an alias, the alias is what the output column will be named. Use the Alias column to give your output a more descriptive name. Aliases are also used for computed columns. This is the same as the AS SQL clause in the SQL pane.
Table	SELECT, INSERT Results, UPDATE, DELETE, and Make Table	This is where you select the name of the table into which your column is placed. You can only select tables from the drop-down list. If you need to add more tables, use the Add Table command on the Query menu. If the column is computed, this column should be left blank.
Output	SELECT, INSERT Results, and Make Table	This column indicates if the column is to be output as part of the result.
Sort Type	SELECT, INSERT Results, and Make Table	If you leave this column empty, the output is not sorted. To specify a sort order, choose Ascending or Descending from the drop-down list. This is the same as the ORDER BY clause in the SQL pane, ASC for ascending or DESC for descending.
Sort Order	SELECT, INSERT Results, and Make Table	This is where you specify in which order the columns are sorted, if you want to sort by more than one column. The columns will be sorted first by the column starting with 1, and then by the column with number 2, and so on. This is the same as the list of columns following the ORDER BY clause in the SQL pane.
Group By	SELECT, INSERT Results, and Make Table	This is the same as the GROUP BY clause in the SQL pane.
Criteria	SELECT, INSERT Results, UPDATE, DELETE, and Make Table	You don't specify the column name, because you add the criteria to the row with the correct table column. If you need to add more than one criteria using the Or operator, you put each criteria in a separate Or. . . column. If you need to add criteria using the And operator, you do it the same column, like this: > 1 AND < 5. This means that the result set will hold rows where the column (indicated in the Column Name column) is greater than 1 and less than 5.
Or. . .	SELECT, INSERT Results, UPDATE, DELETE, and Make Table	This is for adding more than one criterion. You just keep adding one criterion in each of the Or. . . columns until you have added all your criteria.

Table 4-2. Grid Pane Columns Explained (continued)

COLUMN NAME	VALID QUERY TYPES	DESCRIPTION
Append	INSERT Results	This is for appending the results of a row-returning query to an existing table. The result value in Column column is appended to the column named in the Append column in the destination table. Normally this column is filled out by the Query Designer, if it is able to figure out what destination column matches the source column (Column).
New Value	UPDATE and INSERT VALUES	This dictates the new value for the column specified in the Column column. The new value can be an expression that will be evaluated or a literal value.

If you are in doubt about how to create a SQL statement in the SQL pane, then the Grid pane is a good way to learn, because you can see what effect a change in the Grid pane has on the corresponding SQL statement in the SQL pane. Live and learn.

The SQL Pane

The SQL pane is for entering your queries in free text based on the SQL standard for the database to which you are connected. Most relational databases these days rely on the ANSI SQL standard as the base with added functionality. I am not going into details about the SQL standards, as that is a subject for a whole book on its own. If you need specifics on one dialect of a SQL standard, I can only recommend you read the help files and/or documentation that comes with your database, or alternatively buy yourself a copy of a book that covers the subject.

You can do anything in the SQL pane that you can do in the Grid and Diagram panes. One major difference though is that you need to verify the SQL syntax before these other two panes are updated based on the contents of the SQL pane. (See "Verifying the SQL Syntax" later in this chapter for details.) Actually, you can also move to either the Diagram or Grid pane in order to accomplish an update of these panes, but it is not verified as such. You can type the name of an invalid column in a SELECT statement, and this will be shown in the Grid pane. So use the Verify SQL Syntax function frequently when you are editing your queries using the SQL pane. It will save you a lot of hassle.

The Results Pane

The Results pane is quite different from the other three panes in the Query Designer, because it is not intended for editing your query. As the name implies, it is simply an output window. The Results pane is only for row-returning queries, such as SELECT queries and scalar queries with aggregate functions like SELECT COUNT(*) FROM TableName.

In the case of a row-returning query, if such a query has returned rows from a single table, it is actually possible to use the Results pane to add new rows to the source table. If you are familiar with MS Access, then you probably recognize the grid in the Results pane, and you also know that you can add a new row by typing the column values in the last row in the grid (the one marked with an asterisk). If you want to edit the values returned by the query, you can do so by typing the new value in the desired column. Once you have typed in the column values, you simply move to another row, and the Query Designer will try to update the database immediately. If an error occurs when updating, a message box will be displayed, detailing the error. Once you click OK, the cursor is placed in the row in the grid where the error occurred.

Hiding and Showing the Various Panes

All the panes can be hidden, but at least one of the panes has to be visible when the Query Designer is shown. A pane can be hidden by right-clicking on the pane and selecting Hide Pane from the pop-up menu. Actually, you can also hide the panes using the Query toolbar shown in Figure 4-28, which appears by default when you open the Query Designer. The first four buttons from the left on the toolbar are for hiding and showing the Query Designer Panes. The tool tips help you figure out which button does what; to view a tool tip, position the mouse pointer over a button and keep it there for a little while. These buttons are the only way you can show a pane once it is hidden—you cannot use a command on a pop-up menu to show a pane as you can to hide it.

Verifying the SQL Syntax

If you want to make sure that your query is valid, you can use the Verify SQL Syntax function. This is only necessary if you are using the SQL pane to edit your query, as the other panes automatically verify your changes. You can perform the task by clicking on the Verify SQL Syntax button on the Query toolbar or by clicking on Verify SQL Syntax on the Query menu. Alternatively, you can right-click on the SQL pane and select Verify SQL Syntax from the pop-up menu. A message box appears when the query has been validated. It simply tells you that your query is valid or that your query needs to be changed according to the explanation shown in the message box. If your query is invalid, click the Help button in the message box to get a detailed explanation of the problem.

Executing a Query

When you have finished building your query, you might want to execute it. You can execute, or run, your query by clicking the Run Query button on the Query toolbar, by clicking on the Run command on the Query menu, or by right-clicking on a blank space in the Diagram pane and selecting Run from the pop-up menu.

> **WARNING**   *Queries cannot be undone, so if you are deleting rows from one or more tables, make sure they are expendable!*

The query will not execute if the SQL syntax in the SQL pane is invalid. If you are uncertain if your query is correct, then try verifying the syntax before you run the query. See "Verifying the SQL Syntax" earlier in this chapter for details.

Examining the Various Query Types

By default the query created is a SELECT query, but you can change the query type by clicking on the Change Type button on the Query toolbar. You can also change the query type using the Change Type command on the Query menu. In the following sections you will find a short description and example (in the form of SQL statement queries) of all the query types offered by the IDE. Here's a list of them:

- SELECT

- UPDATE

- DELETE

- Make Table

- INSERT

SELECT Query

The SELECT query is always used for returning rows from one or more tables in the database. Sometimes the SELECT statement is combined with or part of an

INSERT query to append the result to an existing table (INSERT Results query) or add the result to a new table (Make Table query, covered shortly).

This is the SELECT query in its very simplest form: SELECT * FROM tblUser. This query returns all rows in the tblUser table. All columns (*) are output.

UPDATE Query

The UPDATE query is for updating column values in specific rows in the destination table. The query UPDATE tblUser SET FirstName='Peter' updates all rows in the tblUser table and sets the FirstName column to "Peter". If you only want to update specific rows, you need to include the WHERE clause, like this:

```
UPDATE tblUser SET FirstName='Peter' WHERE FirstName='John'
```

This will only update the rows where the FirstName column holds the value "John". If you need to update more than one column in each row that matches the criteria in the WHERE clause, you can separate the columns with a comma, like this:

```
UPDATE tblUser SET FirstName='Peter', LastName='Johnson' WHERE FirstName='John'
```

You can only update rows in one table at a time.

DELETE Query

If you want to delete certain rows from a table, this is your best choice. The DELETE query is quite simple and here is an example: DELETE FROM tblUser. This will delete all rows in the tblUser table. As with the update query, you can select which rows to delete using the WHERE clause, like this:

```
DELETE tblUser WHERE FirstName='John'
```

This will delete all rows where the FirstName column holds the value "John". You can only delete rows from one table at a time.

Make Table Query

The Make Table query is actually a little more complex than the name implies. Although a table is created when you use this query, it also selects some rows that are inserted into the new table. The INTO keyword in the following example is what makes the difference; it creates a new table and copies all the rows from the tblUser into the new table (tblTest).

```
SELECT * INTO tblTest FROM tblUser
```

As you can see from the example, the SELECT statement is used for retrieving the rows from the tblUser table that are inserted into the new tblTest table. An error occurs if tblTest already exists in the database. If you need to append the result to an existing table, you need to use an INSERT Results query.

The Make Table query is very good for copying certain rows and/or columns from a source database into a temporary table, where you can manipulate it without messing up the "real" data. It can also be used for backing up data from one or more tables and then restoring it later on.

You can only create one table at a time.

INSERT Queries

There are actually two INSERT queries, one for inserting the result of a row-returning query into another table and one for inserting values into a table.

INSERT Results Query

The INSERT Results query is for appending rows to an existing table. If you need to add rows to a new table, then you must use the Make Table query. The INSERT Results query is structured like this:

```
INSERT INTO tblUser (LoginName, FirstName, LastName, Password) _
SELECT LoginName, FirstName, LastName, Password FROM tblTest
```

In this query I retrieve the columns LoginName, FirstName, and LastName from the table tblTest, and I append it to the tblUser table. The column names in the source table tblTest do NOT have to be same as in the destination table tblUser, but the order of which the columns appear obviously matters.

You can retrieve rows from as many tables as you like, as long as the number of columns match the number of columns in the destination table. There is always only one destination table.

INSERT VALUES Query

The INSERT VALUES query is quite similar to the UPDATE query in the way the SQL statement is constructed:

```
INSERT INTO tblUser (LoginName,FirstName, LastName, Password) _
 VALUES('peterj', 'Peter', 'Johnson', 'password')
```

This query will insert an arrow into the tblUser table with the values "peterj," "Peter," "Johnson," "password" for the columns LoginName, FirstName, LastName, and Password. The order of the values (VALUES) must match how the columns, specified in the first set of parentheses, are ordered. You can leave out the field names and the parentheses after the table name, if you specify values for all the columns in the order in which they appear in the database.

> **NOTE**   *You can only insert one row into the destination table at a time.*

Script Editing Using the SQL Editor

The SQL Editor is a text editor, and it is the same editor that is used for writing your VB code. This means it has the same facilities as the code editor, such as color coding and line numbering. However, there is no IntelliSense! You can change the default behavior of the editor by opening up the Options dialog box, by clicking Options on the Tools menu. See Figure 4-29 for a view of the Options dialog box with the Text Editor node expanded.

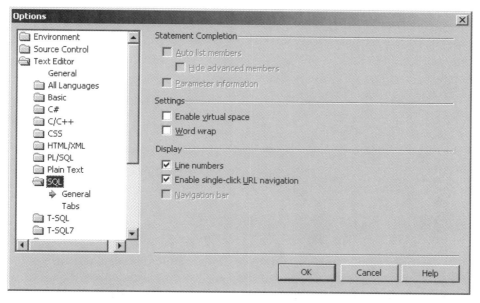

Figure 4-29. The Options dialog box with the Text Editor node expanded

As you can see from Figure 4-29, there are several options available for customization for different SQL dialects such as PL/SQL (Oracle) and various versions of T-SQL (Microsoft SQL Server). There are also some options under the Database Tools node that are relevant to the SQL Editor.

EXERCISE

Add a Create Table Script in the Create Scripts folder named *Create SQL Server Table*. See "Adding New Database Objects" for more information on how to add new database objects to your database project. Once the script has been created, it should look like Figure 4-30.

```
 1   IF EXISTS (SELECT * FROM sysobjects WHERE type = 'U' AND name = 'Table_Name')
 2      BEGIN
 3         PRINT 'Dropping Table Table_Name'
 4         DROP  Table Table_Name
 5      END
 6   GO
 7
 8   /*******************************************************************************
 9   **      File:
10   **      Name: Table_Name
11   **      Desc:
12   **
13   **      This template can be customized:
14   **
15   **
16   **      Auth:
17   **      Date: |
18   ********************************************************************************
19   **      Change History
20   ********************************************************************************
21   **      Date:    Author:          Description:
```

Figure 4-30. The SQL Editor with the Create SQL Server Table script open

EXERCISE

Use the Replace functionality (Ctrl+H) of the Text Editor to replace all occurrences of the string *Table_Name* with *tblTest*. After the starting parentheses, " (", below the CREATE TABLE statement, and before the closing parentheses, ")", type in the following text: **Id int PRIMARY KEY NOT NULL IDENTITY, Test varchar(50) DEFAULT('Test').**

Using the Query Editor to Produce SQL Statements

If you are like me, you cannot remember the syntax for all the various SQL statements there are, but instead of looking it up in the help files for your database, you can use the Query Editor for this purpose. You can access the Query Editor without leaving the SQL Editor by right-clicking anywhere in the SQL Editor and selecting Insert SQL from the pop-up menu. This brings up the Query Editor, or rather the Query Builder as it is called when invoked from within the SQL Editor.

I believe I said that you can right-click anywhere in the SQL Editor to bring up the Query Builder, but perhaps I should point out that the text generated using the Query Builder is placed where you right-click in order to select the Insert SQL command. So make sure that you place the mouse cursor where you want the SQL text inserted before you right-click. When you are done using the Query Builder, close the window and you will be prompted to save the content. Click Yes if you want the generated text inserted into your script or click No, if you don't want to save the text. If you click No, the generated text is discarded, and you cannot retrieve it again! See "Designing Queries with the Query Designer" earlier in this chapter for information on using the Query Editor/Query Builder.

Saving a Script

Once you are done editing your script, or even better, once you have done some work you don't want to lose due to unforeseen circumstances, you should save your script. This is as easy as pressing Ctrl+S. You can also access the save functionality using the menus. Select the Save Create Scripts\Create SQL Server Table.sql command on the File menu. This menu command is obviously dynamically created, so if you called your script something different, then the menu command looks different.

EXERCISE

Save your script.

Editing and Using Script Templates

I have chosen to create a script for MS SQL Server simply because the default template is the SQL Server one. You can change the templates by editing them using any text editor that can save in plain text, such as NotePad. The templates are located in the C:\Program Files\Microsoft Visual Studio.NET\Common7\Tools\Templates\Database Project Items folder. If you placed Visual Studio.NET on a different drive and/or in a different folder when you ran Setup, you obviously need to change the path to the templates accordingly.

Running SQL Scripts

When you have created your script, you can run the script by right-clicking on it in the Solution Explorer and selecting Run On from the pop-up menu. Select the desired database connection or reference from the Run On dialog box and click OK. The script now runs against the selected database connection.

This is a nice little improvement over previous versions of MS Visual Database Tools where you had to explicitly assign a connection to a script. Now you can assign a connection to a script before running it. Mind you, not all scripts are compatible with any database connection or reference.

Okay, this is actually not the only way to run a script. If you have a script open in the SQL Editor, you can right-click anywhere in the editor and select Run from the pop-up menu. If you haven't saved the changes to your script, you will be prompted to do so before the script is run.

When the script is running, all output from the script is being printed in the output window, which is located just below the SQL Editor by default. It is always a good idea to examine the output to see if the script was executed correctly.

Creating Typed Data Sets

If you want to work with typed data sets, you have to create the typed data set manually or at least with the help of some tools (see Chapter 3B for an explanation of typed versus untyped data sets). You cannot create a typed data set from code!

There are a number of steps required in order to generate a typed data set:

1. Get or create the schema.

2. Generate the data set class.

3. Create an instance of the newly generated and derived data set class.

What you can interpret from the preceding steps is that a typed data set is really nothing more than a class that wraps the data access and provides you with strong typing, or the IntelliSense feature and compile time syntax checking, and so on.

There are three tools (actually only two, because the DataSet Designer and the XML Designer are really the same) you can use to create a typed data set:

- Component Designer

- DataSet Designer

- XML Designer

I will not be covering how to do create a typed data set in the Component Designer.

Using the XML Designer to Create a Typed Data Set

Although you can use the XML Designer to create a schema, it is easier to use the DataSet Designer. The DataSet Designer is really the XML Designer with a little extra functionality added, so do yourself a favor and use the DataSet Designer. Because most of the functionality is duplicated in the XML Designer and the DataSet Designer, I will only cover how to use the DataSet Designer to create your typed data sets.

Using the DataSet Designer to Create a Typed Data Set

You can actually use the DataSet Designer to create a new schema from scratch and thus also use it to create a new table or even a new database. I am not going to go through that particular task in this book, but instead I will concentrate on creating a schema based on an existing table.

EXERCISE

Open the Typed DataSet Project located in the Chapter 4 folder.

If you have a project open that is NOT a database project, you can add a new data set if you right-click on the project in the Solution Explorer and select the Add New Item command from the Add submenu. In the Add New Item dialog box, select the DataSet template and give the data set a name before you click Open.

Open the UserManDataSet.xsd Schema and make sure you have it open in Schema view and not XML view. You can change views by clicking the tabs at the bottom of the UserManDataSet.xsd window. See Figure 4-31.

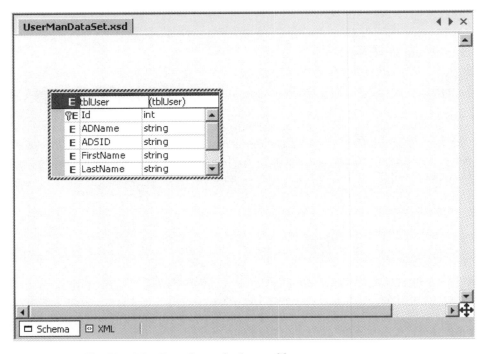

Figure 4-31. The UserManDataSet.xsd schema file

Open the Server Explorer, expand the UserMan database node and the Tables node, and drag the tblUserRights table over the DataSet Designer window and drop it. Now you have two tables in the DataSet Designer window. You need to give this new table a name, and I suggest you use its original name, *tblUserRights*. This is done by clicking the textbox next to the capital *E* in the header of the new table. Delete the current text and type in the new name. Click anywhere else on the DataSet Designer to save the name in memory. Press Ctrl+S to save the schema file to disk. Now you need to build the data set, or rather the Visual Basic DataSet class file. This is done by pressing Ctrl+Shift+B, which starts the build process. Now you have created a typed data set!

> **WARNING** *The DataSet class file is not visible in the Solution Explorer, and you should not edit this file, although it is accessible in the same folder as the schema file. Any changes will be overwritten the next time you build your solution!*

The code in the Form1 Windows form class file obviously needs to be modified in order to use the new typed table that I added. Take a quick look at the code to see how I use the strong typing in the button1_Click event.

Summary

This chapter took you on a journey through all the features of the IDE that are database related. I took a look at the Server Explorer, which holds server resources. The data connections and message queues were the ones specifically discussed. The exercises for this chapter took you through all the steps required to create a database project with database references, scripts, queries, and command files.

You saw how to use the Database Designer to create database diagrams and the Table Designer for creating tables with keys and indexes, constraints, and relationships. I dived into using the SQL Editor for creating scripts and stored procedures. Last but not least I demonstrated how to create a typed data set.

The next chapter demonstrates how to handle exceptions in your applications.

CHAPTER 5

Error Handling

ANY APPLICATION NEEDS to handle errors that occur at runtime. Unfortunately it can be difficult to resolve all the possible errors that can occur. However, it is always a good idea to try to create code that can resolve most errors, so that the user doesn't have to worry about them. You should then attempt to catch the rest of them and display an error message with detailed information to the user about how to continue from this point. The overall purpose of error handlers is to allow the program to gracefully recover from things going awry. This is especially important when dealing with relational databases. Since you are passing through multiple layers of technology, there are many places that an application can break. Although this chapter is about handling data-related exceptions, I will cover the basics for handling all kinds of exceptions briefly.

Now, let's get one thing straight before moving on: For the discussions in this chapter, errors and exceptions are the same. So from this point forward, I only use the word *exception*.

One question that I often hear is this: "Do I need exception handling in all my procedures?" My answer is always a firm *no*, because some procedures are so simple and they do not use variables that can overflow or something similar. These procedures might call a few other very simple procedures, and in such cases you know that no application exceptions will occur. Don't put an exception handler in these types of procedures—it's a waste! Obviously knowing when to use an exception handler is a matter of experience and perhaps preference, but if you are in doubt, just stick one in there! Once you are certain the exception handler is not needed, take it back out.

VB.NET has two programmatic ways of dealing with runtime exceptions: structured exception handling and unstructured exception handling.

Using Both Types of Exception Handling

Although it is possible to use both unstructured and structured exception handling, I recommend that you don't. It will only make your code more difficult to read, maintain, and debug. One thing to notice though is that a single procedure cannot contain both unstructured and structured exception handling. So if you are set on using both approaches, you can only use either (**XOr**) in a single procedure.

Structured Exception Handling

Structured exception handling works like this: It marks blocks of code as *protected*, which means that if any line of code within the block throws an exception, it will be caught by one of the associated exception handlers. The protected block of code is marked using the **Try. . .Catch** statements, and as such the protected code must be inserted between these statements. These statements are part of the **Try. . .Catch. . .Finally. . .End Try** construct. This gives you a control structure that monitors the code in the protected block, catches exceptions when they are thrown, and addresses these through a so-called filter handler. The control structure also separates the code that can be exceptional, er, I mean code that potentially throws exceptions from your "normal" code. I personally like this approach as I think it makes your code so much easier to read.

Listing 5-1 shows you how the **Try. . .Catch. . .Finally. . .End Try** construct is put together.

Listing 5-1. The Try. . .Catch. . .Finally. . .End Try *Construct*

```
' The Try statement on the next line starts the exception handler
Try
... ' This is the protected block of code
Catch
... ' This is where you place your exception handling code. Code that can
    ' resolve and recover from exceptions.
Finally
... ' This block of code is always executed
End Try
```

The **Try** and **End Try** statements, which don't take any arguments, are mandatory if you want to use structured exception handling. Besides those statements, you also need at least either of the **Catch** or **Finally** statements. Here is what the different code blocks do:

- *Try block:* This is where you place the lines of code you want to monitor, because they might throw an exception.

- *Catch block(s):* The **Catch** block is optional, although I don't quite see the point in leaving it out. You can have as many **Catch** blocks as you like, but the filter must be different. I'll get to the exception filtering in "Filtering Exceptions" later in this chapter. In these blocks you place your exception-handling code—code that can possibly resolve the exceptions and let execution continue without notifying a possible user. The **Catch** block is also called the fault handler.

- *Finally block:* The **Finally** block, which is optional, is where you put the lines of code that should run immediately after all exception processing has ended. You may be thinking, "Wait a minute, why not just place those lines of code after the **End Try** statement?" Well, my friend, you could do that, but it doesn't make your code easier to read does it? By placing it in the **Finally** block, you indicate that this code has something to do with the protected code in the **Try** block. Oh, I nearly forgot: If you place the code after the **End Try** statement, it won't be executed if there is an **Exit Sub** or **Exit Function** statement in the **Catch** block that processes the exception. Place the code in the **Finally** block and it will run. So any code that really needs to run, whether or not an exception is thrown in the **Try** block, goes here! The **Finally** block is also called the finally handler.

NOTE *There is NO performance penalty in placing code in the Try block, even if no exception is thrown.*

When you deal with protected blocks of code, there are three types of exception handlers:

- *Fault handler:* This is the same as the **Catch** block when no filter has been specified.

- *Filter handler:* The filter handler is the same as the **Catch** block when a filter has been specified. Actually, there are two types of filter handlers:

    Type-filter handler: This filter handler is used for handling exceptions of a specified class and any subclasses thereof.

    User-filter handler: The user-filter handler is used for handling exceptions of any exception class when you want to specify requirements for the exception. This is done using the **When** keyword.

- *Finally handler:* This is the same as the **Finally** block.

Enabling Structured Exception Handling

Well, perhaps the heading is inaccurate, because you don't really "enable" structured exception handling like you do unstructured exception handling. Instead you place the code you believe might throw an exception in a protected block, called the **Try** block. All code placed in this block is monitored, and any exceptions thrown are passed to the fault handler in your **Try**. . .**Catch**. . .**Finally**. . .**End**

Try construct. Please see the beginning of the section "Structured Exception Handling" earlier in this chapter for more information.

Separating an Exception Handler from Normal Code

This is one of the very neat things about the way structured exception handling is implemented in VB.NET. Whatever you do with your code, the exception handler is separated from your normal code automatically. All exception handling, including enabling exception handling, catching an exception, handling the exception, and finally running some cleanup code, is placed within the same **Try**. . .**Catch**. . .**Finally**. . .**End Try** construct. I think this makes your code so much easier to read compared with unstructured exception handling.

Having More Than One Structured Exception Handler in the Same Procedure

As with unstructured exception handling, it is possible to have more than one structured exception handler in the same procedure. You simply encapsulate your code in the **Try**. . .**Catch**. . .**Finally**. . .**End Try** construct wherever you feel the need. In many cases this is probably overkill, because it is possible to filter the various exceptions, determine the reason for the exception being thrown, and then recover from it, even if you have many lines of code in the **Try** block. I guess it is a matter of preference and making your code readable. Listing 5-2 shows you how two structured exception handlers can coexist in the same procedure.

Listing 5-2. Two Structured Exception Handlers in One Procedure

```
1 Public Sub TwoStructuredExceptionHandlers()
2    Dim lngResult As Long
3    Dim lngValue As Long = 0
4
5    Try ' First exception handler
6        lngResult = 8 / lngValue
7    Catch objFirst As Exception
8        MsgBox(objFirst.Message)
9    End Try
10
11   Try ' Second exception handler
12       lngResult = 8 / lngValue
13   Catch objSecond As Exception
14       MsgBox(objSecond.Source)
15   End Try
16 End Sub
```

There is no hocus-pocus to Listing 5-2; it is simply plain code that shows you how to include more than one structured exception handler in the same procedure.

Examining the Exception Class

The **Exception** class holds information about the last thrown exception. This is why it is usually a good idea to check the properties of this class when you catch an exception in your exception handler. Table 5-1 lists these properties.

Table 5-1. **Exception** *Class Properties*

NAME	DESCRIPTION
HelpLink	The **HelpLink** property returns or sets a link to the help file that is associated with the exception. The data type for this property is **String**, and it must be specified using a URL or a URN.
InnerException	This read-only property returns a reference to the inner exception. This property is often used when an exception handler catches a system exception and stores this information in the **InnerException** property in a new exception object. This new exception object is then used to throw a new exception, one that is user friendly. If the exception handler that catches the new exception wants to know the original exception, it can examine the **InnerException** property.
Message	This read-only property, which can be overridden, is of data type **String**. It returns the error message text that describes the exception in detail.
Source	The **Source** property returns or sets a **String** value that holds the name of the application or the object that threw the exception. If this property is not set, the returned value is a string holding the name of the assembly in which the exception was thrown.
StackTrace	This read-only property, which can be overridden, returns the stack trace. The stack trace pinpoints the location in your code where the exception was thrown, down to the exact line number. The returned value is data type **String**. The stack trace is captured immediately before an exception is thrown.
TargetSite	The **TargetSite** property is read-only and returns an object of data type **MethodBase**. The returned object contains the method that threw the exception. However, if the exception-throwing method is unavailable, the method is obtained from the stack trace. **Nothing** is returned if the method is unavailable and the stack trace is **Nothing**.

The **Exception** class also has the noninherited methods described in Table 5-2.

*Table 5-2. **Exception** Class Methods*

NAME	DESCRIPTION
GetBaseException()	This method returns a reference to the original exception that was thrown. The returned object is of type **Exception**.
GetObjectData(ByVal vobjInfo As SerializationInfo, ByVal vobjContext As StreamingContext)	The **GetObjectData** method sets vobjInfo with all the information about the thrown exception that must be serialized.

Handling Exceptions in the Exception Handler

Once you have enabled your exception handler, it is time to create some code that handles the exceptions when they are thrown. If you can resolve or recover from the exception, you can continue execution, and if not, you have to let the user know and/or perhaps log the exception.

The **Catch** block is where you deal with the thrown exceptions. In its simplest form, the **Catch** block is also called the fault handler. The simplest form is not to specify any filter and simply catch all exceptions, as shown in Listing 5-3.

Listing 5-3. The Catch **Block in Its Simplest Form, Fault Handler**

```
 1 Public Sub SimpleCatchBlock()
 2    Dim lngResult As Long
 3    Dim lngValue As Long = 0
 4
 5    Try
 6        lngResult = 8 / lngValue
 7    Catch
 8        MsgBox("Catch")
 9    End Try
10 End Sub
```

In Listing 5-3 there is only one **Catch** block, and it will receive all exceptions that are thrown in the **Try** block. The problem with this form is you have not specified that you want a copy of the **Exception** object. This means you don't have any access to the exception that was thrown. Well, this is not entirely true, because you can actually get hold of it from within the **Catch** block. Mind you, it is much easier to specify it as part of the **Catch** statement, as in Listing 5-4.

Listing 5-4. The `Catch` *Block with the Default Exception Object*

```
1 Public Sub CatchBlockWithDefaultExceptionObject()
2    Dim lngResult As Long
3    Dim lngValue As Long = 0
4    Dim objE As Exception
5
6    Try
7       lngResult = 8 / lngValue
8    Catch objE
9       MsgBox(objE.ToString)
10   End Try
11 End Sub
```

Listing 5-4 specifies that you want all exceptions and that you want the property values from the thrown exception stored in the `objE` variable. Actually, there is an easier way to do this. All you have to do is replace Line 8 in Listing 5-4 with this:

```
8    Catch objE As Exception
```

This will instantiate the `objE` variable as an object of type **Exception** and then store the values from the thrown exception in `objE`. If you want to specify exactly what kind of exception is handled by a particular **Catch** block, you need to filter the exceptions. See "Filtering Exceptions" later in this chapter for more information on how to filter exceptions.

> **NOTE** *If you have more than one **Catch** block in your exception handler, they will be tried one by one by the CLR when an exception is thrown from the code in the corresponding **Try** block. When I say tried, I mean that the various **Catch** statements will be examined in top-to-bottom fashion, as in a **Select Case** construct, and when a **Catch** statement matches the exception, this **Catch** block is executed. If none of the **Catch** statements match the exception, the CLR will display a standard message box to the user detailing the exception.*

Okay, once you've caught an exception, what do you do with it? In order to be able to recover from an exception, you need to know what kind of exception has been thrown. Table 5-3 shows a list of the standard exception types of interest that the CLR provides.

Table 5-3. Standard Exception Types

EXCEPTION TYPE	BASE TYPE	DESCRIPTION	EXAMPLE
Exception	**Object**	This is the base class for all exceptions. See "Examining the Exception Class" for more information.	See one of the subclasses for more information.
SystemException	**Exception**	The **SystemException** class is the base class for all exceptions thrown by the CLR. It is thrown by the CLR for exceptions that are recoverable by the user application, which means nonfatal exceptions.	See one of the subclasses for more information.
IndexOutOfRangeException	**SystemException**	This exception is thrown by the CLR when you try to access a nonexistent element in an array, meaning an element with an index that is out of bounds. This class cannot be inherited.	See Listing 5-5.
NullReferenceException	**SystemException**	The **NullReferenceException** exception is thrown by the CLR if you try to reference an invalid (Null) object. An invalid object has the value **Nothing**.	See Listing 5-6.
InvalidOperationException	**SystemException**	This exception is thrown by a method if the object that the method belongs to is in an invalid state.	See Listing 5-7.
ArgumentException	**SystemException**	This exception type is the base class for all argument exceptions. You should use one of the subclassed exceptions when throwing an exception if one exists.	See one of the subclasses for more information.
ArgumentNullException	**ArgumentException**	This exception is thrown by methods of an object when you supply a null value for an argument that doesn't allow the argument to be **Nothing**.	See Listing 5-8.
ArgumentOutOfRangeException	**ArgumentException**	The **ArgumentOutOfRangeException** is thrown by a method when one or more of the arguments is not within the valid range.	See Listing 5-9.

In Listing 5-5, I try to set the fourth element of the reference to the arrlngException array, but there are only three elements in the array, so an **IndexOutOfRangeException** exception is thrown.

Listing 5-5. Throwing an IndexOutOfRangeException ***Exception***

```
1 Public Sub ThrowIndexOutOfRangeException()
2    Dim arrlngException(2) As Long
3
4    Try
5        arrlngException(3) = 5
6    Catch objE As Exception
7        MsgBox(objE.ToString)
8    End Try
9 End Sub
```

In Listing 5-6 I try to reference the objException object, but this object hasn't been instantiated yet, so a **NullReferenceException** exception is thrown.

Listing 5-6. Throwing a NullReferenceException ***Exception***

```
1 Public Sub ThrowNullreferenceException()
2    Dim objException As Exception
3
4    Try
5        MsgBox(objException.Message)
6    Catch objE As Exception
7        MsgBox(objE.ToString)
8    End Try
9 End Sub
```

On Line 18 in Listing 5-7 I try to execute a non–row-returning query using the cmmUser command, but the command requires an open and ready connection. Because the connection (cnnUserMan) is busy serving the data reader while the data reader is open, an **InvalidOperationException** exception is thrown.

Listing 5-7. Throwing an InvalidOperationException ***Exception***

```
1 Public Sub ThrowInvalidOperationException()
2    Const strConnection As String = "Data Source=USERMANPC;" & _
3        "User ID=UserMan;Password=userman;Initial Catalog=UserMan"
4    Const strSQLUserSelect As String = "SELECT * FROM tblUser"
5    Dim cnnUserMan As SqlConnection
6    Dim cmmUser As SqlCommand
7    Dim drdUser As SqlDataReader
8
9    Try
```

```
10        ' Instantiate and open the connection
11        cnnUserMan = New SqlConnection(strConnection)
12        cnnUserMan.Open()
13        ' Instantiate command
14        cmmUser = New SqlCommand(strSQLUserSelect, cnnUserMan)
15        ' Instantiate and populate data reader
16        drdUser = cmmUser.ExecuteReader()
17        ' Execute query while data reader is open
18        cmmUser.ExecuteNonQuery()
19     Catch objE As Exception
20        MsgBox(objE.ToString)
21     End Try
22 End Sub
```

On Line 20 in Listing 5-8 I try to update the data source using the data adapter, but the data set supplied as the only argument has not been instantiated. Because the data set object is null (**Nothing**), an **ArgumentNullException** exception is thrown.

Listing 5-8. Throwing an ArgumentNullException ***Exception***

```
1 Public Sub ThrowArgumentNullException()
2    Const strConnection As String = "Data Source=USERMANPC;" & _
3       "User ID=UserMan;Password=userman;Initial Catalog=UserMan"
4    Const strSQLUserSelect As String = "SELECT * FROM tblUser"
5
6    Dim cnnUserMan As SqlConnection
7    Dim cmmUser As SqlCommand
8    Dim dstUser As DataSet
9    Dim dadUser As SqlDataAdapter
10
11   Try
12      ' Instantiate and open the connection
13      cnnUserMan = New SqlConnection(strConnection)
14      cnnUserMan.Open()
15      ' Instantiate command
16      cmmUser = New SqlCommand()
17      ' Instatiate data adapter
18      dadUser = New SqlDataAdapter(cmmUser)
19      ' Update data source
20      dadUser.Update(dstUser)
21   Catch objE As Exception
22      MsgBox(objE.ToString)
23   End Try
24 End Sub
```

In Listing 5-9, on Line 7, I try to display the first 200 characters from the connection string, but there aren't that many characters in the connection string, which is why an **ArgumentOutOfRangeException** exception is thrown.

Listing 5-9. Throwing an `ArgumentOutOfRangeException` ***Exception***

```
 1 Public Sub ThrowArgumentOutOfRangeException()
 2     Const strConnection As String = "Data Source=USERMANPC;" & _
 3      "User ID=UserMan;Password=userman;Initial Catalog=UserMan"
 4
 5     Try
 6        ' Display the first 200 chars from the connection string
 7        MsgBox(strConnection.Substring(1, 200))
 8     Catch objE As Exception
 9        MsgBox(objE.ToString)
10     End Try
11 End Sub
```

Now you know what kind of standard exceptions you can expect to catch. How do you deal with them in the **Catch** block? Well, it depends on what exception you're talking about and how you catch it. First of all you need to look at how you can filter the exceptions so that you make sure that the right **Catch** block handles the right exception. See the next section for more information.

Filtering Exceptions

When you set up your exception handler, it is always good to know what kind of exceptions you can expect, although this isn't always possible. However, depending on the code you put in the **Try** block, it can be quite easy to predict some of the possible exceptions that can be thrown. If you make a call to a method that takes one or more arguments, and the values you pass are variables, it is conceivable that one of the arguments is out of range or even set to **Nothing**. This will throw a standard exception, which you can handily filter using a type filter. Other times you might want to apply user-defined criteria when you are filtering your exceptions. In such cases you need to apply user filtering. Please note that both of these types of filtering can work together.

Type-Filtering Exceptions

Type filtering works by filtering the exceptions by type or class, to be technically correct. If you specify a class in a **Catch** statement, the Catch block will handle the class and all of its subclasses. See Listing 5-10 for an example code.

Listing 5-10. Type-Filtering Exceptions

```
1 Public Sub TypeFilterExceptions()
2    Dim arrlngException(2) As Long
3    Dim objException As Exception
4    Dim lngResult As Long
5    Dim lngValue As Long = 0
6
7    Try
8       arrlngException(3) = 5
9       MsgBox(objException.Message)
10      lngResult = 8 / lngValue
11   Catch objE As NullReferenceException
12      MsgBox("NullReferenceException")
13   Catch objE As IndexOutOfRangeException
14      MsgBox("IndexOutOfRangeException")
15   Catch objE As Exception
16      MsgBox("Exception")
17   End Try
18 End Sub
```

In Listing 5-10 there are three potential exceptions in the **Try** block. Only one of the lines of code will ever be executed, because the code will throw an exception and then you enter the exception handler. You need to comment out the lines of code you don't want to throw an exception, and then run the code.

However, Listing 5-10 shows you how to include more than one **Catch** block, and they each have a different task to do, or rather different types of exceptions to handle. When the first line of code (Line 8) in the **Try** block is executed, an exception is thrown. This means the CLR looks at the available handlers for this block of code. It starts with Line 11, but seeing there is no match between the exception that Line 8 throws (**IndexOutOfRangeException**), it then looks at Line 13, which is a match. As a result, a message box will appear displaying the message "IndexOutOfRangeException".

Notice that I have created a "generic" exception handler at the bottom of the example (Line 15) to catch any exceptions that haven't been caught by the other handlers. You don't have to do this and it isn't always appropriate to have one, but in some cases where you are uncertain about the exceptions that are thrown, it can be a good idea to have this catch-all handler. When it catches an unhandled exception, you can display a message to the user, log the exception, or whatever you fancy doing with it .

User-Filtering Exceptions

Type filtering is a very good way of filtering your exceptions, but sometimes it's just not enough. Imagine you are referencing two objects of the same data type and you know that they are sometimes null (Nothing). You can use a type filter on the exception, which will be a **NullReferenceException**, but how do you tell which of the two objects caused the exception to be thrown? Take a look at Listing 5-11.

Listing 5-11. User-Filtering Exceptions

```
1 Public Sub UserFilterExceptions()
2    Dim objException1 As New Exception()
3    Dim objException2 As Exception
4
5    Try
6      MsgBox(objException1.Message)
7      MsgBox(objException2.Message)
8    Catch objE As NullReferenceException When objException1 Is Nothing
9      MsgBox("objException NullReferenceException1")
10   Catch objE As NullReferenceException When objException2 Is Nothing
11     MsgBox("objException NullReferenceException2")
12   End Try
13 End Sub
```

Listing 5-11 contains two **Catch** blocks that filter on the same exception type, the **NullReferenceException**. Now, in order to know which object caused the exception to be thrown, I have added some user filtering after the type filtering. The **When** keyword specifies a user-defined criteria that must be met before this particular **Catch** block can handle the exception.

In this case, I simply check if the object has been instantiated. The user filter can be virtually any criteria.

Creating Your Own Exception

Sometimes it is necessary to create your own custom exception. Perhaps you are creating a class or component from which you want to throw a custom exception. In such cases you need to create a class that inherits from the **ApplicationException** class, which is the exception class thrown by user applications. Mind you, this is only true when a nonfatal exception is thrown (see Listing 5-12).

Listing 5-12. Creating Your Own Custom Exception Class

```
1 Public Class UserManException
2    Inherits ApplicationException
3
4    Private prstrSource As String = "UserManException"
5
6    Public Overrides ReadOnly Property Message() As String
7      Get
8        Message = "This exception was thrown because you..."
9      End Get
10   End Property
11
12   Public Overrides Property Source() As String
13     Get
14       Source = prstrSource
15     End Get
16
17     Set(ByVal Value As String)
18       prstrSource = Value
19     End Set
20   End Property
21 End Class
```

In Listing 5-12 you can see how to create your own custom exception classes. The sample code shown overrides two of the inherited properties; all other properties and methods are taken from the base class, the **ApplicationException** class. This is a very simple exception class, but it does show the basics for creating your own exception classes.

Throwing a Structured Exception

If you need to throw an exception, you can use the **Throw** statement for this very purpose. The **Throw** statement is quite often used for testing your exception handler using this format:

```
Throw expression
```

The required argument *expression* is the exception you want to throw. The following code will raise a new **IndexOutOfRangeException** exception:

```
Throw New IndexOutOfRangeException()
```

Now, throwing an exception is very easy, and as such it can be used for general communication. However, as the name suggests, exceptions are for exceptional circumstances. So don't use them for general communication purposes. It is guaranteed to confuse the heck out of whoever looks at your code. If you are dealing with classes, then simply create events to handle the communication with the client or use callbacks.

Exiting Structured Exception Handling

At times it can be desirable to exit the exception handler prematurely. This can be done using the **Exit Try** statement. The **Exit Try** statement works pretty much like all the other **Exit** statements in VB.NET: They all exit a structure of some kind.

- **Exit Sub**, **Exit Function**, or **Exit Property** exits and ends the current procedure.

- **Exit Do**, **Exit For**, and **Exit While** exits and ends a loop.

- **Exit Select** exits and ends a **Select Case** structure.

Okay, I think you get it. All these **Exit** statements exit a structure and execution continues on the line following the **End. . .** statement. In the case of an **Exit Try** statement, execution continues with the finally handler, if one exists, and then the first line of code following the **End Try** statement. **Exit Try** can be used in all the exception handler blocks except for the **Finally** block (see Listing 5-13).

Listing 5-13. Exiting a Structured Exception Handler
```
1 Public Sub ExitSEH()
2    Dim lngTest As Long = 1
3
4    Try
5        ' Check to avoid a division by zero exception
6        If lngTest = 0 Then Exit Try
7
8        lngTest = lngTest \ 0
9    Catch objException As Exception
10       MsgBox("This code is executed when an exception is thrown.")
11   Finally
12       MsgBox("This code is ALWAYS executed.")
13   End Try
14
15   MsgBox("This code is executed after the SEH ends.")
16 End Sub
```

In Listing 5-13 I have created some dummy code to demonstrate how to exit a structured exception handler. Line 6 tests if the lngTest variable is 0, and if it is the structured exception handler is exited. If the value of the lngTest variable is not changed before entering the structured exception handler, Line 8 will execute, because the variable holds the value 1. Actually, Line 8 may seem a bit silly, but I have put it there to explicitly throw a division by zero exception. This means only the **Catch** block will be executed.

Try running the code to see what messages are displayed. Then try changing the initial value of the lngTest variable to 0 and see what messages you get.

Recall that the **Exit Try** statement can be put in any of the blocks in the structured exception handler, except for the **Finally** block. If you try to put one in that block, your code won't compile. Now here is another scenario to consider: What happens when you put an **Exit Sub**, **Exit Function**, or **Exit Property** statement in the **Try** block or one of the **Catch** blocks? Well, obviously the execution of the procedure will end and execution will be passed back to the caller of the procedure. But what about the **Finally** block. Will it be executed? Try changing the **Exit Try** statement on Line 6 in Listing 5-13 to **Exit Sub**, setting the initial value of the **lngTest** variable to 0, and running the code again. I think you will find that the **Finally** block IS executed. There is your reason for putting code that must always run in the **Finally** block and not after the structured exception handler ends!

Handling Data-Related Exceptions

Now that I've covered the basics of structured exception handling, it's time to look at how you can use it with data-related exceptions. If you follow my earlier instructions on NOT putting too much code in the same protected block, it is actually quite easy to figure out which data-related procedure or object throws the exception.

Listing 5-14. Catch SqlConnection ***Class Exceptions***

```
1 Public Sub CatchSqlConnectionClassExceptions()
2    Const strConnection As String = "Data Source=USERMANPC;" & _
3     "User ID=UserMan;Password=userman;Initial Catalog=UserMan"
4    Const strSQLUserSelect As String = "SELECT * FROM tblUser"
5
6    Dim cnnUserMan As SqlConnection
7
8    Try
9       ' Instantiate the connection
10      cnnUserMan = New SqlConnection(strConnection & _
11       ";Connection Timeout=-1")
12   Catch objException As ArgumentException
```

```
13        If objException.TargetSite.Name = "SetConnectTimeout" Then
14            MsgBox(objException.StackTrace)
15        End If
16    End Try
17 End Sub
```

In Listing 5-14 I try to instantiate the **SqlConnection** with an invalid **Con-nection Timeout** value. This obviously throws an **ArgumentException**, which I can catch. Because I know that this kind of exception is fairly common and I know that other lines of code can throw it, I also check to see if it was a **Con-nection Timeout** exception (Line 13). Okay, I know the example is rather short, but I am sure you can see where I am heading with this. All the information you need is in the **Exception** object or a subclassed object, so you just have to dig it out!

It's all about filtering the exceptions, as I have shown earlier on in this chapter. I could go on in this chapter and show you how to catch and filter every method of every data-related class in ADO.NET, but why not just stick to a rule of thumb? What you do is look up a particular method and check what kind of exceptions it can throw. You set up your exception handler to filter those exceptions, and then you add some user filtering to the type filtering or if necessary perform an extra check on the **TargetSite.Name**. This will make sure you process an exception with the right exception handler!

CLR Handling of Structured Exceptions

If you have read the previous part of the chapter I am sure you have a pretty good idea of how the CLR handles exceptions, but here is a quick run-through of how it works.

First of all, the CLR uses protected blocks of code and exception objects to handle exceptions. If and when an exception is thrown, the CLR creates an exception object and fills it with information about the exception.

In every executable there is an information table for exceptions, and every method in the executable has an associated array in this information table. This array holds information about the exception handling, but it can be empty. Every element in this array has a description of a protected code block, all the exception filters that are associated with the code, and all the exception handlers.

Recall that the exception table is very efficient, and therefore it sacrifices neither processor time nor memory consumption. You obviously use more resources when an exception is thrown, but if no exception is thrown, the overhead is the same as with "normal" code.

So when an exception is thrown, the CLR starts the exception process. This two-step process begins with the CLR searching through the array. The CLR looks for the first protected block of code, which protects the currently executing line of code, and contains an exception handler and a filter that is associated with the exception.

The second step in this process depends on whether or not such a match is found. If a match is found, the CLR creates the exception object that describes the exception, and then executes all the finally and/or fault statements between the line of code where the exception was thrown and the statement that handles the exception. You must be aware that the order of the exception handlers is very important, because the innermost exception handler is always evaluated first.

If no match is found, the calling method is searched, and if no match is found there either, the CLR aborts the application after dumping the stack trace.

Unstructured Exception Handling

Unstructured exception handling is exactly what the name suggests, unstructured. Although you can organize it to look fairly nice and not make too many jumps in your code, it's still unstructured. Unstructured exception handling (UEH) should be well known to most Visual Basic programmers. Up until now, with the release of Visual Basic.NET, this has been the only built-in mechanism for trapping and handling runtime exceptions. Although you can continue to use unstructured exception handling in VB.NET, I can only recommend it as a means of upgrading old code. This is because unstructured exception handling easily results in code that can be extremely difficult to maintain not to mention debug. Whenever exception handling is discussed in this book, it is built using structured exception handling.

Enabling Unstructured Exception Handling

In order to enable unstructured exception handling, you must use the **On Error Goto *<Label>*** statement (see Listing 5-15) or the **On Error Goto *<LineNumber>*** statement (see Listing 5-16), where *<Label>* is a defined label in the current procedure and *<LineNumber>* is a line number in the current procedure.

Listing 5-15. Enabling Unstructured Exception Handling with a Label

```
1    Public Sub EnableUnstructuredExceptionHandling1()
2       ' Enable local exception handling
3       On Error Goto Err_EnableUnstructuredExceptionHandlingFromLabel
4
5       Exit Sub
6    Err_EnableUnstructuredExceptionHandlingFromLabel:
7    End Sub
```

In Listing 5-15, the line numbers shown are the ones displayed by the IDE, not line numbers supplied by the programmer.

Listing 5-16. Enabling Unstructured Exception Handling with a Line Number

```
1    Public Sub EnableUnstructuredExceptionHandling2()
2        ' Enable local exception handling
3        On Error Goto 5
4
5        Exit Sub
6 5:
7    End Sub
```

A compile-time error occurs if you have not defined the label in the current procedure or if the line number does not exist in the current procedure, as shown in Listings 5-15 and 5-16. Hence you cannot use either of the **On Error Goto <Label>** or **On Error Goto <LineNumber>** statements to jump to a different procedure.

> **NOTE** *When I talk about line numbers in this context, I'm not referring to the line numbers that the IDE visually displays. This is an optional feature of the text editor. I'm talking about the line numbers you can add yourself, like any other label. Basically the line number in this case is a label. You can see this from Listing 5-16, where the line number 5, shown in Line 6 of the example, has been typed in as a label with the name "5". (The colon after the name indicates a label.)*

As you can see from Listings 5-15 and 5-16, I have enabled the exception handler on the very first line in the procedure. This is NOT a requirement, but it is advisable to keep it near the beginning of the procedure. If you are one of those programmers that tend to have procedures made up of hundreds of lines of code, you might want to include more than one exception handler in the same procedure. Actually, I think you should break your procedure into smaller procedures if you do have procedures of that length!

Keep in mind that the exception handler is only active from the line where you enable it, meaning that any exception that occurs as a result of the code in your procedure, before the exception handler is enabled, will be trapped by the CLR, and you won't be able to respond to and/or resolve the exception.

Separating a Exception Handler from Normal Code

When you have an unstructured exception handler in your procedure, it is necessary to separate it from your normal code, because otherwise the exception handler code might be executed even if no exception was thrown. In Listings 5-15 and 5-16 I have separated the exception handler from the normal code by placing it at the end of the procedure and by adding the **Exit Sub** statement on the line before the exception handler label/line number. If I hadn't done that, the exception handler code would be executed with the normal code.

Having More Than One Unstructured Exception Handler in the Same Procedure

Since it is possible for you to have more than one unstructured exception handler in your code, it can quickly become a problem for the readability of your procedure (see Listing 5-17).

Listing 5-17. Two Unstructured Exception Handlers in the Same Procedure

```
1    Public Sub EnableUnstructuredExceptionHandling3()
2        ' Enable local exception handling 1
3        On Error Goto Err_EnableUnstructuredExceptionHandlingFromLabel1
4
5        ' Enable local exception handling 2
6        On Error Goto Err_EnableUnstructuredExceptionHandlingFromLabel2
7
8  Err_EnableUnstructuredExceptionHandlingFromLabel1:
9        Exit Sub
10 Err_EnableUnstructuredExceptionHandlingFromLabel2:
11     End Sub
```

Listing 5-17 contains two unstructured exception handlers, Err_EnableUnstructuredExceptionHandlingFromLabel1 and Err_EnableUnstructuredExceptionHandlingFromLabel2. When there is only one, it is advisable to place the label or line number that begins the exception handler after the last line of "normal" code, that is, non–exception-handling code. It makes your code easier to read, because it is out of the way and as such doesn't interfere with your normal code.

The problem with having more than one unstructured exception handler in the same procedure is the number of labels and where you need to place them. Listing 5-17 contains only two handlers, which I've placed at the end of the procedure in the order they are enabled in the procedure. I had to put an extra **Exit Sub** statement in the code, because otherwise the second exception handler will also be executed when the first exception handler is executed. My point is that even if you do have the label and the **Exit Sub** statements, your code gets more and more complicated to read the more exception handlers you add. I do realize this is a matter of opinion, but I fail to see why anyone would consider this approach easier to maintain than using structured exception handlers.

Another thing I mentioned is that unstructured exception handlers also make your code harder to debug, not for the CLR, but for you to step through the code. You will be branching to one label and back and then to another label and back. It's hard enough stepping through all your custom procedures, don't you think?

One last thing to notice about having more than one unstructured exception handler in your code is this: Only exceptions that are thrown from the code from the line where you enable the first exception handler until the line just before you enable the next exception handler will be handled by the first exception handler. In Listing 5-17 this means exceptions that are thrown on Line 4 will result in Line 9 being executed. If the exception is thrown on Line 7, execution will continue on Line 11. Now, consider what happens if you produce so-called spaghetti code and therefore jump from the second exception handler to code that is located within the block of code that is served by the first exception handler. Take a look at Listing 5-18 to discover the result.

Listing 5-18. Jumping from Code in One Exception Handler to Another

```
1    Public Sub EnableUnstructuredExceptionHandling4()
2        Dim intResult As Integer
3        Dim intValue As Integer
4
5        On Error Goto Err_EnableUnstructuredExceptionHandlingFromLabel1
6        Goto SecondExceptionHandlerBlock
7  FirstExceptionHandlerBlock:
8        intValue = 0
9        intResult = 9 / intValue
10
11       On Error Goto Err_EnableUnstructuredExceptionHandlingFromLabel2
12 SecondExceptionHandlerBlock:
13       intValue = 0
14       intResult = 9 / intValue
15
16       Exit Sub
17 Err_EnableUnstructuredExceptionHandlingFromLabel1:
18       MsgBox("Err_EnableUnstructuredExceptionHandlingFromLabel1")
19       Exit Sub
20 Err_EnableUnstructuredExceptionHandlingFromLabel2:
21       Goto FirstExceptionHandlerBlock
22   End Sub
```

In Listing 5-18, I enable two exception handlers (Lines 5 and 11). After enabling the `Err_EnableUnstructuredExceptionHandlingFromLabel1` exception handler, I jump to the `SecondExceptionHandlerBlock` label (Line 12), and within the block of code served by the `Err_EnableUnstructuredExceptionHandlingFrom-Label2` exception handler I throw an exception by dividing by 0 (Line 14). This means the CLR continues execution from the first line of code in the second error handler, which is Line 21. Now this line of code simply jumps to the `FirstExceptionHandlerBlock` label, which means that Lines 8 and 9 are executed. Line 9 throws an exception by dividing by 0. What happens then? Will the first or second exception handler be invoked? Try running this example code.

I wanted to make the following points by creating this messy example:

- Don't write spaghetti code with **GoTo** statements. These statements can easily be replaced by more naturally flowing code.

- Keep exception handling as simple as possible.

- Don't use unstructured exception handling. Use structured exception handling all the time.

Okay, the message box is actually displayed, which means that the CLR knows what lines of code belong to what exception handler. So even if a second exception handler has been enabled, executing lines of code served by the first exception handler will invoke the first exception handler and NOT the second. If you knew this already, good for you, but if not, did you guess right?

Using Parent Exception Handlers

If you have a procedure that enables an unstructured exception handler, the parent exception handler is the one that will be invoked. This is the case if any of the procedures you call within the block of code that is served by the exception handler throws an exception (see Listing 5-19).

Listing 5-19. Using Parent Exception Handers

```
1    Public Sub UsingParentExceptionHandling()
2        On Error Goto Err_EnableUnstructuredExceptionHandling
3
4        UsesParentExceptionHandling()
5
6        Exit Sub
7 Err_EnableUnstructuredExceptionHandling:
8        MsgBox("Err_EnableUnstructuredExceptionHandling")
9    End Sub
```

```
10
11     Public Sub UsesParentExceptionHandling()
12         Dim intResult As Integer
13         Dim intValue As Integer
14
15         intValue = 0
16         intResult = 9 / intValue
17     End Sub
```

Listing 5-19 enables the `Err_EnableUnstructuredExceptionHandling` exception handler on Line 2 in the `UsingParentExceptionHandling` procedure. Within the block of code that is served by this exception handler, the `UsesParentExceptionHandling` procedure is called, which does not enable any exception handlers. This means when Line 18 in this procedure is executed, an exception is thrown. Because this procedure does not have its own exception handler, the CLR looks to see if the calling procedure does have one, and it does indeed. As a result, this exception is called, which means that the message box containing the text "Err_EnableUnstructuredExceptionHandling" will appear.

Disabling Unstructured Exception Handling

If you want to disable exception handling in the current procedure, you can execute the **On Error Goto 0** statement. This disables all exception handlers in the current procedure. Please note that this statement does NOT tell the CLR to jump to a line with line number 0 if an exception is thrown. This is also true even if your procedure actually has a line with the number 0, as shown Line 11 in Listing 5-20.

Listing 5-20. Disabling Unstructured Exception Handling

```
1      Public Sub DisableUnstructuredExceptionHandling()
2          ' Enable structured exception handling
3          On Error Goto 5
4
5          ' Disable structured Exception handling
6          On Error Goto 0
7
8          Exit Sub
9  5:
10         Exit Sub
11 0:
12         MsgBox("Line Number 0 has been reached!")
13     End Sub
```

Disabling structured exception handling in one procedure like in Listing 5-20 also disables unstructured exception handling in general, not just in the procedure where you execute the **On Error Goto 0** statement. This means you will have to enable exception handling before any exceptions thrown are handed to your application and not handled by the CLR.

Disabling Unstructured, Local Exceptions

If you want to disable any exceptions thrown in a procedure, meaning the exceptions will be ignored, you can use the **On Error GoTo –1** statement. This instructs the CLR to ignore any exceptions in the current procedure and any procedures it might call that don't have an exception handler. The CLR does actually try to clean up after the exception, but it won't hand any exceptions to your application and it won't show a message box detailing the exception.

> **NOTE** *In line with the behavior of the **On Error GoTo 0** statement, the **On Error GoTo –1** statement does NOT tell the CLR to jump to the line with line number –1 if an exception is thrown. This is also true even if your procedure has a line with number –1. Please note that this is only valid for the current procedure, because as soon as the procedure ends, normal exception handling is turned back on.*

Ignoring Exceptions and Continuing Execution

Sometimes it can be a good idea to just ignore an error and continue execution without interruption, and the **On Error Resume Next** statement can help you do just that. If you place this statement in a procedure, execution will continue on the line following the one that caused the exception (see Listing 5-21).

Listing 5-21. Ignoring Exceptions

```
1 Public Sub IgnoreExceptions()
2    Dim intResult As Integer
3    Dim intValue As Integer
4
5    On Error Resume Next
6
7    ' Throw an exception
8    intValue = 0
9    intResult = 9 / intValue
10
11   MsgBox("Was an exception thrown?", MsgBoxStyle.Question)
12 End Sub
```

When an exception is thrown on Line 9 in Listing 5-21, execution will continue on Line 10 and thus the message box will be displayed. Because of this behavior you definitely want to make sure that any **On Error Resume Next** statements in your code are commented out, because otherwise you won't catch many exceptions!

One thing to notice about the **On Error Resume Next** statement is that it only applies to the procedure in which it is placed. If you call another procedure, this other procedure will not inherit the ignored behavior. If the called procedure enables an exception handler, this handler will catch any exceptions thrown in the called procedure. However, if the called procedure does not enable an exception handler, execution halts in the called procedure and the exception is propagated back to the calling procedure, where it is ignored.

Handling Exceptions in the Exception Handler

Once you have enabled your exception handler, it is time to create some code that handles the exceptions when they are thrown. If you can resolve an exception, you can continue execution and if not, you have to let the user know and perhaps log the exception.

If you can resolve the exception, you can use the **Resume** statement to continue execution from the line of code that threw the exception, and as a result this line will be executed again (see Listing 5-22).

Listing 5-22. Resolving Exceptions

```
1    Public Sub ResolveException()
2        On Error Goto Err_EnableUnstructuredExceptionHandling
3
4        Exit Sub
5 Err_EnableUnstructuredExceptionHandling:
6        ' Resolve exception
7        . . .
8
9        ' Continue execution by retrying the offending line of code
10       Resume
11   End Sub
```

Other times it is not feasible to continue execution from the line of code that threw the exception, but you have taken other actions in your exception handler and want execution to continue without executing the offending line of code. You can do this by using the **Resume Next** statement. It will start the execution from the line of code immediately following the offending line (see Listing 5-23).

Listing 5-23. Working around an Exception

```
1    Public Sub WorkingAroundAnException()
2        On Error Goto Err_EnableUnstructuredExceptionHandling
3
4        Exit Sub
5 Err_EnableUnstructuredExceptionHandling:
6        ' Take other actions to work around the exception
7        . . .
8
9        ' Continue execution from the following line
10       Resume Next
11   End Sub
```

One really important thing to know about the unstructured exception handler is that if a new exception is thrown by the code that is part of the exception handler, Lines 6 through 10 in Listing 5-23, the exception handler cannot handle the exception, and it is propagated back to the calling procedure. This can cause some unexpected results, so it is important that you construct your exception handler in a way that eliminates or at least minimizes the risk of throwing a new exception.

Examining the Err Object

The **Err** object holds information about the last occurring exception. This is why you should check the properties of this object whenever you catch an exception in your exception handler.

> **NOTE**   *The* **Err** *object can only be used to handle exceptions that have been caught using the* **On Error GoTo <Label>** *statement.*

Because the **Err** object is "flushed" every time a new exception is thrown, it is important that you save any information from this object that you want to hang on to. The **Err** object has the properties described in Table 5-4.

Table 5-4. **Err** *Object Properties*

NAME	DESCRIPTION
Description	This property returns or sets a **String** value that describes the exception that is thrown.
Erl	This property returns the line number on which the exception was thrown.
HelpContext	The **HelpContext** property is used to indicate a specific help topic in the file indicated by the **HelpFile** property. If both the **HelpFile** and the **HelpContext** properties are valid, or if both the help file exists and the topic exists in this help file, the help topic is shown.
HelpFile	The **HelpFile** property returns or sets the fully qualified path to a valid help file. This help file is shown when the user presses the F1 key on the keyboard or clicks the Help button when the error message dialog box is shown. You should use the **HelpFile** property in conjunction with the **HelpContext** property to make sure that a particular exception number points to the right help topic.
LastDLLError	This read-only property returns the system-generated exception that was thrown when you called a DLL. This property is only set when you call the DLL from within your VB code. System calls to DLLs that throw exceptions are not reflected in this property. The problem with this property is that it does NOT raise an exception when it is set. This means you should check this property immediately after making a call to a DLL in order to ensure you catch any exception thrown.
Number	The **Number** property is the default property of the **Err** object, and it returns or sets a numeric value that indicates the exception that is thrown.
Source	This property returns or sets a **String** value that indicates what object generated or threw the exception.

The **Err** object also has the following two noninherited methods described in Table 5-5.

*Table 5-5. **Err** Object Methods*

NAME	DESCRIPTION	EXAMPLE
Clear()	The **Clear** method is used for clearing the **Err** object, meaning all the properties are reset. This method is automatically invoked when any of the following statements are encountered: **Resume, Resume Next, Resume <LineNumber>, Exit Sub, Exit Function, Exit Property**, and all **On Error xxx** statements.	`Err.Clear()`
Raise(ByVal vintNumber As Integer, Optional ByVal vobjSource As Object = Nothing, Optional ByVal vobjDescription As Object = Nothing, Optional ByVal vobjHelpFile As Object = Nothing, Optional ByVal vobjHelpContext As Object = Nothing)	You use the **Raise** method to raise an exception in your application. This can be particularly helpful when you try to test your exception handler, or if you want to let a calling procedure know that something went wrong. All arguments except for `vintNumber` are optional. Check the corresponding properties for an explanation. Please note that if you don't set all the properties, and any of the properties you don't set already have a value, these values will be used as part of the exception you raise. Always use the **Clear** method and manually set the properties in order to make sure you don't raise an exception with invalid values.	`Err.Raise(vbObjectError + 9)`

The **Err** object is a global object, meaning you do not have to create an instance of it in order to use it. Simply call any of the properties or methods like this: `intExceptionNum = Err.Number` or `Err.Clear()`.

Raising an Unstructured Exception

If for some reason you want an exception thrown, you can use the **Raise** method of the **Err** object to do just this. Actually, the **Error** statement will also throw an exception, but this is an older statement and only supplied for backwards compatibility, so don't use it.

There are two main reasons for raising an exception: to test an exception handler and to notify the caller that an exception was thrown in your object. Whatever your reason, it is fairly simple to raise an exception.

Raising a System Exception

If you want to simulate a system exception, use one of the reserved numbers for system exceptions. This means that you have to call the **Raise** method with a number between 0 and 512, as shown in Listing 5-24.

Listing 5-24. Raising a System Exception

```
1 Public Sub RaiseSystemException(ByVal vintExceptionNum As Integer)
2    Err.Raise(vintExceptionNum)
3 End Sub
```

If you call the RaiseSystemException procedure with a vintExceptionNum argument value of 5, you will raise the dreaded "Invalid procedure call or argument" exception. This exception is usually caused when you pass an invalid number of arguments to a procedure. See your documentation for other system error numbers.

Raising a Valid User Exception

If you want to raise an exception that the receiving exception should recognize as user defined, you can add the value of the **vbObjectError** constant to your error number. This constant has a value of -2147221504, which makes it suitable for simulating a user exception when you raise an exception (see Listing 5-25).

Listing 5-25. Raising a User-Defined Exception

```
1 Public Sub RaiseUserException(ByVal vintExceptionNum As Integer)
2    Err.Raise(vbObjectError + vintExceptionNum)
3 End Sub
```

In Listing 5-25 you can call the RaiseUserException procedure with any number, even numbers that would normally overlap the system error numbers (0–512). This is because the **vbObjectError** constant is added to the passed value before the exception is raised. When you have raised an exception like this, and your own exception handler is set to handle the exception, it is important that you determine if the exception is a user-defined one or if it is a system exception. See the next section, "Determining if a User-Defined Exception Was Thrown," for information on how to do this.

Determining if a User-Defined Exception Was Thrown

So you have caught an exception in your exception handler. Now you need to know if it's a system exception (numbers 0 through 512) or if it's one of your own.

All you need to do is work backwards and subtract the **vbObjectError** constant from the **Number** property of the **Err** object (see Listing 5-26).

Listing 5-26. Determining a User-Defined Exception

```
1 Public Sub DetermineUserException(ByVal vlngExceptionNum As Long)
2    Dim lngExceptionNum As Long
3
4    lngExceptionNum = vlngExceptionNum - vbObjectError
5
6    ' Determine if this is a user-defined exception number
7    If lngExceptionNum > 0 And lngExceptionNum < 65535 Then
8       MsgBox("User-defined Exception")
9    Else
10      MsgBox("Visual Basic Exception")
11   End If
12 End Sub
```

Listing 5-26 saves the difference between the vlngExceptionNum argument value and the **vbObjectError** constant in the lngExceptionNum variable. Line 7 compares the saved value to see if it's in the range 0 through 65,535. If it is, then the exception number is user-defined; otherwise it is a Visual Basic system error.

Catching Exceptions That Occur in DLLs

When you call DLLs through an API call using the **Declare** statement, it is always a good idea to check if anything went wrong in the procedure you called. Because DLLs do not raise exceptions, you need to check the return value; if it's an unexpected value, you should check the **LastDLLError** property of the **Err** object. When I talk about DLLs in this context, I am referring to "plain-vanilla" DLLs, not ActiveX or COM DLLs.

Handling Data-Related Exceptions

Now that I've covered the basics of unstructured exception handling, it's time to look at how you can use this type of handling with data-related exceptions. Listing 5-27 shows an example.

Listing 5-27. Handling Data-Related Exceptions

```
1    Public Sub CatchOpenConnectionException()
2       Const strConnection As String = "Data Source=USERMANPC1;" & _
3          "User ID=UserMan;Password=userman;Initial Catalog=UserMan"
4
5       Dim cnnUserMan As SqlConnection
```

```
 6
 7        On Error Goto Err_EnableUnstructuredExceptionHandling
 8
 9        ' Instantiate and open the connection
10        cnnUserMan = New SqlConnection(strConnection)
11        cnnUserMan.Open()
12
13        Exit Sub
14 Err_EnableUnstructuredExceptionHandling:
15        MsgBox(Err.Description  & vbCrLf & Err.Erl & vbCrLf & Err.Number & _
16           vbCrLf & Err.Source)
17     End Sub
```

If you run the example code in Listing 5-27, you will see a message box that displays the following values:

Timeout expired	(Err.Description)
0	(Err.Erl)
5	(Err.Number)
SQL Server Managed Provider	(Err.Source)

If you look at these values, there isn't a single one of them that is unique. Any of these can be duplicated by a different exception, so it can be hard to resolve this exception. Listing 5-27 only instantiates and opens the connection, but in most procedures you would do at least a little more than that.

How are you going to determine what caused the exception when the property values of the **Err** object are not unique? Here are some potential answers:

- You can enable a new exception handler for every block of code that can be logically grouped (such as an object instantiation and opening).

- You can use the value from the **Erl** property. This way you know the exact offending line of code, assuming you have set up your code with line number labels.

- Check the **Number** property.

Okay, so what is wrong with these suggestions? Well, they would clutter your code and make it very hard to read. Using the **Erl** property would mean that you have to change the exception handler every time you add or remove a line in your procedure, and furthermore you have to have a line number label on at least every nonblank line. Finally, the **Number** property is NOT unique, meaning that quite a few exceptions will cause the **Number** property to be 5. (Refer back to Listing 5-25 and the text that explains this listing.)

Actually, if you are willing to add some extra code to your exception handler, you can determine what caused the exception, but my point here (again) is that it simply takes too much coding. So in this case you could combine the value of the **Source** and **Description** properties to determine the cause of the exception, but why?

Now, here's a little revelation: You can actually get the values from the **Exception** object as you can when you use structured exception handling. So why didn't I tell you this until now? Well, the way I see it, if you are going to use this new **Exception** object, which is much more detailed in its information than the **Err** object, why not go all the way and simply use structured exception handling? You will also get the benefit of having much more control over your exception handler and the exceptions. Do yourself a favor: Forget about unstructured exception handling!

Summary

This chapter has shown you how to use structured exception handling as well as unstructured exception handling. I also gave you some very clear advice on why you should leave the unstructured exception handling behind with your VB6-or-earlier–compatible code.

This chapter also discussed the following points:

- The **Err** object holds information about exceptions when you use the unstructured exception handling.

- If you use structured exception handling, you will be dealing with the **Exception** class, or subclasses thereof.

The next chapter will tell you how to deal with stored procedures, triggers, and views on the server. In other words, you will be shown how to process your data on the server, instead of letting the client do it. If you implement this correctly, it can lead to performance improvements.

CHAPTER 6

Using Stored Procedures, Views, and Triggers

How to use stored procedures, views, and triggers in SQL Server 2000

SERVER-SIDE PROCESSING, which is when you let a server process your queries and the like, is probably a concept you have heard of and is the very topic of this chapter—well, to some extent anyway. I will look into three specific ways of doing server-side processing: stored procedures, triggers, and views. The good thing about server-side processing is that you use the power and resources of your server for processing your queries and thus leave your client free to do other stuff. It's not always appropriate to do so, but in many cases you can benefit from it.

This chapter includes several hands-on exercises that will take you through creating stored procedures, views, and triggers. See the Exercise items that appear throughout the text.

Because this chapter primarily focuses on SQL Server 2000 features, some of the functionality can certainly be reproduced in MS Access and earlier versions of SQL Server. However, if you are unfamiliar with MS Access, I can recommend you read the following book to get you up to speed: *From Access to SQL Server*, by Russell Sinclair, ISBN: 1-893115-240.

Optimization Issues

When I talk about optimizing performance of an application, there are a number of things to consider, but let's just make one thing clear before I go on: I am only talking distributed applications and not stand-alone applications that sit nicely on a single, possibly disconnected, PC. These stand-alone applications are also called single-tier or monolithic applications. The applications I discuss here use a network of some sort to access data and business services.

Okay, now that the basics are out of the way, I can focus on the obstacles that can lead to decreasing performance and how you need to know these obstacles well when you start the optimization process. You should keep such obstacles in mind when you design your application. However, the various resources, such as network bandwidth, processor power, available RAM, and so on, most often change over time, and then you will have to consider whether your application also needs changing.

Table 6-1 lists all the varying factors that can influence the performance of your application, which could be a topic for an entire book. However, although I only describe these factors briefly, I want you to be aware of the resources mentioned; they have great influence on what server-side processing resources you should choose when you design your application.

Table 6-1. Performance Resources Optimization

RESOURCE NAME	DESCRIPTION
Network resources	When speaking of network resources, I am referring to the actual bandwidth of the network. Consider your network setup—whether you are on a LAN or you are accessing resources over a WAN such as the Internet, and so on. If you have a low bandwidth, it is obvious that you want to transfer as little data across the network as possible. If on the other hand you have plenty of bandwidth, you might want to transfer large amounts of data across the network. However, best practices prescribe that you only transfer the data needed across your network, even when you have wide bandwidth.
Local processing resources	If you have the raw power available on your local box, it can be good to do most of the data processing there. Mind you, it all depends on the available bandwidth and the processing resources on the server.
Server processing resources	Server-side processing is desirable, if the server has resources to do so. Another thing you should consider is if it has the resources to serve all your clients, if you let the server do some of the data processing.

Table 6-1 just provides a quick overview. Table 6-2 shows you some different application scenarios.

Table 6-2. Different Application Scenarios

CLIENT MACHINE	SERVER	NETWORK	RECOMMENDATION
Limited processing resources	Plenty of processing resources	Limited bandwidth	Now, this one is obvious. You should use the raw processing power of the server to process your queries and the like and only return the requested data. This will save resources on the network and on the client, but it limits your application's scalability.
Plenty of processing resources	Plenty of processing resources	Limited bandwidth	Hmm, processing could be done on either the client or the server, but it really depends on the amount of data you need to move across the network. If it's a limited amount of data, processing on either side will do, but if it's a lot of data, then let the server do the processing. Another solution could be to store the data locally and then use replication or batch processing to update the server.
Plenty of processing resources	Limited processing resources	Limited bandwidth	In this case, processing should be done on the client, but it really depends on the amount of data you need to move across the network. If it's a limited amount of data, the client should do the processing; but if it's a lot of data, you might consider letting the server do some of the processing.
Plenty of processing resources	Limited processing resources	Plenty of bandwidth	Okay, don't think too hard about this one—processing should be done on the client.

I could add plenty of other scenarios to the list, but I think you get the picture. You'll rarely encounter a situation that matches a straight-forward scenario with a simple answer. It's your job to know about all the potential issues when you design your application and have to decide on where to process your data.

Now, I am going to cover stored procedures, views, and triggers. Let's get started!

Using Stored Procedures

A *stored procedure* (SP) is a precompiled batch of SQL statements that is stored on the database server. Stored procedures have long been a good way of letting the server process your data. They can significantly reduce the workload on the client, and once you get to know them you'll wonder how you ever managed without them.

There is certainly more to a stored procedure than just mentioned, but I do think this is the most significant function of a stored procedure. Think about it: It's a way of grouping a batch of SQL statements, storing it on the database server, and executing it with a single call. The fact that the stored procedure is precompiled will save you time as well when executed. Furthermore, the stored procedure can be executed by any number of users, meaning you will really save a lot of bandwidth just by calling the stored procedure instead of sending the whole SQL statement every time.

A stored procedure can contain any SQL statement that your database server can understand. This means you can use stored procedures for various tasks, such as making queries—both so-called action queries, such as DELETE queries, and row-returning queries, such as **SELECT** statements.

Another task you can use a stored procedure for is database maintenance. Use it to run cleanup SQL statements when the server is least busy and thus save the time and effort of having to do this manually. I will not be covering maintenance tasks in this chapter, but they are important, and you should be aware of the various tasks you can perform with stored procedures. If you are like me, you have been or are working for a small company that does not have a DB admin, in which case you're in charge of keeping the database server running. Granted, it's not an ideal situation, but you certainly get to know your DBMS in different ways than you would just being a programmer, and that's not bad at all.

To sum it up: A stored procedure is a precompiled SQL statement or batch of SQL statements that is stored on the database server. All processing takes place on the server, and any result is then returned to the client.

Why Use a Stored Procedure?

You should use a stored procedure in the following cases (please note that other cases do apply, depending on your circumstances):

- Executing one or more related SQL statements on a regular basis

- Returning the result of your SQL statements because you have a very limited bandwidth on your network

- Delegating data processing to the server because you have very limited processing resources on your client

- Using a number of different clients to execute a batch of SQL statements on a regular basis

Granted, there can be substantially more work in setting up a stored procedure, but my experience has confirmed that the extra work saves you at least tenfold the time once you start coding and using you application.

One last thing I want to mention is the fact that if you base a lot of your data calls on stored procedures, it can be a lot easier to change the data calls at a later date. You can simply change the SP and not the application itself, meaning you don't have to recompile a business service or even your client application, depending on how you have designed your application. On the negative side, stored procedures are often written using database-vendor-specific SQL extensions, which mean that they are hard to migrate to a different RDBMS. This of course is only a real concern if you are planning to move to another RDBMS.

Creating a Stored Procedure

Creating a stored procedure is fairly easy. You might be used to working with the Server Manager, which comes with SQL Server, but if so you may want to check out the facilities in the Server Explorer in the VS.NET IDE. Amongst other things, it is much easier to run and test an SP directly from the text editor. Anyway, here is how you would create a stored procedure for the example UserMan database:

1. Open up the Server Explorer window.

2. Expand the UserMan database on your database server.

3. Right-click on the Stored Procedures node and select New Stored Procedure.

This brings up the Stored Procedure text editor, which incidentally looks a lot like your VB.NET code editor. Except for syntax checking and other minor stuff, they are exactly the same (see Figure 6-1).

```
vb  dbo.StoredPro...ANPC.UserMan}*                          ◀ ▶ ✕
     1   CREATE PROCEDURE dbo.StoredProcedure1
     2   /*
     3      (
     4          @parameter1 datatype = default value,
     5          @parameter2 datatype OUTPUT
     6      )
     7   */
     8   AS
     9      /* SET NOCOUNT ON */
    10      RETURN
    11
```

Figure 6-1. Stored procedure editor with default template

Creating a Simple Stored Procedure

Once you've created a stored procedure, you need to give it a name. As you can
see from your SP editor, the template automatically names it StoredProcedure1.
If you are wondering about the dbo prefix, it simply means that the SP is created
for the dbo user. In SQL Server terms, dbo stands for DataBase Owner. If you have
been working with SQL Server for a while, you probably know the term *broken
ownership chain*. An ownership chain refers to a stored procedure that is
dependent on other database objects such as tables, or other views or
stored procedures.

Generally, the objects that a view or stored procedure depend on are also
owned by the owner of the view or stored procedure. In such a situation there are
no problems, because SQL Server doesn't check permissions when this is the
case. However, when one or more of the dependent database objects are owned
by a user different from the one owning the view or stored procedure, the ownership chain is said to be broken. This means SQL Server has to check the
permissions of any dependent database object that has a different owner. This
can be avoided, if all of your database objects are owned by the same user, such
as dbo. I am not telling you to necessarily take this approach, but it is one option
available to you.

Okay, let's say you've deleted the StoredProcedure1 name and replaced it with SimpleStoredProcedure. To save the SP before continuing, press Ctrl+S. If you saved your stored procedure at this point, you would notice that you don't have to name it using a Save As dialog box, because you have already named it. The editor will make sure that the SP is saved on the database server with the name you've entered, which in this case is SimpleStoredProcedure.

As soon as you have saved it, the very first line of the SP changes. The SQL statement **CREATE PROCEDURE** is changed so that the first line reads:

```
ALTER PROCEDURE dbo.SimpleStoredProcedure
```

Why? Well, you just saved the newly created SP, which means that you can't create another with the same name. Changing **CREATE** to **ALTER** takes care of this—it's that simple. In case you're wondering what happens when you change the name of your SP and the SQL statement still reads **ALTER PROCEDURE. . .**, I can tell you the editor takes care of it for you and creates a new procedure. Try it and see for yourself!

The SimpleStoredProcedure doesn't actually do a lot, does it? Okay, let me show you how to change that. In Figure 6-1, you can see two parts of the SP: The first part is the header and then there is the actual SP itself. The header consists of all text down to and including Line 7. Basically the header declares how the SP should be called, how many arguments to include and what type of arguments, and so on. Since this is a very simple procedure, I don't want any arguments, so I will leave the commented-out text alone.

If you haven't changed the default editor settings, text that is commented out or any comments you have inserted yourself are printed in green. In a SQL Server SP, comments are marked using start and end tags: /* for the comment start tag and */ for the comment end tag. This has one advantage over the way you insert comments in your VB code, because you don't have to have a comment start tag on every line you want to comment out. You only need to have both a start and end tag.

The second part of the SP is the part that starts with the **AS** clause on Line 8. The **AS** clause indicates that the text that follows is the body of the SP, the instructions on what to do when the SP is called and executed.

Create a stored procedure, name it SimpleStoredProcedure, and save it as described earlier. Type the following text on Line 10 in the SimpleStoredProcedure in place of the **RETURN** statement:

```
SELECT COUNT(*) FROM tblUser
```

Now the stored procedure should look like the example in Figure 6-2. The stored procedure will return the number of rows in the tblUser table.

Don't forget to save the changes using Ctrl+S.

```
vb   dbo.SimpleSt...ANPC.UserMan)*                              ◄ ► ✕
      1   ALTER PROCEDURE dbo.SimpleStoredProcedure
      2   /*
      3       (
      4           @parameter1 datatype = default value,
      5           @parameter2 datatype OUTPUT
      6       )
      7   */
      8   AS
      9       /* SET NOCOUNT ON */
     10   SELECT COUNT(*) FROM tblUser
     11
```

Figure 6-2. Stored procedure that returns the number of rows in the tblUser table

Running a Simple Stored Procedure from the IDE

Of course, there's no point in having a stored procedure that just sits there, so here's what you do to run it: If you have the SP open in the SP editor window, you can right-click anywhere in the editor window and select Run Stored Procedure from the pop-up menu. If you do this with the stored procedure you created in the exercise in the previous section, the Output window, located just below editor window, should display output from the SP as shown in Figure 6-3.

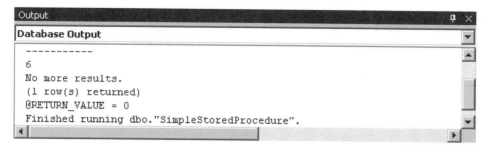

Figure 6-3. Output window with output from SimpleStoredProcedure

If you have closed down the SP editor window, you can run the SP from the Server Explorer. Expand the database node, right-click on the Stored Procedures node, and select Run Stored Procedure from the pop-up menu. This will execute the stored procedure the exact same way as if you were running it from the editor window.

Running a Simple Stored Procedure from Code

Okay, now that you have a fully functional SP, you can try and run it from code. Listing 6-1 shows you some very simple code that will run the SP.

Listing 6-1. Running a Simple Stored Procedure

```
1 Public Sub ExecuteSimpleSP()
2    Const STR_CONNECTION As String = "Data Source=USERMANPC;" & _
3      "User ID=UserMan;Password=userman;Initial Catalog=UserMan"
4
5    Dim cnnUserMan As SqlConnection
6    Dim cmmUser As SqlCommand
7    Dim lngNumUsers As Long
8
9    ' Instantiate and open the connection
10   cnnUserMan = New SqlConnection(STR_CONNECTION)
11   cnnUserMan.Open()
12
13   ' Instantiate and initialize command
14   cmmUser = New SqlCommand("SimpleStoredProcedure", cnnUserMan)
15   cmmUser.CommandType = CommandType.StoredProcedure
16
17   ' Save result
18   lngNumUsers = cmmUser.ExecuteScalar()
19 End Sub
```

The code in Listing 6-1 retrieves the return value from the SP. Now, this is really not a task you want to use a stored procedure for, but it demonstrates what a simple SP looks like. The SP itself could just as well have had a DELETE FROM tblUser WHERE LastName='Johnson'" SQL statement. If you were to execute this from code, you have to notice if the SP returns a value or not. It doesn't in this case, so you need to use the **ExecuteNonQuery** method of the **SqlCommand** class.

EXERCISE

Create a new stored procedure and save it with the name uspGetUsers. Type in the following text on Line 10 in place of the **RETURN** statement:

```
SELECT * FROM tblUser
```

Now the stored procedure should look like the one in Figure 6-4. This stored procedure will return all rows in the tblUser table.

Don't forget to save the changes using Ctrl+S.

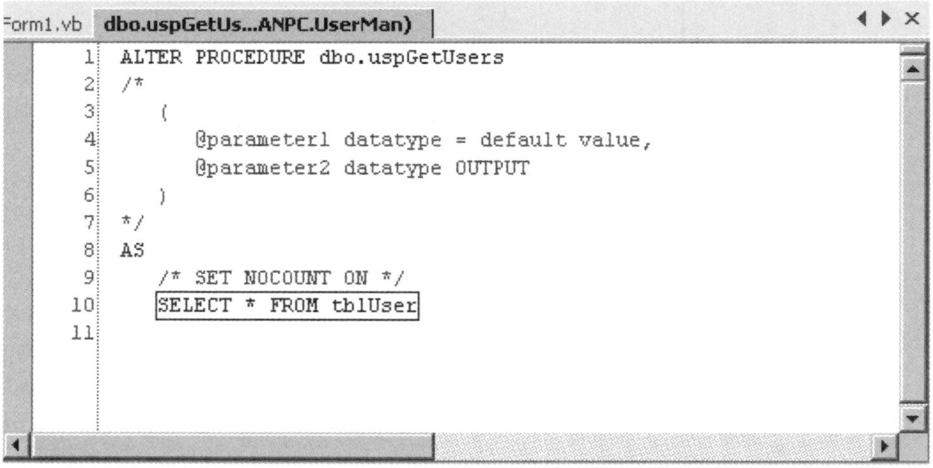

```
Form1.vb   dbo.uspGetUs...ANPC.UserMan)                          ◀ ▶ ✕
    1   ALTER PROCEDURE dbo.uspGetUsers
    2   /*
    3       (
    4           @parameter1 datatype = default value,
    5           @parameter2 datatype OUTPUT
    6       )
    7   */
    8   AS
    9       /* SET NOCOUNT ON */
   10      SELECT * FROM tblUser
   11
```

Figure 6-4. The uspGetUsers stored procedure

What you need now is some code to retrieve the rows from the SP (see Listing 6-2).

Listing 6-2. Retrieving Rows from a Stored Procedure

```
1 Public Sub ExecuteSimpleRowReturningSP()
2    Const STR_CONNECTION As String = "Data Source=USERMANPC;" & _
3      "User ID=UserMan;Password=userman;Initial Catalog=UserMan"
4
5    Dim cnnUserMan As SqlConnection
6    Dim cmmUser As SqlCommand
7    Dim drdUser As SqlDataReader
8
9    ' Instantiate and open the connection
10   cnnUserMan = New SqlConnection(STR_CONNECTION)
11   cnnUserMan.Open()
12
13   ' Instantiate and initialize command
14   cmmUser = New SqlCommand("uspGetUsers", cnnUserMan)
15   cmmUser.CommandType = CommandType.StoredProcedure
16
17   ' Retrieve all user rows
18   drdUser = cmmUser.ExecuteReader()
19 End Sub
```

The example in Listing 6-2 retrieves the rows returned from the SP by using the **ExecuteReader** method of the **SqlCommand** class. Please note that this is currently the only way to retrieve rows as the result of a function call with the command class.

Creating a Stored Procedure with Arguments

Sometimes it is a good idea to create a stored procedure with arguments instead of having more SPs essentially doing the same. It also gives you some flexibility with regards to making minor changes to your application without having to recompile one or more parts of it, because you can add to the number of arguments and keep existing applications running smoothly by specifying a default value for the new arguments.

Create a new stored procedure and save it with the name uspGetUsersByLastName. Type in the following text on Lines 10 and 11 in place of the **RETURN** statement:

```
SELECT * FROM tblUser
WHERE LastName = @strLastName
```

Uncomment Lines 2 to 7, and insert the following text instead of Lines 3 and 4:

```
@strLastName varchar(50)
```

The stored procedure should look like the one in Figure 6-5. This stored procedure will return all rows in the tblUser table where the LastName column matches the strLastName argument.

Don't forget to save your changes using Ctrl+S.

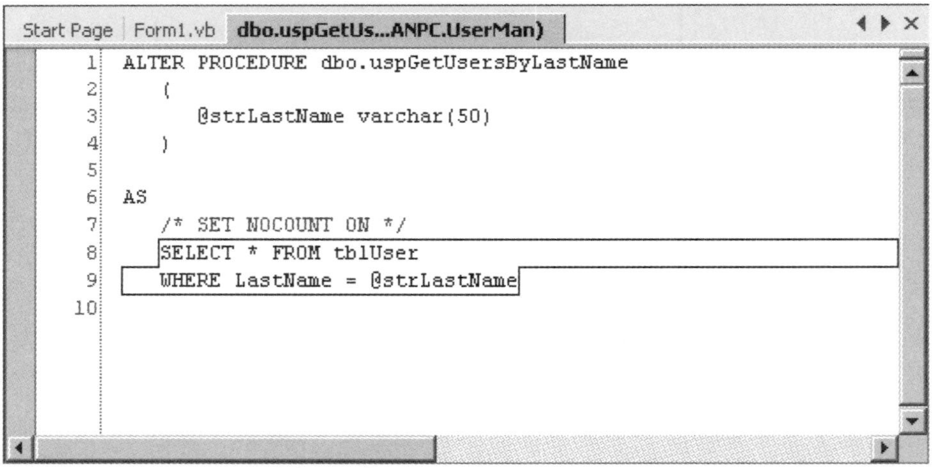

Figure 6-5. The uspGetUsersByLastName stored procedure

Arguments in stored procedures can be either input or output. If you include an input argument, you don't have to specify anything after the data type, but if you use an output argument, you need to specify the **OUTPUT** keyword after the data type.

> **NOTE** *I only cover the absolute basics of how to create a stored procedure in this chapter. If you need more information, I suggest you look up the* **CREATE PROCEDURE** *statement in the Books Online help application that comes with SQL Server.*

Running a Stored Procedure with Arguments from the IDE

Try and run the stored procedure you created in the last exercise and see how the argument affects how it is run. You can try running the SP from either the editor window or the Server Explorer window. The Run dialog box asks you for a value for the strLastName argument. Type **Doe** in the text box and click OK. Now all users with the last name of Doe are returned as the result of the SP.

Using a Stored Procedure with Arguments

The uspGetUsersByLastName stored procedure seems to work, so try and run it from code. Listing 6-3 shows how you would do this.

Listing 6-3. Retrieving Rows from a Stored Procedure with an Input Argument

```
1 Public Sub GetUsersByLastName()
2    Const STR_CONNECTION As String = "Data Source=USERMANPC;" & _
3      "User ID=UserMan;Password=userman;Initial Catalog=UserMan"
4
5    Dim cnnUserMan As SqlConnection
6    Dim cmmUser As SqlCommand
7    Dim drdUser As SqlDataReader
8    Dim prmLastName As SqlParameter
9
10   ' Instantiate and open the connection
11   cnnUserMan = New SqlConnection(STR_CONNECTION)
12   cnnUserMan.Open()
13
14   ' Instantiate and initialize command
15   cmmUser = New SqlCommand("uspGetUsersByLastName", cnnUserMan)
16   cmmUser.CommandType = CommandType.StoredProcedure
17   ' Instantiate, initialize and add parameter to command
18   prmLastName = cmmUser.Parameters.Add("@strLastName", _
19   SqlDbType.VarChar, 50)
20   ' Indicate this is an input parameter
```

```
21    prmLastName.Direction = ParameterDirection.Input
22   ' Set the value of the parameter
23   prmLastName.Value = "Doe"
24
25   ' Return all users with a last name of Doe
26   drdUser = cmmUser.ExecuteReader()
27 End Sub
```

In Listing 6-3 a **SqlParameter** object specifies the input parameter of the stored procedure. On Lines 18 and 19 I ask the command object to create and associate a parameter with the @strLastName argument. The value of this parameter is set to "Doe", which effectively means that only rows containing a last name of Doe are returned.

As you can see, I have specified that the parameter is an input argument using the **ParameterDirection** enum. Don't worry too much about parameter and argument; they are essentially the same thing.

Creating a Stored Procedure with Arguments and Return Values

So far I have created SPs that return a single value or a result set (rows) and a stored procedure that takes an input argument. In many cases this is all you want, but sometimes it's not enough. What if you want a value and a result set returned at the same time? Actually, you may want several values and a result set, but I'm sure you get the idea.

In such instances, you can use output arguments.

Actually, you can return as many different values and result sets as you want by including multiple **SELECT** statements after the **AS** clause, but I personally think this approach looks messy. If I return rows and one or more values, I generally use output arguments for the values. I guess this is a matter of preference.

Instead of using the following example code to return a scalar value, two result sets, and another scalar value in that order:

```
. . .
AS
   SELECT 19
   SELECT * FROM tblUser
   SELECT * FROM tblUserRights
   SELECT 21
```

I would use something like this:

```
. . .
AS
    SELECT * FROM tblUser
    SELECT * FROM tblUserRights
```

The two return values should then be returned as output arguments. But it's your call, my friend, as to which approach you prefer to use.

Create a new stored procedure and save it with the name uspGetUsersAndRights. This stored procedure should return the value 55 for the output argument lngNumRows, and then all rows in the tblUser table and all rows in the tblUserRights table.

The stored procedure should look like the one in Figure 6-6.

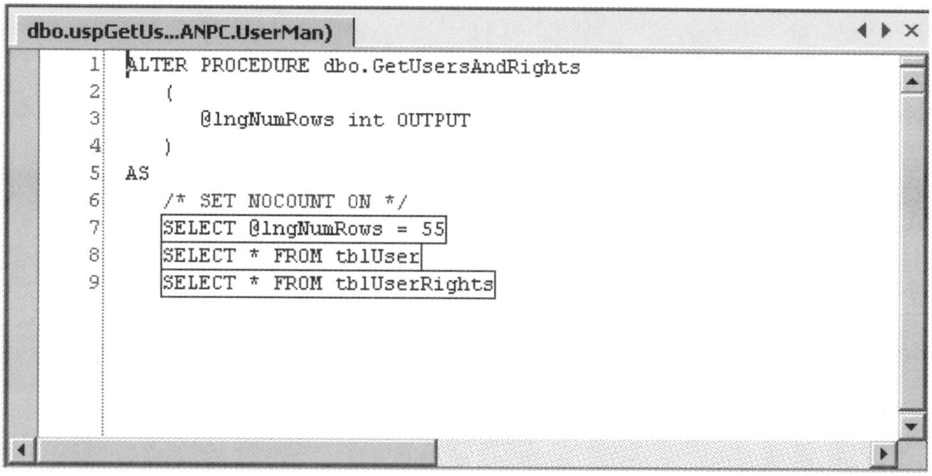

```
dbo.uspGetUs...ANPC.UserMan)                              ◀ ▶ ×
    1   ALTER PROCEDURE dbo.GetUsersAndRights
    2   (
    3        @lngNumRows int OUTPUT
    4   )
    5   AS
    6   /* SET NOCOUNT ON */
    7   SELECT @lngNumRows = 55
    8   SELECT * FROM tblUser
    9   SELECT * FROM tblUserRights
```

Figure 6-6. The uspGetUsersAndRights stored procedure

Running a Stored Procedure with Arguments and Return Values from the IDE

If you've created and saved the stored procedure in the previous exercise, test it by running it. You can try running the SP from either the editor window or the Server Explorer window. The Output window, located just below editor window, will display the output from the SP, and it should look similar to the output in Figure 6-7.

> **NOTE** *Syntax testing of your stored procedure is done when you save it, and I have a feeling you have already encountered this. If not, just know that's how it is—syntax errors are caught when you try to save your SP.*

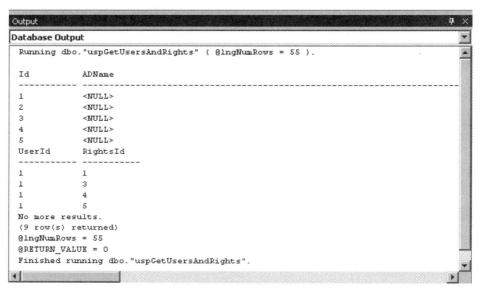

Figure 6-7. Output window with output from the uspGetUsersAndRights SP

Using a Stored Procedure with Arguments and Return Values

Listing 6-4 shows the code to execute the uspGetUsersAndRights SP.

Listing 6-4. Retrieving Rows and Output Values from a Stored Procedure

```
1 Public Sub GetUsersAndRights()
2    Const STR_CONNECTION As String = "Data Source=USERMANPC;" & _
3      "User ID=UserMan;Password=userman;Initial Catalog=UserMan"
4
5    Dim cnnUserMan As SqlConnection
6    Dim cmmUser As SqlCommand
7    Dim drdUser As SqlDataReader
8    Dim prmNumRows As SqlParameter
9
10    ' Instantiate and open the connection
11    cnnUserMan = New SqlConnection(STR_CONNECTION)
12    cnnUserMan.Open()
13
```

```
14    ' Instantiate and initialize command
15    cmmUser = New SqlCommand("uspGetUsersAndRights", cnnUserMan)
16    cmmUser.CommandType = CommandType.StoredProcedure
17    ' Instantiate, initialize and add parameter to command
18    prmNumRows = cmmUser.Parameters.Add("@lngNumRows", SqlDbType.Int)
19    ' Indicate this is an output parameter
20    prmNumRows.Direction = ParameterDirection.Output
21    ' Get first batch of rows (users)
22    drdUser = cmmUser.ExecuteReader()
23
24    ' Display the last name of all user rows
25    Do While drdUser.Read()
26       MsgBox(drdUser("LastName").ToString)
27    Loop
28
29    ' Get next batch of rows (user rights)
30    If drdUser.NextResult() Then
31       ' Display the id of all rights
32       Do While drdUser.Read()
33          MsgBox(drdUser("RightsId").ToString)
34       Loop
35    End If
36 End Sub
```

In Listing 6-4 two result sets are returned, and therefore I use the **NextResult** method of the data reader class to advance to the second result set on Line 30. Otherwise this stored procedure works pretty much the same as one with input parameters, although the parameter direction is specified as an output on Line 20.

Retrieving a Value Specified with RETURN

In a stored procedure you can use the **RETURN** statement to return a scalar value. However, this value cannot be retrieved using the **ExecuteScalar** method of the command class, as it would when you use the **SELECT** statement (refer back to Figure 6-2). Of course there is a way to retrieve this value, which I show you after the following exercise.

EXERCISE

Create a new stored procedure and save it with the name uspGetRETURN_VALUE. This stored procedure should return the value 55 as the RETURN_VALUE. The stored procedure should look like the one in Figure 6-8.

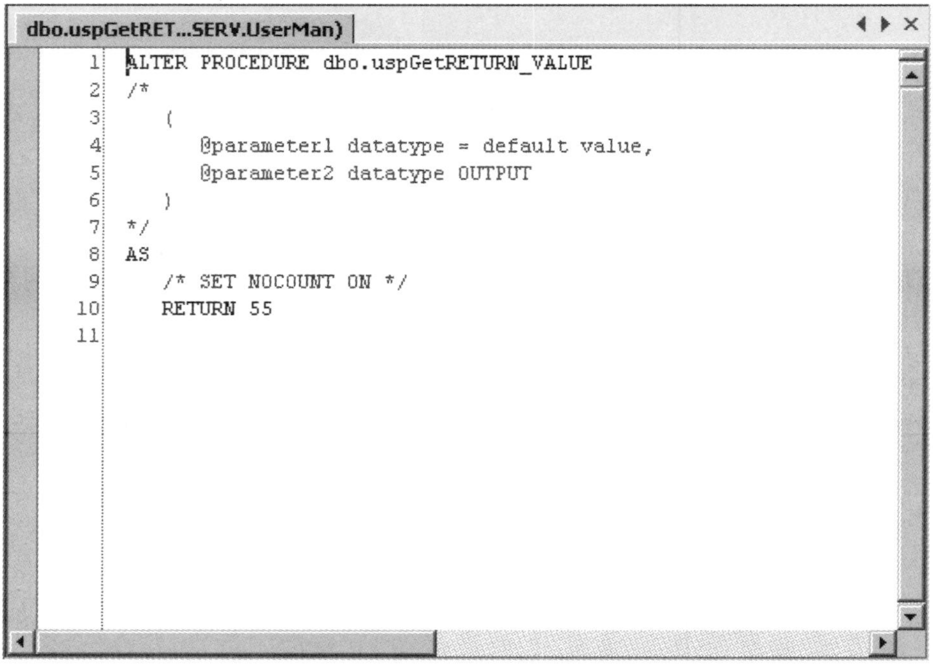

```
dbo.uspGetRET...SERV.UserMan)                                    ◀ ▶ ✕

 1  ALTER PROCEDURE dbo.uspGetRETURN_VALUE
 2  /*
 3      (
 4          @parameter1 datatype = default value,
 5          @parameter2 datatype OUTPUT
 6      )
 7  */
 8  AS
 9      /* SET NOCOUNT ON */
10      RETURN 55
11
```

Figure 6-8. The uspGetRETURN_VALUE stored procedure

Listing 6-5 shows you how to retrieve the value from code.

Listing 6-5. Retrieving RETURN_VALUE from a Stored Procedure

```
1  Public Sub GetRETURN_VALUE()
2     Const STR_CONNECTION As String = "Data Source=USERMANPC;" & _
3       "User ID=UserMan;Password=userman;Initial Catalog=UserMan"
4
5     Dim cnnUserMan As SqlConnection
6     Dim cmmUser As SqlCommand
7     Dim drdUser As SqlDataReader
8     Dim prmNumRows As SqlParameter
9     Dim lngResult As Long
10
11    ' Instantiate and open the connection
12    cnnUserMan = New SqlConnection(STR_CONNECTION)
13    cnnUserMan.Open()
14
15    ' Instantiate and initialize command
16    cmmUser = New SqlCommand("uspGetRETURN_VALUE", cnnUserMan)
17    cmmUser.CommandType = CommandType.StoredProcedure
18    ' Instantiate, initialize and add parameter to command
```

```
19    prmNumRows = cmmUser.Parameters.Add("@RETURN_VALUE", SqlDbType.Int)
20    ' Indicate this is a return value parameter
21    prmNumRows.Direction = ParameterDirection.ReturnValue
22    ' Get RETURN_VALUE
23    lngResult = cmmUser.ExecuteScalar()
24 End Sub
```

In Listing 6-5 the **ExecuteScalar** method gets the return value from a stored procedure. Normally, you would use this method to return the value in the lngResult variable, but this variable will contain the default value, 0, in this case. However, because I have specified the **Direction** property of the prmNumRows parameter with the **ReturnValue** member of the **ParameterDirection** enum, I can simply look at the **Value** property of the parameter after executing the command.

Changing the Name of a Stored Procedure

If you change the name of your stored procedure in the editor window, the stored procedure is saved with the new name when you save (Ctrl+S). However, if you are not using this method to copy an existing SP, you should be aware that the old SP still exists. So you will have to delete it if you don't want it.

Using Views

A *view* is, as the word suggests, a display of data in your database. Perhaps it helps to think of a view as a virtual table. It can be a subset of a table or an entire table, or it can be a subset of several joined tables. Basically, a view can represent just about any subset of data in your database, and you can include other views in a view. Including a view in another view is called *nesting,* and it can be a valuable way of grouping display data, but nesting too deeply can also result in performance problems and can certainly make it a real challenge to track down errors. There isn't really any magic to a view or any big secrets that I can let you in on; it's simply just a great tool for manipulating your data. Like stored procedures, views are used for server-side processing of your data, but whereas SPs mainly are used for security and performance reasons, views are generally used to secure access to your data and to hide complexity of queries that contain many joins. In the rest of this section, I am going to look at why, when, where, and how you should use a view.

View Restrictions

A view is almost identical to a row-returning query, with just a few exceptions.

Some of the restrictions are detailed here:

- **COMPUTE** and **COMPUTE BY** clauses cannot be included in your view.

- **ORDER BY** clauses are not allowed in a view, unless you specify the **TOP** clause as part of the **SELECT** statement.

- The **INTO** keyword cannot be used to create a new table.

- Temporary tables cannot be referenced.

There are other restrictions, but please check with your SQL Server documentation and/or Help Files.

Why Use a View?

You may want to use a view for a variety of reasons:

- *Security:* You don't want your users to access the tables directly, and with the help of a view you can restrict users to seeing only the parts of a table they are allowed to see. You can restrict access to specific columns and/or rows.

- *Encryption:* You can encrypt a view so that no one can see where the underlying data comes from. Keep in mind that this is an irreversible action!

There are other reasons for creating a view, but the preceding reasons are certainly two of the most common.

Creating a View

It is easy to create a view. If you are used to working with the SQL Server's Server Manager, you should check out what the Server Explorer has to offer you. Here is how you create a view using the UserMan database as an example:

1. Open up the Server Explorer window.

2. Expand the UserMan database on your database server.

3.   Right-click on the Views node and select New View.

This brings up the View Designer, which in fact is the same as the Query Designer.

NOTE   *The Query Designer is described in detail in Chapter 4. Although the View Designer and Query Designer have the same look and feel, you cannot create views that do not adhere to the view restrictions mentioned in the section, "View Restrictions."*

The Add Table dialog box is also shown right when the View Designer is displayed. In this dialog box, simply select the tables you want to retrieve data from and click on Add. Click Close when all the required tables have been added.

As you start selecting in the Diagram pane the columns that should be output when the view is run, the SQL pane and the Grid pane change accordingly. When you are done selecting the columns to output, you should save the view using Ctrl+S.

EXERCISE

Create a new view. This view should contain the following tables: tblUser, tblRights, and tblUserRights. The following fields should be output:

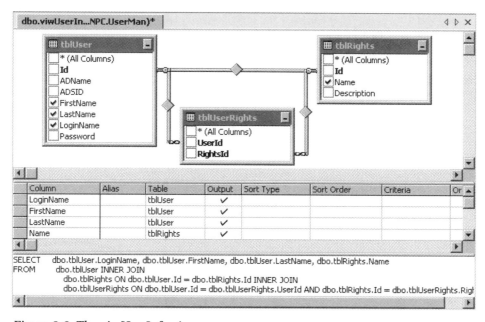

Figure 6-9. The viwUserInfo view

tblUser.LoginName, tblUser.FirstName, tblUser.LastName, and tblRights.Name. Save the view under the name viwUserInfo. The new view should look like the one in Figure 6-9.

Running a View from the IDE

Running a view is perhaps not the most appropriate phrase when you think about it. On the other hand, the view does have to retrieve the data from all the tables referenced in the view, so I guess "running a view" will have to do.

Anyway, you can run a view from the View Designer by right-clicking on a blank area of the View Designer and selecting Run from the pop-up menu. The data retrieved by the view is then displayed in the Results pane of the View Designer.

EXERCISE

Run the viwUserInfo view from the View Designer. The Results pane now displays

	LoginName	FirstName	LastName	Name
▶	UserMan	John	Doe	AddUser
*				

Figure 6-10. The results of running the viwUserInfo view

rows like the ones in Figure 6-10. Notice that the Name field of the tblRights table seems a bit confusing, because it doesn't really show what Name means. To make things clearer, in the Grid pane add the text **RightsName** to the Alias column in the Name row. Run the view again and notice how the new column name appears in the Results pane. Save the view with Ctrl+S.

Using a View from Code

Actually, it is very easy to use a view in code, because a view is referenced like any standard table in your database, which means that you can retrieve data using a command object or a data adapter that fills a data set, and so on.

NOTE *Please see Chapter 3B for specific information on how to manipulate data in a table.*

Retrieving Read-Only Data from a View in Code

The simplest use of a view is for display purposes, like when you just need to display some information from one or more related tables. Because in the example code I don't have to worry about updates, I don't have to set up anything particular. Listing 6-6 demonstrates how to return all rows from a view and populate a data reader.

Listing 6-6. Retrieving Rows From a View

```
1 Public Sub RetrieveRowsFromView()
2    Const STR_CONNECTION As String = "Data Source=USERMANPC;" & _
3      "User ID=UserMan;Password=userman;Initial Catalog=UserMan"
4
5    Dim cnnUserMan As SqlConnection
6    Dim cmmUser As SqlCommand
7    Dim drdUser As SqlDataReader
8
9    ' Instantiate and open the connection
10   cnnUserMan = New SqlConnection(STR_CONNECTION)
11   cnnUserMan.Open()
12
13   ' Instantiate and initialize command
14   cmmUser = New SqlCommand("SELECT * FROM viwUserInfo", cnnUserMan)
15   ' Get rows
16   drdUser = cmmUser.ExecuteReader()
17 End Sub
```

Listing 6-6 is just like any other row-returning query, except that a view is queried instead of a table.

Manipulating Data in a View from Code

Listing 6-6 shows you how to retrieve data from a view put it into a data reader, and this means the data cannot be updated, because the data reader doesn't allow updates. However, it is possible to update data in a view. The problem with this is that various versions of SQL Server support different levels of update sup-

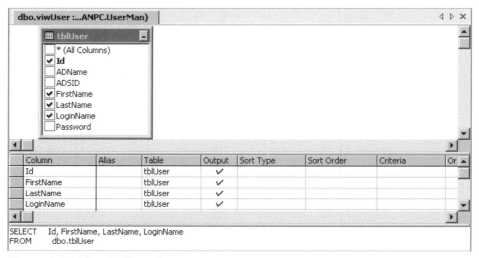

Figure 6-11. The viwUser view

port for views. If you only have one table in a view, this is not a problem at all; however, if you have multiple tables in a view, only SQL Server 2000 supports updating rows in more than one of the source tables. Besides the mentioned problems, you will certainly run into even bigger problems if you need to migrate to a different RDBMS. Generally I would discourage updating data in views.

EXERCISE

Create a new view. This view should contain the tblUser table. The following fields should be output: Id, FirstName, LastName, and LoginName. Save the view under the name viwUser. The new view should look like the one in Figure 6-11.

This view, which can be located on SQL Server 7.0 as well as SQL Server 2000, can be manipulated using the code in Listing 6-7.

Listing 6-7. Manipulating Data in a View Based on a Single Table

```
1  Public Sub ManipulatingDataInAViewBasedOnSingleTable()
2    Const STR_CONNECTION As String = "Data Source=USERMANPC;" & _
3      "User ID=UserMan;Password=userman;Initial Catalog=UserMan"
4
5    Const STR_SQL_USER_SELECT As String = "SELECT * FROM viwUser"
6    Const STR_SQL_USER_DELETE As String = "DELETE FROM viwUser WHERE Id=@Id"
7    Const STR_SQL_USER_INSERT As String = "INSERT INTO viwUser(FirstName," & _
8      " LastName, LoginName, Logged, Description) VALUES(@FirstName, " & _
9      "@LastName, @LoginName)"
10   Const STR_SQL_USER_UPDATE As String = "UPDATE viwUser SET " & _
11     "FirstName=@FirstName, LastName=@LastName, LoginName=@LoginName " & _
12     "WHERE Id=@Id"
13
14   Dim cnnUserMan As SqlConnection
15   Dim cmmUser As SqlCommand
16   Dim dadUser As SqlDataAdapter
17   Dim dstUser As DataSet
18
19   Dim cmmUserSelect As SqlCommand
20   Dim cmmUserDelete As SqlCommand
21   Dim cmmUserInsert As SqlCommand
22   Dim cmmUserUpdate As SqlCommand
23
24   Dim prmSQLDelete, prmSQLUpdate, prmSQLInsert As SqlParameter
25
26   ' Instantiate and open the connection
27   cnnUserMan = New SqlConnection(STR_CONNECTION)
28   cnnUserMan.Open()
29
30   ' Instantiate and initialize command
31   cmmUser = New SqlCommand("SELECT * FROM viwUser", cnnUserMan)
32   ' Instantiate the commands
33   cmmUserSelect = New SqlCommand(STR_SQL_USER_SELECT, cnnUserMan)
34   cmmUserDelete = New SqlCommand(STR_SQL_USER_DELETE, cnnUserMan)
35   cmmUserInsert = New SqlCommand(STR_SQL_USER_INSERT, cnnUserMan)
36   cmmUserUpdate = New SqlCommand(STR_SQL_USER_UPDATE, cnnUserMan)
37   ' Instantiate command and data set
38   cmmUser = New SqlCommand(STR_SQL_USER_SELECT, cnnUserMan)
39   dstUser = New DataSet()
40
41   dadUser = New SqlDataAdapter()
42   dadUser.SelectCommand = cmmUserSelect
43   dadUser.InsertCommand = cmmUserInsert
```

```
44    dadUser.DeleteCommand = cmmUserDelete
45    dadUser.UpdateCommand = cmmUserUpdate
46
47    ' Add parameters
48    cmmUserDelete.Parameters.Add("@FirstName", SqlDbType.VarChar, 50, _
49      "FirstName")
50    cmmUserDelete.Parameters.Add("@LastName", SqlDbType.VarChar, 50, _
51      "LastName")
52    cmmUserDelete.Parameters.Add("@LoginName", SqlDbType.VarChar, 50, _
53      "LoginName")
54    prmSQLDelete = dadUser.DeleteCommand.Parameters.Add("@Id", _
55      SqlDbType.Int, 0, "Id")
56    prmSQLDelete.Direction = ParameterDirection.Input
57    prmSQLDelete.SourceVersion = DataRowVersion.Original
58
59    cmmUserUpdate.Parameters.Add("@FirstName", SqlDbType.VarChar, 50, _
60      "FirstName")
61    cmmUserUpdate.Parameters.Add("@LastName", SqlDbType.VarChar, 50, _
62      "LastName")
63    cmmUserUpdate.Parameters.Add("@LoginName", SqlDbType.VarChar, 50, _
64      "LoginName")
65    prmSQLUpdate = dadUser.UpdateCommand.Parameters.Add("@Id", _
66      SqlDbType.Int, 0, "Id")
67    prmSQLUpdate.Direction = ParameterDirection.Input
68    prmSQLUpdate.SourceVersion = DataRowVersion.Original
69
70    cmmUserInsert.Parameters.Add("@FirstName", SqlDbType.VarChar, 50, _
71      "FirstName")
72    cmmUserInsert.Parameters.Add("@LastName", SqlDbType.VarChar, 50, _
73      "LastName")
74    cmmUserInsert.Parameters.Add("@LoginName", SqlDbType.VarChar, 50, _
75      "LoginName")
76
77    ' Populate the data set from the view
78    dadUser.Fill(dstUser, "viwUser")
79
80    ' Change the last name of user in the second row
81    dstUser.Tables("viwUser").Rows(1)("LastName") = "Thomsen"
82    ' Propagate changes back to the data source
83    dadUser.Update(dstUser, "viwUser")
84 End Sub
```

In Listing 6-7 a data adapter and a data set were set up to retrieve and hold data from the viwUser view. The LastName column of row 2 is then updated as well as the data source with the changes in the data set. This simple demonstration was designed to show you how to work with views based on a single table.

Using Triggers

A *trigger* is actually a stored procedure that automatically invokes (triggers) when a certain change is applied to your data. Triggers are the final server-side processing functionality I will discuss in this chapter. Until SQL Server 2000 was released, triggers were a vital part of enforcing referential integrity, but with the release of SQL Server 2000, you now have that capability built in. In the rest of this section I will show you what a trigger is and when and how you can use it.

Triggers respond to data modifications using INSERT, UPDATE, and DELETE operations. Basically, you can say that a trigger helps you write less code; you can incorporate business rules as triggers and thus prevent the inclusion of data that is invalid because it violates your business rules.

Here's a perfect situation for a business rule: You need to check if a member of an organization has paid his or her annual fee and therefore is allowed to order material from the organization's library. An INSERT trigger could perform the lookup in the members table when a member tries to order material and check if the member has paid the annual fee. This is exactly what makes a trigger more useful than a constraint in some situations, because a trigger can access columns in other tables, unlike constraints, which can only access columns in the current table or row.

SQL Server implements AFTER triggers, meaning that the trigger is invoked after the modification has occurred. However, this doesn't mean that a change can't be rolled back, because the trigger has direct access to the modified row and as such can roll back any modification. I stated that SQL Server implements after triggers, and until SQL Server 2000 was released, these were the only type of triggers supported by SQL Server. However, SQL Server 2000 also supports the notion

of BEFORE triggers, which you might know from the Oracle RDBMS. In SQL Server 2000 they are called INSTEAD OF triggers.

Why Use a Trigger?

Triggers are automatic, so you don't have to apply the business logic in your code. Think about the example mentioned before, where a member of an organization orders some material from the organization's library. If your code is to handle your business rule, this would mean that you need to look up the member's information in the members table before you can insert the order in the orders table. With the trigger, this lookup is done automatically, and an exception is thrown if you try to insert an order for library material if the member hasn't paid his or her annual fee.

To make it short, use a trigger for keeping all your data valid or to comply with your business rules. Think of triggers as an extra validation tool, while at the same time making sure you have set up referential integrity.

NOTE *With SQL Server 2000, you shouldn't use triggers for referential integrity (see Chapter 2), because you can set that up with the Database Designer. See Chapter 4 for information on the Database Designer.*

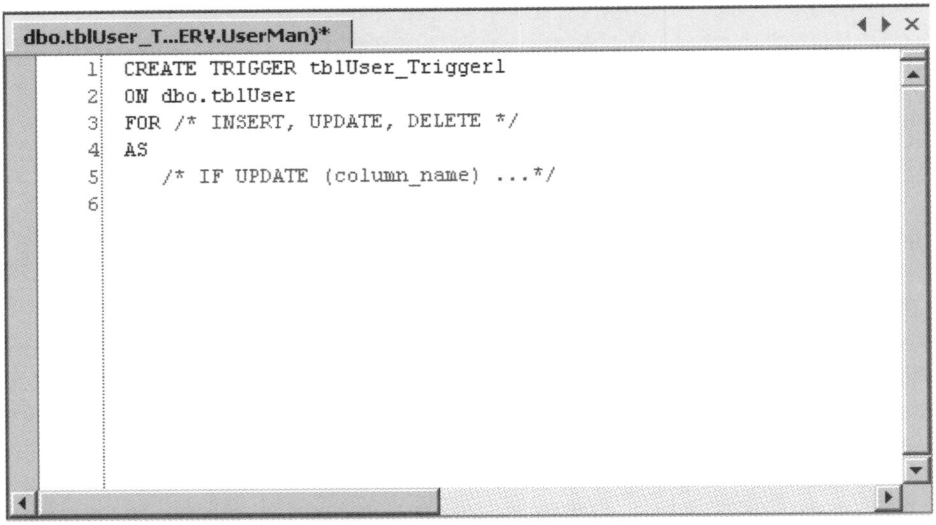

```
1  CREATE TRIGGER tblUser_Trigger1
2  ON dbo.tblUser
3  FOR /* INSERT, UPDATE, DELETE */
4  AS
5      /* IF UPDATE (column_name) ...*/
6
```

Figure 6-12. Trigger editor with default template

Creating a Trigger

It is quite easy to create a trigger. This can be done using the Server Manager that comes with SQL Server, but I will use the Server Explorer. Here is how you create a trigger for the example UserMan database:

1. Open up the Server Explorer window.

2. Expand the UserMan database on your database server.

3. Expand the Tables node.

4. Right-click on the table you want to create a trigger and select New Trigger from the pop-up menu.

This brings up the Trigger text editor, which is more or less the same editor you use for your VB.NET code (see Figure 6-12).

In the trigger editor, you can see that the template automatically names a new trigger Trigger1 prefixed with the name of the table. Actually, if another trigger with this name already exists, the new trigger is named Trigger2, and so on.

Once you are done editing your trigger, you need to save it by pressing Ctrl+S. As soon as you have saved it, the very first line of the SP changes. The SQL statement **CREATE TRIGGER** is changed so that the first line reads as follows:

```
ALTER TRIGGER dbo. . . .
```

NOTE *The trigger editor performs syntax checking when you save your trigger, meaning if the syntax of your trigger is invalid, you are not allowed to save it to your database.*

EXERCISE

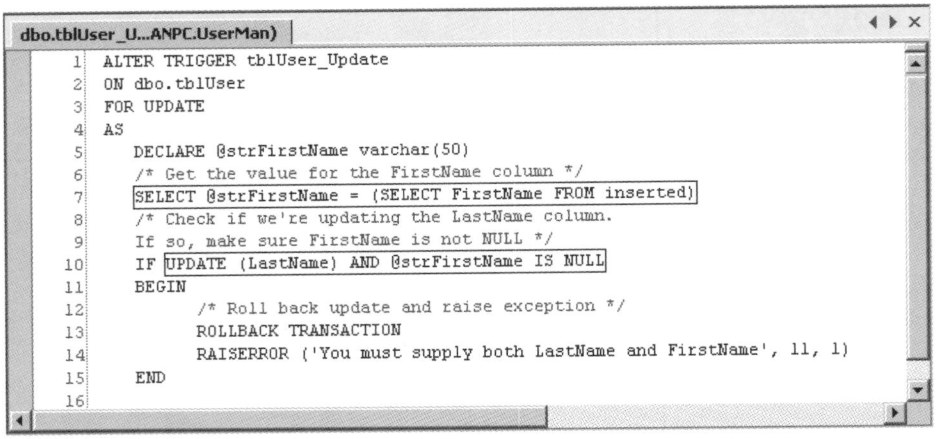

Figure 6-13. The tblUser_Update trigger

Create a new trigger for the tblUser table and save it with the name tblUser_Update. This is an update trigger, so you need to change the text on Line 3 to **FOR UPDATE**. Replace the text on Line 5 and down with the following:

```
DECLARE @strFirstName varchar(50)
/* Get the value for the FirstName column */
SELECT @strFirstName = (SELECT FirstName FROM inserted)
/* Check if we're updating the LastName column.
If so, make sure FirstName is not NULL */
IF UPDATE (LastName) AND @strFirstName IS NULL
BEGIN
   /* Roll back update and raise exception */
   ROLLBACK TRANSACTION
   RAISERROR ('You must fill in both LastName and FirstName', 11, 1)
END
```

Now the stored procedure should look like the one in Figure 6-13. Don't forget to save the changes using Ctrl+S.

When a trigger has been saved to the database, you can locate it under the table to which it belongs in the Server Explorer.

The tblUser_Update trigger is invoked when updating a row in the user table. The trigger first tests to see if the LastName column is updated. If it is, then the trigger checks to see if the FirstName column is empty, because if it is the update is rolled back and an exception is raised. Please note that this trigger is designed to work with only one updated or inserted row at a time. If more rows are inserted at the same time, the trigger will have to be redesigned to accommodate this.

However, this trigger only serves as a demonstration. The functionality of this trigger can easily be implemented using constraints, because the check I perform is done in the same table. If I had looked up a value in a different table, then the trigger would be your only choice.

Please see your SQL Server documentation if you need more information on how to create triggers. Listing 6-7 shows you how to execute the new trigger, demonstrating how to raise an exception you can catch in code.

Listing 6-7. Manipulating Data in a View Based on a Single Table

```
1  Public Sub TestUpdateTrigger()
2    Const STR_CONNECTION As String = "Data Source=USERMANPC;" & _
3      "User ID=UserMan;Password=userman;Initial Catalog=UserMan"
4
5    Const STR_SQL_USER_SELECT As String = "SELECT * FROM tblUser"
6    Const STR_SQL_USER_DELETE As String = _
7      "DELETE FROM tblUser WHERE Id=@Id"
8    Const STR_SQL_USER_INSERT As String = "INSERT INTO tblUser(" & _
9      "FirstName, LastName, LoginName) VALUES(@FirstName, " & _
10     "@LastName, @LoginName)"
11   Const STR_SQL_USER_UPDATE As String = "UPDATE tblUser SET " & _
12     "FirstName=@FirstName, LastName=@LastName, " & _
13     "LoginName=@LoginName WHERE Id=@Id"
14
15   Dim cnnUserMan As SqlConnection
16   Dim cmmUser As SqlCommand
17   Dim dadUser As SqlDataAdapter
18   Dim dstUser As DataSet
19
20   Dim cmmUserSelect As SqlCommand
21   Dim cmmUserDelete As SqlCommand
22   Dim cmmUserInsert As SqlCommand
23   Dim cmmUserUpdate As SqlCommand
24
25   Dim prmSQLDelete, prmSQLUpdate, prmSQLInsert As SqlParameter
26
27   ' Instantiate and open the connection
28   cnnUserMan = New SqlConnection(STR_CONNECTION)
29   cnnUserMan.Open()
30
31   ' Instantiate and initialize command
32   cmmUser = New SqlCommand("SELECT * FROM tblUser", cnnUserMan)
33   ' Instantiate the commands
34   cmmUserSelect = New SqlCommand(STR_SQL_USER_SELECT, cnnUserMan)
35   cmmUserDelete = New SqlCommand(STR_SQL_USER_DELETE, cnnUserMan)
```

```
36    cmmUserInsert = New SqlCommand(STR_SQL_USER_INSERT, cnnUserMan)
37    cmmUserUpdate = New SqlCommand(STR_SQL_USER_UPDATE, cnnUserMan)
38    ' Instantiate command and data set
39    cmmUser = New SqlCommand(STR_SQL_USER_SELECT, cnnUserMan)
40    dstUser = New DataSet()
41
42    dadUser = New SqlDataAdapter()
43    dadUser.SelectCommand = cmmUserSelect
44    dadUser.InsertCommand = cmmUserInsert
45    dadUser.DeleteCommand = cmmUserDelete
46    dadUser.UpdateCommand = cmmUserUpdate
47
48    ' Add parameters
49    cmmUserDelete.Parameters.Add("@FirstName", SqlDbType.VarChar, _
50      50, "FirstName")
51    cmmUserDelete.Parameters.Add("@LastName", SqlDbType.VarChar, _
52      50, "LastName")
53    cmmUserDelete.Parameters.Add("@LoginName", SqlDbType.VarChar, _
54      50, "LoginName")
55    prmSQLDelete = dadUser.DeleteCommand.Parameters.Add("@Id", _
56      SqlDbType.Int, 0, "Id")
57    prmSQLDelete.Direction = ParameterDirection.Input
58    prmSQLDelete.SourceVersion = DataRowVersion.Original
59
60    cmmUserUpdate.Parameters.Add("@FirstName", SqlDbType.VarChar, _
61      50, "FirstName")
62    cmmUserUpdate.Parameters.Add("@LastName", SqlDbType.VarChar, _
63      50, "LastName")
64    cmmUserUpdate.Parameters.Add("@LoginName", SqlDbType.VarChar, _
65      50, "LoginName")
66    prmSQLUpdate = dadUser.UpdateCommand.Parameters.Add("@Id", _
67      SqlDbType.Int, 0, "Id")
68    prmSQLUpdate.Direction = ParameterDirection.Input
69    prmSQLUpdate.SourceVersion = DataRowVersion.Original
70
71    cmmUserInsert.Parameters.Add("@FirstName", SqlDbType.VarChar, _
72      50, "FirstName")
73    cmmUserInsert.Parameters.Add("@LastName", SqlDbType.VarChar, _
74      50, "LastName")
75    cmmUserInsert.Parameters.Add("@LoginName", SqlDbType.VarChar, _
76      50, "LoginName")
77
78    ' Populate the data set from the view
79    dadUser.Fill(dstUser, "tblUser")
```

```
80
81    ' Change the name of user in the second row
82    dstUser.Tables("tblUser").Rows(1)("LastName") = "Thomsen"
83    dstUser.Tables("tblUser").Rows(1)("FirstName") = Nothing
84
85    Try
86        ' Propagate changes back to the data source
87        dadUser.Update(dstUser, "tblUser")
88    Catch objE As Exception
89        MsgBox(objE.Message)
90    End Try
91 End Sub
```

In Listing 6-7 the second row is updated, and the LastName column is set to "Thomsen" and the FirstName to a NULL value. This will invoke the update trigger that throws an exception, which is caught in code and displays the error message.

This should give you a taste for using triggers, and they really aren't that hard to work with. Just make sure you have a well-designed database that doesn't use triggers for purposes that can easily be achieved by other means such as referential integrity.

Summary

In this chapter I discussed how to create various server-side objects for server-side processing of your data. I demonstrated stored procedures, views, and triggers, and showed you how to create, run, and execute a stored procedure from code; how to create, run, and use a view from code, including updating the view; and finally how to create triggers.

I didn't go into much detail about stored procedures, views, and triggers, but if you need more information and sample code, I can certainly recommend you read this Apress book: *Code Centric: T-SQL Programming with Stored Procedures and Triggers* by Garth Wells, ISBN: 1-893115-836.

The next chapter is about hierarchical databases. I will discuss how you access the LDAP protocol and access a network directory database like the Active Directory.

CHAPTER 7

Hierarchical Databases

How to access Active Directory through the Lightweight Directory Access Protocol

IN THIS CHAPTER I will discuss the LDAP directory protocol and how it can be used for connecting to Active Directory, Microsoft's network directory service. Active Directory is a hierarchical database, and you can find a general description of such in Chapter 2.

Looking at LDAP

Since you will be accessing Active Directory in the example application, I believe providing some brief background on Active Directory and the Lightweight Directory Access Protocol (LDAP) is in order. Active Directory is a network directory service, like the Domain Name System (DNS) and Novell Directory Services (NDS). A *network directory service* holds objects such as users, printers, clients, servers, and so on. In short, a network directory service holds information, which is used to manage or access a network. This chapter contains example code that will take you through accessing Active Directory.

Active Directory was first introduced with the Microsoft Windows 2000 operating system. Active Directory is an X.500-compliant network directory based on open standards protocols such as LDAP. The Active Directory is X.500 compliant, which means it is a hierarchical database with a tree-like structure. When the specifications for the X.500 directory were under development, an access protocol for accessing a network directory based on the X.500 specification was needed, and thus the Directory Access Protocol (DAP) was created. However, the specification for DAP was too overwhelming and the overhead too big, which resulted in only very few clients and/or applications being able to connect to DAP. If you need more information about the X.500 directory standard as it is defined by the International Organization for Standardization (ISO) and the

International Telecommunication Union (ITU), you can visit this address: `http://www.nexor.com/x500frame.htm`.

This challenge was met by a group of people at the University of Michigan who realized that reducing the DAP overhead could result in retrieving the same directory information quicker and the clients would be a lot smaller. So they created a new protocol specification, the Lightweight Directory Access Protocol.

> **NOTE**   *See Chapter 2 for information on how a hierarchical database is structured.*

LDAP runs directly over the TCP/IP stack. The network directory service needs to host an LDAP service if you want to use LDAP to access the directory, though, which means that LDAP is client-server based.

These days LDAP is becoming the de facto standard for clients to access directory information. This is true for clients working over both the Internet and intranets, with standard LAN directory access now also moving towards LDAP.

One of the most important aspects of the LDAP protocol standard is that it gives us an API that is common and most notably platform independent. As a result, applications that access a directory service such as MS Active Directory or Novell Directory Services (NDS) will be a lot easier and inexpensive to develop.

> **NOTE**   *The LDAP directory service protocol gives you access to an existing directory; it cannot create a new directory.*

Exploring Active Directory

The fact that Active Directory is currently available only with Windows 2000 means you need at least a Windows 2000 Server, with AD installed, in order to follow this discussion.

Not only is AD accessible, it is also extendable, which is significant. If you have an object that you want to expose to a network, you can extend the schema of the AD and make it available to anyone who can access the AD implementation in question. The schema in AD defines all the object classes and attributes that can be stored in the directory. This doesn't mean that all the objects defined in the schema are actually present in AD, but the schema allows them to be created, so to speak. For each object class, the schema also defines where the object can be created in the directory tree by specifying the class's valid or legal parents. Furthermore, the content of a class is defined by a list of attributes that the class must or may contain. This means that an AD object is a named set of attributes. This set of attributes is distinct and is used to describe a user or printer, for instance. Anything on the network that is concrete can be specified as an object in AD.

As I will not be going into much more detail about AD, you should check out information at the following hyperlink if you want more specifics: `http://www.microsoft.com/windows2000/technologies/directory/default.asp`.

So to sum up quickly: Active Directory is a network directory service, based on the X.500 specifications, that can be accessed using the client-server–based LDAP directory service protocol.

Accessing AD Programmatically

The Active Directory can of course be accessed programmatically from VB.NET, as is the case with VB6. However, unlike VB6, VB.NET has some built-in features that let you access Active Directory without having to go through the Windows API. The **System.DirectoryServices** namespace has everything you need for this purpose.

Examining the System.DirectoryServices namespace

The **System.DirectoryServices** namespace holds a number of classes that let you access the Active Directory. Table 7-1 lists some of the classes important to this namespace.

*Table 7-1. **System.DirectoryServices** Classes*

CLASS NAME	DESCRIPTION
DirectoryEntries	This collection class contains the child entries of an Active Directory entry (**DirectoryEntry.Children** property). Please note that the collection only contains immediate children.
DirectoryEntry	The **DirectoryEntry** class encapsulates an object or a node in the Active Directory database hierarchy.
DirectorySearcher	This class is used for performing queries against Active Directory.
PropertyCollection	This collection holds all the properties of a single **DirectoryEntry** class (**DirectoryEntry.Properties** property).
PropertyValueCollection	The **PropertyValueCollection** collection holds values for a multivalued property (**DirectoryEntry.Properties.Values** property).
ResultPropertyCollection	This collection holds the properties of a **SearchResult** object (**SearchResultCollection.Item(0).Properties** property).
ResultPropertyValueCollection	The **ResultPropertyValueCollection** collection holds values for a multivalued property ().
SchemaNameCollection	This collection holds a list of schema names that is used for the **DirectoryEntries** classes **SchemaFilter** property.
SearchResult	This class encapsulates a node in the Active Directory database hierarchy. This node is returned as the result of a search performed by an instance of the **DirectorySearcher** class. Use the **SearchResult** class with the **FindOne** method of the **DirectorySearcher** class.
SearchResultCollection	This collection contains the instances of the **SearchResult** class that are returned when querying the Active Directory hierarchy using the **DirectorySearcher.FindAll** method.
SortOption	The **SortOption** class specifies how a query should be sorted.

In order to use these classes, you need to be aware of the following restrictions:

- The Active Directory Services Interface Software Development Kit (ADSI SDK) or the ADSI runtime must be installed on your computer. If you're running Windows 2000, it is installed by default. If you're running an earlier version of Windows, you can install the SDK by downloading it from the MS Web site: `http://www.microsoft.com/windows2000/techinfo` `/howitworks/activedirectory/adsilinks.asp` .

- A directory service provider, such as Active Directory or LDAP, must be installed on your computer.

I won't be explaining all the classes in the **System.DirectoryServices** name-space, but the **DirectoryEntry** class is quite important, so I discuss this class in the following section.

Studying the DirectoryEntry Class

Recall that the **DirectoryEntry** class encapsulates an object in the Active Directory database hierarchy. You can use this class for binding to objects in the AD or for manipulating object attributes. This class and the helper classes can be used with the following providers: **IIS**, **LDAP**, **NDS**, and **WinNT**. More providers will probably follow. As you may have guessed, I will only be demonstrating the use of LDAP to access AD in this chapter.

Table 7-2 shows you the noninherited, public properties of the **DirectoryEntry** class.

*Table 7-2. **DirectoryEntry** Class Properties*

PROPERTY NAME	DESCRIPTION
AuthenticationType	This property returns or sets the type of authentication to be used. The value must be a member of the **AuthenticationTypes** enum. The default value is **None**, and these are the other values of the enum: **Anonymous**, **Delegation**, **Encryption**, **FastBind**, **ReadonlyServer**, **Sealing**, **Secure**, **SecureSocketsLayer**, **ServerBind**, and **Signing**.
Children	This read-only property returns a **DirectoryEntries** class (collection) that holds the child entries of the node in the Active Directory database hierarchy. Only immediate children are returned.

Table 7-2. **DirectoryEntry** *Class Properties (continued)*

PROPERTY NAME	DESCRIPTION
Guid	The **Guid** property returns the Globally Unique Identifier of the **DirectoryEntry** class. If you're binding to an object in AD, you should use the **NativeGuid** property instead. This property is read-only.
Name	This read-only property returns the name of the object. The value returned is the name of the **DirectoryEntry** object that appears in the underlying directory service. Note that the **SchemaClassName** together with this property are what make the directory entry unique; in other words, these two names make it possible to tell one directory entry apart from its siblings.
NativeGuid	The **NativeGuid** property returns the Globally Unique Identifier of the **DirectoryEntry** class as it is returned from the provider. This property is read-only.
NativeObject	This read-only property returns the native ADSI object. You can use this property when you want to work with a COM interface.
Parent	The **Parent** property returns the **DirectoryEntry** object's parent in the Active Directory database hierarchy. This property is read-only.
Password	This property returns or sets the password that is used when the client is authenticated. When the **Password** and **Username** properties are set, all other instances of the **DirectoryEntry** class that are retrieved from the current instance will automatically be created with the same values for these properties.
Path	The **Path** property returns or sets the path for the **DirectoryEntry** class. The default is an empty **String**.
Properties	This property returns a **PropertyCollection** class holding the properties that have been set for the **DirectoryEntry** object.
SchemaClassName	The **SchemaClassName** property returns the name of the schema that is used for the **DirectoryEntry** object.
SchemaEntry	This property returns the **DirectoryEntry** object that is holding the schema information for the current **DirectoryEntry** object. The **SchemaClassName** property of a **DirectoryEntry** class determines the properties that are valid for the **DirectoryEntry** instance.
UsePropertyCache	This property returns or sets a **Boolean** value that indicates if the cache should be committed after each operation or not. The default is **True**.
Username	The **Username** property returns or sets the user name that is used for authenticating the client. When the **Password** and **Username** properties are set, all other instances of the **DirectoryEntry** class that are retrieved from the current instance will automatically be created with the same values for these properties.

In order to sum up what the **DirectoryEntry** contains, check out the methods for this class. Table 7-3 shows you the noninherited, public methods of the **DirectoryEntry** class.

*Table 7-3. **DirectoryEntry** Class Methods*

METHOD NAME	DESCRIPTION	EXAMPLE
Close()	This method closes the **DirectoryEntry** object. This means that any system resources used by the **DirectoryEntry** object are released at this point.	`objAD.Close()`
CommitChanges()	The **CommitChanges** method saves any changes you have made to the **DirectoryEntry** object to the Active Directory database.	`objAD.CommitChanges()`
CopyTo() As DirectoryEntry	This overloaded method is used for creating a copy of the **DirectoryEntry** object as a child of `objADParent` with or without a new name (`strNewName`).	`objADCopy = objAD.CopyTo (objADParent)` or `objADCopy = objAD.CopyTo (objADParent, strNewName)`
DeleteTree()	The **DeleteTree** method does exactly what it says: It deletes the **DirectoryEntry** object and the entire subtree from the Active Directory database hierarchy.	`objAD.DeleteTree()`
Invoke(ByVal vstrMethodName As String, ByVal ParamArray varrArgs() As Object) As Object	This method calls the `vstrMethodName` method on the native Active Directory with the `varrArgs` arguments.	
MoveTo()	This overloaded method is used for moving the **DirectoryEntry** object to the `objADParent` parent with or without a new name (`strNewName`).	`objAD.MoveTo(objADParent)` or `objAD.MoveTo (objADParent, strNewName)`
RefreshCache()	This overloaded method loads property values for the **DirectoryEntry** object into the property cache. Either all property values are loaded or just the ones specified with the `arrstrProperties` argument.	`objAD.RefreshCache()` or `objAD.RefreshCache (arrstrProperties)`
Rename(ByVal vstrNewName As String)	The **Rename** method renames or changes the name of the **DirectoryEntry** object to `vstrNewName`.	`objAD.Rename(strNewName)`

Looking at the LDAP Syntax

In order to bind to or search the AD, you need to know about the LDAP syntax used for binding and querying, so let's take a closer look at it.

Each object in AD is identified by two names when you use LDAP for access. This is the Relative Distinguished Name (RDN) and the Distinguished Name (DN). The DN actually consists of both the RDN and all of its parents and ancestors. Here is an example:

- The RDN for the UserMan object is `CN=UserMan`.

- The DN for the UserMan object in my AD might look like this:
  `\C=DK\O=UserMan\OU=developers\CN=UserMan`.

Each node in the hierarchy is separated by a backslash (\). The DN is unique across the directory service. This means that for each node the object name is unique. If you look at the DN, the Common Name (CN) `UserMan` must be unique in the developer's node. The Organizational Unit (OU) `developers` must be unique in the `UserMan` node, and so on. The O in `O=UserMan` represents an organization and the C in `C=DK` represents a country, Denmark in this case. For the United States, you would use `C=US`.

These prefixes are called *monikers,* and they are used to identify the object category. CN, which as stated previously stands for Common Name, is the most common moniker of them all. This moniker is used by most of the objects below an organizational unit (OU) node in the hierarchy. Table 7-4 list some additional monikers.

Table 7-4. Common Monikers

MONIKER NAME	DESCRIPTION	EXAMPLE
Common Name (CN)	The most common of all the monikers is logically called Common Name. It is used for most of the objects below the O or OU nodes or objects.	`CN=UserMan`
Country (C)	This moniker is used to describe the top-level node.	`C=DK` or `C=US`
Domain Component (DC)	The DC moniker is used to describe a domain. Because you are not allowed to use periods in a RDN, you need to use two DC monikers to describe your domain.	`DC=userman, DC=com`
Organization (O)	The O moniker is used for describing an organization, and usually this is the company name.	`O=UserMan`
Organizational Unit (OU)	If your organization has more units, the OU moniker is used to describe these.	`OU=developers`

Here is an example of a complete LDAP path for the UserMan user on my system:

```
LDAP://CN=UserMan,CN=Users,DC=userman,DC=com
```

Actually, I have changed the domain name, but I am sure you get the picture. The example starts by indicating that LDAP is the protocol (LDAP://) I want to use followed by a comma-delimited list of RDNs to make up the DN. Translating the query into plain English: the path looks for the user UserMan belonging to the Users group in the userman.com domain.

Sometimes I use commas and sometimes slashes (forward or backward slashes) as delimiters. Actually, you can use both kinds, but you have to be aware that the order in which the DN is put together changes. For example, if you use a comma as the delimiter, the DN starts with the end object or the object that is lowest in the hierarchy, and then you traverse up the tree node until you have added the top-level node. On the other hand, if you use a slash as the delimiter, the reverse order is expected:

```
LDAP://DC=com/DC=userman/CN=Users/CN=UserMan
```

I can't tell you what separator to use—in most cases it's simply a matter of preference.

Binding to an Object in Active Directory

In order to do anything in AD using a class from the **System.DirectoryServices** namespace, you must first bind to an object. Not that it is hard to do the binding, but if you're new to LDAP and specifically LDAP syntax, you're in for a surprise. Make sure you read "Looking at the LDAP Syntax" earlier before you start binding to AD. Check out Listing 7-1 for a very simple example of how to bind to a specific user in AD.

Listing 7-1. Binding to an Object in AD
```
1 Dim objEntry As DirectoryEntry
2
3 ' Bind to the user man object
4 objEntry = New DirectoryEntry("LDAP://CN=UserMan,CN=Users,DC=userman," & _
5   "DC=com", "Administrator", "adminpwd")
```

In Listing 7-1 I have instantiated the **DirectoryEntry** object and bound it to the **UserMan** user object in AD. I have also specified the user, Administrator, and the password for this account. You will have to change these credentials to an account on your system with at least read access to the Active Directory. As you can see, it is pretty simple, once you know what object to bind to.

Searching for an Object in AD

When you want to search for a specific object in Active Directory, you can use an instance of the **DirectorySearcher** class, as shown in Listing 7-2.

Listing 7-2. Searching for a Specific Object in AD

```
1 Public Sub SearchForSpecificObjectInAD()
2    Dim objEntry As DirectoryEntry
3    Dim objSearcher As DirectorySearcher
4    Dim objSearchResult As SearchResult
5
6    ' Instantiate and bind to Users node in AD
7    objEntry = New DirectoryEntry("LDAP://CN=Users,DC=userman,DC=com", _
8     "UserMan", "userman")
9
10   ' Set up to search for UserMan on the Users node
11   objSearcher = New DirectorySearcher(objEntry, _
12    "(&(objectClass=user)(objectCategory=person)" & _
13    "(userPrincipalName=userman@userman.com))")
14
15   ' Find the user
16   objSearchResult = objSearcher.FindOne()
17
18   ' Check if the user was found
19   If Not objSearchResult Is Nothing Then
20      ' Display path for user
21      MsgBox("Users Path: " & objSearchResult.Path)
22   Else
23      MsgBox("User not found!")
24      End If
25 End Sub
```

In Listing 7-2 I include an instance of the **DirectorySearcher** object to locate the UserMan user on the Users node. I use the **FindOne** method to return exactly one result that matches **userPrincipalName**. Please see Table 7-4 earlier for more information on **userPrincipalName**. If more objects are found when searching, only the first object found is returned. If you want more objects returned, you need to use the **FindAll** method. See Listing 7-3 for an example.

Listing 7-3. Searching for All Objects of a Specific Class in AD

```
1 Public Sub SearchForAllUserObjectsInAD()
2    Dim objEntry As DirectoryEntry
3    Dim objSearcher As DirectorySearcher
4    Dim objSearchResult As SearchResult
5    Dim objSearchResults As SearchResultCollection
6
7    ' Instantiate and bind to domain root in AD
8    objEntry = New DirectoryEntry("LDAP://DC=userman,DC=com", _
9      "UserMan", "userman")
10
11   ' Set up to search for UserMan on the Users node
12   objSearcher = New DirectorySearcher(objEntry, _
13     "(&(objectClass=user)(objectCategory=person))")
14
15   ' Find all objects of class user
16   objSearchResults = objSearcher.FindAll()
17
18   ' Check if any users were found
19   If Not objSearchResults Is Nothing Then
20       ' Loop through all users returned
21       For Each objSearchResult In objSearchResults
22           ' Display path for user
23           MsgBox("Users Path: " & objSearchResult.Path)
24       Next
25   Else
26       MsgBox("No users were found!")
27   End If
28 End Sub
```

In Listing 7-3 all objects in AD of the class user and category person were returned. However, what you don't see from the example code is that not all properties of the objects were returned. By default, only the **adsPath** and **Name** properties are returned. If you want other properties returned, you have to specify them, as in Listing 7-4.

Listing 7-4. Returning Nondefault Properties from an AD Node or Object

```
1 Public Sub ReturnNonDefaultNodeProperties()
2    Dim objEntry As DirectoryEntry
3    Dim objSearcher As DirectorySearcher
4    Dim objSearchResult As SearchResult
5    Dim objProperty As DictionaryEntry
6
```

```
7    ' Instantiate and bind to Users node in AD
8    objEntry = New DirectoryEntry("LDAP://CN=Users,DC=vb-joker,DC=com", _
9     "UserMan", "userman")
10
11   ' Set up to search for UserMan on the Users node and
12   ' return non-default properties
13   objSearcher = New DirectorySearcher(objEntry, "(&(objectClass=user)" & _
14    (objectCategory=person)(userPrincipalName=userman@vb-joker.com))", _
15    New String(2) {"sn", "telephoneNumber", "givenName"})
16
17   ' Find the user
18   objSearchResult = objSearcher.FindOne()
19
20   ' Check if the user was found
21   If Not objSearchResult Is Nothing Then
22       ' Display user properties
23       For Each objProperty In objSearchResult.Properties
24           MsgBox(objProperty.Key.ToString)
25       Next
26   Else
27       MsgBox("User not found!")
28   End If
29 End Sub
```

If you need a list of LDAP display names that can represent a user in AD, please try this link: http://msdn.microsoft.com/library/default.asp?url= /library/en-us/netdir/w2k/DN_person.asp.

In Listing 7-4 I specify the extra properties I want returned with the object found. This is done on Line 15, where a **String** array consisting of three properties is added as an argument to the **DirectorySearcher** constructor. Alternatively, you can add the objects by using the **Add** or **AddRange** methods of the **PropertiesToLoad** property, as follows:

```
' Add properties one by one
objSearcher.PropertiesToLoad.Add("sn")
objSearcher.PropertiesToLoad.Add("telephoneName")
objSearcher.PropertiesToLoad.Add("givenName")
' Add properties in one go
objSearcher.PropertiesToLoad.AddRange(New String(2) _
 {"sn", "telephoneNumber", "givenName"})
```

The following links provide more information on how to construct your LDAP query filter:

- http://msdn.microsoft.com/library/psdk/adsi/glquery_0j3m.htm

- http://msdn.microsoft.com/library/psdk/adsi/ds2prggd_0hfc.htm

- http://msdn.microsoft.com/library/psdk/adsi/ds2prggd_56lw.htm

Manipulating Object Property Values

Oftentimes it is okay to just read the data returned from the Active Directory. However, sometimes you may want to manipulate the data as well. Once you have bound to an object, you can actually edit, delete, or add the object's property values.

Checking for the Existence of a Property

One of the first things you need to learn is to check whether a certain property has been returned with the object. For this purpose you would use the **Contains** method of the **Properties** collection. This method and collection are part of the **DirectoryEntry** and the **SearchResult** classes. Here is how you check to see if the **telePhoneNumber** property was returned:

```
If objEntry.Properties.Contains("telePhoneNumber") Then
If objSearchResult.Properties.Contains("telePhoneNumber") Then
```

If you don't check whether a property is in the **Properties** collection before accessing it, you risk throwing an exception!

Using a Local Cache for the Properties

When you work with instances of the **DirectoryEntry** class, the properties and the property values are by default cached locally. This means access to the **DirectoryEntry** object is faster, because any change will only be applied to the local cache and not committed to the Active Directory database. The properties are cached when you first read a property.

The default behavior can, however, be changed using the **UsePropertyCache** property. The default value is **True,** which means properties are cached locally. If you set this property to **False**, all changes to the cache will be committed to the Active Directory database after each operation.

If there has been a change to the Active Directory database, you can update the cache by calling the **RefreshCache** method. If you have made changes to the content of the cache, you should call the **CommitChanges** method before you call **RefreshCache**. Otherwise, you will overwrite the noncommitted changes in the cache.

Editing an Existing Property

Editing an existing property of an object in the AD is quite easy; see Listing 7-5 for an example.

Listing 7-5. Editing an Existing User Property

```
1 Public Sub EditUserProperty()
2    Dim objEntry As DirectoryEntry
3    Dim objPropertyValues As PropertyValueCollection
4
5    ' Bind to UserMan user object
6    objEntry = New DirectoryEntry("LDAP://CN=UserMan,CN=Users," & _
7     "DC=userman,DC=com", "UserMan", "userman")
8
9    ' Change the e-mail address for the user
10   objEntry.Properties("mail")(0) = "userman@userman.com"
11   ' Commit the changes to the AD database
12   objEntry.CommitChanges()
13 End Sub
```

The example code in Listing 7-5 binds to the UserMan AD object on Lines 6 and 7, and on Line 10 I change the e-mail address of the user. The changes are committed on Line 12.

Adding a New Property

If you want to add a new property to an existing object in the AD, you can use the **Add** method of the **DirectoryEntry** class. See Listing 7-6 for an example.

Listing 7-6. Adding a New User Property

```
1 Public Sub AddNewUserProperty()
2    Dim objEntry As DirectoryEntry
3    Dim objPropertyValues As PropertyValueCollection
4
5    ' Bind to UserMan user object
6    objEntry = New DirectoryEntry("LDAP://CN=UserMan,CN=Users," & _
7     "DC=userman,DC=com", "UserMan", "userman")
8
9    ' Add new e-mail address
10   objEntry.Properties("mail").Add("userman@userman.com")
```

```
11    ' Commit the changes to the AD database
12    objEntry.CommitChanges()
13 End Sub
```

In Listing 7-6 I add an e-mail address to the UserMan user by including the
Add method of the objEntry object. This happens on Line 10, but before I can do
that I have to bind to the UserMan user object in AD, and this is done on Lines
6 and 7. Finally I use the **CommitChanges** method on Line 12 to propagate the
changes back to the AD database.

Updating the Active Directory Database

If the **UsePropertyCache** property of a **DirectoryEntry** object is set to **False**, you
don't have to worry about committing your changes to the Active Directory database, as it is done automatically. However, if the **UsePropertyCache** property is
set to **True**, which is the default, you must manually commit the changes. You
can do this by calling the **CommitChanges** method of the **DirectoryEntry** class.

Accessing Active Directory Using the OLE DB .NET Data Provider

Although you can achieve just about anything in relation to the Active Directory
with the classes in the **System.DirectoryServices** namespace, it can be a lot easier to use the OLE DB .NET Data Provider instead because it allows you to
implement standard SQL syntax to extract the wanted data. See Listing 7-7
for an example.

Listing 7-7. Using OLE DB .NET to Access AD

```
1 Dim cnnAD As OleDbConnection
2 Dim cmmAD As OleDbCommand
3 Dim drdAD As OleDbDataReader
4
5 ' Instantiate and open connection
6 cnnAD = New OleDbConnection("Provider=ADsDSOObject;" & _
7   "User Id=UserMan;Password=userman")
8 cnnAD.Open()
9 ' Instantiate command
10 cmmAD = New OleDbCommand("SELECT cn, adsPath FROM " & _
11   "'LDAP://userman.com' WHERE objectCategory='person' AND " & _
12   "objectClass='user' AND cn='UserMan'", cnnAD)
13 ' Retrieve rows in data reader
14 drdAD = cmmAD.ExecuteReader()
```

Listing 7-7 shows you how to retrieve all rows from AD for the userman.com domain with the user name UserMan. You need to change the user ID and password on Line 7 to match a user with read access to your AD. On Line 11 you will need to change the domain name to match the name of the domain to which you are connecting.

The **objectCategory** and **objectClass** references on Lines 11 and 12 are standard LDAP style query calls, and they ensure only user objects are searched.

Specifying an OLEDB Provider for the Connection

There is only one provider to use with the OLE DB .NET Data Provider for accessing AD, **ADsDSOObject**, which you can see on Line 6 in Listing 7-7.

Basically, you can use the following code to open a connection to the AD:

```
cnnAD = New OleDbConnection("Provider=ADsDSOObject")
cnnAD.Open()
```

Obviously, you need to be logged on to a system that uses AD with an account that has permission to read from AD, but it's really that simple! If you are not logged on or don't have read access to AD, you can always use the syntax specified in Lines 6 and 7 in Listing 7-7.

Specifying What Domain to Access with the LDAP Protocol

When you try to access AD after opening an **OleDbConnection**, you need to specify the protocol and the domain name of the AD to access. This is done where you would normally specify the table name in a SELECT statement, like this:

```
FROM 'LDAP://userman.com'
```

As you can see, I have put the protocol name and domain name in single quotes. This is a must, because if you don't, an exception will be thrown! Specifying the protocol is the same as it is when you use your browser; you specify HTTP or FTP to use either protocol, followed by a colon and two slashes (://).

See Listing 7-7 for a complete example of how to construct a SELECT statement that retrieves rows from AD.

Specifying What Information to Retrieve from AD

As in any other SELECT statement, you can tell the command which "columns"
you want returned.

Table 7-5 shows a list of some of the information you can retrieve from AD.
Please note that this list is not exhaustive, but merely a starting point for how
to get user information. The "User Properties dialog equivalent" column refers to
the information you can find using the **Active Directory Users and Computers**
MMC snap-in. You then double-click on the user you want to see information for
and the user dialog box pops up.

Table 7-5. User Information Available from the Active Directory

NAME	DESCRIPTION	USER PROPERTIES DIALOG BOX EQUIVALENT
adsPath	This is the full path to the object, including protocol header.	None
mail	This is the user's e-mail account. Please note that this has nothing to do with any e-mail accounts created in Exchange Server.	General tab, e-mail text box
objectSid	This represents the user's Security Identifier (SID). Please note that this is returned as an array of bytes. You need to convert the SID if you want to display it in a human readable format (S-1-5-21-. . .)	None
samAccountName	This is the name used by the Security Account Manager (SAM)	Account tab, User logon name (pre-Windows 2000) text box.
userPrincipalName	The user principal name (UPN) is an Internet-style login name for a user. The UPN is based on the Internet standard RFC 822, and is most often the same as **mail**.	Account tab, User logon name text box and drop-down list. This is most often the same as the user's e-mail address, as it comes from the concept of one logon name to access all your services.

Please note that you cannot specify the asterisks (*) to retrieve all "columns"
as you would in a standard SQL statement. If you do, the query will only return
adsPath. Check out the SQL Dialect at this address:
`http://msdn.microsoft.com/library/psdk/adsi/ds2prggd_55pw.htm.`

If you want more information about the schema, its objects, the objects' attributes, and so on, there is plenty of information about the Active Directory schema at this address: `http://msdn.microsoft.com/library/default.asp?url=` `/library/en-us/netdir/hh/adsi/glschema3_868x.asp`.

Updating an Active Directory Object

The current OLE DB provider for ADSI, the one that comes with MDAC 2.6 and 2.7, is read-only, meaning you cannot use it to issue an UPDATE statement. Microsoft says this will change, but I haven't found any information detailing if this is to change with ADSI in Windows 2002 or if ADSI with Windows 2000 is also part of these plans. Stay alert, my friend!

Retrieving the SID for a User

You have probably noticed that the tblUser table in the UserMan database holds two columns that are named ADName and ADSID. They are there to hold the SID (objectSid) and the SAM Account Name (samAccountName) for the user (see Table 7-5 for a description of objectSid and samAccountName). Take a look at Listing 7-8 to see how to retrieve these two values for the UserMan user. You obviously need to have added the UserMan user to Active Directory on your network for this to work!

Listing 7-8. Retrieving SAM Account Name and SID from AD

```
1 Public Sub GetSIDAndSAMAccountNameFromAD()
2     Dim cnnAD As OleDbConnection
3     Dim cmmAD As OleDbCommand
4     Dim drdAD As OleDbDataReader
5     Dim strSAMAccountName As String
6     Dim strSID As String
7
8     ' Instantiate and open connection
9     cnnAD = New OleDbConnection("Provider=ADsDSOObject;" & _
10      "User Id=UserMan;Password=userman")
11    cnnAD.Open()
12    ' Instantiate commands
13    cmmAD = New OleDbCommand("SELECT objectSid, samAccountName " & _
14      "FROM 'LDAP://vb-joker.com' WHERE objectCategory='person' " & _
15      "AND objectClass='user' AND cn='UserMan'", cnnAD)
16
17    ' Retrieve rows in data reader
18    drdAD = cmmAD.ExecuteReader()
19    ' Go to first row
```

```
20    drdAD.Read()
21    ' Get SAM Account name
22    strSAMAccountName = drdAD("samAccountName").ToString
23    ' Get SID
24    strSID = drdAD("objectSid").ToString
25 End Sub
```

In Listing 7-8 the SID and SAM Account Name are retrieved from AD using the OLE DB provider for Microsoft Directory Services. Once returned, I save the values in local variables. In Chapter 11, I will expand on this example and show you how to save the values to your UserMan database.

Summary

This chapter contains a very brief technology backgrounder on LDAP and Active Directory and how these are used in conjunction. I discussed the **System.DirectoryServices** namespace and the classes it encompasses, specifically showing you the **DirectoryEntry** class and its properties and methods.

I also explained how to establish a connection programmatically using both the classes in the **System.DirectoryServices** namespace and using the OLE DB .NET Data Provider.

I can conclude by saying that although the Active Directory is a unique way of storing some of your data, it will not replace your relational database. Active Directory is for storing data objects long term and objects that are only changed infrequently.

At the time of writing this chapter, the Active Directory objects in the .NET Framework Class Library weren't fully functional, meaning that some of the code in this chapter might not work for you at all. I managed to get it working and I would have liked to have included more detailed examples, but time and bugs didn't allow me to. However, I will be updating the example code for this chapter and for the rest of the book, and you can find the updates at the Apress Web site.

The following chapter is about message queues and how you can use them for connectionless programming.

Message Queues

Using message queues for connectionless programming

MESSAGE QUEUES ARE GREAT whenever you don't have a permanent connection or in loosely coupled situations. They're also handy when you simply want to dump your input and return to your application without waiting for the output from whatever application or server will be processing your input. You can make message queues the basis of a fail-safe application that uses them whenever your regular database fails. This can help ensure that no data is lost and you have very little or no downtime at all, if you use transactional queues. Obviously not all applications can use message queues to such advantage, but for storing or accepting customer input it can be a great solution. One situation springs to mind in which using message queues would not be beneficial and that is a banking transaction that needs to be processed in real-time.

Microsoft's messaging technology is called *Message Queuing*. Mind you, in line with other traditional Microsoft marketing stunts, this technology has had other names before Windows 2000 was shipped. However, the release that ships with Windows 2000 is built upon a previous version of the technology and includes the Active Directory (AD) integration. AD integration is good because it is now easier to locate public message queues across your domain and it ensures easy Enterprise-wide backup.

Is MSMQ Dead?

Microsoft Message Queue Server (MSMQ) is the name Microsoft gave version 1.0 of its message queuing technology. It was originally included with the Enterprise Edition of Windows NT 4. With version 2.0 it became an add-on to any server version of Windows NT 4, and it was part of the Windows NT Option Pack. The Windows NT Option Pack could be freely downloaded from the Microsoft Web site. Since then the message queuing technology has been integrated into the OS, as is the case with Windows 2000 and the upcoming Windows 2002 and Windows XP. Not only has MSMQ been integrated into the

OS, it has changed its name to Message Queuing and been extended in numerous ways. One extension is the integration with Active Directory instead of being SQL Server based.

So to answer the question, "Is MSMQ Dead?" the answer is *yes* and *no.* Yes, because it is no longer a stand-alone product, and no because the features of the original MSMQ have been incorporated into the OS as a service called Message Queuing.

Connectionless Programming

Connectionless programming involves using a queue to hold your input to another application or server. Connectionless in this context means you don't have a permanent connection to the application or server. Instead, you log your input in a queue, and the other application or server then takes it from the queue, processes it, and sometimes puts it back in the same or a different queue.

The opposite of connectionless is *connection oriented,* and basically any standard database system these days falls into this category. You have probably heard these two terms in relation to TCP/IP (Transmission Control Protocol/Internet Protocol). The UDP (User Datagram Protocol) part of the protocol is connectionless, and the TCP part is connection oriented. However, there is a major difference between message queuing and the UDP protocol. Whereas the UDP protocol does not guarantee delivery, and a packet sent over the network using the UDP transport protocol can be lost, the message queue doesn't lose any packets. The reason why a message queue is said to be connectionless is that your client doesn't "speak" directly with your server. There is no direct connection, as there is with a standard database.

Now that you have an understanding of connectionless programming, let's move on to an overview of the **MessageQueue** class.

Taking a Quick Look at the MessageQueue Class

The **MessageQueue** class is part of the **System.Messaging** namespace. That namespace also holds the **Message** class, which is used in conjunction with the **MessageQueue** class. The **System.Messaging** namespace holds a number of classes that are exclusively used for accessing and manipulating message queues.

The **MessageQueue** class is a wrapper around **Message Queuing**, which is an optional component of Windows 2000 and Windows NT. With Windows NT it's part of the Option Pack. At any rate, you need to make sure you have installed Message Queuing on a server on your network before you can try the examples in this chapter.

When to Use a Message Queue

Use a message queue in your application if you need to perform any of these tasks:

- *Storing less-important information in a message queue while your DBMS is busy serving customers during the day:* The information in the message queue is then batch-processed when the DBMS is less busy. This is ideal for processing all real-time requests and storing all other requests in a message queue for later processing.

- *Connecting to a DBMS over a WAN, such as the Internet, and the connection is not always available for whatever reason:* You can do two things when you design your application. You can set up your application to access the DBMS the usual way, and if you get a time-out or another connection failure, you store the request in a message queue. You then start a component that checks for when the DBMS is available, and when it is, it will forward the requests that are stored in the message queue and return a possible result to your application. At this point your application can resume normal operation and shut down the message queue component. The other possibility is to design your application as an offline one, meaning that all DBMS requests are stored in a local message queue and forwarded by your message queue component to the DBMS.

- *Exchanging data with a mainframe system, like SAP:* You can use a message queue to hold SAP IDocs. These are then sent to and received from the SAP system by the queue manager/component. Anyone who ever worked with SAP will know that real-time communications with SAP is often a problem, because the server is often overloaded at specific intervals during the day. So basically you use the message queue for storing and forwarding requests to and from the SAP system. Recall that SAP is originally a mainframe system, but these days SAP is often found running on midsized computers or PCs. The five most popular platforms for R/3 are Windows NT, Sun Solaris, HP-UX, AS/400, and AIX.

I am sure you yourself can come up with a few applications that would benefit from message queuing based on your current or previous work experience. How about sales people in the field? Wouldn't it be good if they could save some info in a message queue and have it batch processed when they are back in the office?

Why Use a Message Queue and Not a Database Table?

A message queue can be of good use in many situations, but what makes it different from using a database table? When you call a DBMS, it is normally done synchronously, but with a message queue it is done asynchronously. This means it is generally faster to access a message queue than to access a database table. With synchronous access the client application has to wait for the server to respond, whereas with asynchronous access a query or the like is sent to the server, and the client application then continues its normal duties. When the server has finished processing the query, it will notify you and pass you the result.

When you use a database table, you must comply with a fairly strict format for adding data. There are certain fields that must be supplied, and you don't really have the ability to add extra information. Although the same can be said about message queues, when it comes to supplying certain fields, it is much easier to supply extra information that you have a hard time storing in a database table.

This approach is valid for Windows forms and Web forms, though it depends on the *application type*. Distributed applications, standard client-server applications on a local network, and stand-alone applications constitute some of the different application types. If your application is not distributed and you are accessing a standard DBMS on a local server or on your client, I don't see a reason for using a message queue. Actually, one reason might be that your DBMS is busy during the day, and hence you store your requests and messages in a message queue for batch processing when the DBMS is less busy.

In short, application infrastructure and business requirements in general determines whether you should use message queuing. Having said this, I realize that sometimes it is a good idea to work with a tool for a while so that you can get to know the situations when you should use it. So if you're new to message queuing, make sure you try the example code that follows later on in this chapter.

A message queue works using the First In, First Out (FIFO) principle, which means that the first message in the queue is the message you will retrieve if you use the **Receive** or **Peek** method of the **MessageQueue** class. See "Retrieving a Message" and "Peeking at Messages" later in this chapter for more information on these methods.

Because FIFO is the principle applied to how the messages are placed in the queue, a new message is placed at the bottom, or end, of the message queue when added, right? Well, this is correct, but there is more to it than just the arrival time in the queue. Each message also has a priority that determines its place in the queue. The priority takes precedence over the arrival time, so it is possible to place a message at the top of the message queue even if there are already other messages in the queue. If I were to make up a **SELECT** statement that describes how the messages are inserted into a queue and returned to you, it would look something like this:

```
SELECT * FROM MessageQueue ORDER BY Priority, ArrivalTime
```

Obviously this statement is just an example, but it does show you how the messages are ordered, first by priority and then by arrival time. Priority is not normally something you would set, so most messages would have the same priority, but there may be times when it is necessary to "jump" the queue. See "Prioritizing Messages," later in this chapter for more information on how to prioritize your messages.

How to Use a Message Queue

Of course, you need to set up the Message Queue before you can use it in your application. Maybe you already have a queue to connect to, but first I will show you how to set up a queue. Please note that you cannot view or manage public queues if you're in a workgroup environment. Public queues only exist in a domain environment. See your Windows 2000 or Windows NT documentation for installing Message Queuing. If you are running in workgroup mode, you cannot use Server Explorer to view a queue, not even private ones. I will get to private and public queues in the next section.

Private Queue vs. Public Queue

You need to know a distinction between the two types of queues you can create before continuing. There are private and public queues, and Table 8-1 compares some of the features of both types of message queues.

Table 8-1. Private vs. Public Message Queues

PRIVATE MESSAGE QUEUE	PUBLIC MESSAGE QUEUE
Not published in the Message Queue. Information Service (MQIS) database.	Published in the Message Queue Information Service (MQIS) database.
Can only be created on the local machine.	Must be registered with the Directory Service.
Can be created and deleted off-line.	Must be created and deleted while you're online.
Cannot be located by other message queuing applications, unless they are provided the full path of the message queue.	Can be located by other message queuing applications through the Message Queue Information Service (MQIS) database.
Is persistent, but backing up, although possible, is not an easy task.	Is persistent and can be backed up on an Enterprise level with the Active Directory.

Creating the Queue Programmatically

Chapter 4 covers how to create a message queue from the Server Explorer, but if you want to do it programmatically, please read on.

It is easy to create a message queue programmatically. Listings 8-1 and 8-2 show you two different ways of creating a private queue on the local machine, USERMANPC.

Listing 8-1. Creating a Private Message Queue Using the Machine Name

```
1 Public Sub CreatePrivateQueueWithName()
2     Dim queUserMan As New MessageQueue()
3
4     queUserMan.Create("USERMANPC\Private$\UserMan")
5 End Sub
```

Listing 8-2. Creating a Private Message Queue Using the Default Name

```
1 Public Sub CreatePrivateQueue()
2     Dim queUserMan As New MessageQueue()
3
4     queUserMan.Create(".\Private$\UserMan")
5 End Sub
```

In Listing 8-1 I specify the machine as part of the path argument, whereas I simply use a period in Listing 8-2. The period serves as a shortcut for letting the **MessageQueue** object know that you want it created on the local machine. The other thing you should notice is that I prefix the queue with Private$. This must be done to indicate that the queue is private. Exclusion of the prefix indicates you are creating a public queue. The different parts of the path are separated using the back slash, as in a standard DOS file path:

```
MachineName\Private$\QueueName
```

A public queue is created more or less the same way, except you leave out the \Private$ part of the path. You can also use the period to specify that you want it created on the local machine, as shown in Listing 8-3.

Listing 8-3. Creating a Public Message Queue Using the Default Name

```
1 Public Sub CreatePublicQueue()
2    Dim queUserMan As New MessageQueue()
3
4    queUserMan.Create(".\UserMan")
5 End Sub
```

As stated, the period could have been substituted with the name of the local machine or indeed the name of a different machine on which you want to create the queue.

> **NOTE** *If you try to create an already existing message queue, a **QueExists** exception is thrown.*

There are two overloaded versions of the **MessageQueue** class's **Create** method, and you have seen the simpler one. The other one takes a second argument, a **Boolean** value indicating whether the message queue is transactional. I will go into message queue transactions in the "Making Message Queues Transactional" section later on in this chapter, but for now take a look at Listing 8-4, which shows you how to make the queue transactional:

Listing 8-4. Creating a Transactional Private Message Queue

```
1 Public Sub CreateTransactionalPrivateQueue()
2    Dim queUserMan As New MessageQueue()
3
4    queUserMan.Create(".\Private$\UserMan", True)
5 End Sub
```

In Listing 8-4 a private message queue named UserMan is created on the local machine with transaction support. If you run the example code in Listing 8-4, you might want to remove it afterwards, as it might otherwise have an impact on the rest of the examples in this chapter.

Displaying or Changing the Properties of Your Message Queue

Some of the properties of your message queue can be changed after you have created it. You can do this by using the Computer Management MMC snap-in that is part of the Administrative Tools under Windows 2000. When you have opened the Computer Management snap-in, do the following:

1. Expand the Services and Applications node.

2. Expand the Message Queuing node.

3. Expand the node with the requested queue and select the queue. The Computer Management MMC snap-in should now look like the one shown in Figure 8-1.

4. Right-click on the queue and select Properties from the pop-up menu. This brings up the queue Properties dialog box (see Figure 8-2).

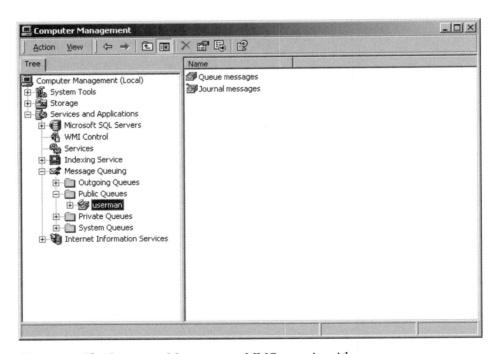

Figure 8-1. The Computer Management MMC snap-in with message queue selected

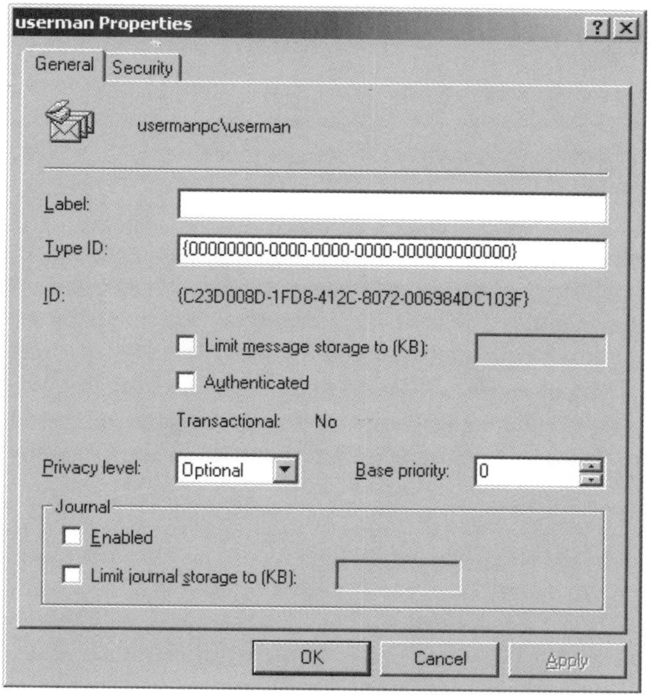

Figure 8-2. The Properties dialog box for the message queue

As you can see from Figure 8-2, one of the options that cannot be changed after the queue has been created is whether the queue is transactional or not. This makes it all the more important for you to know if you will need transaction support before you create the queue.

Assigning a Label to Your Message Queue

If you want to bind to your message queue using a label, you first need to assign a label to the queue. Looking back at Figure 8-2, notice you can enter the text for your label in the Label text box. One thing you have to remember is that it is not necessary for the label to be unique across all your message queues, but you are guaranteed problems if you try to bind and send messages to a queue using the same label. So the lesson learned here is make sure your label is unique!

You can also change the label of a message queue programmatically. See Listing 8-5 for example code.

Listing 8-5. Changing the Label of an Existing Queue

```
1 Public Sub ChangingQueueLabel()
2    Dim queUserMan As New MessageQueue(".\Private$\UserMan")
3
4    queUserMan.Label = "USERMAN1"
5 End Sub
```

In Listing 8-5 the friendly name is used to bind to an existing private queue on the local machine. A friendly name is a name that makes it easier for humans to read and interpret it. In the case of the example code in Listing 8-5, the friendly name tells you that the queue is created on the local machine (.), it is private ((Private$), and the name of it is UserMan. You must use the friendly name to bind to the message queue if you want to change the label programmatically! Line 4 is where the actual changing of the label takes place simply by setting the label property.

Retrieving the ID of a Message Queue

If you want to bind to your public message queue using its ID, you can retrieve this using the Computer Management MMC snap-in. See "Displaying or Changing the Properties of Your Message Queue" later in this chapter for more information on how to display message queue properties. If you refer back to Figure 8-2, you can see the ID just below the Type ID text box! Mind you, this ID is only available if you are connected to the AD Domain Controller. If you're not connected, you cannot view the properties for a public message queue. If you try to view the ID for a private message queue, this space is simply blank.

You can also retrieve the ID of a message queue programmatically, as shown in Listing 8-6.

Listing 8-6. Retrieving the ID of an Existing Queue

```
1 Public Sub RetrieveQueueId()
2    Dim queUserMan As New _
3      MessageQueue(".\UserMan")
4    Dim uidMessageQueue As Guid
5
6    ' Save the Id of the message queue
7    uidMessageQueue = queUserMan.Id
8 End Sub
```

As you can see from Listing 8-6 the ID is a GUID, so you need to declare your variable to be data type **Guid** if you want to store the ID. You must be connected to the AD Domain Controller in order to retrieve the ID of a message queue, otherwise an exception is thrown. If you try to retrieve the ID of a private message queue, an "empty" GUID is returned: **00000000-0000-0000-0000-000000000000**. You can display a GUID using the **ToString** method of the **Guid** class.

Binding to an Existing Message Queue

Once you have created a message queue or if you want to access an existing queue, you can now bind to it, as described in the following sections.

Binding Using Friendly Name

Listing 8-7 shows you three different ways of binding to an existing queue: using the New constructor, using a so-called friendly name (.\Private$\UserMan), or specifying the path of the queue and the name assigned to the queue when it was created.

Listing 8-7. Binding to an Existing Queue

```
1 Public Sub BindToExistingQueue()
2    Dim queUserManNoArguments As New MessageQueue()
3    Dim queUserManPath As New MessageQueue(".\Private$\UserMan")
4    Dim queUserManPathAndAccess As New MessageQueue(".\Private$\UserMan", _
5      True)
6
7    ' Initialize the queue
8    queUserManNoArguments.Path = ".\Private$\UserMan"
9 End Sub
```

Line 2 is the simplest method, but it requires an extra line of code because you haven't actually told the message queue object what queue to bind to. Line 8 takes care of specifying the queue using the **Path** property. On Line 4, I have specified the queue as well as the read-access restrictions. When the second argument is set to **True**, as is the case with the example in Listing 8-7, exclusive read access is granted to the first application that accesses the queue. This means that no other instance of the **MessageQueue** class can read from the queue, so be careful when you use this option.

Binding Using the Format Name

Since you cannot create or bind to a message queue on a machine in Workgroup mode, you need to access a queue on a machine that is part of Active Directory. However, this creates a problem when the message queue server you want to access cannot access the primary domain controller. Because Active Directory is used for resolving the path, you won't be able to use the syntax shown in Listing 8-6 to bind to a message queue.

Thankfully there's a way around this. Instead of using the friendly name syntax as in the previous listings, you can use the format name or the label for this purpose. Listing 8-8 shows you how to bind to existing queues using the format name.

Listing 8-8. Binding to an Existing Queue Using the Format Name

```
1 Public Sub BindToExistingQueueUsingFormat()
2   Dim queUserManFormatTCP As New _
3     MessageQueue("FormatName:DIRECT=TCP:10.8.1.15\Private$\UserMan")
4   Dim queUserManFormatOS As New _
5     MessageQueue("FormatName:DIRECT=OS:USERMANPC\UserMan")
6   Dim queUserManFormatID As New _
7     MessageQueue("FormatName:Public=AB6B9EF6-B167-43A4-8116-5B72D5C1F81C")
8 End Sub
```

In Listing 8-8 I bind to the private queue named UserMan on the machine with the IP address 10.8.1.15 using the TCP protocol, as shown is on Lines 2 and 3. On Lines 4 and 5 I bind the public queue named UserMan on the machine with name USERMANPC. There is also an option of binding using the SPX protocol. If you want to use the SPX network protocol, you must use the following syntax: FormatName:DIRECT=SPX:NetworkNumber;HostNumber\QueueName.

You can connect to both public and private queues with all format name options, so in the example code in Listing 8-8 you could swap the public and private queue binding among the three different format names. The last format name shown in Listing 8-8 is on Lines 6 and 7 where I use the ID of the message queue as the queue identifier. The ID used in the sample code is fictive and it will look different on your network. The ID, which is a GUID, is generated at creation time by the MQIS. See "Retrieving the ID of a Message Queue" for more information on how to get the ID of your message queue.

Binding Using the Label

One last way to bind to an existing message queue is to use the label syntax. This syntax cannot be used when you're offline, only when connected to the Active Directory Domain Controller. Listing 8-9 shows you how to connect to the message queue with the UserMan label. See "Assigning a Label to Your Message Queue" earlier in this chapter for more information on how to set the label of a message queue.

Listing 8-9. Binding to an Existing Queue Using the Label

```
1 Public Sub BindToExistingQueueUsingLabel()
2    Dim queUserManLabel As New MessageQueue("Label:UserMan")
3 End Sub
```

That rounds up how to bind to a message queue. Now it gets interesting, because next I will show you how to send, retrieve, and otherwise deal with messages.

Sending a Message

Sending a message is obviously one of the most important aspects of a message queue. If you can't send a message, why have a message queue? Let's take a look at the simplest form of sending a message to a message queue. The **Send** method of the **MessageQueue** class is used for this purpose, as demonstrated in Listing 8-10.

Listing 8-10. Sending a Simple Message to a Message Queue

```
1 Public Sub SendSimpleMessage()
2    Dim queUserMan As New _
3      MessageQueue(".\Private$\UserMan")
4
5    ' Send simple message to queue
6    queUserMan.Send("Test")
7 End Sub
```

After binding to the private UserMan queue on the local machine, I send a **String** object containing the text "Test" to the queue. Obviously this is not exactly useful, but you can apply this example to testing whether something is actually sent to the queue. As you have probably guessed, the **Send** method is overloaded, and I have used the version that only takes one argument and is an object.

If you execute the code in Listing 8-10, you can see the resulting message using the Server Explorer or the Computer Management MMC snap-in. Expand the private UserMan message queue and select the Queue Messages node. Now the Computer Management snap-in should resemble what is shown in Figure 8-3; if you're using the Server Explorer, it should resemble Figure 8-4. Please note that in Server Explorer, you need to expand the Queue Messages node to see the messages in the queue, as done in Figure 8-4.

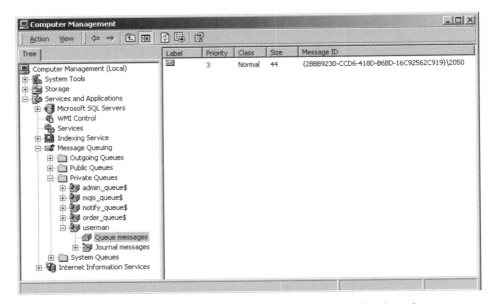

Figure 8-3. Computer Management with Queue Messages node selected

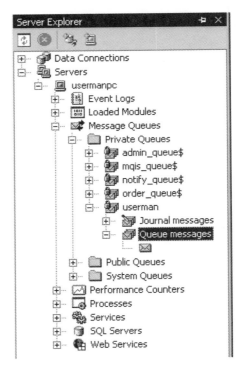

Figure 8-4. Server Explorer with Queue Messages node selected

> **NOTE** *One major advantage Computer Management has over the Server Explorer when it comes to message queues is that you can use it when you're not connected to the AD Domain Controller. This is NOT possible with the Server Explorer, even if you want to look at private message queues!*

Retrieving a Message

Obviously it is a good idea to be able to retrieve the messages that have been posted to a message queue. Otherwise the messages simply stack up your message queue server and do absolutely no good to anyone. There are actually a number of ways you can retrieve a message from a message queue, but let's start out with retrieving the message sent in Listing 8-10. See Listing 8-11 for the code that retrieves the first message from the message queue.

Listing 8-11. Retrieving the First Message from a Message Queue

```
1 Public Sub RetrieveSimpleMessage()
2    Dim queUserMan As New MessageQueue(".\Private$\UserMan")
3    Dim msgUserMan As Message
4
5    ' Retrieve first message from queue
6    msgUserMan = queUserMan.Receive()
7 End Sub
```

In Listing 8-11 I bind to the private UserMan message queue and retrieve the first message from the queue. When the message is retrieved from the message queue, it is also removed from the queue. If you need to read a message from the queue without removing it, you should take a look at "Peeking at Messages" later in this chapter for more information.

Although the example code in Listing 8-11 will retrieve the first message from the message queue, there isn't a lot you can do with it. If you try to access any of the properties of the msgUserMan message, an exception is thrown, because you have not set up a so-called formatter that can read the message. A message can take on a variety of different forms, so it is a must that you set up a formatter before you retrieve a message from the queue. See the next section, "Setting Up a Message Formatter," for more information on how to do this.

Receive and Peek

The **Receive** and **Peek** methods of the **MessageQueue** class are synchronous, meaning that they will block all other activity until the message has been retrieved. If there are no messages in the message queue, the **Receive** and **Peek** methods will wait until a message arrives in the queue. If you need asynchronous access you must use the **BeginReceive** method instead. Actually, you can specify a time-out value when you call the **Receive** or **Peek** methods to make sure you don't wait indefinitely. Both of these overloaded methods have a version that takes a **TimeSpan** argument. This means the method will return if a message is found in the queue or when the time specified in the **TimeSpan** argument has elapsed. An exception is thrown if the time elapses.

Setting Up a Message Formatter

Recall that you need to set up a formatter in order to be able to read the messages that you retrieve from your message queue. This is a fairly easy yet important task. The **Formatter** property of the **MessageQueue** class is used for this very purpose. When you instantiate an instance of the **MessageQueue** class, a default formatter is created for you, but this formatter cannot be used to read from the queue, only to write or send to the queue. This means you have to either change the default formatter or set up a new formatter.

See Listing 8-12 for example code that can retrieve and read the message sent in Listing 8-10. Mind you, if you have already retrieved that message from the queue, the queue is now empty, and you need to send another message before you try to receive again. If the message queue is empty, the **Receive** method will await the arrival of a new message in the queue.

Listing 8-12. Setting Up a New Formatter and Retrieving the First Message from a Queue

```
1 Public Sub RetrieveMessage()
2    Dim queUserMan As New MessageQueue(".\Private$\UserMan")
3    Dim msgUserMan As Message
4    Dim strBody As String
5
6    ' Set up the formatter
7    queUserMan.Formatter = New XmlMessageFormatter(New Type() _
8      {GetType(String)})
9
10   ' Retrieve first message from queue
11   msgUserMan = queUserMan.Receive
12   ' Save the message body
13   strBody = msgUserMan.Body.ToString
14 End Sub
```

In Listing 8-12 I specify that the formatter should be of type **XmlMessageFormatter**. This is the default formatter for a message queue, and it is used for serializing and deserializing the message body using XML format. I have also specified that the message formatter should accept message bodies of data type **String**. This is done on Lines 7 and 8. If I hadn't done this, I wouldn't be able to access the message body.

Generally you should use the same formatter for sending and receiving, but because this is a very simple example, the formatter is not needed for sending to the message queue. Now, let's see in which situations the **Formatter** property is really useful. In Listing 8-13 I set up the formatter so it will be able to read to different types of message bodies: A body of data type **String** and of data type **Integer**. This is done by adding both data types to the **Type** array as the only argument to the **XmlMessageFormatter** constructor.

Listing 8-13. Sending and Retrieving Different Messages from One Message Queue

```
1 Public Sub SendDifferentMessages()
2    Dim queUserMan As New MessageQueue(".\Private$\UserMan")
3    Dim msgUserMan As New Message()
4
5    ' Set up the formatter
6    queUserMan.Formatter = New XmlMessageFormatter(New Type() _
7      {GetType(String), GetType(Integer)})
8
9    ' Create body as a text message
10   msgUserMan.Body = "Test"
11   ' Send message to queue
12   queUserMan.Send(msgUserMan)
13   ' Create body as an integer
14   msgUserMan.Body = 12
15   ' Send message to queue
16   queUserMan.Send(msgUserMan)
17 End Sub
18
19 Public Sub RetrieveDifferentMessages()
20   Dim queUserMan As New MessageQueue(".\Private$\UserMan")
21   Dim msgUserMan As Message
22   Dim strBody As String
23   Dim intBody As Integer
24
25   ' Set up the formatter
26   queUserMan.Formatter = New XmlMessageFormatter(New Type() _
```

```
27    {GetType(String), GetType(Integer)})
28
29    ' Retrieve first message from queue
30    msgUserMan = queUserMan.Receive
31    strBody = msgUserMan.Body.ToString
32    ' Retrieve next message from queue
33    msgUserMan = queUserMan.Receive
34    intBody = msgUserMan.Body
35 End Sub
```

In Listing 8-13 I use the SendDifferentMessages procedure to send to two messages to the queue: one with a body of data type **String** and one with a body of data type **Integer**. In the RetrieveDifferentMessages procedure I retrieve these two messages in the same order they were sent to the message queue. The fact that you can send messages with a different body is what makes a message queue even more suitable than a database table for data exchange situations where the data exchanged has very different structures.

In the example code in Listing 8-13 I have used data types **String** and **Integer** as the body formats that can be deserialized when the messages are read from the queue, but you can in fact use any base data type as well as structures and managed objects. If you need to pass older COM/ActiveX objects, you should use the **ActiveXMessageFormatter** class instead. There is also the **BinaryMessageFormatter** class that you can use for serializing and deserializing messages using binary format, as opposed to the XML format used by the **XmlMessageFormatter** class.

Peeking at Messages

Sometimes it is not desirable to remove a message from the queue after you have had a look at the contents, as will happen when you use the **Receive** method of the **MessageQueue** class. However, there is another way: You can use the **Peek** method instead. This method does exactly the same as the **Receive** method except for removing the message from the queue. In addition, repeated calls to the **Peek** method will return the same message, unless a new message with a higher priority is inserted into the queue. See "Prioritizing Messages" later in this chapter for more information on that topic.

Listing 8-14 is actually a nearly complete copy of Listing 8-12 except for the call to the **Peek** method on Line 11. So if you want to look at the first message in the queue, the **Peek** and **Receive** methods work exactly the same, except for the removal of the message. See "Clearing Messages from the Queue" for details about removing messages.

Listing 8-14. Peeking at a Message in the Queue

```
1    Public Sub PeekMessage()
2    Dim queUserMan As New MessageQueue(".\Private$\UserMan")
3    Dim msgUserMan As Message
4    Dim strBody As String
5
6    ' Set up the formatter
7    queUserMan.Formatter = New XmlMessageFormatter(New Type() _
8      {GetType(String)})
9
10   ' Peek first message from queue
11   msgUserMan = queUserMan.Peek
12   ' Save the message body
13   strBody = msgUserMan.Body.ToString
14 End Sub
```

Picking Specific Messages from a Queue

A message queue is designed with a stack-like structure in mind. It doesn't have any search facilities as such, meaning that messages are retrieved from the top of the stack, or rather the top of the message queue. However, it is possible to pick specific messages from your queue. To do so, use the **ReceiveById** method, which takes a message ID as its only argument. The message ID is generated by Message Queuing and it is assigned to an instance of the **Message class** when it is sent to the queue. Listing 8-15 shows you how to retrieve the ID from a message and later use that ID to retrieve this message, even though it is not at the top of the message queue.

Listing 8-15. Retrieving a Message from the Queue by Message ID

```
1 Public Sub RetrieveMessageById()
2    Dim queUserMan As New MessageQueue(".\Private$\UserMan")
3    Dim msgUserMan As New Message()
4    Dim strId As String
5
6    ' Set up the formatter
7    queUserMan.Formatter = New XmlMessageFormatter(New Type() _
8      {GetType(String)})
9
10   ' Create body as a text message
11   msgUserMan.Body = "Test 1"
12   ' Send message to queue
```

```
13    queUserMan.Send(msgUserMan)
14
15    ' Create body as a text message
16    msgUserMan.Body = "Test 2"
17
18    ' Send message to queue
19    queUserMan.Send(msgUserMan)
20    strId = msgUserMan.Id
21    ' Create body as a text message
22    msgUserMan.Body = "Test 3"
23    ' Send message to queue
24    queUserMan.Send(msgUserMan)
25
26    msgUserMan = queUserMan.ReceiveById(strId)
27    MsgBox("Saved Id=" & strId & vbCrLf & "Retrieved Id=" & msgUserMan.Id)
28 End Sub
```

In Listing 8-15 I bind to the existing private UserMan queue, set up the formatter to accept data type **String**, create three messages and send them to the queue. Just after the second message is sent to the queue, the message ID is saved, and then this ID is used to retrieve the associated message. This message is second in the message queue. On Line 27 I simply display the saved message ID and the retrieved message to show that they are the same.

If you use the **ReceiveById** or indeed the **PeekById** method, you must be aware that an **InvalidOperationException** exception is thrown if the message does not exist in the queue. So whenever you use one of these methods, you should use a structured error handler, as demonstrated in Listing 8-16.

Listing 8-16. Retrieving a Message by Message ID in a Safe Manner

```
1 Public Function RetrieveMessageByIdSafe(ByVal vstrId As String) As Message
2    Dim queUserMan As New MessageQueue(".\Private$\UserMan")
3    Dim msgUserMan As New Message()
4
5    ' Set up the formatter
6    queUserMan.Formatter = New XmlMessageFormatter(New Type() _
7     {GetType(String)})
8
9    Try
10       msgUserMan = queUserMan.ReceiveById(vstrId)
11    Catch objE As InvalidOperationException
12       ' Message not found, return a Null value
13       RetrieveMessageByIdSafe = Nothing
14
15       Exit Function
```

```
16    End Try
17
18    ' Return message
19    RetrieveMessageByIdSafe = msgUserMan
20 End Function
```

Listing 8-16 catches an attempt to locate a nonexisting message by ID and simply returns a null value to the caller. If the passed message ID can be found in the queue, the retrieved message is returned to the caller.

The ID of a message is of data type **String**, but it is internally a GUID as you can see from Listing 8-15. At any rate, the **Id** property of a message is read-only, so you cannot assign your own IDs to your messages. I guess this is one way of ensuring all messages are unique. Your only option is to save the ID of a particular message and then later use this ID to retrieve the message.

> **NOTE**   *The **PeekById** method works the same as the **ReceiveById** method, except that the message is not removed from the message queue.*

Sending and Retrieving Messages Asynchronously

Sometimes it is desirable to be able to send and receive your messages in asynchronous fashion. This makes sure your application isn't held up until delivery or retrieval has been completed. In order to use asynchronous communication with a message queue, you need to set up an event handler that deals with the result of the asynchronous operation. This can done using the **AddHandler** statement. See Listing 8-17 for an example.

*Listing 8-17. Receive a Message Asynchronously Using **AddHandler***

```
1 Public Sub MessageReceiveCompleteEvent(ByVal vobjSource As Object, _
2  ByVal vobjEventArgs As ReceiveCompletedEventArgs)
3    Dim msgUserMan As New Message()
4    Dim queUserMan As New MessageQueue()
5
6    ' Make sure we bind to the right message queue
7    queUserMan = CType(vobjSource, MessageQueue)
8
9    ' End async receive
10   msgUserMan = queUserMan.EndReceive(vobjEventArgs.AsyncResult)
11 End Sub
12
13 Public Sub RetrieveMessagesAsync()
```

```
14    Dim queUserMan As New MessageQueue(".\Private$\UserMan")
15    Dim msgUserMan As New Message()
16
17    ' Set up the formatter
18    queUserMan.Formatter = New XmlMessageFormatter(New Type() _
19      {GetType(String)})
20
21    ' Add an event handler
22    AddHandler queUserMan.ReceiveCompleted, _
23      AddressOf MessageReceiveCompleteEvent
24
25    queUserMan.BeginReceive(New TimeSpan(0, 0, 10))
26 End Sub
```

In Listing 8-17 I have first set up the procedure that will receive the Receive-Complete event. This procedure takes care of binding to the passed queue, which is the queue used to begin the retrieval, and then the asynchronous retrieval is ended by calling the **EndReceive** method. This method also returns the message from the queue.

In the RetrieveMessagesAsync procedure I set up the message queue, and on Line 22 I add the event handler that calls MessageReceiveCompleteEvent procedure on completion of the message retrieval. Finally the asynchronous message retrieval is started by calling the **BeginReceive** method on Line 25. I have specified that the call should time-out after 10 seconds using a new instance of the **TimeSpan** class.

Listing 8-17 makes use of the **BeginReceive** and **EndReceive** methods, but you can use the example code with only very few modifications if you want to peek instead of receive the messages from the queue (see Listing 8-18).

*Listing 8-18. Peeking Asynchronously Using **AddHandler***

```
1 Public Sub MessagePeekCompleteEvent(ByVal vobjSource As Object, _
2  ByVal vobjEventArgs As PeekCompletedEventArgs)
3    Dim msgUserMan As New Message()
4    Dim queUserMan As New MessageQueue()
5
6    ' Make sure we bind to the right message queue
7    queUserMan = CType(vobjSource, MessageQueue)
8
9    ' End async peek
10   msgUserMan = queUserMan.EndPeek(vobjEventArgs.AsyncResult)
11 End Sub
12
13 Public Sub PeekMessagesAsync()
14    Dim queUserMan As New MessageQueue(".\Private$\UserMan")
```

```
15    Dim msgUserMan As New Message()
16
17    ' Set up the formatter
18    queUserMan.Formatter = New XmlMessageFormatter(New Type() _
19      {GetType(String)})
20
21    ' Add an event handler
22    AddHandler queUserMan.PeekCompleted, _
23      AddressOf MessagePeekCompleteEvent
24
25    queUserMan.BeginPeek(New TimeSpan(0, 0, 10))
26 End Sub
```

Clearing Messages from the Queue

Messages can be removed from a message queue in two ways: You can remove them one by one or you can clear the whole queue in one go.

Removing a Single Message from the Queue

Removing a single message from the queue can only be done programmatically and not using either Server Explorer or Computer Management.

You can use the **Receive** method to remove messages from the queue. Although this method is generally used to retrieve messages from the queue, it also removes the message. See "Retrieving a Message" earlier in this chapter for more information.

You can also use the **ReceiveById** method to remove a message. Alternatively, you can use the **PeekById** method to find a specific message and then use **ReceiveById** to remove it. See "Picking Specific Messages from a Queue" earlier in this chapter for more information on how to use the **ReceiveById** and **PeekById** methods.

Removing All Messages from the Queue

Removing all messages from the queue can be done either manually using Server Explorer or Computer Management, or programmatically.

> **CAUTION**   *Clearing all messages from a queue is an irreversible action, and once you confirm the deletion, the messages are permanently lost. So be careful when you perform this action!*

Removing All Messages Manually

If you want to manually remove all messages from a queue, you can use either the Server Explorer or Computer Management. Select the Queue Messages node (refer back to Figures 8-3 and 8-4), right-click on this node, and select All Tasks/Purge (Computer Management) or Clear Messages (Server Explorer) from the pop-up menu. Then click **Yes** or **OK** in the confirmation dialog box to clear all messages from the queue.

Removing All Messages Programmatically

If you want to clear all messages from a queue programmatically, you can use the **Purge** method for this purpose. Listing 8-19 shows you how to bind to a message queue and clear all messages from it.

Listing 8-19. Clearing All Messages from a Queue

```
1 Public Sub ClearMessageQueue()
2    Dim queUserMan As New MessageQueue(".\Private$\UserMan")
3    Dim msgUserMan As Message
4
5    ' Clear all messages from queue
6    queUserMan.Purge()
7 End Sub
```

In Listing 8-19 I have used the **Purge** method of the **MessageQueue** class to clear all messages from the queue. This method works with any number of messages in the queue, meaning that it doesn't matter if the queue is empty when you call this method.

Prioritizing Messages

Every now and then it is important that a particular message is read ASAP. Normally when you send a message, it ends up at the end of the message queue, because messages are sorted by arrival time. However, since messages are first and foremost sorted by priority, you can specify a higher priority to make sure that this message is added to the message queue at the top.

You can set the priority of a message using the **Priority** method of the **Message** class. See Listing 8-20 for a code example that sends two messages to the queue, one with normal priority and one with highest priority.

Listing 8-20. Sending Messages with Different Priority

```
1 Public Sub SendPriorityMessages()
2    Dim queUserMan As New MessageQueue(".\Private$\UserMan")
3    Dim msgUserMan As New Message()
4
5    ' Set up the formatter
6    queUserMan.Formatter = New XmlMessageFormatter(New Type() _
7    {GetType(String), GetType(Integer)})
8
9    ' Create first body
10   msgUserMan.Body = "First Message"
11   ' Send message to queue
12   queUserMan.Send(msgUserMan)
13
14   ' Create second body
15   msgUserMan.Body = "Second Message"
16   ' Set priority to highest
17   msgUserMan.Priority = MessagePriority.Highest
18   ' Send message to queue
19   queUserMan.Send(msgUserMan)
20 End Sub
21
22 Public Sub RetrievePriorityMessage()
23   Dim queUserMan As New MessageQueue(".\Private$\UserMan")
24   Dim msgUserMan As Message
25
26   ' Set up the formatter
27   queUserMan.Formatter = New XmlMessageFormatter(New Type() _
28   {GetType(String)})
29
30   ' Retrieve first message from queue
31   msgUserMan = queUserMan.Receive
32   ' Display the message body
33   MsgBox(msgUserMan.Body.ToString)
34 End Sub
```

If you run the code in Listing 8-20, you will see that setting the priority of the second message to highest makes sure that it goes to the top of the message queue. The message box will display the text "Second Message". Actually, this is only true if your message queue isn't transactional. If it is, the text displayed will be "First Message."

The priority of the second message is set on Line 17. When you set the **Priority** property of a **Message** object, it must be set to a member of the **MessagePriority** enum. The default is **Normal**.

Locating a Message Queue

Sometime you don't know the path to a particular queue or you just need to verify that a specific queue still exists. Let's start with the easy task: how to check if a particular queue exists (see Listing 8-21).

Listing 8-21. Checking If a Message Queue Exists

```
1 Public Function CheckQueueExists(ByVal vstrPath As String) As Boolean
2    CheckQueueExists = MessageQueue.Exists(vstrPath)
3 End Function
```

In Listing 8-21 I use the **Exists** method of the **MessageQueue** class. Because this is a public shared function, you don't actually have to instantiate a message queue object in order to use this method.

The CheckQueueExists procedure will return **True** or **False** depending on if the passed vstrPath argument matches an existing message queue.

Now this is pretty simple, because you already know the path. However, sometimes you don't know the path, just the name of the machine where message queuing is installed. See Listing 8-22 for an example of how to retrieve a list of all the private queues on a specific machine.

Listing 8-22. Retrieve All Private Queues on a Machine

```
 1 Public Sub BrowsePrivateQueues()
 2    Dim arquePrivate() As MessageQueue = _
 3     MessageQueue.GetPrivateQueuesByMachine("USERMANPC")
 4    Dim queUserMan As MessageQueue
 5
 6    ' Display the name of all the private queues on the machine
 7      For Each queUserMan In arquePrivate
 8        MsgBox(queUserMan.Label)
 9      Next
10 End Sub
```

In Listing 8-22 I retrieve all the message queues on the USERMANPC machine and display their label. As you can see from Line 2, all the queues are saved in an array of **MessageQueue** class instances. If you need the public queues instead, simply replace the **GetPrivateQueuesByMachine** method call with a call to the **GetPublicQueuesByMachine** method.

The public queues can also be located on the whole network instead of just one machine. There are three different methods that can be used to locate public queues network wide:

- **GetPublicQueues**

- **GetPublicQueuesByCategory**

- **GetPublicQueuesByLabel**

See Listings 8-23, 8-24, and 8-25 for code that shows you how to use these methods.

Listing 8-23. Retrieve All Public Queues on a Network

```
 1 Public Sub BrowsePublicQueuesNetworkWide()
 2    Dim arrquePublic() As MessageQueue = _
 3     MessageQueue.GetPublicQueues()
 4    Dim queUserMan As MessageQueue
 5
 6    ' Display the name of all the public queues on the network
 7    For Each queUserMan In arrquePublic
 8       MsgBox(queUserMan.QueueName)
 9    Next
10 End Sub
```

Listing 8-23 uses the **GetPublicQueues** method to retrieve all public queues on the network and then displays the name of each queue.

Listing 8-24 retrieves all public queues on a network by category using the **GetPublicQueuesByCategory** method. For each returned message queue in the "00000000-0000-0000-0000-000000000001" category, I display the queue name. The category being referred to is the same as the Type ID in Figure 8-2 and the **Category** property of the **MessageQueue** class. This is a way for you to group your message queues, particularly for administrative purposes.

Listing 8-24. Retrieving All Public Queues on a Network by Category

```
 1 Public Sub BrowsePublicQueuesByCategoryNetworkWide()
 2    Dim arrquePublic() As MessageQueue = _
 3     MessageQueue.GetPublicQueuesByCategory( _
 4     New Guid("00000000-0000-0000-0000-000000000001"))
 5    Dim queUserMan As MessageQueue
 6
 7    ' Display the name of all the public queues
 8    ' on the network within a specific category
 9    For Each queUserMan In arrquePublic
```

359

```
10       MsgBox(queUserMan.QueueName)
11    Next
12 End Sub
```

Listing 8-25 shows you how to find all the public queues on the network that have the "userman" label. The name of the machine where each queue is located is then displayed one by one.

Listing 8-25. Retrieve All Public Queues on a Network by Label

```
 1 Public Sub BrowsePublicQueuesByLabelNetworkWide()
 2    Dim arquePublic() As MessageQueue = _
 3     MessageQueue.GetPublicQueuesByLabel("userman")
 4    Dim queUserMan As MessageQueue
 5
 6    ' Display the name of all the public queues
 7    ' on the network with a specific label
 8    For Each queUserMan In arquePublic
 9       MsgBox(queUserMan.MachineName)
10    Next
11 End Sub
```

Removing a Message Queue

Now and then you might need to remove a message queue from a machine, and for this purpose you have several options. A message queue can be deleted either manually using Server Explorer or Computer Management or programmatically.

> **CAUTION** *Clearing a message queue is an irreversible action, and once you confirm the deletion, the queue and all its messages are permanently lost!*

Removing a Message Queue Manually

If you want to manually remove a queue, you can use either the Server Explorer or Computer Management. Select the queue node (refer back to Figures 8-1 and 8-5), right-click on this node, and select **Delete** from the pop-up menu. Then click **Yes** in the confirmation dialog box to remove the message queue and all its messages.

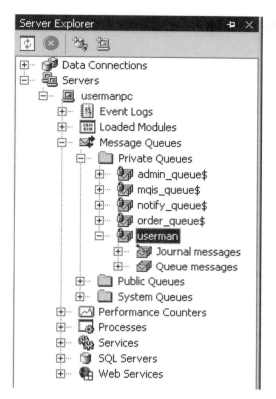

Figure 8-5. The Server Explorer with message queue selected

Removing a Message Queue Programmatically

If you want to clear all messages from a queue programmatically, you can use the **Purge** method for this purpose. Listing 8-26 shows you how to bind to a message queue and clear all messages from it.

Listing 8-26. Removing a Message Queue

```
1 Public Sub RemoveMessageQueue(ByVal vstrPath As String)
2     MessageQueue.Delete(vstrPath)
3 End Sub
```

In Listing 8-26 I have used the **Delete** method of the **MessageQueue** class to remove the queue with the vstrPath path. Keep in mind that if the queue doesn't exist, an exception is thrown, so I can only recommend that you don't use the example code in Listing 8-26 without being sure the queue actually exists. See how to use the **Exists** method in the section "Locating a Message Queue" later in this chapter. Alternatively, you can set up a structured error handler like the one in Listing 8-27.

Listing 8-27. Removing a Message Queue in a Safe Manner

```
1 Public Sub RemoveMessageQueueSafely(ByVal vstrPath As String)
2    Try
3       MessageQueue.Delete(vstrPath)
4    Catch objE As Exception
5       MsgBox(objE.Message)
6    End Try
7 End Sub
```

In Listing 8-27 I catch any exception being thrown when I try to remove the message queue specified using the **vstrPath** argument. I am only displaying the error message, but I am sure you can take it from there.

Making Message Queues Transactional

As with normal database access, it is possible to make your message queues transactional. This means you can send several messages as a single transaction, and then act upon the result of the transmission of these messages by determining if you should commit or rollback the messages. Whether a message queue is transactional or not is determined at creation time. You cannot change this after the queue has been created.

There are two types of transactions when it comes to message queues: internal and external. Please see the following sections for a brief description of the two types of message queue transactions.

Internal Transactions

Internal transactions refers to transactions that you manage manually or explicitly and only involves messages sent between a client and a message queue. This means that no other resources, such as database manipulation, can be part of an internal transaction and that you must explicitly begin and then commit or roll back a transaction. Internal transactions are handled by the Message Queuing's Transaction Coordinator.

Internal transactions are faster than external transactions, which are discussed next.

External Transactions

External transactions are exactly what the name suggests: external. Resources other than message queue resources are part of external transactions. This could be database access, Active Directory access, and so on. Furthermore, external transactions are NOT handled by the Message Queuing's Transaction Coordinator, but by a coordinator such as the Microsoft Distributed Transaction Coordinator (MS DTC), and external transactions are implicit or automatic.

External transactions are slower than internal transactions. In this chapter I will only be covering internal transactions, since external transactions fall outside the scope of this book and could by themselves be the subject of an entire book.

Creating a Transactional Message Queue

If you are creating your queue programmatically, see Listing 8-4 for an example of how to make it transactional. If you want to create your transactional message queue using Server Explorer, Chapter 4 gives you the details. Of course it is also possible to use the Computer Management MMC snap-in. Open the snap-in and follow these steps:

1. Expand the Services and Applications node

2. Expand the Message Queuing node

3. Select either the Public Queues or the Private Queues node.

4. Right-click on the node and select New/Public Queue or New/Private Queue from the pop-up menu. This brings up the Queue Name dialog box, as shown in Figure 8-6.

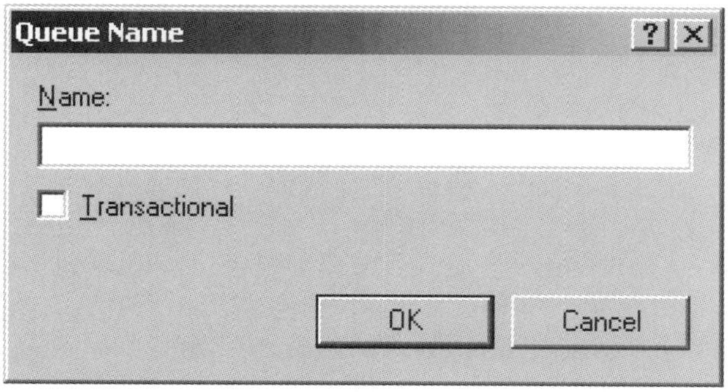

*Figure 8-6. The **Queue Name** dialog box*

Give the message queue a name by typing one in the Name text box, and make sure you check the Transactional check box before you click **OK** to create the message queue.

Starting a Transaction

Because internal transactions are explicit or manual, you must begin a transaction from code before you start sending and retrieving messages that are to be part of the transaction. Actually, the very first thing you should check is if your message queue is transactional. This can be done using the **Transactional** property, which returns a **Boolean** value indicating if the queue is transactional or not:

```
If queUserMan.Transactional Then
```

The next thing you need to do is to create an instance of the **MessageQueueTransaction** class. The constructor for this class is not overloaded, so it's created like this:

```
Dim qtrUserMan As New MessageQueueTransaction()
```

Now it's time to start the transaction, and this is done using the **Begin** method of the **MessageQueueTransaction** class, as follows:

```
qtrUserMan.Begin()
```

You may be wondering how you would reference this transaction object from the message queue object. I do understand if you are confused, but it's really not that difficult. You simply pass the transaction object when you send or retrieve a message, like this:

```
msgUserMan = queUserMan.Receive(qtrUserMan)
```

or

```
queUserMan.Send(msgUserMan, qtrUserMan)
```

As you can see from these short examples, you do as you normally would when you write your code without transactions, with the exception that you pass the transaction object when you perform an operation that needs to be part of the transaction. This has some advantages over having the transaction coupled directly with the message queue: You decide what operations are part of the transaction, therefore you can send or receive messages that are part of the transaction and send or receive other messages that are not. You can also use your transaction with more than one message queue.

Ending a Transaction

When you have started a transaction, you must also end it. That's pretty logical if you ask me. However, how the transaction should be ended is not quite so direct. If you didn't run into any problems during the operations that are part of the transaction, you would normally commit the transaction or apply the changes to the message queue(s). If you do run into a problem with any of the transactional operations, you would normally abort the transaction as soon as the problem occurs. When I refer to problems I am not only talking about exceptions that are thrown by the **MessageQueue** object, but also other operations external to the message queue operations that can make you abort the transaction.

Committing a Transaction

Committing a transaction is straightforward, and it is done using the **Commit** method of the **MessageQueue** class, as follows:

```
qtrUserMan.Commit()
```

The **Commit** method is not overloaded and it doesn't take any parameters. However, a **MessageQueueException** exception is thrown if you try to commit a transaction that hasn't been started (**Begin** method).

Aborting a Transaction

In situations where you have to abort a transaction, you can use the **Abort** method of the **MessageQueue** class, like this:

```
qtrUserMan.Abort()
```

The **Abort** method is not overloaded and it doesn't take any parameters. However, like the **Commit** method, a **MessageQueueException** exception is thrown if you try to abort a transaction that hasn't been started (**Begin** method).

Using the MessageQueueTransaction Class

I have just gone over all the methods that are important to managing a transaction, but there is one property that I haven't mentioned and that is the **Status** property. This read-only property returns a member of the **MessageQueueTransactionStatus** enum that tells you the status of the transaction. The **Status** property can be read from the time you create your instance of the **MessageQueueTransaction** class and until the object has been destroyed. You can see the **MessageQueueTransactionStatus** enum members in Table 8-1.

*Table 8-1. Members of the **MessageQueueTransactionStatus** Enum*

MEMBER NAME	DESCRIPTION
Aborted	The transaction has been aborted. This can be done by the user with the **Abort** method.
Committed	The transaction has been committed. This is done using the **Commit** method.
Initialized	The transaction object has been instantiated, but no transaction has yet been started. In this state you should not pass the transaction object to the message queue methods.
Pending	The transaction has been started and is now pending an **Abort** or **Commit**. When the transaction is pending, you can pass the transaction object to the message queue methods.

See Listing 8-28 for an example of how to use transactions combined with a structured exception handler. The example code can only be run if you have created a private, transactional message queue named UserMan on the local machine.

Listing 8-28. Using Message Queue Transactions

```
1 Public Sub UseMQTransactions()
2    Dim qtrUserMan As New MessageQueueTransaction()
3    Dim queUserMan As New MessageQueue(".\Private$\UserMan")
4    Dim msgUserMan As New Message()
5
6    ' Set up the queue formatter
7    queUserMan.Formatter = New XmlMessageFormatter(New Type() _
8      {GetType(String)})
9
10   ' Clear the message queue
11   queUserMan.Purge()
12   ' Start the transaction
13   qtrUserMan.Begin()
14
15   Try
16      ' Create message body
17      msgUserMan.Body = "First Message"
18      ' Send message to queue
```

```
19       queUserMan.Send(msgUserMan, qtrUserMan)
20
21       ' Create message body
22       msgUserMan.Body = "Second Message"
23       ' Send message to queue
24       queUserMan.Send(msgUserMan)
25
26       ' Retrieve message from queue
27       msgUserMan = queUserMan.Receive()
28       ' Display message body
29       MsgBox(msgUserMan.Body)
30
31       ' Commit transaction
32       qtrUserMan.Commit()
33
34       ' Retrieve message from queue
35       msgUserMan = queUserMan.Receive()
36       ' Display message body
37       MsgBox(msgUserMan.Body)
38     Catch objE As Exception
39       ' Abort the transaction
40       qtrUserMan.Abort()
41     End Try
42 End Sub
```

In Listing 8-28 I have demonstrated how you can send messages with and without transactions to the same message queue. When you run the code, you will see the text "Second Message" displayed before the "First Message" text, because when the first message is retrieved from the queue on Line 27, the first message has not yet been committed to the queue. The transaction is then committed and the first message sent to the queue.

Looking at System-Generated Queues

So far I have only been looking at user-created queues, but there is another group of queues that needs attention: system-generated queues. These queues are maintained by **Message Queuing**. The following queues are system queues:

- Dead-letter messages

- Journal messages

- Transactional dead-letter messages

The two dead-letter message queues, seen in the Server Explorer in Figure 8-7 on the System Queues node, are used for storing messages that cannot be delivered. One queue holds the nontransactional messages and the other one holds the transactional ones. See the next section for an explanation of the Journal messages queues.

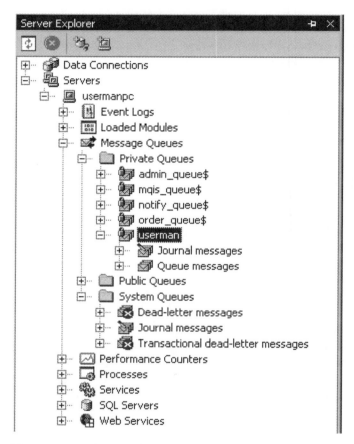

Figure 8-7. The system and journal queues

Using Journal Storage

Journal storage is a great facility for keeping copies of messages that are sent to or removed from a message queue. It can be very helpful if for some reason you need to resend a message. The message delivery might have failed, and you receive a negative acknowledgement. Because an acknowledgement does not contain the message body, you cannot use this message to resend the original message. However, you can use it to find a copy of the original message in the Journal messages queue.

Every message queuing client (machine) has a global journal queue called the system journal. The system journal stores copies of all messages sent from the message queuing client. This is true whether the message is delivered or not.

Besides the system journal, all message queues have their own journal queue. The journal queue associated with each message queue stores copies of all messages removed from the message queue, but only if journaling is enabled on the message queue. See the next section, "Enabling Journaling on a Message Queue," for more information on how to enable journaling on a message queue.

The last way to use journal storage is to programmatically enable journaling on a per-message basis. If you do this, copies of messages sent from your system will be saved in the system journal on the machine that sends the message.

Enabling Journaling on a Message Queue

Journaling can be enabled on a message queue either manually or programmatically. If you want to do it manually, you can do it from the Computer Management MMC snap-in. In Figure 8-2 you can see the Properties dialog box for an existing queue or a queue that is about to be created. If you want to enable journaling you should check the Enabled check box in the Journal group and click on Apply.

You can also programmatically enable journaling on an existing queue by setting the **UseJournalQueue** property of an existing message queue to **True**, like this:

```
Dim queUserMan As New MessageQueue(".\Private$\UserMan")

queUserMan.UseJournalQueue = True
```

Enabling Journaling on a Per-Message Basis

It is also possible to use journaling on a per-message basis, and this is done programmatically, by setting the **UseJournalQueue** property of an existing message to **True** before sending it to the queue, as shown in Listing 8-29.

Listing 8-29. Enabling Message Journaling

```
1 Public Sub EnableMessageJournaling()
2    Dim queUserMan As New MessageQueue(".\Private$\UserMan")
3    Dim msgUserMan As New Message()
4
5    ' Set up the formatter
6    queUserMan.Formatter = New XmlMessageFormatter(New Type() _
7    {GetType(String)})
8
9    ' Create message body
10   msgUserMan.Body = "Message"
11   ' Enable message journaling
12   msgUserMan.UseJournalQueue = True
13   ' Send message to queue
14   queUserMan.Send(msgUserMan)
15 End Sub
```

In Listing 8-29 I enable message journaling on the msgUserMan message on Line 12, just before I send it to the queue. This saves a copy of the message in the system journal on the local machine. Well, actually it won't be saved until the message is sent to the queue (Line 14).

Retrieving a Message from Journal Storage

Now, enabling journaling is easy enough, but how do you actually retrieve the messages from the journal when needed? Well, you can access these journal queues and other system queues by specifying the correct path to the queue. For example, the following code accesses the journal storage for the private message queue UserMan on the local machine:

```
Dim queUserMan As New MessageQueue(".\Private$\UserMan\Journal$")
```

Securing Your Message Queuing

So far in this chapter you have been shown how to create private and public queues, both transactional and nontransactional ones, and you have seen how you send and receive messages to and from a queue, including peeking at messages without removing them from the queue. However, I have yet to mention message queuing security, which is what I am going to cover in this section.

Message Queuing uses built-in features of the Windows OS for securing messaging. This includes the following:

- Authentication

- Encryption

- Access control

- Auditing

Using Authentication

Authentication is the process by which a message's integrity is ensured and the sender of a message can be verified. This can be achieved by setting the message queue's **Authenticate** property to **True**. The default value for this property is **False**, meaning no authentication is required. When this property is set to **True**, the queue will only accept authenticated messages—nonauthenticated messages are rejected. In other words, the message queue on the server requires messages to be authenticated, not just the message queue object you use to set the **Authenticate** property. Basically this means that when you set the property, you affect all other message queue objects that are working on the same message queue. You can programmatically enable authentication as it's done in Listing 8-30.

Listing 8-30. Enable Authentication on a Messsage Queue

```
1 Public Sub EnableQueueAuthentication()
2     Dim queUserMan As New MessageQueue(".\Private$\UserMan")
3     Dim msgUserMan As New Message()
4
5     ' Enable queue authentication
6     queUserMan.Authenticate = True
7 End Sub
```

You can also request authentication by setting this property from the Computer Management MMC snap-in. See Figure 8-2 and the section "Displaying or Changing the Properties of Your Message Queue" for more information on how to set the properties of an existing message queue. In Figure 8-2 you can see the Authenticated check box, which you need to enable before clicking OK to request that messages on this queue are authenticated.

If a message is not authenticated, it is rejected and therefore lost. However, you can specify that the rejected message should be placed in the dead-letter queue, as shown in Listing 8-31.

Listing 8-31. Rejecting a Nonauthenticated Message

```
1  Public Sub RejectNonauthenticatedMessage()
2    Dim queUserMan As New MessageQueue(".\Private$\UserMan")
3    Dim msgUserMan As New Message()
4
5    ' Enable queue authentication
6    queUserMan.Authenticate = True
7    ' Set up the queue formatter
8    queUserMan.Formatter = New XmlMessageFormatter(New Type() {GetType(String)})
9
10   ' Create message body
11   msgUserMan.Body = "Message Body"
12   ' Make sure a rejected message is placed in the dead-letter queue
13   msgUserMan.UseDeadLetterQueue = True
14
15   ' Send message to queue
16   queUserMan.Send(msgUserMan)
```

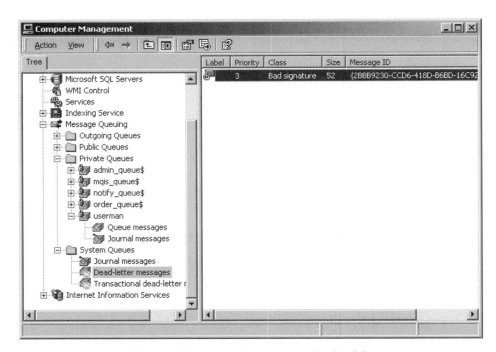

Figure 8-8. A rejected nonauthenticated message in the dead-letter queue

```
17 End Sub
```

In Listing 8-31 the **UseDeadLetterQueue** property is set to **True**, meaning that if the message is rejected, it is placed in the dead-letter queue (see Figure 8-8).

In Figure 8-8 you can see that the message in the dead-letter queue has been rejected because of a bad signature. Another way of dealing with rejected messages is to request notification of the message rejection. Setting the **AcknowledgeType** and **AdministrationQueue** properties does this (see Listing 8-32).

Listing 8-32. Receiving Rejection Notification in the Admin Queue

```
 1 Public Sub PlaceNonauthenticatedMessageInAdminQueue()
 2    Dim queUserManAdmin As New MessageQueue(".\Private$\UserManAdmin")
 3    Dim queUserMan As New MessageQueue(".\Private$\UserMan")
 4    Dim msgUserMan As New Message()
 5
 6    ' Enable queue authentication
 7    queUserMan.Authenticate = True
 8    ' Set up the queue formatter
 9    queUserMan.Formatter = New XmlMessageFormatter(New Type() {GetType(String)})
10
11    ' Create message body
12    msgUserMan.Body = "Message Body"
13    ' Make sure a rejected message is placed in the admin queue
14    msgUserMan.AdministrationQueue = queUserManAdmin
15    ' These types of rejected messages
16    msgUserMan.AcknowledgeType = AcknowledgeTypes.NotAcknowledgeReachQueue
17
18    ' Send message to queue
19    queUserMan.Send(msgUserMan)
20 End Sub
```

In Listing 8-32 I have set up the private queue UserManAdmin to receive notification of rejection. Please note that you need to have created this message queue as a nontransactional queue before you run the example code.

As is the case with the code in Listing 8-31, the code in Listing 8-32 rejects the messages that you send. That seems okay, because you requested that all messages should be authenticated, but you "forgot" to authenticate your message.

Setting the **AttachSenderId** property to **True** does this, because it results in Message Queuing setting the **SenderId** property. However, this is not enough, because you also need to set the **UseAuthentication** property to **True**. This ensures the message is digitally signed before it is sent to the queue. Likewise, the digital signature that Message Queuing has assigned is used for authenticating the message when it is received. Listing 8-33 shows you how to send an authenticated message.

Listing 8-33. Sending an Authenticated Message

```
1 Public Sub AcceptAuthenticatedMessage()
2    Dim queUserMan As New MessageQueue(".\Private$\UserMan")
3    Dim msgUserMan As New Message()
4
5    ' Enable queue authentication
6    queUserMan.Authenticate = True
7    ' Set up the queue formatter
8    queUserMan.Formatter = New XmlMessageFormatter(New Type() {GetType(String)})
9
10   ' Make sure a rejected message is placed in the dead-letter queue
11   msgUserMan.UseDeadLetterQueue = True
12   ' Make sure that message queuing attaches the sender id and
13   ' is digitally signed before it is sent
14   msgUserMan.UseAuthentication = True
15   msgUserMan.AttachSenderId = True
16   ' Create message body
17   msgUserMan.Body = "Message Body"
18
19   ' Send message to queue
20   queUserMan.Send(msgUserMan)
21 End Sub
```

In Listing 8-33 I set the **UseAuthentication** and **AttachSenderId** properties of the **Message** object to **True** in order to ensure that the message is digitally signed and can be authenticated by Message Queuing. In this situation the message queue, unlike in the examples in Listings 8-31 and 8-32, will not reject the message, even if it only accepts authenticated messages. If authentication has already been set up on the message queue, you can leave out Lines 5 and 6.

Now it's obviously good to know if a message has been authenticated or not, but you don't actually have to check anything to find out. If you have set up authentication on the message queue, all messages in the queue have been authenticated when they arrived in the queue, meaning you can trust any message you receive from the queue.

Using Encryption

Encryption is another way of securing messages sent between message queuing computers. With encryption, anyone trying to spy on the traffic on the network between the message queuing computers will receive encrypted messages. Now, while someone might be able to decrypt your messages, encryption certainly makes it harder to obtain sensitive information.

There is some overhead involved when you encrypt your messages at the sending end and decrypt them at the receiving end, but if your network is public and you are sending sensitive information, you should definitely consider using encrypted messages.

As is the case with authentication, encryption requirements can be applied to the queue, meaning that all nonencrypted messages will be rejected by the queue. Setting the **EncryptionRequired** property of the **MessageQueue** object to **EncryptionRequired.Body**, as in Listing 8-34, does this.

Listing 8-34. Making Sure Nonencrypted Messages Are Rejected by the Queue

```
1 Public Sub EnableRequireBodyEncryption()
2    Dim queUserMan As New MessageQueue(".\Private$\UserMan")
3    Dim msgUserMan As New Message()
4
5    ' Enable body encryption requirement
6    queUserMan.EncryptionRequired = EncryptionRequired.Body
7 End Sub
```

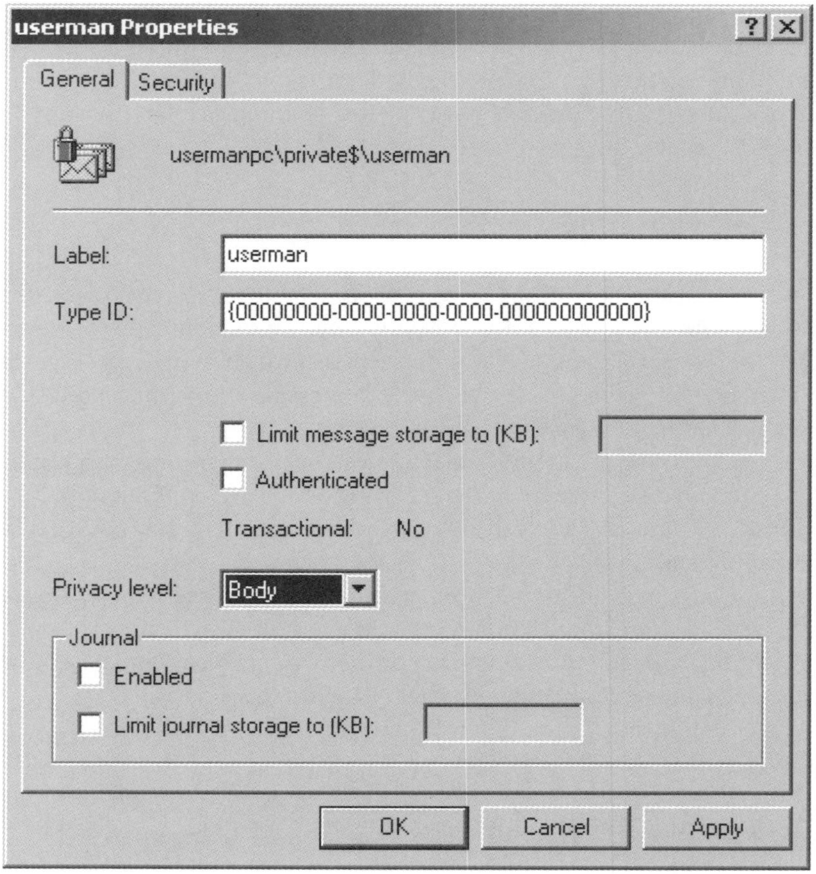

Figure 8-9. The privacy level set to Body

In Listing 8-34 I set the **EncryptionRequired** property of the **MessageQueue** object to **EncryptionRequired.Body**. As a result, the body of any message sent to the queue must be encrypted; otherwise it is rejected. Message Queue encryption is also called privacy, meaning a private message, not to be confused with a private message queue, is an encrypted message. Instead of setting the encryption property of the message queue programmatically, you can also set it from the Computer Management MMC snap-in (see Figure 8-9).

In Figure 8-9 Body has been selected from the Privacy level drop-down list, which has the same results as running the example code in Listing 8-34. Please note that I have unchecked the Authentication check box in this example. This doesn't mean that you can't use encryption and authentication at the same time; I have simply done so to simplify the code in the following listings.

Unlike with authentication, it is possible to use encryption even if the message queue doesn't require it, but only if the privacy level is set to Optional. This can be done from the Computer Management MMC snap-in or programmatically, as follows:

```
' Set message body encryption to optional
queUserMan.EncryptionRequired = EncryptionRequired.Optional
```

If you specify Optional as the privacy level, you can send encrypted and nonencrypted messages to the message queue. However, if you set the privacy level to None, you can only send nonencrypted messages to the queue. If you send an encrypted message to a queue with a privacy level of None, the message is rejected.

The example in Listing 8-35 shows you how to send and receive an encrypted message.

Listing 8-35. Sending and Receiving Encrypted Messages

```
1 Public Sub SendAndReceiveEncryptedMessage()
2    Dim queUserMan As New MessageQueue(".\Private$\UserMan")
3    Dim msgUserMan As New Message()
4
5    ' Require message body encryption
6    queUserMan.EncryptionRequired = EncryptionRequired.Body
7    ' Set up the queue formatter
8    queUserMan.Formatter = New XmlMessageFormatter(New Type() {GetType(String)})
9
10   ' Make sure that message is encrypted before it is sent
11   msgUserMan.UseEncryption = True
12   ' Create message body
13   msgUserMan.Body = "Message Body"
14
15   ' Send message to queue
16   queUserMan.Send(msgUserMan)
17
18   ' Retrieve message from queue
19   msgUserMan = queUserMan.Receive()
20   ' Show decrypted message body
21   MsgBox(msgUserMan.Body.ToString)
22 End Sub
```

In Listing 8-35 I encrypt a message, send it to the queue, and receive it from the queue. During the transport to and from the queue, the message body is encrypted, but the message is automatically decrypted by the receiving **Message-Queue** object. This means decryption of an encrypted message is always performed automatically when the message is received.

Using Access Control

Controlling access to the message queue is probably the best way to secure your messages. As with most other Windows operations, such as creating new users, the reading and writing of messages can be access controlled. Access control happens when a user tries to perform an operation, such as reading a message from a queue. Each user under Windows 2000 or Windows NT has an Access Control List (ACL), which contains all the operations the user can perform. The ACL is checked when the user tries to read a message. If the user has read access, the user can read the message from the queue. However, if the user isn't allowed to read from the queue, the read is disallowed.

Access control can be applied at the message queue level or even at the message level, but it can also be applied at the Message Queuing level, meaning that all message queues in the Active Directory will abide by the permissions you set. Take a look at Figure 8-10, where you can see the Access Control List for the User-Man user of the UserMan domain. The permissions shown are for the UserMan private message queue.

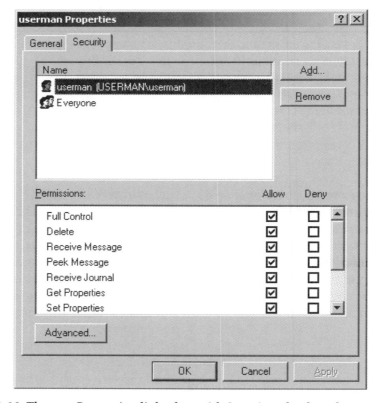

Figure 8-10. The user Properties dialog box with Security tab selected

You can bring up the ACL by opening the Computer Management MMC snap-in, selecting the private UserMan queue, right-clicking on the queue, and selecting Properties from the pop-up menu. This brings up the Properties dialog box, in which you must click Security to get to the ACL (see Figure 8-10).

As you can see from the ACL in Figure 8-10, there are permissions for just about any thing you can do with the message queue, such as write, read, and peek at messages. Next to the operation there are two check boxes, one for allowing the operation and one for denying the operation. All you have to do is select the user or group you want to set the permissions for in the list box in top part of the dialog box. If the user or group is not listed, you can add it by clicking the Add button. If you need to remove a user or group, you can click the Delete button.

You need to be especially careful when you set the permissions for groups, because as always with ACLs in Windows, the more restrictive permission takes precedence. For instance, if you set the Delete operation to Allow for the User-Man user and then set the same permission for the Everyone group to Deny, the UserMan user is denied the right to delete the message queue. All users in the domain are part of the Everyone group, so you need to be especially careful with this option. Setting group and user permissions are really outside the scope of this book, so if you need more information on how ACLs work and permissions are set with respect to users and groups, you should look in the documentation that comes with your Windows OS.

Using the SetPermissions Method

Instead of setting the user permissions from Computer Management, you can also perform this task programmatically using the **SetPermissions** method of your **MessageQueue** object. Listing 8-36 shows you how to do it.

Listing 8-36. Setting User Permissions Programmatically

```
1 Public Sub SetUserPermissions()
2   Dim queUserMan As New MessageQueue(".\Private$\UserMan")
3   Dim msgUserMan As New Message()
4   Dim aclUserMan As New AccessControlList()
5
6   ' Give UserMan user full control over private UserMan queue
7   queUserMan.SetPermissions("userman", MessageQueueAccessRights.FullControl)
8   ' Give UserMan user full control over private UserMan queue
9   queUserMan.SetPermissions(New MessageQueueAccessControlEntry( _
10   New Trustee("userman"), MessageQueueAccessRights.FullControl))
11   ' Deny UserMan deleting the private UserMan queue
12   queUserMan.SetPermissions("userman", MessageQueueAccessRights.DeleteQueue, _
```

```
13        AccessControlEntryType.Deny)
14     ' Deny UserMan all access rights on the private UserMan queue
15     aclUserMan.Add(New AccessControlEntry(New Trustee("userman"), _
16        GenericAccessRights.All, StandardAccessRights.All,
          AccessControlEntryType.Deny))
17     queUserMan.SetPermissions(aclUserMan)
18  End Sub
```

In Listing 8-36 I have used all four overloads of the **SetPermissions** method. The first two (Lines 7 and 9) take the name of the user or group and the rights to assign to this user or group. They are basically the same and can only be used to assign rights to a user or group, not revoke rights. The next overloaded version of the method (Line 12) can be used to allow, deny, revoke, or set a specific permission for a particular user or group. The last version of the method (Lines 15 through 17) can be used to allow, deny, revoke, or set generic and standard access rights for a user or group. Actually, the last overloads can be used for changing permissions for several users and/or groups in one go. You simply need to add as many Access Control Entries (ACE) as necessary to the ACL (Line 15), before you set the permission using the ACL (Line 17).

I have only constructed the example code in Listing 8-36 for you to see how all four of the overloaded versions of the **SetPermissions** method can be used. You shouldn't be using them at the same time. If a conflict occurs between the rights you assign or revoke, only the last rights assigned or revoked will count.

Using Auditing

In the context of this chapter, auditing is used for logging access to a message queue. This means allows you to check the Event Log to see who has been accessing it, or even better, who has been trying to access it and been denied the access. Auditing really falls beyond the scope of this book, as it is a generic tool used for logging access to any kind of service or object in the Windows OS.

You can set up auditing from the Computer Management MMC snap-in. Select the message queue you want to audit or indeed all of Message Queuing by selecting the node by this name. Right-click on the selected node and select Properties from the pop-up menu. This brings up the Properties dialog box, in which you should select the Security tab. On the Security tab click the Advanced button. This brings up the Access Control Settings dialog box. Select the Auditing tab to bring up the dialog box shown in Figure 8-11. Normally there are no Auditing Entries on the list, but in Figure 8-11 I have added an entry that logs when any user (Everyone group) fails to write a message to the message queue.

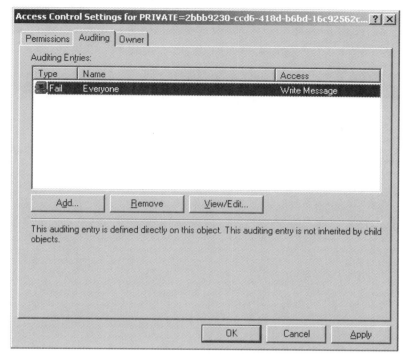

Figure 8-11. The Access Control Settings dialog box

There are two types of audits: Success and Failure. Try playing around with these audits and don't forget to check the entries added to Event Log (the Application Log). You can view the Event Log using the Event Viewer.

If you want further information about auditing or just Message Queuing security in general, I suggest you read the documentation for Windows 2000.

Summary

This chapter introduced you to the concept of connectionless programming using message queues. I showed you how to create message queues from the Server Explorer and the Computer Management MMC snap-in, and how to do it programmatically.

I discussed how you can locate message queues on the network; how messages queues work with transactions; why you should use a message queue and not a database table; how the messages are ordered or sorted in a queue; and finally how you work with the various properties and methods of both the **MessageQueue** and **Message** classes.

In the next chapter I will show you how to wrap your data access functionality in classes. I will be covering OOP fundamentals such as polymorphism very briefly and show you how to use them in your UserMan application.

CHAPTER 9

Data Wrappers

Creating classes (wrappers) for your data access

IN THIS CHAPTER I WILL BE going over how to wrap, or encapsulate, your data access in classes and components. You will see example code that covers some of the principles of Object Oriented Programming (OOP). *Wrapper* is generally a term used by programmers for the more proper term *class*. In the context of this book, a wrapper is a class. This chapter contains important information that I will use in Chapter 11 to finish the UserMan example application. You'll also find hands-on exercises in this chapter that will take you through creating a database project, and adding scripts, queries, and command files.

Why Use Data Wrappers?

There are a number of reasons for using data wrappers and classes or components in general. Wrapping your data access in a class can prevent direct access to your data. You can set up permissions on the data so that it can be accessed only by an administrator or by your component. This gives you much better control over how the data is accessed and prevents potential tampering with your data.

Wrapping the data accessed in a component allows you to place the component where it is most appropriate in your network. By most appropriate, I mean the place on the server where the component is easy to access for the clients, easy for you to update, and the workload resulting from clients using the component is proficiently handled. This obviously involves how you are distributing your application and what kind of application model you are using—client-server, n-tier, and so on.

Looking at Object Oriented Programming

In this section I will cover some of the basic principles of OOP. This is only a short introduction, and if you are completely new to OOP, I suggest you do some reading in order to fully exploit the potential of Visual Basic.NET. Suggested reading includes the following titles from Apress:

- *Moving to VB.NET: Strategies, Concepts, and Code*, by Dan Appleman. ISBN 1-893-115-97-6. Published June 2001.

- *Doing Web Development: Client-Side Techniques*, by Debbie Kurata. ISBN 1-893-115-87-9. Published July 2001.

- *Programming VB.NET: A Guide for Experienced Programmers*, by Gary Cornell and Jonathan Morrison. ISBN 1-893-115-99-2. Published July 2001. Chapters 4 and 6 in this book discuss OOP.

I will compare OOP to general programming guidelines and show you how you can apply OOP to the UserMan example application. This chapter is therefore a brief OOP introduction in preparation for Chapter 11; the principles discussed in this chapter will be applied to the completion of the example application.

Okay, so let's have a look at the basic principles in OOP: polymorphism, inheritance, and encapsulation.

Polymorphism

Polymorphism, which is also called *many forms*, is the ability to call a particular method on an object instantiated from any class that is derived from a base class, without knowing which class the object was instantiated from.

Let me illustrate this using the standard **Object** class that is part of the Framework base classes. All other classes in the Framework are derived from this class, and they all expose the **ToString** method. This method simply returns a **String** representation of the instantiated object. The idea is that you can always call the **ToString** method on an object to get the **String** representation without really knowing what subclass your object is derived from.

This means classes that inherit from another class should expose the same properties and methods as the base class, which makes it easy for a programmer to use standard methods and properties on any of your objects.

You can extend the inherited methods and properties if they can be overridden, which means that you don't have to expose the functionality of the base class. (Inheritance is discussed in the next section.)

My explanation is very simply put, but essentially this is what polymorphism is. See the section "Visual Basic.NET Keywords Related to OOP" later in this chapter for more information on how polymorphism is implemented in VB.NET.

Inheritance

Inheritance is the ability for a class to be derived from another class, or as the name inheritance suggests, inherit the characteristics of another class. You will encounter words such as *superclass* or *base class* to describe the class that is inherited from, and *subclass* or *derived class* for the class that inherits from another class.

There is support for two types of inheritance in VB.NET: *interface inheritance* and *implementation inheritance.*

Interface vs. Implementation Inheritance

In previous versions of Visual Basic, there was only support for interface inheritance through the **Implements** keyword, but now there is also implementation inheritance. Interface inheritance is also called *has a. . .* inheritance, whereas implementation inheritance is often called *is a. . .* inheritance.

Interface Inheritance

An *interface* is a set of related public methods, properties, events, and indexers that the inheriting class must implement. An interface is a contract, so if you choose to implement an interface in your class, you are bound by the contract offered by the interface. This means you must implement all the methods and such specified in the interface.

An interface doesn't include any implementation, which means that you cannot directly instantiate an interface. Instead, an interface must be implemented by a class, and it is this class you can instantiate. An interface is an abstract data type, and it provides for a very loose coupling between the interface and the classes that implement it. See Listing 9-1 for an example of how to implement interface inheritance.

Listing 9-1. Creating and Implementing an Interface

```
1 Public Interface IUserMan
2    Property TestProperty() As String
3    Sub TestMethod()
4 End Interface
5
6 Public Class CUserMan
7    Implements IUserMan
8
9    Private prstrUserName As String
10
11    Public Property UserName() As String Implements IUserMan.TestProperty
12       Get
13          UserName = prstrUserName
14       End Get
15
16       Set(ByVal vstrUserName As String)
17          prstrUserName = vstrUserName
18       End Set
19    End Property
20
21    Public Sub CalculateOnlineTime() Implements IUserMan.TestMethod
22    End Sub
23 End Class
24
25 Public Sub CreateUserManObject()
26    Dim objUserMan As New CUserMan()
27 End Sub
```

In Listing 9-1 I have created the IUserMan interface, which defines the Test-Property property and the TestMethod method. In the CUserMan class (Lines 6 through 23), I have implemented the IUserMan interface using the **Implements** statement on Line 7. As you can see from the code, it is necessary to implement public signatures (methods, properties, events, and indexers) in the class that implements the interface, but you are not required to keep the names of the signatures. See Lines 11 and 21, where I use the **Implements** keyword following a property and method declaration to indicate what signature in the interface is being implemented by the property and method.

I then create a procedure that creates an instance of the class that implements the interface (Lines 25 through 27). This is the ONLY way to instantiate an interface, so to speak.

Implementation Inheritance

Implementation inheritance should be used when you can use the **Is a. . .** phrase to refer to a subclass or derived class. By this I mean the subclass is a superclass or that the subclass is of the same type as the superclass. For example, say you have a superclass called CBird and subclasses called CHedgeHawk and CPigeon. It's obvious that the hedge hawk and the pigeon are of type bird. That's what the **Is a. . .** phrase indicates.

Implementation inheritance is especially great when a lot of functionality can be put into the base class, which in turn allows the derived classes to inherit this functionality without extending it. Not that you can't extend the code in the base class, but if you find you're extending most of the code from the base class, is implementation inheritance really what you need? Would interface inheritance not be better? Actually, it's not always so easy to make this choice. Keep the **Is a. . .** phrase in mind when considering implementation inheritance. It might just make your decision a little bit easier.

The obvious advantage implementation inheritance has over interface inheritance is that you avoid potential duplication of code by placing all your standard code in the superclass.

Implementation inheritance results in tight coupling between the superclass and the subclass. See Listings 9-4 and 9-5 later in this chapter for examples of how implementation inheritance can be used.

Encapsulation

The term *encapsulation* has been used and abused over the years. You might get many different definitions if you ask different people about this OOP term. I will try to give you a brief explanation of encapsulation and how it is implemented and used in VB.NET.

Encapsulation, also called information hiding, is the ability to hide your code or implementation from the user of your class. This means that when you create your classes, you expose some public properties and methods, but your code decides how your private variables and such are manipulated. If you look at Listing 9-5 later in the chapter, you will see I have declared the private **String** variable prstrTest on Line 2; because this variable is declared private, it cannot be accessed directly from a user of your class. Instead I have created the Test property, which provides access to the variable. I haven't actually implemented any checking of the value passed when setting the property, but this is generally the idea of encapsulation: no direct access to private members, only through exposed methods or properties for which you can validate the input. See Listing 9-2 for an example that validates the passed argument in the property **Set** procedure.

*Listing 9-2. Validating the Argument of a **Property Set** Procedure*

```
1 Set(ByVal vstrTest As String)
2    ' Check if the string contains any invalid chars
3    If InStr(vstrTest, "@") = 0 Then
4        prstrTest = vstrTest
5    End If
6 End Set
```

Visual Basic.NET Keywords Related to OOP

In Visual basic.NET a few keywords are related to OOP, either directly or indirectly. These keywords are as follows:

- *MustInherit:* Any class that is marked with **MustInherit** can only act as a base class, and it cannot be instantiated. If you try to instantiate such a class using the **New** operator, a compile-time exception is thrown. **MustInherit** cannot be used for declaring methods or properties in a class. See Listing 9-3 to see an example of how NOT to use this method and Listing 9-4 for an example that shows the right way.

- *Overridable:* A property or method marked with this keyword can be overridden in a derived class. It does not mean you have to override it, however. If you want to make sure it is overridden in a derived class, you must use the **MustOverride** keyword in your declaration. See Listing 9-5 for how to override a property in a derived class.

- *MustOverride:* A property or method marked with this keyword MUST be overridden in a derived class. If you only want to give the programmer deriving your class the option of overriding the method or property, you must use the **Overridable** keyword in your declaration.

- *NotOverridable:* If you mark a property or method with this keyword, you are explicitly telling the deriving class that the method or property cannot be overridden. You don't actually have to specify this, because this is the default behavior. However, it does make your code more readable.

- *Overrides:* The method or property marked with this keyword overrides the method or property in the base class with the same name. You should always use this keyword when overriding a method or property declared in the base class. See Listing 9-5 for how to override a property in a derived class.

- *Overloads:* The **Overloads** statement is for declaring several procedures with the same name within the same class. The parameter list is the only difference between the procedures. The compiler then makes the choice when your code calls the procedure, depending on the supplied arguments.

- *Inherits:* This keyword is used for inheriting from another class, called the superclass or base class. See Listing 9-4 for an example.

- *Implements:* The **Implements** keyword is used for specifying that a class, method, property, event, or indexer implements the corresponding feature in an interface. See Listing 9-1 earlier for an example that uses the **Implements** keyword.

- *Interface:* The **Interface** keyword is used for specifying an interface. See Listing 9-1 earlier for an example that uses the **Implements** keyword.

*Listing 9-3. A **MustInherit** Class That Cannot Be Instantiated*

```
1 Public MustInherit Class CMustInherit
2    Private prstrTest As String
3
4    Public Property Test() As String
5      Get
6          Test = prstrTest
7      End Get
8
9      Set(ByVal vstrTest As String)
10          prstrTest = vstrTest
11      End Set
12    End Property
13 End Class
14
15 Public Sub InstantiateMustInheritClass()
16    Dim objMustInherit As New CMustInherit()
18 End Sub
```

In Listing 9-3 the CMustInherit class has been declared with the **MustInherit** keyword, which means when an instance of the class is instantiated, it can only be inherited by another class. This means Line 16 will throw an exception at compile time because the syntax is wrong. However, if you do as in Listing 9-4 where I have wrapped the CMustInherit class in the CWrapper class, you can inherit from and instantiate the CWrapper class as shown on Line 7.

*Listing 9-4. A **MustInherit** Class That Can Be Instantiated*

```
1 Public Class CWrapper
2    Inherits CMustInherit
3    ' Place your other code here
4 End Class
5
6 Public Sub InstantiateMustInheritClassWrapper()
7    Dim objMustInherit As New CWrapper()
8
9 End Sub
```

Listing 9-4 is wrong and throws a compile time exception. Listing 9-5 shows you how to do it the right way.

Listing 9-5. Overriding a Property in a Derived Class

```
1 Public Class COverridable
2    Private prstrTest As String
3
4    Public Overridable Property Test() As String
5       Get
6          Test = prstrTest
7       End Get
8
9       Set(ByVal vstrTest As String)
10         prstrTest = vstrTest
11      End Set
12   End Property
13 End Class
14
15 Public Class CWrapper
16   Inherits COverridable
17
18   Private prstrTest As String
19
20   Public Overrides Property Test() As String
21      Get
22         Test = prstrTest & "Overridden"
23      End Get
24
25      Set(ByVal vstrTest As String)
26         prstrTest = vstrTest
27      End Set
28   End Property
29 End Class
```

In Listing 9-5 two classes have been declared, COverridable and CWrapper. COverridable is the base class from which CWrapper inherits. On Line 4 the Test property is declared as overridable, and in the derived class on Line 20 this property has indeed been overridden using the **Overrides** keyword. The **Overrides** keyword is always necessary when you are overriding a method or property—it doesn't matter if the property or method is declared using either the **MustOverride** or **Overridable** keyword. So if you were to remove the **Overrides** keyword from Line 20, you would get a compile-time error.

Wrapping a Database

Now that some of the initial details are out of the way, let's take a look at what to wrap and how in a database. If you've familiarized yourself with the database concepts in Chapter 2, you will be well off when I enter the analysis and design stage. Basically, wrapping your database access is like grouping your data in related tables. Actually, since you have already broken down your data into tables you have more or less found a way of defining your classes and wrappers.

Having a class for each table in your database is often the most satisfying solution from a maintenance viewpoint and in regard to the users of your classes and or components. Now that I mention components, I also have to add that one class doesn't necessary constitute one component. Quite often you will have more than one class in your component, but that depends on how you decide to distribute your business and data services.

Okay, so what needs to happen here? Classes and possibly components that hold the classes first need to be created. Since this book is strictly about data manipulation, I won't be covering business services, only data services. If you look at the schema for the UserMan database, you will see the following tables: tblLog, tblRights, tblUser, and tblUserRights.

To follow my own advice, I need to create a class for each of these tables; for the purpose of showing you the what and how, I am just going to create the CUser class.

Creating the CUser Class

The tblUser table has the following columns: Id, ADName, ADSID, FirstName, LastName, LoginName, and Password.

What I need to do now is find out what columns I will have to expose from the class, and if a column is exposed, whether will it be read-write, read-only, or write-only access. See Table 9-1 for a list of columns, data types, and access types.

Table 9-1. The tblUser Columns

COLUMN NAME	DATA TYPE	NULLABLE	ACCESS TYPE	DESCRIPTION
Id	int	No	Read-only	This is the Id used for looking up values in related tables. This is an IDENTITY column, so you will never have to set the value for it.
ADName	varchar	Yes	Read-write	This is the Active Directory name for the user, if he or she is a member of the AD.
ADSID	uniqueidentifier	Yes	Read-write	This is the Active Directory Security IDentifier (SID) for the user, if he or she is a member of the AD.
FirstName	varchar	Yes	Read-write	This is the user's first, or given, name.
LastName	varchar	Yes	Read-write	This is the user's last name, or surname.
LoginName	varchar	No	Read-write	This is the user's login name, which he or she must use in conjunction with the password when logging on to the system.
Password	varchar	No	Read-write	This is the user's password, which he or she must use in conjunction with the logon name when logging on to the system.

Now, if you look at Table 9-1, there are a couple of columns for which the access type needs to be discussed in further detail. ADName and ADSID can change depending on the AD connected, but why do I want the user of the class to be able to do this? First of all, I need to make sure that it is possible to set these values. Who's allowed to do it will be taken care of from the application.

Next, a new Class Library project needs to be created and a new class added to it that holds the methods, properties, and so on of the CUser class.

EXERCISE

Create a new Class Library project called UserMan and rename the existing class (Class1) CUser. Open the CUser class and change the class name to CUser as well.

It's time to add private variables, methods, and properties that can handle access to the database table. For all the columns, it's best to create properties, because all they do is read or write a value. Before creating the properties, it's a good idea to create private variables that hold the values in order to avoid having to access the database every time a variable is read. See Listing 9-6 for some example code that creates private variables to hold the user values from the database table.

EXERCISE

Add a private variable to the CUser class for every column in the tblUser table. See Listing 9-6 for an example.

Listing 9-6. Creating Private Variables to Hold the User Values

```
' User table column values
Private prlngId As Long
Private prstrADName As String
Private prguiADSID As Guid
Private prstrFirstName As String
Private prstrLastName As String
Private prstrLoginName As String
Private prstrPassword As String
```

Listing 9-6 is simply a list of private variables that correspond directly to the columns in the tblUser table. Now properties need to be added to set and retrieve the values from the variables. See Listing 9-7 for an example of the **Id** property.

*Listing 9-7. The Read-Only **Id** Property*

```
Public ReadOnly Property Id() As Long
    Get
        Id = prlngId
    End Get
End Property
```

EXERCISE

Add properties for all the columns in the tblUser table to the CUser class. See Listing 9-7 and 9-8 examples.

---

*Listing 9-8. The Read-Write **ADName** Property*

```
Public Property ADName() As String
   Get
      ADName = prstrADName
   End Get

   Set(ByVal vstrADName As String)
      prstrADName = vstrADName
   End Set
End Property
```

Listing 9-8 shows you how the ADName column in the database table can be accessed using a property. This is not quite true, because only a private variable is being accessed. However, the code for accessing the database table and Active Directory will be added in Chapter 11.

All the properties of data type **String** that can be set to a maximum length in the database, so it's a good idea to add a check if the passed string is shorter than or equal to this length. This also means that you need to hold the maximum length values in private variables, as in Listing 9-9.

EXERCISE

Add a private variable to the CUser class for every column in the tblUser table that has a maximum length. See Listing 9-9 for an example.

Listing 9-9. Creating Private Variables to Hold the Maximum Length of Table Columns

```
' User table column max lengths
Private prshtADNameMaxLen As Short
Private prshtFirstNameMaxLen As Short
Private prshtLastNameMaxLen As Short
Private prshtLoginNameMaxLen As Short
Private prshtPasswordMaxLen As Short
```

I now need to create the length check for the **Property Set** procedures. This can be done as shown in Listing 9-10.

Add a check of the length of the passed argument in the **Property Set** procedures. Keep in mind only those procedures set a variable that corresponds to a column in the database table with a maximum length. See Listing 9-10 for example code.

*Listing 9-10. Creating Maximum Length Checks of **Property Set** Arguments*

```
Set(ByVal vstrADName As String)
    If Len(vstrADName) <= prshtADNameMaxLen Then
        prstrADName = vstrADName
    Else
        prstrADName = Left(vstrADName, prshtADNameMaxLen)
    End If
End Set
```

In Listing 9-10 I check if the length of the passed vstrADName argument is shorter than or equal to the maximum length of the table column by comparing the length with the value of the private variable prshtADNameMaxLen. If it is shorter, the value is stored, and if not, the first prshtADNameMaxLen number of characters from the vstrADName string are stored. I suppose you could throw an exception here, but is it really that bad to pass a string with too many characters? The reason I need to perform this check is that if I try to pass a string that is too long to the database, an exception will be thrown. Alright, this check can certainly be done in different ways, and I am sure you know one or two other ways you might normally use, but this is merely to demonstrate how you can build up your properties.

The CUser class isn't finished yet—a lot more code needs to be added to it, such as methods and so on, but I am sure you get the idea of how to create wrappers for all your data access. I will be giving you more ideas and hints in Chapter 11, when I finish the UserMan example application.

Summary

This chapter took you on a short journey through OOP and how to apply OOP to your data access code. The three main concepts of OOP were discussed: polymorphism, inheritance, and encapsulation. With regards to inheritance, I briefly outlined the differences between interface and implementation inheritance.

I also went over how to wrap your data access code in classes in the context of creating a class for accessing the tblUser database table in the UserMan example application. This work will be finished in Chapter 11.

The next chapter is about creating and using data-bound controls.

CHAPTER 10

Data-Bound Controls

Creating and working with data-bound controls

IN THIS CHAPTER I WILL discuss data-bound controls and why they are so popular with some developers and extremely unpopular with others. I will explore how to use the various data-bound controls that come with Visual Basic.NET. I will also show you how to create your own data-bound controls. Keep an eye out for the hands-on exercises that appear throughout this chapter.

Data-Bound Controls vs. Manual Data Hooking

A *data-bound control*, such as a list box, a grid or a text box, is a control that is hooked up to a data source. This means the developer doesn't have to take care of updating the control when the underlying data changes or updating the data source when user input has changed the data in the control. Data-bound controls are there to make your life as a developer easier.

Manual data hooking is an alternative to data-bound controls that has always been around. *Manual data hooking* describes the process by which you as a developer retrieve values from a data source and display them in one or more UI controls. However, when Visual Basic started shipping with controls that were data bound, the developer community suddenly had an extra tool to use for displaying and manipulating data.

I think that data-bound controls are a great idea, because it saves you from having to develop lots of code that otherwise takes care of the manual data hooking. With manual data hooking you have full control over how the data is handled, whereas data-bound controls often severely limit your ability to intervene and manipulate the data before being displayed or before being written back to the data source. This has been an annoying "extra feature" of data-bound controls for a long time, and I bet you know someone who tells you NOT to use data-bound controls because of this drawback. I have been using data-bound controls mainly for display purposes or read-only data, because I then don't have to worry about problems with updating the data source once the user changes the displayed data.

Traditionally, all data-bound controls were bound to a single data control that took care of the binding to the data source, as shown in Figure 10-1.

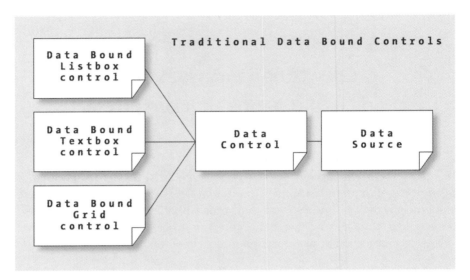

Figure 10-1. Traditional data-bound controls

In Figure 10-1 you can see how the data control takes care of the communication between the data source and the data-bound controls. This effectively means that you as a programmer do not have control over the way data is transferred from the data source to the bound controls and back again. The data control encapsulates all this for you, but it leaves you with very few options regarding how the data source is updated.

Different Controls for Different UIs

Visual Studio.NET supports several UIs, and they each require different controls. The Web and Windows are two of the UIs that VS.NET supports. For example, if you look at the Toolbox in the IDE you can see different tabs of controls for different purposes. Figure 10-2 shows the Toolbox with the Windows Forms tab expanded. If you display the Toolbox in your IDE and look at the Windows Forms tab and the Web Forms tab, many of the controls are named the same. This doesn't mean they are the same controls—on the contrary, they are not. However, they do serve a similar purpose. Read on to find out more about the important distinctions.

Figure 10-2. The Toolbox with the Window Forms tab expanded

Using Data-Bound Controls with Windows Forms

Data binding in Windows forms requires a data provider and a data consumer. The data provider is not just a so-called traditional data source, such as a database table. In fact, data binding on Windows forms can be much more than that. It can involve a collection or an array and any of the data structures from ADO.NET. These data structures include the **DataReader** and **DataSet** classes. I will be covering data binding with the ADO.NET data structures in this section.

All Windows forms have a **BindingContext** object. When you bind a control on a Windows form to a data source, this control will have an associated **CurrencyManager** object. The **CurrencyManager** object handles the communication with the data source and is responsible for keeping the data-bound controls synchronized. All the bound controls display data from the same row at the same time, and one Windows form can have more than one currency manager. This happens when the Windows form has more than one data source, because the form maintains one currency manager for each data source associated with the form.

Another important aspect of the currency manager is its ability to know the current position in the data source. You can read the position using the **Position** property of the **CurrencyManager** class. This is especially useful with ADO.NET data structures, such as the **DataTable** class, because they do not provide cursor functionality—that is, you cannot retrieve a cursor or pointer to the current row. However, this can be achieved with the currency manager. You'll see how the **CurrencyManager** object is used in the section "Looking at the Code Created by the Data Form Wizard" later in this chapter.

Examining the Binding Context

The *binding context* keeps track of all the currency managers on a Windows form. Even if there aren't any currency managers and data sources, your Windows form will always have a **BindingContext** object associated with it. As a matter of fact, this is true for all classes derived from the **Control** class, which is also part of the **System.Windows.Forms** namespace.

It is the binding context with which the data-bound control communicates. The binding context talks to the currency manager, which in turn talks to the data source, as shown in Figure 10-3. I will show you how the **BindingContext** object is used in code in the section "Looking at the Code Created by the Data Form Wizard" later in this chapter.

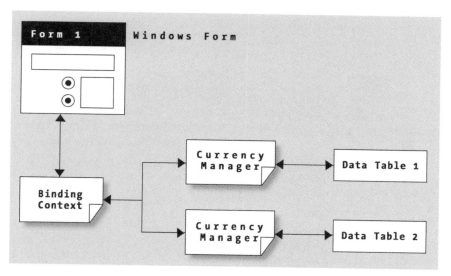

Figure 10-3. How data-bound controls communicate with the data source

Creating a Form Using the Data Form Wizard

Instead of doing all the hard work yourself, you can let the Data Form Wizard create your form with one or more data-bound controls. I will take you through this process, because it will help you understand how controls are bound to data in Windows forms. Here is how to create a new form:

1. Add a new item to your project and make sure you select the Data Form Wizard template.

2. Give the new form a name. This brings up the Data Form Wizard. Click Next.

3. The Choose the dataset you want to use dialog box appears (see Figure 10-4). Select the Create a new dataset named option if you want to create a new data set, and type the name of the data set in the text box. Or select the Use the following dataset option and choose an existing data set from the drop-down list box. (This option is only available if you already have a data set in your project.) Click Next.

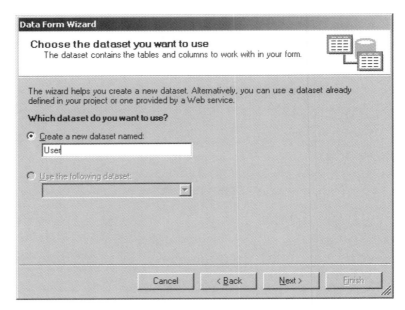

Figure 10-4. Choosing a data set in the Data Form Wizard

4. The Choose a data connection dialog box appears (see Figure 10-5). Select the desired database connection in the Which connection should the wizard use? drop-down list box. Click Next.

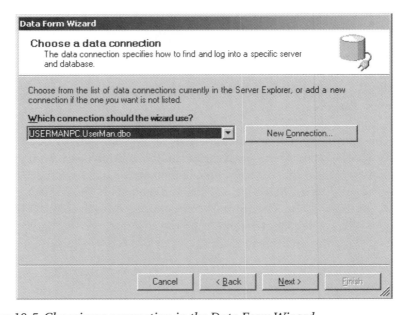

Figure 10-5. Choosing a connection in the Data Form Wizard

5. The Choose tables or views dialog box appears (see Figure 10-6). Select the desired tables and/or views from the Available item(s) tree view, and choose the data form from the Selected item(s) tree view. Click on the right arrow button to make your selections. Click Next.

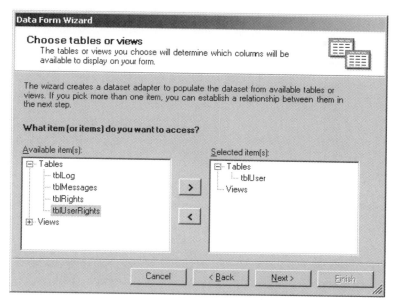

Figure 10-6. Choosing tables and views in the Data Form Wizard

6. The Choose tables and columns to display on the form dialog box appears (see Figure 10-7). Select a table from the Master or single table drop-down list box. If you only want data from one table in your form, this is all you need to do. If you want to create a master detail form, you must also select a table in the Detail table drop-down list box.

7. Check the columns you want displayed on your form in the Columns list boxes. (The right-hand Columns list box will be activated only if you selected a table from the Detail table drop-down list.) Click Next.

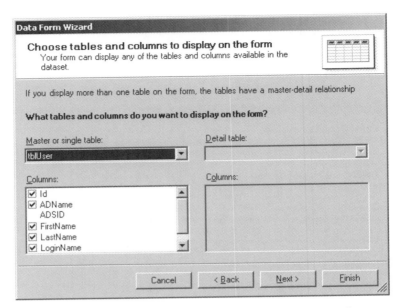

Figure 10-7. Choosing tables and columns in the Data Form Wizard

8. The Choose the display style dialog box appears (see Figure 10-8). Select the All records in a grid option if you want your data displayed in a grid. Select the Single record in individual controls option if you want to be able to navigate and manipulate the data. Check or uncheck the Cancel All check box depending on whether you want the data to be read-only or not.

9. Click Finish.

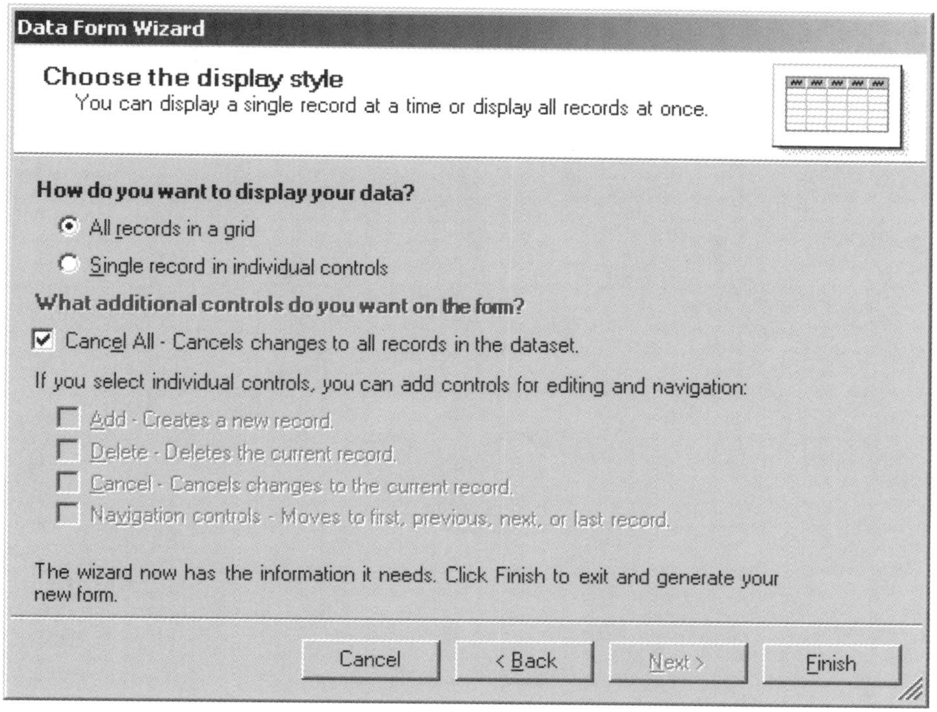

Figure 10-8. Choosing how to display the data in the Data Form Wizard

The data form will now be created and shown in the IDE. As you can see at the bottom of Figure 10-9, the wizard creates the objUser data set, the OleDb-Connection1 connection, and the OleDbDataAdapter1 adapter. These objects are only for use by the new form. If you open up the code behind file (.vb), you will see how all the code is at your mercy. You can change it to your liking, because it's all there. This is definitely a big difference from the way it was done in previous versions of Visual Basic. You can see how the wizard has created all the OLEDB .NET Data Provider data objects such as the insert, update, delete, and select commands, the data adapter, and connection objects.

> **NOTE** *See Chapter 3A for a discussion of data adapters.*

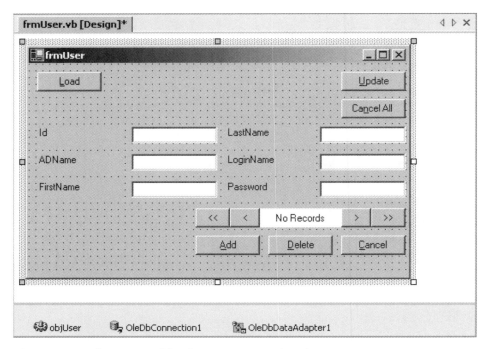

Figure 10-9. A form created by the Data Form Wizard

The wizard also creates a strongly typed XML data set file (.xsd). Another file it creates that is not normally shown in the Solution Explorer is the class file, which encapsulates or wraps the data access. This file is named the same as the data set file (.xsd), but with a .vb extension. You can see this file in the folder you have selected to save your project in, or you can click the Show All Files button in the Solution Explorer. This button is located at the very top of the Solution Explorer window, as shown in Figure 10-10.

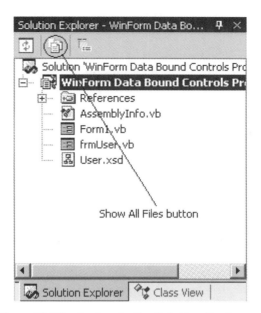

Figure 10-10. The Show All Files button in the Solution Explorer window

EXERCISE

1. Create a new connection to the UserMan database from the Server Explorer if you don't already have one.

2. Add a new form using the Data Form Wizard and name the form frmUser.

3. Create a new data set called User in the wizard dialog box.

4. Select the UserMan database connection and add the tblUser table.

5. Display the data as a single record in individual controls.

   The new form should look like what appears in Figure 10-9.

One thing you might have noticed is that the wizard always uses the OLE DB .NET Data Provider. This is also true when you connect to a SQL Server, which is obviously not ideal. However, this can be fixed using the search and replace functionality of the IDE. I have customized the wizard-generated code to use the SQL Server .NET Data Provider, and you can find this code on the Apress Web site (http://www.apress.com).

Looking at the Code Created by the Data Form Wizard

I will now go through the code created by the Data Form Wizard, and if you want to follow along, I suggest you open the project in which you created the frmUser form from the previous exercise. If you didn't perform the exercise, now would be a good time to do so, as I will cover how the **CurrencyManager** and **BindingContext** objects are used in code.

If you open the frmUser form in the Code Editor, not in Design View, you will see several hundreds lines of code. Just think about that for a minute—how long do you think it would take you to type this in yourself? What I am getting at here is that even if the code generated by the Data Form Wizard often needs to be adjusted slightly, it will save you a lot of time compared to typing it all in yourself.

To get a better look at the code in the Code Editor, expand the Windows Forms Designer generated code region by clicking the plus sign next to the line number where you see the text "Windows Forms Designer generated code." This is similar to what you would do in Windows Explorer when you go file hunting. If the code region is already expanded, a minus sign is shown instead.

If you are following along, scroll down the code until you reach the **New** constructor (**Sub**) and the **Dispose** method. Notice that just after these methods the wizard has put the declaration of all the objects used by the form. This includes the data objects such as the data adapter, connection, and command objects as well as all the buttons and labels shown on the form. All these objects and controls are declared using the **Friend** access modifier, which means that the objects are only accessible to the form class itself and other classes and so on within the same project. They are also declared using the **WithEvents** statement, which means that all events are exposed in code, and thus you can respond to events from these objects programmatically.

There is one declaration I want you to look closer at and that is the objUser object. This object is of type *<ProjectName>*.User, where *ProjectName* is the name of your project and User is the class. Can't recall creating this class? Don't worry, that's because the wizard did. Right-click on the class and select Go To Definition. This brings up the User class in the Code Editor window. This class is derived from the **DataSet** class in the **System.Data** namespace, which basically means this class is the disconnected part of the data source you will be binding to. The User class is located in the User.vb file, which also holds the following classes:

- *tblUserDataTable:* Derived from **System.Data.DataTable**. Implements such public properties as **Count** and the default property **Item**. The class also holds procedures such as an enumerator, and procedures for manipulating rows in the table.

- *tblUserRow:* Derived from **System.Data.DataRow**. Implements properties for getting and setting column values in rows in the tblUser table, a constructor (**New**), Boolean functions to check for Null values in columns, and functions to set the column values to Null.

- *tblUserRowChangeEvent:* Derived from **System.EventArgs**. This class is the base class for event data, which means this class is used for controlling events in connection with data manipulation in the tblUser table through the User class.

In the **InitializeComponent Sub** procedure, all the objects are instantiated and initialized.

Last, but not least, you have all the private **Sub** procedures for the **Click** events of the buttons on the form; a **Sub** procedure for updating the current row position label; **Sub** procedures for updating, loading, or filling the **DataSet**; and finally a **Sub** procedure for updating the data source.

You should really take a long and close look at these files and classes, because there is loads of information in them. If you do a search in the frmUser.vb file for the **BindingContext** object, you will see what operations it actually performs with regards to manipulating the data.

Binding a Windows Form Control to a Data Source

Any Windows form control that is derived from the **Control** class, which is a member of the **System.Windows.Forms** namespace, can be bound to any property of an object and thus a data source. If you go back to the code generated by the Data Form Wizard earlier in this chapter, you can search the code and find how the **DataBindings** property of all the buttons on the form is being used to bind to the objUser object mentioned in the previous section. The **DataBindings** property returns a **ControlBindingsCollection**, and this collection has an **Add** method, which you can see used in the generated code to add a **Binding** object. This **Binding** object is the real trick of the data binding. It is created by the **Add** method of the **ControlBindingsCollection**, and it specifies how a certain control property is bound to a certain member of a data source. The following example code is taken from the code generated by the Data Form Wizard:

```
Me.mfp_editId.DataBindings.Add(_
 New System.Windows.Forms.Binding("Text", Me.objUser, "tblUser.Id"))
```

The mfp_editId item is a **TextBox** control, but as stated previously, you can bind data to any control derived from the **Control** class. In the example, the text box is bound to the Id column of the tblUser table (data member) from the objUser object (data source). The first argument, which reads "Text," specifies that it is the **Text** property of the mfp_editId **TextBox** control bound to the Id column.

Using the BindingContext Object

The **BindingContext** object can be associated with a Windows form and when it is, it is a global object, meaning you don't have to instantiate it. If you do a search, you'll see many instances of **Me.BindingContext** in the code, which indicates the **BindingContext** object is indeed associated with or rather a part of the current Windows form object. The noninherited, public properties of the **BindingContext** class are shown in Table 10-1 and the noninherited, public method is shown in Table 10-2.

*Table 10-1. Properties of the **BindingContext** Class*

PROPERTY NAME	DESCRIPTION
IsReadOnly	This read-only property returns a **Boolean** value indicating if the **BindingContext** is read-only.
Item	This overloaded, read-only property returns a specific **BindingManagerBase.** This property is the default, meaning you don't have to specify it. You can use either BindingContext.Item() or BindingContext(). This property comes in two versions (overloads): One that takes a data source object and one that takes the data source object as well as the data member string.

*Table 10-2. Method of the **BindingContext** Class*

METHOD NAME	DESCRIPTION
Contains()	This overloaded method returns a **Boolean** value indicating if the **BindingContext** object contains the specified **BindingManagerBase**.

As you can see from Tables 10-1 and 10-2, there just aren't that many public properties and methods to use, but this is not really a problem. Remember that the **BindingContext** object holds a **CurrencyManager** object for each data source on the form. This means you don't really have to manipulate the **BindingContext** object at all, but you have to use this object's **Item** property to get to the **CurrencyManager** objects and/or the **Contains** method to check if a specific **CurrencyManager** exists. Does this make sense to you? It probably would have if I hadn't used two terms for virtually the same thing: **CurrencyManager** and **BindingManagerBase**.

The **BindingManagerBase** class is abstract, meaning it must be derived or inherited before you can use it. Yes, you guessed it: The **CurrencyManager** class does indeed inherit from the **BindingManagerBase** class. So for the purpose of discussing data-bound controls on Windows forms, these two classes are more or less the same. In fact they expose the same properties, and only one method sets them apart, the **Refresh** method of the **CurrencyManager** class.

Okay, so before continuing on with the **CurrencyManager** class, let me explain how to get to it using the **BindingContext** object. In the case of the source code created by the Data Form Wizard, I will use **Me.BindingContext** to refer to the **BindingContext** object of the frmUser form. Listings 10-1 and 10-2 show you two different ways of accessing the currency manager.

Listing 10-1. Saving a Reference to the Currency Manager

```
Dim objCurrencyManager As CurrencyManager
objCurrencyManager = Me.BindingContext(objUser, "tblUser")
```

*Listing 10-2. Accessing the **Count** Property of the Currency Manager through the Binding Context*

```
Me.BindingContext(objUser, "tblUser").Count
```

As you can see from Listings 10-1 and 10-2, you can either choose to reference the currency manager through the **BindingContext** object (as shown in Listing 10-2) or save a reference to it and use it directly (as shown in Listing 10-1). Whether you choose one method over the other doesn't really make a difference—it's a matter of preference. One thing to notice about the **CurrencyManager** class is that it doesn't have a constructor (**New Sub** procedure), so you can only instantiate an object of data type **CurrencyManager** using the **Item** property of a **BindingContext** object. Although the example in Listing 10-1 may not appear to follow this convention, remember that the **Item** property is the default and thus does not have to be specified. Therefore the code in Listing 10-3 does the exact same thing as the code in Listing 10-1.

*Listing 10-3. Saving a Reference to the Currency Manager Specifying the **Item** Property*

```
Dim objCurrencyManager As CurrencyManager
objCurrencyManager = Me.BindingContext.Item(objUser, "tblUser")
```

Let me take an opportunity to reiterate what I am doing and how I am doing it. I never liked using default properties in previous versions of Visual Basic, but for some reason the **Item** property always eluded me, and this will continue in the new version of VB. So no **Item** property in my example code from here on out.

One last thing I want to discuss about the **Item** property is the way it can be called. It's overloaded, but in the code generated by the Data Form Wizard, you only see one of the overloaded versions of the property. That's the one that takes both the data source object and the data member string. The other version of the property only takes the data source object as an argument. This version should be used if the data source is a **DataTable** object, because then you don't have to specify a table name as you do when the data source is a data set.

Using the CurrencyManager Object

Now look at the **CurrencyManager** class, because that's the juicy one—the one with all the properties and methods you will be using extensively in your code when you create data-bound controls. Table 10-3 lists all the noninherited, public properties of the currency manager and Table 10-4 shows you all the noninherited, public methods.

*Table 10-3. Properties of the **CurrencyManager** Class*

PROPERTY NAME	DESCRIPTION
Bindings	This read-only property returns a **BindingsCollection** object that holds all the **Bindings** objects being managed by the **CurrencyManager**.
Count	The **Count** property, which is read-only, returns an **Integer** value that indicates the number of rows managed by the **CurrencyManager**.
Current	This property returns the current object. Because the returned object is of data type **Object**, you need to cast it to the same data type as the data type contained by the data source before you can use it.
Position	The **Position** property retrieves or sets the current position in the data source. The value is zero-based and of data type **Integer**.

*Table 10-4. Methods of the **CurrencyManager** Class*

METHOD NAME	DESCRIPTION	EXAMPLE
AddNew()	The **AddNew** method adds a new item to the	

```
Me.BindingContext(objUser,
```

underlying list. In the case of a **DataTable**, the new item is a **DataRow**.

"tblUser").AddNew() (taken from the code generated by the Data Form Wizard)

CancelCurrentEdit() — This method cancels the current edit operation. The data is NOT saved in its current condition. Data is reverted back to the condition it was in when you started the edit operation. If you need to end the edit operation and save any changes, you should use the **EndCurrentEdit** method for this purpose instead.

Me.BindingContext(objUser, "tblUser").
CancelCurrentEdit() (taken from the code generated by the Data Form Wizard)

EndCurrentEdit() — The **EndCurrentEdit** method is used for ending the current edit operation. The data is saved in its current condition, so this does NOT cancel the edits. Use the **CancelCurrentEdit** method for this purpose instead.

Me.BindingContext(objUser, "tblUser").
EndCurrentEdit() (taken from the code generated by the Data Form Wizard)

GetItemProperties() — This overloaded method retrieves or sets a collection of property descriptors for the binding. The returned value is of data type **PropertyDescriptorCollection**.

Dim objPropertyDescriptor Collection As PropertyDescriptor Collection = Me.BindingContext(objUser, "tblUser").
GetItemProperties()

Refresh() — The **Refresh** method refreshes or rather repopulates the bound controls. This method is for use with data sources that do not support change notification, such as an array. Data sets and data tables do support change notification, meaning this method is not needed with objects of these data types.

Me.BindingContext(objUser, "tblUser").Refresh()

RemoveAt(ByVal vintIndex As Integer) — This method deletes the item at the specified index position.

Me.BindingContext(objUser, "tblUser").RemoveAt(0)

ResumeBinding() — This method and the **SuspendBinding** method are used for temporarily suspending the data binding. You should use these two methods if you want to let a user perform several edits without validating these edits until binding is resumed. This method resumes suspended binding.

Me.BindingContext(objUser, "tblUser").ResumeBinding()

*Table 10-4. Methods of the **CurrencyManager** Class (continued)*

METHOD NAME	DESCRIPTION	EXAMPLE
SuspendBinding()	This method and the **ResumeBinding** method are used for temporarily suspending the data binding. You should use these two methods if you want to let a user perform several edits without validating these edits until binding is resumed. This method suspends binding.	`Me.BindingContext(objUser, "tblUser"). SuspendBinding()`

As you can see from Tables 10-3 and 10-4, the **CurrencyManager** class has method and properties for performing just about any action on the data source.

Retrieving the Number of Rows in the Data Source

Occasionally it is desirable to retrieve the number of rows in the data source to which the controls are bound for display purposes, such as to show that the current row is number *n* of the actual number of rows. This can be easily achieved using the **Count** property of the **CurrencyManager** class, as follows:

```
MsgBox("This is row number " & CStr(Me.BindingContext(objUser,& _
"tblUser").Position + 1) & _

" of " & Me.BindingContext(objUser, "tblUser").Count.ToString & " rows.")
```

This code obviously uses both the **Position** and **Count** properties to display the current row position and the number of rows. Because the **Position** property is zero-based, I have added the value 1 to this property at display time. This is done to make sure that the current position is one-based as it is with the **Count** property.

Retrieving the Current Row of a Data Source

Sometimes you need to manipulate the content of the current row in the data source. This can be done using the **Current** property of the **CurrencyManager** class. However, this property returns a value of data **Object**, which means you have to cast this value to the same data type used by the data source. When you are binding to a **DataSet**, **DataTable**, or **DataViewManager**, or rather when the data source is set to an object of one of these data types, you are actually binding to a **DataView** object. In this situation, you have to cast the returned object to a **DataRowView** object.

```
Dim drwCurrent As DataRowView = CType(Me.BindingContext (objUser,&_
"tblUser").Current, DataRowView)
```

In the example code, `drwCurrent` will now hold the current row in the data source.

Retrieving and Setting the Current Position in a Data Source

You can retrieve and set the current position in the data source using the **Position** property of the **CurrencyManager** class. See the section "Retrieving the Number of Rows in the Data Source" earlier in this chapter for example code of how to read the **Position** property.

However, retrieving the current position in the data source is not the only thing you can do with the **Position** property—you can also set the position. That's right, you can use the **Position** property to move around the data source. The best of it all, it's extremely easy to do so, as this example demonstrates:

```
Me.BindingContext(objUser, "tblUser").Position = 3
```

This code makes the fourth row the current one (the **Position** property is zero-based). Table 10-5 shows you how to make specific rows current.

Table 10-5. Navigating to Specific Rows in the Data Source in a Bound Control

POSITION	EXAMPLE
First row	`Me.BindingContext(objUser, "tblUser").Position = 0`
Last row	`Me.BindingContext(objUser, "tblUser").Position =` `Me.BindingContext(objUser, "tblUser").Count - 1`
Next row	`Me.BindingContext(objUser, "tblUser").Position += 1`
Previous row	`Me.BindingContext(objUser, "tblUser").Position -= 1`

In connection with moving around the data source, it is necessary to check the validity of the move before you actually perform it. This is not necessary with moving to the first or last row, because that is always valid, but moving to the previous or next row can throw an exception if there is no such row.

So if you want to move to the previous row, make sure you are not at position 0, which is the first row. Check it like this:

```
If Not Me.BindingContext(objUser, "tblUser").Position = 0 Then
```

If you want to move to the next row, check if you're currently at the last row, as follows:

```
If Not Me.BindingContext(objUser, "tblUser").Position = _
 Me.BindingContext(objUser, "tblUser").Count - 1 Then
```

Controlling Validation of Edit Operations

When you edit the data in the data source, the **CurrentChanged** and **Item-Changed** events are triggered. This is good, because you can respond to these events and perform whatever actions you need to in your application. However, sometimes it is NOT desirable to have events fired. If you are doing a bulk update, it is better to respond to these events after the update has been applied. You can do this using the **SuspendBinding** and the **ResumeBinding** methods. These methods are used for temporarily suspending the data binding. See Listing 10-4 for an example of how to suspend and resume data binding.

Listing 10-4. Suspend and Resume Data Binding

```
1 ' Suspend data binding
2 Me.BindingContext(objUser, "tblUser").SuspendBinding()
3 ' Perform bulk edits
4 . . .
5 ' Resume data binding
6 Me.BindingContext(objUser, "tblUser").ResumeBinding()
```

Listing 10-4 shows you how to first suspend the data binding before performing your bulk edits and then finally resume the data binding. No events are triggered between Lines 2 and 6.

Creating Your Own Data Bound Windows Form Control

As I have already shown, it is fairly easy to create a data-bound Windows form control. I suggest you always use the Data Form Wizard for this purpose, if you are creating a control with a form-like UI. Even if it means you have to change some of the wizard-generated code afterwards, it will nearly always be quicker and easier to use this approach.

Obviously, when you are using a form-like approach, you will be creating a component with a UI, and that won't do in some cases. This is when you need to create a Windows user control. You can do so in any Windows project by following these simple steps:

1. Add a new item to the project. When the Add New Item dialog box appears, select the User Control template, give the user control a name, and click OK.

2. Drag the required Windows form controls from the Toolbox onto the Windows user control when it's in design mode.

3. Create a class like the objUser class in the wizard-generated code that is the data source.

4. Bind one or more properties of each of the Windows form controls you have placed on the Windows user control to a property of the data source class.

That is all there is to it!

EXERCISE

Create a new user control and name it UserManId. Add a **TextBox** control to the user control and bind it to the Id column of the tblUser table. You can find an example of how to do this in the downloads section on the Apress Web site (http://www.apress.com).

Using Data-Bound Controls with Web Forms

Data binding your Web controls is quite different behind the scenes than with Windows forms, although not too difficult. Some ASP.NET Server–related controls have a **DataSource** property. (See Chapter 1 for more information on ASP.NET.) The **DataSource** property is used for binding to a **DataSet** object.

> **NOTE** *See Chapter 3B for more information on the **DataSet** object.*

Before I go on, I want to demonstrate how to create a Web form with data-bound controls as I did with the Windows form.

Creating a Form Using the Data Form Wizard

Instead of doing all the hard work yourself, let the Data Form Wizard create your Web form with one or more data-bound controls for you as you would with a Windows form. This wizard does more or less the same thing for Web forms as it does with Windows forms, but it will only let you create read-only Web forms. This means you have to take care of creating updateable pages yourself. I suggest you try running the Data Form Wizard in a Web application project and perform the same steps as you did with the wizard for the Windows form (see "Creating a Form Using the Data Form Wizard" earlier in this chapter). Mind you, you will have to skip Steps 10 through 12, because they don't apply to Web forms. In addition to restricting your Web forms to read-only, another drawback of the Data Form Wizard is it allows only a data grid as a control on your Web form.

Anyway, try running the wizard and run the project after the wizard finishes to see how nicely it displays your data as read-only in a data grid.

> **NOTE** *I have created a new project on the Apress Web site that is an extension of the wizard-generated code. It lets you edit and update your data source.*

Maintaining State

The problem with any data binding in ASP.NET is maintaining the state. Web forms, and ultimately the ASP.NET page framework, communicate with the client, such as a browser, using the Hypertext Transfer Protocol (HTTP). The problem concerning data binding with the HTTP protocol is that it is stateless. This means information is lost every time the page or your Web form is refreshed, including the data to which your controls are bound. The Web form is refreshed when the user of the client requests new or more information from the server, such as when a user clicks the Send button in a browser after filling in his or her personal details.

The problem in this scenario is that the user might have entered some invalid data or even left out some required data. Your Web form would then need to inform the user about the error and at the same time redisplay the form with the entered information. Because the information is lost when the Web form is refreshed, you need to handle this yourself, meaning you have to save the information elsewhere.

How to save this information is not exactly difficult, but choosing the right way of doing so can be a very tricky task, because there are several options available to you:

- Saving the information in the Web form's **ViewState** property

- Enabling the grid's view state by setting the **EnableViewState** property of the data grid to **True** if you are using a **DataGrid** control (part of the **System.Web.UI.WebControls** namespace). **True** is the default value.

- Saving information in a Web form's *state bag*. A state bag is as the term suggests a place to save the state of your form. It is a data structure that is maintained by the page (Web form) for saving values between server roundtrips.

- Storing any information in the **Session** and **Application** objects. These objects are probably familiar to you, if you have been developing Web sites using Visual InterDev. I won't be covering these objects, but you can find plenty of information about them in the Visual Studio.NET MSDN Library.

Which of these options you should choose really depends on your circumstances. I can make one simple recommendation, and that is to try out the different options if and when performance is an issue. Testing is the key word here.

Recall that a Web form loses its state when it is being refreshed, but this is not quite true. The current properties of the page (Web form), the page itself, and the base properties of the server controls and their state are automatically saved between roundtrips. All you need to worry about is when you have information that is NOT part of the mentioned controls and/or properties, such as private variables and contents of standard HTML elements.

Creating Your Own Data Bound Web Form Control

Because the Data Form Wizard for Web forms always creates read-only forms with a **DataGrid** control, it can be a lot of work making it updateable and/or using separate controls instead of the data grid, but the initial code to build upon is there and its easier to extend the wizard generated code than to do it all by hand.

When you are using a form-like approach as suggested in the preceding section, you will be creating a page UI, and that won't do in some cases. Sometimes you need a control that can be dragged from the Toolbox onto a Web form. In those instances, you need to create a Web user control. You can create a Web user control in any Web project by adding a new item to your project. When the Add New Item dialog box appears, you select the Web User Control template, give the user control a name, and click OK. Here is what else you need to do:

1. Drag the required Web form controls from the Toolbox onto the Web user control when it's in design mode.

2. Create a data set for binding the controls to. To do so, drag the table you want as your data set from the Server Explorer onto the Web user control. This creates a new connection and a new data adapter object, as shown in Figure 10-11. These objects are set to point at the data source you dragged from the Server Explorer, meaning you do not have to initialize them.

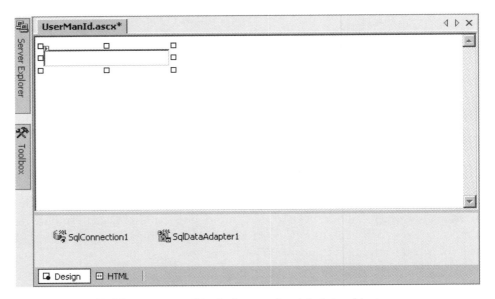

Figure 10-11. A Web user control in design mode with data objects

3. Create a data set from the data adapter object. Select the SqlDataAdapter1 object, right-click on it, and then select Generate Dataset from the pop-up menu.

4. In the Generate Dataset dialog box (shown in Figure 10-12), specify that you want to create a new data set by selecting New and then giving the data set a name in the text field beside the New option. Click OK.

5. The data set, User1 in this example, is now visually added to the data design view next to the data adapter object.

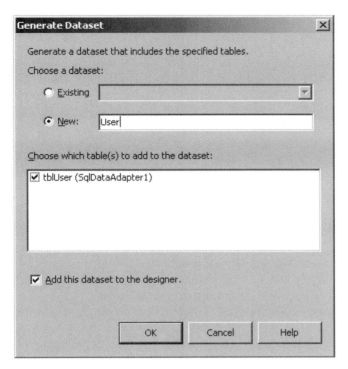

Figure 10-12. The Generate Dataset dialog box

6. Bind one or more properties of each of the Web form controls you have placed on the Web user control to a property of the data source class. Do so by following these steps:

   1. Select the Web user control in design mode.

   2. Select the Properties window and place the cursor in the DataBindings textbox.

   3. Click the button with three dots (. . .) next to the text box. This brings up the DataBindings dialog box.

   4. Select the **Text** property in the Bindable Properties tree view.

   5. Check the Simple binding radio button and expand the User1 data set in the tree view below the Simple binding radio button.

   6. Keep expanding the nodes so you can select the Id column of the tblUser table from the data set, as shown in Figure 10-13. Click OK.

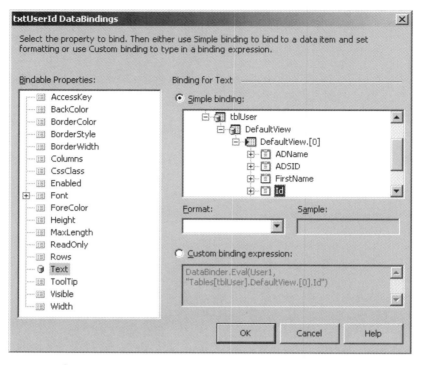

Figure 10-13. The DataBindings dialog box

7.   Place the code from Listing 10-5 in the Page_Load **Sub** procedure in the code for the Web user control.

Listing 10-5. Finishing the Data Binding in a Web User Control
```
' Open connection
SqlConnection1.Open()
' Fill data set
SqlDataAdapter1.Fill(User1, "tblUser")
' Bind controls to data source
txtUserId.DataBind()
```

The example in Listing 10-5 is pretty simple, but this really is all you need if you perform the other steps. You now have yourself a data-bound user control you can use on any Web page.

The question is if you really want to do it this way. You may have other considerations: whether you really want to open a connection for just one control, when to close the connection, and so forth. You know the drill—the example code is simply to show how easily it can be done. How you finish the user control is entirely up to you.

EXERCISE

Create a new user control and name it UserManId. Add a TextBox control to the user control and bind it to the Id column of the tblUser table. You can find an example of how to do this on the Apress Web site (`http://www.apress.com`).

Summary

In this chapter I explained what data-bound controls are, how you use them in Windows forms and Web forms, and how they differ from data-bound controls in previous versions of Visual Basic. I showed you the **CurrencyManager** and **BindingContext** classes in regards to data binding in Windows forms and demonstrated how they are used for data binding. I also discussed the **DataBindings** property of the Windows form control derived from the **Control** class, and showed you how to manually bind a Windows form control to a data source.

In the next chapter I will finish the UserMan example application that I have been referring to throughout the book, and I will give you some ideas and tips on how to take the example further if you want to build your own application on the basis of the UserMan application.

Part Three

Example Application

CHAPTER 11

UserMan

Finishing the example application

IN THIS CHAPTER, I WILL be finishing the UserMan example application that we have built upon throughout this book, assuming you've followed along with me and performed the exercises as you went. I will also give you some ideas as to how to take it further, if you feel the application can be the building block that you need for your very own .NET application.

The example application created throughout the book is all about implementing a user administration system that works with user information extracted from Active Directory, the new directory system in Windows 2000.

Identifying the UserMan Information

Let me state all the particulars about what the UserMan application should do, how it should do it, and so on. UserMan is a user management system that performs the following tasks:

- Logging on and off from the system (checking the tblUser table)

- Adding, editing, and deleting a user (tblUser table)

- Updating and checking a user's permissions (tblUserRights table)

- Logging all user activity (tblLog table)

- Adding, updating, and deleting user rights or permissions (tblRights table)

These are just the duties of the UserMan application as I have written it, but it obviously needs more than this to be considered for any sort of deployment in any organization.

Discovering the Objects

This section covers the items in the UserMan application that you can identify as actual objects.

Database Objects

The database has already been written and it consists of the following tables:

- tblUser

- tblUserRights

- tblRights

- tblLog

You can see the database schema in the last part of Chapter 2 (Figure 2-10). Keeping the guidelines from Chapter 9 in mind, your next step in developing this application is figuring out how to wrap the access to these tables in one or more classes. Actually, this is fairly easy, because it almost always makes sense to wrap each table in a class. I have had to wrap more than one table in the same class, but in most cases I have wrapped one table per class. The tables in the UserMan database are clearly defined, and although they are related, they should be accessed individually for adding, updating, and deleting rows. So you need to include four classes in the relational database:

- CUser

- CUserRights

- CRights

- CLog

Finishing the CUser Class

I started creating the CUser class in Chapter 9, so let's finish this particular class now. The rest of the classes look quite alike, and they can be found in the downloads section on the Apress site (`http://www.apress.com`). First you need to add some database connectivity. Listing 11-1 shows you the private constants and variables needed.

Listing 11-1. Private Database Constants and Variables
for the CUser Class

```
' Database constants
Private Const PR_STR_CONNECTION As String = "Data Source=USERMANPC;" & _
  "User ID=UserMan;Password=userman;Initial Catalog=UserMan"
Private Const PR_STR_SQL_USER_SELECT As String = "SELECT * FROM tblUser"
Private Const PR_STR_SQL_USER_DELETE As String = _
  "DELETE FROM tblUser WHERE Id=@Id"
Private Const PR_STR_SQL_USER_INSERT As String = _
  "INSERT INTO tblUser(FirstName, LastName, LoginName, Password) " & _
  "VALUES(@FirstName, @LastName, @LoginName, @Password)"
Private Const PR_STR_SQL_USER_UPDATE As String = _
  "UPDATE tblUser SET FirstName=@FirstName, LastName=@LastName, " & _
  "LoginName=@LoginName, Password=@Password WHERE Id=@Id"
' Database variables
Private Shared prshcnnUserMan As SqlConnection
Private prdadUserMan As SqlDataAdapter
Private prdstUserMan As DataSet

' For direct user table manipulation
Private prcmmUser As SqlCommand
' The command objects for the dataset manipulation
Private prcmmUserSelect As SqlCommand
Private prcmmUserDelete As SqlCommand
Private prcmmUserInsert As SqlCommand
Private prcmmUserUpdate As SqlCommand
' Parameter objects for dataset manipulation
Private prprmSQLDelete, prprmSQLUpdate, prprmSQLInsert As SqlParameter
```

In Listing 11-1 there are a few constants, one for the connection string
(PR_STR_CONNECTION) and the command strings for selecting, inserting, updating,
and deleting rows from the user table (PR_STR_SQL_USER_...). There are also a few
database objects, such as the connection (prshcnnUserMan), the data adapter
(prdadUserMan), the data set (prdstUserMan), and so on.

> **NOTE** *If you need more information on any of these objects, I suggest you*
> *read Chapters 3A and 3B. These chapters cover most classes in ADO.NET.*

Making the Connection Object Shared

If you look at the connection object again, you will see that I have declared it using the **Shared** access modifier. I have done this so the connection object will be shared amongst all instances of the CUser class—that is, they will all use the same single connection. Also, this keeps the connection object alive until the last instance of the class has been destroyed. Is this good or bad? Well, you be the judge. Just make sure you think about such issues as scalability, performance, and the overall number of users when you decide to change the declaration or leave it for that matter.

> **NOTE** *Programming is an art on its own, and it's up to you to make the most of your application. What is good for one application might be extremely bad for another. I hope this book will give you some things to consider when you design and implement your application, if nothing else.*

If you have been adding these private variables and constants to your CUser class, I am sure you have found out that **SqlConnection**, **SqlCommand**, and other such data types are not being recognized. To rectify this, you need to import the **System.Data.SqlClient** namespace by adding the following as the very first line of code in your CUser class:

```
Imports System.Data.SqlClient
```

Actually, this might not be the very first line of code in your class, because if you have any **Option**. . . statements such as **Option Strict On** in your class, they must come before any **Imports** statements.

Opening the Database Connection

If you have added all the database variables needed for accessing the UserMan database on a SQL Server 2000, the next step is to set up the code for establishing the database connection, as shown in Listing 11-2.

Listing 11-2. Connecting to the Database

```
1 Private Sub OpenDatabaseConnection()
2    Try
3       ' Check if the connection has already been instantiated
4       If prshcnnUserMan Is Nothing Then
5          ' Instantiate the connection
6          prshcnnUserMan = New SqlConnection(PR_STR_CONNECTION)
7          ' Check if the connection is closed
8          If CBool(prshcnnUserMan.State And ConnectionState.Closed) Then
9             ' Open the connection
10            prshcnnUserMan.Open()
11         End If
12      End If
13   Catch objSqlException As SqlException
14      ' A Connection low-level exception was thrown. Add a description and
15      ' re-throw the exception to the caller of this class
16      Throw New Exception("The connection to the UserMan database could " & _
17         "not be established, due to a connection low-level error", _
18         objSqlException)
19   Catch objE As Exception
20      ' Any other exception thrown is handled here
21      Throw New Exception("The connection to the UserMan database " & _
22         "could not be established.", objE)
23   End Try
24 End Sub
```

In Listing 11-2 I open the connection in the private **Sub** procedure OpenData-baseConnection. I have chosen to make the procedure private because there is no need for clients to perform this operation. It should be handled when you instantiate the class (see Listing 11-3 in the next section). I make sure that the connection has not been instantiated before I do so, and that it is closed before I try to open it. If it isn't closed when I open it, an exception is thrown. If an exception occurs, I throw a new exception with a message detailing what went on, and then I add the current exception to the **InnerException** property of the new exception. This way the caller of this class can see the original exception thrown and my error message as well.

Instantiating Your Class

Any initialization of variables and such that is not handled by an initializer should be placed in the **New Sub** constructor, as shown in Listing 11-3.

Listing 11-3. Open Database Connection at Class Instantiation

```
1 Public Sub New()
2   ' Perform standard inherited instantiation
3   MyBase.New()
4   ' Open the connection to the database
5   OpenDatabaseConnection()
6 End Sub
```

Listing 11-3 shows you how to make sure that the database connection is open and ready for use after the client has instantiated the class. Placing a call to the custom OpenDatabaseConnection procedure in the **New Sub** constructor does this. I have added a call to the base class's constructor in the form of **MyBase.New()**, which ensures that the base class instantiation is performed. This call must be the first line of code in your custom constructor.

Closing the Database Connection

Just as you need to open your database connection, it must also be closed again to preserve connection resources. Listing 11-4 shows you how to do this.

Listing 11-4. Closing the Database Connection

```
1 Private Sub CloseDatabaseConnection()
2   Try
3       ' Close the connection
4       prshcnnUserMan.Close()
5   Catch objE As Exception
6       Throw New Exception("The connection to the UserMan database " & _
7         "could not be closed properly.", objE)
8   End Try
9 End Sub
```

Listing 11-4 closes the database connection using the **Close** method of the connection class. This method isn't really known for throwing that many exceptions, so the exception handler might be overkill. You be the judge, and take it out if it bothers you.

As you can see, I have also chosen to make this procedure private, as is the case with the OpenDatabaseConnection procedure. I have done this for the same reason: The client shouldn't be able to call this method—it should be done automatically by your code when the class is disposed of.

Disposing of Your Class

When your class is disposed of, you must make sure that your connection is closed. Placing a call to a procedure that performs the closing of the connection in the class's **Finalize** method does this (see Listing 11-5).

Listing 11-5. Disposing of a Class

```
1 Protected Overrides Sub Finalize()
2    ' Close the database connection
3    CloseDatabaseConnection()
4    MyBase.Finalize()
5 End Sub
```

In Listing 11-5 I close the database connection from within the **Finalize** method of the class. The **Finalize** method is called when an object is disposed of, such as when a client sets the object to **Nothing**. You need to close the database connection explicitly; otherwise it will stay open and not be returned to the pool.

> **NOTE** *Chapter 3A tells you more about connections and connection pools.*

Instantiating the Command Objects

The command objects used by the data adapter for manipulating the data source and the generic command object need to be instantiated, as demonstrated in Listing 11-6.

Listing 11-6. Instantiating the Command Objects

```
1 Private Sub InstantiateCommands()
2    ' Instantiate the data adapter command objects
3    prcmmUserSelect = New SqlCommand(PR_STR_SQL_USER_SELECT, prshcnnUserMan)
4    prcmmUserDelete = New SqlCommand(PR_STR_SQL_USER_DELETE, prshcnnUserMan)
5    prcmmUserInsert = New SqlCommand(PR_STR_SQL_USER_INSERT, prshcnnUserMan)
6    prcmmUserUpdate = New SqlCommand(PR_STR_SQL_USER_UPDATE, _
7     prshcnnUserMan)
8    ' Instantiate and initialize generic command object
9    prcmmUser = New SqlCommand()
10   prcmmUser.Connection = prshcnnUserMan
11 End Sub
```

In Listing 11-6 I instantiate the command objects used by the data adapter for selecting, adding, updating, and deleting rows in the data source. I then instantiate the generic command object that can be used directly on the data source so that, for example, I can retrieve only certain columns from a table in a data reader using the command object's **ExecuteReader** method. I haven't specified any command text as this can be done when the command is executed, but I do specify the shared connection as the command's connection, because this

is the connection I will use for all queries through this command. The InstantiateCommands procedure should be added to the **New** constructor in Listing 11-3 after the call to open the database connection.

Instantiating the DataSet Object

In line with most other objects, **DataSet** objects need to be instantiated as well before you can use them. Listing 11-7 shows you how to do this.

Listing 11-7. Instantiating the Data Set

```
1 Private Sub InstantiateDataSet()
2    prdstUserMan = New DataSet()
3 End Sub
```

As you can see from Listing 11-7, there isn't much code in the Instantiate-DataSet procedure. You don't really need any more code and as such you can consider taking the single line of code out of the procedure and placing it where you would normally place a call to the procedure. In any case, the instantiation code should be placed in the **New** constructor.

Instantiating and Initializing the Data Adapter

I just showed you to instantiate the data set, but the data set needs to be populated from the data source, and this must be done using the data adapter. So let's go ahead and instantiate and initialize the data adapter as shown in Listing 11-8.

Listing 11-8. Instantiating and Initializing the Data Adapter

```
1 Private Sub InstantiateAndInitializeDataAdapter()
2    prdadUserMan = New SqlDataAdapter()
3    prdadUserMan.SelectCommand = prcmmUserSelect
4    prdadUserMan.InsertCommand = prcmmUserInsert
5    prdadUserMan.DeleteCommand = prcmmUserDelete
6    prdadUserMan.UpdateCommand = prcmmUserUpdate
7 End Sub
```

In Listing 11-8 I instantiate the data adapter and initialize the command properties by setting them to the already instantiated command objects.

Adding Command Object Parameters

Chapters 3A and 3B show you how to add parameters to your command objects so that the data adapter knows exactly how to query your data source. Listing 11-9 shows you how to perform this task for UserMan.

Listing 11-9. Adding Command Object Parameters

```
1 Private Sub AddCommandObjectParameters()
2    ' Add delete command parameters
3    prcmmUserDelete.Parameters.Add("@FirstName", SqlDbType.VarChar, 50, _
4     "FirstName")
5    prcmmUserDelete.Parameters.Add("@LastName", SqlDbType.VarChar, 50, _
6     "LastName")
7    prcmmUserDelete.Parameters.Add("@LoginName", SqlDbType.VarChar, 50, _
8     "LoginName")
9    prcmmUserDelete.Parameters.Add("@Password", SqlDbType.VarChar, 50, _
10    "Password")
11   prprmSQLDelete = prdadUserMan.DeleteCommand.Parameters.Add("@Id", _
12    SqlDbType.Int, 0, "Id")
13   prprmSQLDelete.Direction = ParameterDirection.Input
14   prprmSQLDelete.SourceVersion = DataRowVersion.Original
15
16    ' Add update command parameters
17   prcmmUserUpdate.Parameters.Add("@FirstName", SqlDbType.VarChar, 50, _
18    "FirstName")
19   prcmmUserUpdate.Parameters.Add("@LastName", SqlDbType.VarChar, 50, _
20    "LastName")
21   prcmmUserUpdate.Parameters.Add("@LoginName", SqlDbType.VarChar, 50, _
22    "LoginName")
23   prcmmUserUpdate.Parameters.Add("@Password", SqlDbType.VarChar, 50, _
24    "Password")
25   prprmSQLUpdate = prdadUserMan.UpdateCommand.Parameters.Add("@Id", _
26    SqlDbType.Int, 0, "Id")
27   prprmSQLUpdate.Direction = ParameterDirection.Input
28   prprmSQLUpdate.SourceVersion = DataRowVersion.Original
29
30    ' Add insert command parameters
31   prcmmUserInsert.Parameters.Add("@FirstName", SqlDbType.VarChar, 50, _
32    "FirstName")
33   prcmmUserInsert.Parameters.Add("@LastName", SqlDbType.VarChar, 50, _
34    "LastName")
35   prcmmUserInsert.Parameters.Add("@LoginName", SqlDbType.VarChar, 50, _
36    "LoginName")
```

```
37    prcmmUserInsert.Parameters.Add("@Password", SqlDbType.VarChar, 50, _
38      "Password")
39 End Sub
```

In Listing 11-9, I add the parameters needed by the data adapter for manipulating the data source to the command objects. This call should be added to the **New** constructor.

Filling the Data Set

Now that everything has been set up, all you need to do is fill the data set with data from the data source. See Listing 11-10 for example code that accomplishes this task.

Listing 11-10. Populating the Data Set with Data from the Data Source
```
 1 Private Sub PopulateDataSet()
 2    Try
 3       prdadUserMan.Fill(prdstUserMan, "tblUser")
 4    Catch objSystemException As SystemException
 5      Throw New Exception("The dataset could not be populated, " & _
 6       "because the source table was invalid.", objSystemException)
 7    Catch objE As Exception
 8      Throw New Exception("The dataset could not be populated.", objE)
 9    End Try
10 End Sub
```

Listing 11-10 is pretty simple—I try to fill the data set with data from the tblUser table in the data source. If an exception is thrown, I rethrow it with the original exception. This method should also be added to the **New** constructor.

Hooking Up the Public Properties to the Data Set

Now that the data set has been populated, the public properties can now be hooked up to the data set. All the properties read and set private variables, so you need to read the values from the populated data set and save them in the corresponding private variables, as demonstrated in Listing 11-11.

Listing 11-11. Saving the Data Set Values
```
 1 Private Sub SaveDataSetValues()
 2    ' Save user id
 3    prlngId = CType(prdstUserMan.Tables("tbluser").Rows(0).Item("Id"), Long)
 4    ' Check if ADName is Null
```

```
5    If prdstUserMan.Tables("tbluser").Rows(0).IsNull("ADName") Then
6        prstrADName = ""
7    Else
8        prstrADName = _
9        CType(prdstUserMan.Tables("tbluser").Rows(0).Item("ADName"), _
10       String)
11   End If
12   ' Check if ADSID is Null
13   If Not prdstUserMan.Tables("tbluser").Rows(0).IsNull("ADSID") Then
14       prguiADSID = _
15       CType(prdstUserMan.Tables("tbluser").Rows(0).Item("ADSID"), Guid)
16   End If
17   ' Check if first name is Null
18   If prdstUserMan.Tables("tbluser").Rows(0).IsNull("FirstName") Then
19       prstrFirstName = ""
20   Else
21       prstrFirstName = _
22       CType(prdstUserMan.Tables("tbluser").Rows(0).Item("FirstName"), _
23       String)
24   End If
25    Check if last name is Null
26   If prdstUserMan.Tables("tbluser").Rows(0).IsNull("LastName") Then
27       prstrLastName = ""
28   Else
29       prstrLastName = CType(prdstUserMan.Tables("tbluser").Rows(0).Item( _
30       "LastName"), String)
31   End If
32   ' Check if login name is Null
33   If prdstUserMan.Tables("tbluser").Rows(0).IsNull("LoginName") Then
34       prstrLoginName = ""
35   Else
36       prstrLoginName = CType(prdstUserMan.Tables("tbluser").Rows(0).Item( _
37       "LoginName"), String)
38   End If
39   ' Check if password is Null
40   If prdstUserMan.Tables("tbluser").Rows(0).IsNull("Password") Then
41       prstrPassword = ""
42   Else
43       prstrPassword = CType(prdstUserMan.Tables("tbluser").Rows(0).Item( _
44       "Password"), String)
45   End If
46 End Sub
```

In Listing 11-11, I simply read the values from the data set and save them in the corresponding private variables. Please note that I read from the very first row in the data set. I do this in order to facilitate sorting and filtering, which can be added later on. I have added a check for null values for the columns in the database that allow this.

Specifying the Parent Class

I don't know if you are wondering about what class your CUser class is derived from. If you've followed along with the example, you haven't actually included an **Inherits** statement to specify a class to inherit from. For the purposes of the UserMan application, you don't have to, because you want to inherit from the **Object** class, which is done implicitly. This means you don't have to add the Inherits Object statement to your class. However, if there is a different class you want to inherit from, you need to add the **Inherits** statement to your class as the first line of code following the class definition (Public Class CUser).

> **NOTE** *I discuss these issues in Chapter 9, where I started creating the CUser class.*

What Else Is Needed?

Obviously the CUser class isn't finished yet, although you have added a lot of code to it. What you need now is to add code to allow filtering and sorting of the rows in the data set and, more importantly, code for updating the data source.

> **NOTE** *I have already added this code and a few other procedures to the CUser class to be found in the downloads section on the Apress Web site* (http://www.apress.com).

Active Directory Object

You need an object for reading the values for the ADSID and ADName columns in the tblUser table. Listing 11-12 shows example code for this purpose.

> **NOTE** *You will find more information about Active Directory access in Chapter 7.*

Listing 11-12. The Active Directory Class

```
1 Imports System.Data.OleDb
2
3 Public Class CActiveDirectory
4    ' Database objects
5    Private prcnnAD As OleDbConnection
6    Private prcmmAD As OleDbCommand
7    Private prdrdAD As OleDbDataReader
8
9    Private Sub OpenConnection()
10      ' Instantiate and open connection
11      prcnnAD = New OleDbConnection("Provider=ADsDSOObject;" & _
12       "User Id=UserMan;Password=userman")
13      prcnnAD.Open()
14   End Sub
15
16   Private Sub RetrieveUserInformation()
17      ' Instantiate command
18      prcmmAD = New OleDbCommand("SELECT cn, adsPath FROM " & _
19       "'LDAP://userman.com' WHERE objectCategory='person' AND " & _
20       "objectClass='user' AND cn='UserMan'", prcnnAD)
21      ' Retrieve UserMan info in data reader
22      prdrdAD = prcmmAD.ExecuteReader()
23   End Sub
24 End Class
```

As you can see from Listing 11-12, I have used the OLE DB .NET Data Provider for retrieving the user information from AD. This provider is read-only, but this is okay because I only want to retrieve information. This class is far from finished; you still need to retrieve the correct values (ADName and ADSID) and save the retrieved values in private variables. Furthermore, you need to set up read-only properties so that the client who uses the class can read these values. This client can be the CUser class.

You also need to create properties and/or methods that take the name of the user you want to retrieve information for, instead of hard-coding the name of the user, and thus making it possible to read any user's information.

> **NOTE** *A finished* CActiveDirectory *class can be found in the downloads section on the Apress Web site (*http://www.apress.com*).*

Other Objects

You need to create more classes than the ones you've already created, because you haven't finished wrapping all your data access. Here are some suggestions:

- Message queuing

- Data-bound controls

You will find implementations of these classes in the downloads section on the Apress Web site (`http://www.apress.com`).

Wrapping Classes as Components

When you are done creating all your classes, you need to decide if one or more of them need to be wrapped as a component for deployment on a server. It's really beyond the scope of this book to cover component building, but for your pleasure, I have included all the table classes wrapped in one component for deployment to be found in the downloads section on the Apress Web site (`http://www.apress.com`). In most cases, the architecture your application determines if a class is wrapped in a component.

Creating the Client

At this point, the database has been put together, and I have shown you how to create wrapper classes for some of the data-related access I have covered in this book. So now I need to show you how to create the client application. I have decided to show you how to create both a Windows client based on a Windows form and a Web client based on a Web form because these are the UIs I have covered in this book.

Creating a Windows Client

There isn't much in creating the Windows client that has anything to do with accessing the data in the UserMan application. I have therefore decided to leave out any example code from the Windows client in this chapter. However, you can find a finished example of the UserMan Windows client in the downloads section on the Apress Web site. The code holds plenty of comments for helping you understand the example.

Creating a Web Client

As is the case with the Web client, I haven't found any potential in showing you example code from the Web client here in this chapter, but you can find a finished version of the UserMan Web client in the downloads section on the Apress Web site (http://www.apress.com). The code is fairly well documented through the use of comments.

Tips and Ideas

In this section I will give you some tips and ideas for further developing the UserMan application so that you can perhaps use it for your own purposes. I have grouped the suggestions so that they will be easier for you to go through.

Database Suggestions

In this section you will find all the suggestions that are related to database improvements and/or enhancements.

Password Column in User Table

As you have probably noticed, the Password column in the tblUser table is a varchar(50) column that anyone with read access to the table can read. This means the password of any user, including the administrator's (UserMan), can be read by a user with read access. This is obviously not the way it should be. There are several third-party vendors that produce encryption components. At the time of this writing, I haven't seen any for the .NET Framework, but when you read this there probably will be one, or you could use a COM Component though COM Interop (COM Interop is covered in Chapter 3B).

Another option is to create your own password encryption scheme. If you feel access to your network is fairly secure, a handy little routine of your own might be all that's needed. I am not going to implement one for you or even try to tell you how to do it, because I am simply no good at that stuff.

Logging to the Event Log

Instead of logging to the tblLog table in the UserMan database, you could log events in the Windows NT Event Log. This will make your events available to all users able to read the Event Log on your network. Check out the **EventLog** class in the **System.Diagnostics** namespace for more information on how to read from and write to the Event Log.

Passing the Connection Object to the Various Classes

Instead of having a connection in each of your classes, you should consider passing an open connection to them for their use. This way you can share a connection between the classes. Again, this depends on how you have created your application, how it's been deployed, and the amount of traffic you expect on a single connection.

One last thing to consider if you want to implement this enhancement is if you include a data reader, it will use the connection exclusively while it's open. So with data readers this is obviously not an option.

Create Stored Procedures for Accessing Your Database Tables

As the classes have been implemented right now, they access the data directly. However, you can change the implementation of the classes to use stored procedures (SPs) instead. You might not want to do this until you see how performance is, but perhaps later you decide that you could improve performance by using SPs instead. One of the really good things about using classes for database access in your application is you can change the implementation of your classes as long as you leave the interface intact, and the client applications won't detect that anything has changed.

Set Up Triggers to Enforce Business Rules

In Chapter 6, I showed you how to implement simple triggers, such as enforcing the inclusion of both a first name and a last name for a user, if you supply either. This is just one of many simple tasks that you can let a trigger handle for you instead of placing this functionality in your classes or, even worse, in your client code.

Set Up Database Security

I haven't done anything to implement security on the database level, meaning that more or less anyone with access to your network and SQL Server can access your UserMan database. I suggest one of the first things you do is add some sort of security if you haven't already done so. Ask your system administrator or read the Books Online help that comes with SQL Server for more information on how to implement security at the database level.

Use Constants for Table and Column Names

Replace all hard-coded table and column names such as tblUser and Id with constants. It makes your code easier to update and maintain, and I personally think it makes your code easier to read.

Use Local Transactions

It's always a good thing to use transactions with any operations that write to a database. This has not been implemented in the classes for UserMan, and I strongly suggest you consider adding local transaction support.

> **NOTE**   *Chapter 3A discusses local transactions, which are transactions that are explicitly started and ended using the connection object.*

General Suggestions

This section contains ideas and suggestions that don't really fit in elsewhere.

Let Active Directory Validate Users

Instead of having your own validation routine, why not let Active Directory perform one for you? This of course means that all users of your application need to be stored in Active Directory. Simply extend the Active Directory class to allow writing as well as reading.

Use Web Services to Expose Some Functionality

You could expose some of the application functionality from one or more Web Services. I won't be going into details about Web Services in this book, but basically you use Web Services as methods of a Web Server to expose certain functionality across the Internet, intranet, or indeed any network using Simple Object Access Protocol (SOAP) over HTTP. This guarantees that you can use this functionality through a firewall.

> **NOTE**   *I am currently writing a book on basic Web Services,* Building Web Services with Visual Basic.NET, *to be published by Apress, and it will be available by the end of 2002.*

Exception Handling

The two client applications have very little exception handling, and this is obviously not good. Go through the code and place exception handlers where you feel it is necessary. For your own sake, please use structured exception handling and not unstructured exception handling. Looking over the various classes for places to add exception handling is probably not a bad idea either!

Use Automatic Transactions

All .NET Framework classes can be part of an automatic transaction. This means you can roll back or commit changes made in classes just as you can with database operations. All you have to do is make your class transactional. See the documentation for more information on how to do this.

Summary

This chapter finished the example application that the rest of the chapters in this book had been built upon. I showed you how to use some of the data-related tools and/or methods introduced in earlier chapters, such as Active Directory access and SQL Server access, to build and finish the example application.

I went on to give you some ideas and tips on how to take the UserMan application further and customize it for your own use.

Here we are at the end of the last chapter of this book. I sincerely hope you have enjoyed reading it as much as I have enjoyed writing it. I would love to hear from you if you have any queries and/or suggestions regarding this book. You can reach me at dbpwvbnet@vb-joker.com. I am also interested in hearing from you if you have any improvements to the example application that you want to share with other readers.

Index

Web Form design mode
    use of Toolbox window in, 23
Web forms
    creating with the Data Form Wizard,
        417–418
    options for saving information,
        418–419
    using data-bound controls with,
        417–423
Web services
    manipulating in the Server Explorer
        window, 22
Web site address
    for Active Directory information,
        315
    Apress, 423
    for downloading ADSI SDK, 317
    for Erwin, 34
    for ICT WizERD, 34
    for information about constructing
        an LDAP query filter, 325
    for information about the X.500
        directory specification, 313–314
    for Information Management
        System (IMS) software, 33
    for Visible Analyst® DB Engineer, 34
Web user control
    finishing the data binding in, 422
Web User Control template
    creating your own data-bound Web
        form control with, 419–422
Wells, Garth
    *Code Centric: T-SQL Programming
        with Stored Procedures and
        Triggers* by, 311
Windows client
    creating, 440–441
Windows CLR, 8
Windows form control
    binding to a data source, 409–410
Windows Form design mode
    use of Toolbox window in, 23
Windows forms
    data binding on, 399–401

    using data-bound controls with,
        399–401
Workstation
    ConnectionString property
        value, 61
WorkstationID
    SqlConnection class property, 64
wrapping
    a database, 391–395
WriteXml() method
    DataSet class, 151
WriteXmlSchema() method
    DataSet class, 151

X

X.500 directory specification
    Web site address for information
        about, 313–314
XML Designer
    creating typed data sets
        with, 243
    function of Dynamic Help in, 19
XML format
    use of by ADO.NET, 145
XmlLang property
    XmlReader class, 125
XmlMessageFormatter constructor
    using for sending and receiving
        messages, 349–350
XmlNodeReader class, 123
XmlReader
    closing, 131
    reading rows in, 130–131
XmlReader class, 123
    methods, 126–129
    properties, 123–125
XmlReader object
    declaring and instantiating,
        130
XmlSpace property
    XmlReader class, 125
XmlTextReader class, 123
XmlValidatingReader class, 123

books for professionals by professionals™

About Apress

Apress, located in Berkeley, CA, is an innovative publishing company devoted to meeting the needs of existing and potential programming professionals. Simply put, the "A" in Apress stands for the "Author's Press™." Apress' unique author-centric approach to publishing grew from conversations between Dan Appleman and Gary Cornell, authors of best-selling, highly regarded computer books. In 1998, they set out to create a publishing company that emphasized quality above all else, a company with books that would be considered the best in their market. Dan and Gary's vision has resulted in over 30 widely acclaimed titles by some of the industry's leading software professionals.

Do You Have What It Takes to Write for Apress?

Apress is rapidly expanding its publishing program. If you can write and refuse to compromise on the quality of your work, if you believe in doing more then rehashing existing documentation, and if you're looking for opportunities and rewards that go far beyond those offered by traditional publishing houses, we want to hear from you!

Consider these innovations that we offer all of our authors:

- **Top royalties with *no* hidden switch statements**
  Authors typically only receive half of their normal royalty rate on foreign sales. In contrast, Apress' royalty rate remains the same for both foreign and domestic sales.

- **A mechanism for authors to obtain equity in Apress**
  Unlike the software industry, where stock options are essential to motivate and retain software professionals, the publishing industry has adhered to an outdated compensation model based on royalties alone. In the spirit of most software companies, Apress reserves a significant portion of its equity for authors.

- **Serious treatment of the technical review process**
  Each Apress book has a technical reviewing team whose remuneration depends in part on the success of the book since they too receive royalties.

Moreover, through a partnership with Springer-Verlag, one of the world's major publishing houses, Apress has significant venture capital behind it. Thus, we have the resources to produce the highest quality books *and* market them aggressively.

If you fit the model of the Apress author who can write a book that gives the "professional what he or she needs to know™," then please contact one of our Editorial Directors, Gary Cornell (gary_cornell@apress.com), Dan Appleman (dan_appleman@apress.com), Karen Watterson (karen_watterson@apress.com) or Jason Gilmore (jason_gilmore@apress.com) for more information.

Apress Titles

ISBN	LIST PRICE	AUTHOR	TITLE
1-893115-01-1	$39.95	Appleman	Appleman's Win32 API Puzzle Book and Tutorial for Visual Basic Programmers
1-893115-23-2	$29.95	Appleman	How Computer Programming Works
1-893115-97-6	$39.95	Appleman	Moving to VB.NET: Strategies, Concepts and Code
1-893115-09-7	$29.95	Baum	Dave Baum's Definitive Guide to LEGO MINDSTORMS
1-893115-84-4	$29.95	Baum, Gasperi, Hempel, and Villa	Extreme MINDSTORMS
1-893115-82-8	$59.95	Ben-Gan/Moreau	Advanced Transact-SQL for SQL Server 2000
1-893115-85-2	$34.95	Gilmore	A Programmer's Introduction to PHP 4.0
1-893115-17-8	$59.95	Gross	A Programmer's Introduction to Windows DNA
1-893115-62-3	$39.95	Gunnerson	A Programmer's Introduction to C#, Second Edition
1-893115-10-0	$34.95	Holub	Taming Java Threads
1-893115-04-6	$34.95	Hyman/Vaddadi	Mike and Phani's Essential C++ Techniques
1-893115-50-X	$34.95	Knudsen	Wireless Java: Developing with Java 2, Micro Edition
1-893115-79-8	$49.95	Kofler	Definitive Guide to Excel VBA
1-893115-57-7	$39.95	Kofler/Kramer	MySQL
1-893115-75-5	$44.95	Kurniawan	Internet Programming with VB
1-893115-19-4	$49.95	Macdonald	Serious ADO: Universal Data Access with Visual Basic
1-893115-06-2	$39.95	Marquis/Smith	A Visual Basic 6.0 Programmer's Toolkit
1-893115-22-4	$27.95	McCarter	David McCarter's VB Tips and Techniques
1-893115-76-3	$49.95	Morrison	C++ For VB Programmers
1-893115-80-1	$39.95	Newmarch	A Programmer's Guide to Jini Technology

ISBN	LIST PRICE	AUTHOR	TITLE
1-893115-81-X	$39.95	Pike	SQL Server: Common Problems, Tested Solutions
1-893115-20-8	$34.95	Rischpater	Wireless Web Development
1-893115-93-3	$34.95	Rischpater	Wireless Web Development with PHP and WAP
1-893115-24-0	$49.95	Sinclair	From Access to SQL Server
1-893115-94-1	$29.95	Spolsky	User Interface Design for Programmers
1-893115-53-4	$39.95	Sweeney	Visual Basic for Testers
1-893115-65-8	$39.95	Tiffany	Pocket PC Database Development with eMbedded Visual Basic
1-893115-59-3	$59.95	Troelsen	C# and the .NET Platform
1-893115-54-2	$49.95	Trueblood/Lovett	Data Mining and Statistical Analysis Using SQL
1-893115-16-X	$49.95	Vaughn	ADO Examples and Best Practices
1-893115-83-6	$44.95	Wells	Code Centric: T-SQL Programming with Stored Procedures and Triggers
1-893115-95-X	$49.95	Welschenbach	Cryptography in C and C++
1-893115-05-4	$39.95	Williamson	Writing Cross-Browser Dynamic HTML
1-893115-78-X	$49.95	Zukowski	Definitive Guide to Swing for Java 2, Second Edition
1-893115-92-5	$49.95	Zukowski	Java Collections

Available at bookstores nationwide or from Springer Verlag New York, Inc. at 1-800-777-4643; fax 1-212-533-3503. Contact us for more information at sales@apress.com.

Apress Titles Publishing SOON!

ISBN	AUTHOR	TITLE
1-893115-99-2	Cornell/Morrison	Programming VB.NET: A Guide for Experienced Programmers
1-893115-72-0	Curtin	Building Trust: Online Security for Developers
1-893115-55-0	Frenz	Visual Basic for Scientists
1-893115-96-8	Jorelid	J2EE FrontEnd Technologies: A Programmer's Guide to Servlets, JavaServer Pages, and Enterprise
1-893115-87-9	Kurata	Doing Web Development: Client-Side Techniques
1-893115-58-5	Oellerman	Fundamental Web Services with XML
1-893115-89-5	Shemitz	Kylix: The Professional Developer's Guide and Reference
1-893115-29-1	Thomsen	Database Programming with VB.NET

Available at bookstores nationwide or from Springer Verlag New York, Inc. at 1-800-777-4643; fax 1-212-533-3503. Contact us for more information at sales@apress.com.

The Ultimate Resource for VB.NET

In *Programming VB.NET: A Guide for Experienced Programmers,* Gary Cornell and Jonathan Morrison carefully explain the exciting new features of Visual Basic.NET. Cornell and Morrison write from the point of view of the experienced programmer, with constant references to the changes from earlier versions of VB. Developers will learn how to use VB.NET for database programming through ADO.NET and Web programming through ASP.NET. After reading *Programming VB.NET: A Guide for Experienced Programmers,* developers will have a firm grasp of the exciting new VB.NET language and its uses in creating powerful .NET applications.

Programming VB.NET: A Guide for Experienced Programmers
by Gary Cornell and Jonathan Morrison
ISBN: 1-893115-99-2 $39.95 US / 400 p.
Available August 2001

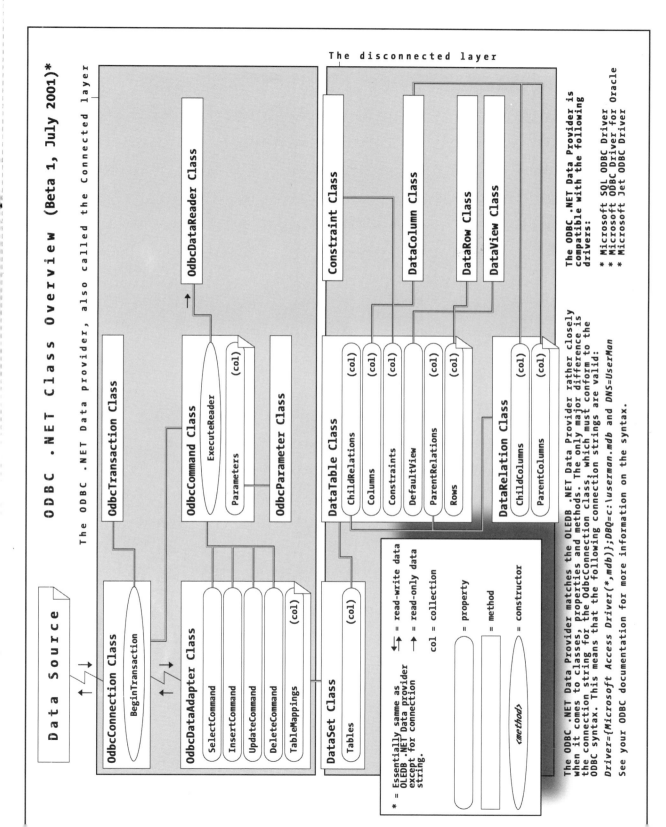

ODBC .NET Class Overview (Beta 1, July 2001)*

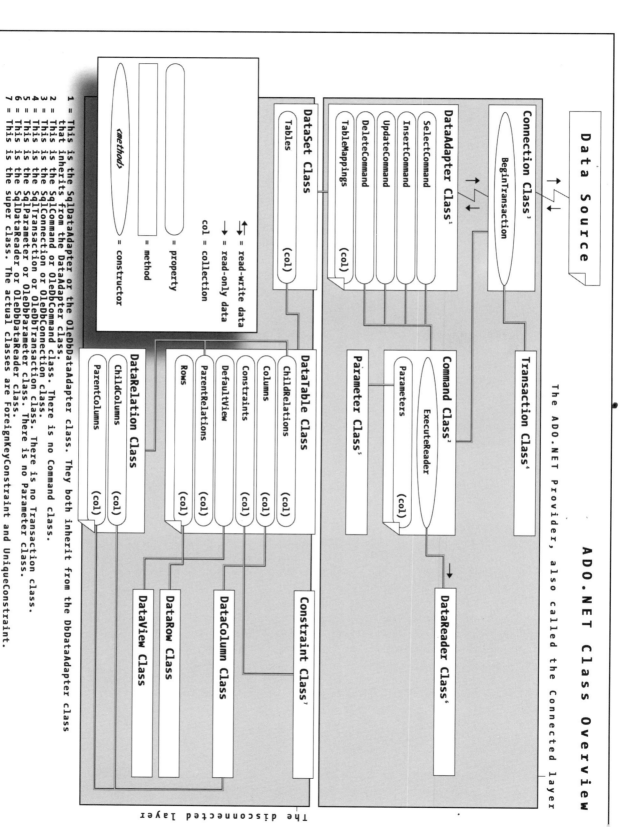

Data Source

ADO.NET Class Overview

The ADO.NET Provider, also called the Connected layer

Connection Class³

BeginTransaction

DataAdapter Class¹

SelectCommand
InsertCommand
UpdateCommand
DeleteCommand
TableMappings (col)

DataSet Class

Tables (col)

Transaction Class⁴

Parameter Class⁵

Parameters (col)

Command Class²

ExecuteReader

DataReader Class⁶

DataTable Class

ChildRelations (col)
Columns (col)
Constraints (col)
DefaultView
ParentRelations (col)
Rows (col)

DataRelation Class

ChildColumns (col)
ParentColumns (col)

Constraint Class⁷

DataColumn Class

DataRow Class

DataView Class

‹methods›

col = collection

= read-write data
= read-only data

= constructor
= method
= property

The disconnected layer

1 = This is the SqlDataAdapter or the OleDbDataAdapter class. They both inherit from the DbDataAdapter class
    that inherits from the DataAdapter class.
2 = This is the SqlCommand or OleDbCommand class. There is no Command class.
3 = This is the SqlConnection or OleDbConnection class.
4 = This is the SqlTransaction or OleDbTransaction class. There is no Transaction class.
5 = This is the SqlParameter or OleDbParameter class. There is no Parameter class.
6 = This is the SqlDataReader or OleDbDataReader class.
7 = This is the super class. The actual classes are ForeignKeyConstraint and UniqueConstraint.